Rethinking Political Theory

SERIES IN CONTINENTAL THOUGHT

RETHINKING
POLITICAL
THEORY:

Essays in Phenomenology and the Study of Politics

Hwa Yol Jung

OHIO UNIVERSITY PRESS

ATHENS

Ohio University Press books are printed on acid-free paper ∞

Library of Congress Cataloging-in-Publication Data

Jung, Hwa Yol.
   Rethinking political theory : essays in phenomenology and the
study of politics / Hwa Yol Jung.
      p.   cm. — (Series in continental thought : 18)
   Includes bibliographical references and index.
   ISBN 0-8214-1052-0
   1. Political science—Philosophy.   2. Phenomenology.   I. Title.
II. Series.
JA71.J853   1993
320'.01—dc20   92-44901
                                                      CIP

For Petee—my lifelong *"ukkae dongmu"*
who is celebrating her special birthday
this year

CONTENTS

ACKNOWLEDGMENTS

I AM GRATEFUL TO THE EDITORS of Northwestern University Press and to the following journals for having given me permission to reprint my essays: "The Political Relevance of Existential Phenomenology," *The Review of Politics*, 33 (1971): 538–63, and "Leo Strauss's Conception of Political Philosophy: A Critique," *The Review of Politics*, 29 (1967): 492–517; "Phenomenology as a Critique of Politics," *Human Studies*, 5 (1982): 161–81; "A Critique of the Behavioral Persuasion in Politics: A Phenomenological View," in *Phenomenology and the Social Sciences*, 2 vols., ed. Maurice Natanson (Evanston: Northwestern University Press, 1973), vol. 2, pp. 133–73; "The Question of Ethnocentrism and the Production of Intercultural Texts," *IUJ* (International University of Japan) *Annual Review*, 5 (1988): 133–63; "Communications" Note, *American Political Science Review*, 67 (1973): 964–65; "Being, Praxis, and Truth: Toward a Dialogue Between Phenomenology and Marxism," *Dialectical Anthropology*, 12 (1988): 307–28; "The Question of the Moral Subject in Foucault's Analytics of Power," *Canadian Journal of Political and Social Theory*, 11 (1987): 28–45; "Mikhail Bakhtin's Body Politic: A Phenomenological Dialogics," *Man and World*, 23 (1990): 85–99; "The Genealogy of Technological Rationality in the Human Sciences," *Research in Philosophy and Technology*, 9 (1989): 59–82; and "Language, Politics, and Technology," *Research in Philosophy and Technology*, 5 (1982): 43–63. Since most of these papers were originally read at the annual meetings of the American Political Science Association, the Society for Phenomenology and Existential Philosophy, and the International Association for Philosophy and Literature, I would like to acknowledge my sincere gratitude to numerous commentators who contributed directly or indirectly to the ultimate shaping of my ideas.

Fred Dallmayr of the University of Notre Dame has been a unique source of my intellectual inspiration and camaraderie since the late 1960s when he sought me out at an annual meeting of the American Political Science Association to chat about our mutual interests, as well as about an article I wrote on Maurice Merleau-Ponty's radical humanization of politics. Ever since we have been close friends. It was the spring of 1975 when he invited me to try out some of the ideas and themes found in this volume with undergraduate and graduate students at Purdue University. I wish to thank Kaz Okuda of the International University of Japan, without whose encouragement Chapter 5 would have never been written. I would also like to take this opportunity to thank Professor Maurice Natanson of Yale University, who introduced me to the social phenomenology of Alfred Schutz. His inclusion of my essay in the classic and comprehensive two-volume work on phenomenology and the social sciences that he edited in 1973 greatly uplifted the spirit and confidence of my scholarship in phenomenology. This essay appears in Chapter 3 of this book. I owe many thanks to Lester Embree, who is Director of the Center for Advanced Research in Phenomenology, for his initial encouragement to collect my essays into one volume and for his infinite forbearance for its completion. To my wife, Petee: I am always pleased with her unfailing intellectual fellowship as well as her caring and abiding friendship. She read with utmost care all the essays contained in this volume from their very inception. The visit to Seoul National University during the spring of 1989 was our joint venture: she in mathematics and I in political science. Teaching and learning together on the same campus was fun and a memorable experience for both of us, adding extra flavor to our stay in Seoul.

I wish to thank my students and fellow colleagues at Seoul National University —particularly to Kim Hongwoo, Cha In-Suk, and Kim Chae-Yoon— not only for their intellectual collegiality, but also for their warm hospitality during my visit in the spring of 1989. But for the persistent and indefatigable effort of Hongwoo, my wife and I would have never been able to visit that fine institution of education. In addition, I am also indebted to Vice President Kim Young Kook; Lee Jung Bok, who was Chairman of the Department of Political Science; and Chey Myung, who was Director of the Social Science Research Institute, for their willing generosity and help beyond intellectual fellowship. I would also like to mention three dear friends who made our stay in Seoul very enjoyable: Lee Hongkoo, whom I have known since my undergraduate days at Emory University; Lee Jae-Chang, who was a onetime colleague at Moravian College and is now Dean of Planning at Korea University; and Chee Kwang-Yul, whose close friendship goes back to the indigent and difficult days of the Korean war and who has now become a successful businessman. All in all, they made our visit to my birthplace unforgettable. I would be remiss if I forgot to acknowledge my indebtedness to my hardworking secretaries—Mickey Ortiz, Carol Newell, Jeanette Ludwig, and Clara

Masessa—without whose skill in "electric language" this manuscript would never have been completed. Among student helpers who kept themselves busy in producing the final draft of the manuscript, I want to single out Anna Grunwald and Lisa Bittenbender. Most of all, I am thankful to my colleague John Stoneback of the Computer Science Department for his relentless effort to find student helpers for me. Finally, I wish to thank Betsy Behnke, my copyeditor, who has a sharp eye for details, for having gone through every word with care.

Acknowledgments

Most thought-provoking is that we are still not
thinking—*not even yet, although the state of the
world is becoming constantly more
thought-provoking.*

—Martin Heidegger,
What Is Called Thinking?

PREFACE AS A POSTSCRIPT

THE VERY FIRST LESSON I LEARNED about phenomenology was the
simple fact that it is a philosophical *movement*. As a movement, it
is never stagnant but always dynamic. In its transformative character, its vitality is being preserved. From Edmund Husserl to Martin Heidegger, Maurice Merleau-Ponty, Alfred Schutz, Hans-Georg
Gadamer, Paul Ricoeur, Emmanuel Levinas, and Jacques Derrida,
phenomenology has gone through transcendental, existential,
hermeneutical, and deconstructive stages covering a vast array of
such themes as the nature of Being, human existence, language, science, religion, ethics, history, society, politics, art, and technology.
Whatever disagreements arise and develop from them should be
deemed more or less family quarrels. In retrospect, Husserl's seminal critique of scientism, for example, is an incomparable exercise
in deconstruction.

To be true to the originary evidence of human experience, phenomenology attempts to *show* the experiential basis of all conceptualization, both philosophical and scientific. It is truly a radical
empiricism. What geography is to the natural landscape, all conceptualization is to firsthand, preconceptual experience. Herein lies
the importance of Husserl's historic formulation of the life-world
(*Lebenswelt*) as inherently socio-historico-cultural. As applied to
social-scientific theorizing, the phenomenology of the life-world
does not ignore the common-sense understanding of actors on the
social scene, because all scientific conceptualization depends on
and is an elaboration of preconceptual knowledge.

Moreover, reflexivity is endemic to phenomenology. Phenomenology takes the burden of *Selbstdenken* seriously by becoming
self-conscious of its own activity and of the theoretical attitude of

the thinking subject who interprets the world. Thus the task of a phenomenologist, as Husserl himself understood it, is surely infinite, and the phenomenologist is a perpetual beginner. In the same vein, Heidegger spoke of questioning as the piety of thinking and Merleau-Ponty conceived of the end of philosophical interrogation as the account of its own beginning.

Phenomenology makes its distinct contribution to the human sciences in a twofold way: since it is concerned with both the question of "truth" and the question of "method," it is both substantive and methodological. When I was first introduced to phenomenology by way of studying Heidegger's *Being and Time* and Merleau-Ponty's *Phenomenology of Perception* in the early 60s, I quickly came to the realization that it is *the* alternative, though far less traveled and virtually unknown in political theorizing, to political behavioralism and to the essentialism of Leo Strauss, which then happened to be the two major competing paradigms in the study of politics. By killing two birds with one stone, phenomenology—I thought—was destined not only to be another paradigm, but also to bring about a paradigm shift in the study of politics. Behavioralism, on the one hand, is a species of scientism. In the first place, it assumes a unitary method for all the sciences because it is oblivious to the ontological distinction between the human and the natural. In the second place, and correlatively, behavioralism contends that it is ethically neutral since ethics has no place in scientific inquiry as such. It is, in brief, stricken with ethical amnesia. On the other hand, Strauss's essentialism is proposed as a critique of both "positivism" and "historicism" and faults them for their respective "ethical neutralism" and "ethical relativism." Since "to be" is "always to be," Strauss's essentialism fails to take into account the human being's historicity or time-boundedness, and thus is incapable of understanding or taking account of history as transformation. *Verum* is *factum,* indeed: time is within the reach of humans, whereas eternity belongs only to God. In the final analysis, the unity of human knowledge can be postulated only because language, which is human-made, is the necessary medium for constructing reality both social and natural. Insofar as the truth of nature as well as of history must be communicated by way of language, it is inevitably a *social* construction. It cannot be otherwise. Herein lies the necessity of hermeneutics for the (social) construction of all knowledge as propounded by such contemporary writers as Gadamer, Thomas S. Kuhn, and Stephen Toulmin.

The movement of history is predicated upon the fact that the human being is an agent or acting subject who is capable of triggering or initiating transformation. Historical movement or transformation without the subject is a fatal abstraction. Structuralism prematurely announced the disappearance of "man" the subject. Fortunately, its erasure of the subject was short-lived. Subjectivity is not dead. Although the early Michel Foucault was critical of phenomenological subjectivity, the later Foucault spoke of "new forms of subjectivity," and the *"résumé"* of his courses between 1970 and 1982 at the Collège de France includes *"Subjectivité et vérité"* (1980–81), *"L'herméneutique du sujet"* (1981–82), and *"Le gouvernement de soi et des autres"* (1982–83). The notion of decentered subjectivity that surges forth in such work strikes a judicious, though somewhat tamed, balance between human agency and social structure. It may be said that social structure without agency is meaningless, while agency without social structure is vacuous.

The body, too, is a living subject. The most distinctive discovery of phenomenology is, I submit, the notion that the body—the shadowy *other* of the mind or the soul—is not just an object among other objects in the world, but a sentient subject (*Leib, corps vécu*). The human being is fully human precisely because s/he is embodied. Only because humans are fully embodied are they naturally rooted in the world both social and natural. This lived body is the natural linkage to the world; it makes us—you and me—visible as humans. In other words, it is the most fundamental mode of our being-in-the-world, and its implications for ethics and political philosophy have yet to be fully explored. Ultimately, it makes sense to say that the world itself is "one body" rather than "one mind." Because the word is made flesh, it becomes performative, that is, it incorporates the ethical. In the beginning was the word, and it was born ethical.

The concept of the lived body runs counter to the tradition of logocentrism, which accords the legitimacy of "rationality" only to the mind in isolation from the body—that is, it runs counter to the mainstream tradition of disembodied reason. The mind without the body is another fatal abstraction. All conception—mental or physical—is always and necessarily corporeal. But contemporary social theory unfortunately values corporeality or the lived body far too lightly. For example, corporeality is totally missing from Jürgen Habermas's communicative theory of human action; it knows no "body politic." And despite the unusual insights concerning the clinical body, the incarcerated body, and the sexual body, the lived body is not woven into the conceptual fabric of Foucault's body politic. His body politic would have been enriched if it were firmly and securely placed in the native soil of the lived body.

The lived body is our active mode of being-in-the-world. By way of it we relate ourselves to other people and other things in the world. It was Ludwig Feuerbach who discovered the paradigmatic significance of a "Thou"—a discovery that has rightly been hailed as the "Copernican revolution" of social thought and whose tradition has been preserved, continued, and expanded by Marx, William James, Martin Buber, and Mikhail Bakhtin. What heliocentrism is to geocentrism, heterocentric dialogism is to egocentric monologism, which is connected in the Cartesian *Cogito* with ocularcentrism. In Heidegger's formulation, the word *Unterschied* has the double meaning of difference and the between (*Unter/schied*): it works like a hinge that connects and conserves difference and the relational, that is, difference as dif/ference (*Differenz* as *Unter/schied*). The relational—which may be interhuman, intersexual, or interspecies—is marked by the play of difference: the more difference, the more reciprocity and the more the other, the more the self. In the world of identity, which is the opposite of difference, nothing or nobody is truly relational. Without alterity as difference, that is, without the otherness of the Other, the question of ethics is unthinkable, simply because there would be no genuine reciprocity. In the universe of one person unpopulated by others—were it imaginable—there would be neither reciprocity nor ethics. But for reciprocity, there would be no need for ethics. Plurality, Hannah Arendt affirms, *is* "the human condition," which is also the title of her path-breaking work. She defines human plurality as having the twofold character of *equality* and *distinction*. While the principle of equality makes human communication *possible,* the principle of distinction makes human communication *necessary.* Alterity as difference thus belongs to the realm of necessity: without distinction, everybody would become nobody. In view of this, *pluralism*— in all of its manifestation and forms—*acquires a radically new meaning.* Sustained by the play of difference, it shuns identity, homogeneity, uniformity, centralization, conformity, and totalization.

As a revolt against modernity, postmodernity lives and thrives on the diet of difference. In significant measure, it is an attempt to dispel (dis-spell) the Cartesian anxiety about difference, since for the *Cogito*, desire is nothing but the desire for identity—the identity, for instance, between thought and existence that results inescapably in egocentric monologism. Inasmuch as postmodernity is anti-Cartesian, it is largely post-epistemological. In other words, it is ethical. Today the ethical concern is phenomenological as much as it is postmodern. In this respect, Levinas's philosophy may be singled out as the exemplar of ethical thinking based on alterity as the otherness of the Other.

In her controversial reporting of the 1961 Adolf Eichmann trial in Jerusalem, Arendt discerned and confronted the issue of "thoughtlessness" or the "banality of evil" in Eichmann's crimes against humanity, an issue that has often been obfuscated by and misunderstood in her friends' and foes' commentaries. Thinking or thoughfulness itself—particularly in relation to human conduct, that is, ethical thinking—is indeed frail and arduous, as is evidenced in Heidegger's involvement in Nazism. Heidegger's Nazi affair has an ironic twist because he, who was also a mentor of Arendt and whose indelible imprints are visible, I think, in her *The Human Condition* (1958), is a quintessential exponent of thinking. Be that as it may, thinking does not, for Arendt, refer to the human being's special gift and ability for theoretical conceptualization. Rather, for her, it is the natural gift of all humans, all men and women, as common-sense wisdom (the true meaning of which is revealed in the original Latin expression *sensus communis*). Most importantly, Arendt faults Eichmann's thoughtlessness for his lack or absence of other-directed thinking, that is, heterocentric thinking: his thoughtlessness is identified with *his inability to think from the standpoint of others.*

xvii

Preface as a Postscript

Feminism today, too, is a search and struggle for recognition and distinction by affirming "a different voice" as opposed to the "phallacious" logic of identity that perpetuates male domination. It is a heresiarchical play of difference: it is the oppositional voice of desiring to be the Other and go beyond the phallus, beyond "the second sex"—to use the unsurpassable expression and meaning of Simone de Beauvoir. "Gynesis" as *jouissance* marks feminine difference from masculine identity. In the first place, gynesis as the valorization of the feminine intends to subvert the canonical institution of philosophy as the *specular theory* of knowing and doing, as the ethics of *specular man*. In the second place, gynesis as *jouissance,* which is truly "Freude/an," signifies not only the enjoyment of things carnal but also—as it is also spelled *"j'ouïs sens"* ("I hear meaning")—a protest against and the subversion of ocularcentrism. It ultimately promises to show vision's *cul-de-sac.* Gynesis auscultates the "different voice" of the feminine; it is the joy of hearing (and voicing) but not of seeing. The feminine hearing has taken a *dumb rap* from the masculine seeing for too long! Gynesis, all in all, is the keyword for the "Freude/an" body politic, and it holds a promising future for transforming many traditional views.

The carnivalesque is the heresiarchical play of difference, of alterity as difference. Insofar, as alterity implies transgression and transformation, it is a technique of the body politic to deconstruct the world: *both* to *destroy* a "real" world *and* to *construct* a "possible," eu/topian world at the same time. Once Leszek Kolakowski contended that the most perennial theme that philosophy as a cultural critique plays out is the antagonism between the "priestly" and the "jesterly." The priestly is the guardian of the absolute and stands for stability and identity, whereas the jesterly—the unelimeninable *other* of the priestly—is irreverent to everything priestly and relishes contradiction and difference. The jesterly is the sinew of dialogue, and it preserves, enlivens, and nourishes human plurality in a nonviolent way. When suffering is not skin deep, rebellion is its natural and inevitable outcome: suffering and rebellion are born as twin brothers/sisters. Rebellion is that fine median that treads between totalitarian *submission* and revolutionary *destruction*. Carnival may indeed be "a licensed affair"—to borrow Terry Eagleton's critical expression. As a *licensed* affair, it has a double meaning: one is permission or authorization, and the other "unrestrained by law" and "disregarding accepted rules." Carnival is then "licentious," and it is capable of transgressing or reversing the repressive status quo.

Václav Havel's politics of "living in truth" and of his "Charter 77" group in Czechoslovakia, whose intellectual pillar was Jan Patočka—once an assistant of Husserl and a student of Heidegger—vindicates the efficacy of the jesterly against the high priesthood of totalitarian politics, of "the power of the powerless," and of the existential politics of conscience and nonviolent resistance for the creation of a "post-totalitarian" political order. It is no accident that Havel's speech delivered to the Joint Session of the U.S. Congress on February 21, 1990, was sloganized as "consciousness precedes being." In an interview published as "The Politics of Hope," he also talked about the role of an intellectual as a perpetual "irritant" rebel who is explicitly and self-consciously detached from the established order of any kind and who is always suspicious of belonging to the "winning side." Havel shows that—to borrow the eloquent language of Roger Scruton in writing about T. G. Masaryk and Patočka—"the individual soul is the foundation of social order and . . . the care of the soul, and the care of the *polis*, are two aspects of a single concern"—*The Philosopher on Dover Beach*, p. 88.

In the end, Husserl sums up concisely the quintessential mission of a philosopher, particularly in time of crisis and need: the "civil servant of humanity." Here he prescribes philosophizing with a human face. In this Husserlian spirit, the phenomenologist is one who is willing to take on the challenge and responsibility of strengthening the moral solidarity of humanity. In so doing, the phenomenologist is well-tempered to the postmodern disposition and climate of thinking, and stands ready and eager to transcend disciplinary boundaries, abandon conceptual condominia, and tear down continental divides of culture in the age of academic specialization and compartmentalization.

Part I
Phenomenology as a
Critique of Politics

Only connect! . . . Live in fragments no longer. Only connect, and the beast and the monk, robbed of the isolation that is life to either, will die.

—E. M. Forster,
Howards End

One

THE POLITICAL RELEVANCE OF EXISTENTIAL PHENOMENOLOGY

I. Introduction

FOR SOME OF ITS SEVERE CRITICS, existentialism represents a temporary outburst of the dark side of humanity that is indicative of a passing phenomenon of our age, and particularly of the postwar angry generation living on the morbid edges of death, anxiety, and the absurdity of human existence. They contend that existentialism is not a philosophy, or at least not a serious and disciplined philosophy. Professor Henry S. Kariel characterized existential psychology as "negativism" and its counterpart, behavioral psychology, as "positivism"; similarly, Professor Eugene J. Meehan described the phenomenology of Edmund Husserl as having sought to find philosophical certainty "in feeling rather than in thought," an assessment that falsely indicts phenomenology as an irrationalism.[1] I have singled out these two political theorists as representatives of a widespread misconception of existential philosophy and phenomenology, held as well, I suspect, by many American political theorists. This essay is not designed as a direct rebuttal to these misunderstandings and criticisms; it is rather an attempt to show what I consider to be the significant and positive contributions of existential philosophy and phenomenology to the foundation of political theory.

3

Over the years, the terms *existential philosophy, phenomenology,* and *radical empiricism* have on many occasions been used more and more synonymously, although they have separate historical origins in Kierkegaard, Husserl and William James, respectively. Not only is there a close affinity between Husserl's phenomenology and James's radical empiricism, but James has actually been called the first American existential philosopher. Indeed, phenomenology as it has developed in Europe and in this country now represents a far broader movement than when Husserl first initiated it. In this essay I rely heavily on the second school of phenomenology, called existential phenomenology, which attempts to synthesize and go beyond the existential thought initiated by Kierkegaard and the phenomenological thought initiated by Husserl. Martin Heidegger in Germany, Jean-Paul Sartre, Maurice Merleau-Ponty, and Paul Ricoeur in France, and John Wild in this country are among the outstanding representatives of existential phenomenology.[2] For existential phenomenologists, phenomenology is essentially a descriptive method by which to explore the different regions of human existence. These thinkers do not aim at description for its own sake, however, but rather for the sake of elucidating the meaning of human being-in-the-world. Ricoeur says that "existential phenomenology makes the transition between transcendental phenomenology, born of the reduction of everything to its appearing to me, and ontology, which restores the question of the sense of being for all that is said to 'exist.' "[3]

In setting forth the implications of existential phenomenology for political theory, I have divided the balance of this discussion into five issues: (1) the *Lebenswelt* (life-world); (2) phenomenology as radical empiricism; (3) phenomenology and philosophy of political science; (4) the meaning of human action; and (5) the meaning of sociality. In Section II, I shall discuss the idea of the life-world as the all-encompassing horizon of meaning within which the rituals of our action and interaction take place in the midst of other people, cultural objects, and natural things. Since the life-world refers to human culture, it has a political dimension as well as historical and social dimensions. Section III deals with phenomenology as a philosophy of lived experience. Phenomenology in the first place attempts to examine and justify its own activity as a philosophy, and secondly it acknowledges the dependence of the conceptual on the preconceptual. Section IV is concerned with the phenomenological insistence that the study of human behavior, and political science in particular, must adopt methods radically different from those of the natural sciences because there is a qualitative difference between the human (or behavioral) and the natural. Section V is devoted to the structure of human action, since political science, in common with the other behavioral sciences, is concerned with the meaning-structure of individual action in relation to the political system. Section V discusses the concept of sociality as the structure of human beings' relationships to one another, the elucidation of which is most elemental to social and political theory.

II. The Lebenswelt (Life-World)

The phenomenology of the everyday life-world has a direct relevance and significance to the theory of politics because it is a philosophy that attempts to describe rigorously the meaning of concrete human experience, political or otherwise, in our everyday life. The task of describing this human life-world, however, has been neglected in Western philosophy since the time of Plato, who considered it a cave world of impermanent shadows and images. Now phenomenology pays serious attention to the exploration of the everyday life-world.

The relevance of the phenomenology of the life-world to the theory of politics is twofold. In the first place, the life-world is the basic matrix of all theoretical endeavors, including political theorizing. It has a privileged status in the sense that all conceptual activity is founded upon the preconceptual world called the life-world. Husserl himself regarded this everyday life-world as the most universal problem of philosophy and as the foundation of all theoretical enterprises. Second, the life-world is a historical, social, and cultural world that encompasses the whole of political reality as the object of political theorizing. The phenomenology of the life-world is a philosophy of social reality in the broadest sense of the term *social*.

The totality of the world consists of subuniverses or subworlds. The world is the comprehensive and inclusive horizon of all possible and actual experiences. This world contains in it innumerable realities, that is, as many as there are orders of experience. There is the world of individual opinion, the world of dreams, the play world of the child, the world of the insane, etc.[4] What is experienced is real, and conversely, what is real is experienceable. Because reality is constituted by the meaning of our experiences, we can speak of "finite provinces of meaning," each of which is in its own way "a specific accent of reality." Each province of meaning is called finite because it has, within boundaries of its own, a particular cognitive style that appears fictitious, inconsistent, and incompatible with another (finite) province of meaning. The world of the insane, for instance, appears "unreal" to the world of the sane, and *vice versa*.

Among these multiple realities, the reality of everyday existence is of direct and immediate importance to political and social theory. It is the archetype of reality, and other realities may be considered as its modifications. This paramount reality of everyday existence is characterized by working, that is, by overt action requiring bodily movement. In contrast to the world of dreams, the world of working is characterized by a state of wide-awake consciousness that attends to the requirements of our activities. As working is most vital for the constitution of the reality of everyday existence, political actions and interactions are necessarily founded upon acts of working.

Husserl's famous urging to go back "to the things themselves" means to return to the primordial and original world of everyday existence that is prior to the derivative and secondary expression of theorizing activity in philosophy and science. This life-world is an ultimate horizon in which natural things, cultural objects, and individual persons are understood in the "natural attitude." By the "natural attitude" is meant a prereflective and naive point of view toward the world where all objects originally appear to us in our perception and where our doings have practical meanings. In the "natural attitude" the typical contents of the world are accepted as a matter of course or are taken for granted as familiar. Husserl says that

> it [the life-world] is pregiven to us all quite naturally, as persons within the horizon of our fellow men, i.e., in every actual connection with others, as "the" world common to us all. Thus it is . . . the constant ground of validity, an ever available source of what is taken for granted, to which we, whether as practical men or as scientists, lay claim as a matter of course.[5]

For the purpose of relating phenomenology to the theory of politics, the following characteristics of the life-world deserve special attention. First, the life-world is preconceptual. It is pregiven to the world of conceptualization. Because it precedes conceptual knowledge, the life-world is a prephilosophical, prelogical, and prescientific world. It is the world not of what "I think" but of what "I live through." In this mundane, lived world we experience things and other people immediately rather than mediately. It is foremost the theater of action, for example, the world of political actors in contrast to the conceptual world of political theorists. The theorist *as* theorist does not participate in this life-world as an actor.

Hence the second and real importance of the life-world lies in its status as the meaningful basis of human action. As active doers, human beings are always in the making or on the way. They are what they make of themselves, and they mold their future by their actions. Thus the human being has neither fixed properties nor a predetermined future. The idea that the human being is always an open possibility constitutes our radical historicity. Furthermore, value occupies the center of action. And since value is not an accidental appendage but rather is endemic to a human culture, the structure of action *is* a structure of approvals and disapprovals.[6]

Third, the world is not the private world of an individual, but is from the outset an intersubjective or socialized world. Accordingly, our knowledge of it, whether conceptual or common-sense, is not private but is also socialized. Thus social reality is an original datum of the life-world from which the theorist's conceptual knowledge is constructed. The investigation of social reality constitutes the primary object of social and political theory. As with all human activity in society, the stuff of politics *is* other people. Politics is inevitably a mingling with other people. In the meeting of the past and the present, we inherit from our predecessors a certain political system with its traditions, beliefs, and fixed values, all of which we ordinarily accept as normal. These given patterns of a political culture, however, are in principle questionable—that is, they become problematical to us. They may be called into question, for example, in a time of crisis, and a new pattern of meanings and values may emerge. To put it differently, when the traditional patterns of behavior are no longer applicable to resolving new problems, the situation is called a crisis. Thus the life-world as the theater of action is dynamic and changing, which means that it is historical. As there are different cultures in history, moreover, there are different versions of the life-world. To summarize, the life-world is *active, social,* and *historical.* Although they are conceptually distinguishable, these characteristics of the life-world are in reality inseparable from one another.

III. Phenomenology as Radical Empiricism

Phenomenology is a radical empiricism. To be rightly called radical, an empiricism must meet two requirements. First, the radicality of an empirical philosophy demands a self-examination and self-clarification of its own theorizing activity. To be radical, then, phenomenology must attempt to question its own presuppositions. Second, to be radical, an empirical philosophy should include in its theory no more and no less than what is directly experienced. Therefore, radical empiricism recognizes the dependence of reflection on directly lived experience, that is to say, it accepts the idea that reflection is founded upon lived experience. What is experiential is the primary material of reflection: immediate experience provides the material for later conceptual activity.

Above all, phenomenology examines the nature of theorizing as an activity. It clarifies the nature not only of theorizing in general, but of political theorizing in particular, for no other reason than that political theorizing is a form of theorizing. As the *logos* of the phenomenon, phenomenology deals with the object as it appears to consciousness. The object or the world that appears to consciousness is not a thing but the object-as-meant or the world-as-meant.

And since "phenomena" are lived meanings, then phenomenology is concerned with meanings. Meaning is made possible by the intentional structure of consciousness. Intentionality is the essence of consciousness, and by intentionality is understood the active directionality of consciousness toward an object. Because consciousness is intentional, it is always consciousness *of* something, whether it be real or ideal, existent or imaginary; for example, thinking is thinking *of* something. To use the language of phenomenology, the act of intending is called *noesis;* its correlate, the object as intended, is called *noema.* Intentionality suggests an inseparable noetic-noematic bond. In the act of reflection, there is a unity of the thinker (*ego*), thinking (*cogito*), and the object of which s/he thinks (*cogitatum*). Though these three aspects are distinguishable, they are existentially inseparable in the concrete act of thinking. Existentially speaking, intentionality is at the heart of consciousness. It is the source that gives meaning to human experience.

The idea that conceptual knowledge is derived from and founded upon preconceptual knowledge is a prerequisite to the method of radical empiricism as a philosophy of experience. William James speaks of the dependence of "knowledge-about" on "knowledge by acquaintance." According to him, knowledge by acquaintance is knowing things by seeing their colors and by tasting them, and knowing other people in their presence. Since pure experience is feeling, knowledge by acquaintance is "felt knowledge," whereas "knowledge-about" is "thought knowledge": "Through feelings we become acquainted with things, but only by our thoughts do we know about them. Feelings are the germ and starting point of cognition, thoughts the developed tree."[7] To say that the conceptual is dependent upon the preconceptual simply means that any explicit act of conceptualization, including political theorizing, presupposes something that is directly experienced prior to conceptualization.

The felt dimension of our experience plays an important function in what we think, observe, and perceive and in how we behave. Meaning involves experiencing that is preconceptual, presymbolic, and preverbal (that is, something felt). Although it is yet to be articulated, this felt "mass" of our experience is richer and broader than our thought, observation, speech, and action. It makes sense to say that "we know more than we can tell" or that "we mean more than we can say." We often grope for words to express the meaning we experience and feel dissatisfied with our verbal or written expressions of it. Meaning is not limited to symbolically expressive meaning, that is, it is not concerned merely with the logical, syntactical, and semantic structures of symbols. If it were, our thought process would be like the working of programmed computers and our speech would be like the mechanical voice of a record. Certainly, felt meaning can be symbolized. For since feeling and symbolizing go hand in hand, we are capable of symbolizing our felt meaning or expressing it in words. But our thought is the mediation between felt meaning and symbols, and the latter have a direct reference to the former. Let us illustrate this from the way we define a political concept such as democracy. In order to define (or conceptualize about) "democracy," we first refer directly to the implicit or tacit meaning we associate with it. Before we articulate the conceptual meaning of democracy, we have some positive but inarticulate understanding of it. We do not conceptualize in a vacuum or without any basic reference to something we already know tacitly. A definition of democracy begins from our felt or tacit meaning of it. Our felt meaning of democracy, therefore, is not necessarily logically prior to our conceptual definition of democracy, but it is *experientially* prior to our definition of it.

The dependence of reflection on lived experience, or of the "objective" meaning of symbolization on "subjective" felt meaning, leads us to the heart of the controversial issue between subjectivity and objectivity. Not only is phenomenology criticized as a "subjectivism," but we also treat subjectivity as if it were anathema to all scientific inquiry. But, on the contrary, as the notion of intentionality suggests, subjectivity and objectivity are only two moments of the same phenomenon. Subjectivity refers to the "intrinsic relatedness" of our experiences and actions to our awareness of them, on the one hand, and on the other hand, objectivity refers to what is observable from outside. The affirmation of the latter to the exclusion of the former (objectivism) is misleading because it ignores the place of subjectivity in thought and observation. What is observable (a datum), for example, is always related to the awareness of an observer. A datum of observation is not yet a fact, and a fact is meaningful only in relation to the observer for whom it is a fact. Thus a fact is nothing but meaning given to a datum (or data) by the observer in the process of observation. Further, the truth of a fact or thought for one observer is sanctioned intersubjectively, that is, by a scientific or intellectual community. Since consciousness is intentional, reflective thought—whether philosophical or scientific—is neither entirely subjective nor entirely objective.

The existential revolt of Kierkegaard was directed against the intellectualist objectivism of Hegel, against Hegel's "abstract thought"—as Kierkegaard called it—which has no reference to the concrete existence of the thinker him/herself, and in which s/he becomes merely a thinking substance or thing. Intellectualism defines human existence in terms of thought and converts the certainty of existence and the world into the certainty of thought "about" them or into the "ideas" of them. In other words, it recognizes reality only in the process of thought, and in this process, the human being is reduced to a "little abstract effigy." A philosophy whose starting point is cognitive experience tends to exalt thought over action, theory over practice.

The rejection of intellectualism does not mean, however, that the philosophy of existence is the tyranny of practice over theory, that is, a kind of utilitarian pragmatism or instrumentalism that discredits the value of disinterested intellectual pursuit.[8] Rather, existential philosophy makes a serious attempt to achieve the unity of theory and practice by defining human beings in terms of how they act and ought to act. The human being is not just a thinking subject, but is active and affective as well as intellectual. Existentialism is a philosophy, not of the "I think," but of the *"we are"* (*our* being-in-the-world), which includes theoretical activity as an essential component. To say that humans are active doers means that we are capable of entering relationships with others. Action and sociality imply each other, for the field of action calls for the reciprocity of the existing self with the other. For this reason, the structure of action is always relational. As John Macmurray puts it: "The Self must be conceived, not theoretically as subject, but practically, as agent. . . . [H]uman behaviour is comprehensible only in terms of a dynamic social reference; the isolated, purely individual self is a fiction."[9] Because existential philosophy unites thought with action, it is particularly relevant to the theory of politics. Political theory aims at reflection with a view to action as well as with a view to knowledge. It is an attempt to link the self as thinker with the self as actor. This also is the central question of existential philosophy.[10]

IV. Phenomenology and Philosophy of Political Science

Philosophy can no more pass over facts than the empirical sciences can leave out broad epistemological questions raised in philosophy. There must be an alliance between philosophy and the social sciences, or between the philosopher who *reflects* and the social scientist who *observes*. Since the philosopher and the social scientist are the bearers of reflection on the same life-world from which their knowledge is constructed, there can be neither segregation nor cold war between philosophy and the social sciences. Like the social scientist, the philosopher speaks about human action, history, and the social world. Conversely, the social scientist is already a philosopher at the very moment of the interpretation of social facts.[11]

The contribution of phenomenological investigation to the theory of politics, society, and culture lies especially in its focusing on the meaning of human action. The most basic thesis of phenomenology in the social sciences is set forth by Alfred Schutz when he says that

> it is the main problem of the social sciences to develop a method in order to deal in an objective way with the subjective meaning of human action and . . . the thought objects of the social sciences have to remain consistent with the thought objects of common sense, formed by men in everyday life in order to come to terms with social reality. . . . The thought objects constructed by the social scientist, in order to grasp this social reality, have to be founded upon the thought objects constructed by the common sense thinking of men, living their daily life within their social world. Thus, the constructs of the social sciences are, so to speak, constructs of the second degree, that is, constructs of the constructs made by the actors on the social scene, whose behavior the social scientist has to observe and to explain in accordance with the procedural rules of his science.[12]

It follows then that all conceptual frameworks in political science must presuppose and ought to be consonant with our preconceptual understanding about political things. The ordinary language of political humankind precedes the objectified language of political science, and the latter must be consistent with the former.[13] The language of political science can refine, improve, and supplement but cannot ignore the ordinary discourse of political humankind. The usefulness of the former is justified by the extent to which it elucidates the reality of the political system.

The recent methodology of political science, however, is far from being immune from abstract conceptualization. One example of the tendency to abstract and reify concepts is found in the *analytic* conception of "philosophy of political science." According to this view, political science is a descriptive discipline that seeks to increase factual knowledge about the political world, whereas political ethics (or political philosophy) is purely normative in that it attends to the substantive issues of what makes a good political society. In contrast, however, the philosophy of political science is a strictly formalistic undertaking, for it deals with the logical and linguistic analysis of concepts and statements about political phenomena. Unlike the first two, it is neither factual nor normative. Viewed in this way, values are on the one hand *scientifically* meaningless, that is, they are unrelated to political science as a factual discipline because they express personal beliefs and preferences rather than report the state of affairs. On the other hand, both facts and values are *philosophically* irrelevant because the function of philosophy is logical and linguistic rather than empirical and normative.[14] As factual and normative inquiries are relegated to political science and political ethics respectively, the analytic philosophy of political science emphasizes the linguistic aspect of political analysis. Another example of abstract theorizing is Anthony Downs's "positive" conception of political science.[15] To be "positive," according to him, the model is constructed for the purpose of accurate prediction rather than of describing political reality accurately or understanding the meaning of political phenomena under observation. It is constructed by selecting a few crucial variables as relevant while ignoring others that may in fact have a vital influence on the real world of politics. Since for Downs the utility of theoretical constructs is dependent upon "the accuracy of their prediction rather than the reality of their assumptions," the preconceptual reality of how *real* people behave in the *real* world of politics is materially irrelevant to his conceptual framework.

Now it goes without saying that language is an indispensable instrument in political theorizing and in political life, and that the clarification of linguistic uses or misuses helps to settle the issues in question, although the idea that all philosophical problems arise out of linguistic confusions is highly presumptuous. Be that as it may, it would be a mistake to treat language as if it were independent of the reality it purports to describe, just as it would be a mistake to think that preconceptual reality can be ignored as materially irrelevant to theoretical constructs in political science. The language of politics itself is a part of the complex reality of the political world that the political theorist is to elucidate. Insofar as preconceptual language is the landscape of conceptual thought, the language of political theory is inseparably linked to the political reality it objectifies. By the same token, the question of how far political reality is intelligible cannot be answered without at the same time answering how political reality and theoretical concepts are interdependent. The political concepts of "power," "freedom," "justice," "democracy," etc. (that is, those concepts that are used in the literature of political theory), all have a point of reference somewhere in political life itself. This thesis, of course, does not destroy or diminish the importance of conceptual language, but instead only recognizes the primacy of the ordinary language of political humankind. Whether a political theorist is willing to admit it or not, preconceptual political reality serves as the background of his/her political theorizing, for s/he is first and foremost a member of the political society that s/he objectifies. Precisely because the ordinary discourse of political life is the primary word, though not the last word, both how ordinary language functions in political life and how it is related to political theorizing are two basic but long neglected issues that political theory cannot afford to continue to overlook.[16]

Warning must be given that the emphasis on the meaning of human action within phenomenology is not a call for a new kind of knowledge in the social sciences, but is rather an insistence on the qualitative difference between the orders of reality investigated by natural scientists on the one hand and by social scientists on the other. The difference between the natural sciences and the social sciences is not that they seek different kinds of knowledge, but that they have radically different objects to investigate. Only human beings are capable of endowing with meaning what they do, feel, and perceive, while things in nature are not. This radical difference between the human and the merely natural is taken into account in the phenomenological method of the social sciences. Like the sociological method of Max Weber, phenomenology accommodates its methodological rigor to this basic fact. Schutz writes:

> The concept of Nature, for instance, with which the natural sciences have to deal is, as Husserl has shown, an idealizing abstraction from the *Lebenswelt,* an abstraction which, on principle and of course legitimately, excludes persons with their personal life and all objects of culture which originate as such in practical human activity. Exactly this layer of the *Lebenswelt,* however, from which the natural sciences have to abstract, is the social reality which the social sciences have to investigate.[17]

Phenomenology is thus opposed to the scientific doctrine that defines the truth of the social sciences essentially according to the procedural rules of the physical sciences, because the methodology of the natural sciences fails to acknowledge the meaning-structure of human phenomena, which is absent in natural phenomena. This does not mean that phenomenology resorts to the method of introspection. Nor does it reject *in toto* the "behavioristic" interpretation of human behavior. The phenomenological approach only pinpoints the limits and blind spots of behaviorism. The behavioristic interpretation of human action is correct and valid so long as it refers to the external indications of movement, but it goes wrong when it identifies what is external with the intended meaning the actor imputes to his/her action. The intended meaning of action cannot be inferred merely from its external indications. Only by combining what is external and what is intended is it possible to understand fully the meaning of human behavior.

In order to see more clearly the implications of phenomenology for political science, it might be well to compare phenomenology with Heinz Eulau's views of the behavioral approach to politics.[18] The following exposition of the similarities and ultimate divergences of these approaches illustrates the value of phenomenology to the theory of politics.

Eulau maintains that the radical goal of political science is humanity, and that the function of political science is to understand and interpret the political world rather than to change it. Not unlike the phenomenologist, Eulau defines the basic stuff of politics in terms of the conditions and consequences of individual action and the roles that the political actor performs in the social, cultural, and personal milieu. Most significantly, he emphasizes the importance of the *meaning* the actor attaches to his/her action. The presence of meaning makes the study of human behavior different from the study of natural objects and events. For this very reason, according to Eulau, the distinct merit of the behavioral persuasion lies in its focus on the meaning of human behavior. Moreover, he holds that the observation of political behavior must meet the test of intersubjective agreement between observer and observed. In other words, there must be an agreement between the meaning given to behavior by the observer and that given by the actor him/herself. This does not require, however, that the observational language of political science should be the same as the language of the political actor, but rather that their meanings must be consonant with each other.

In sum, according to both the behavioral persuasion of Eulau and the basic view of phenomenology, the meaning-world of the political observer must be consistent with the meaning-world of the political actor. But the critical difference that separates these two approaches lies in their assessment of objective methods in handling political data: the phenomenologist insists that because there is a qualitative difference between things human and things merely natural, the method of the behavioral sciences must be radically different from that of natural science techniques, whereas while Eulau recognizes this difference, he insists that nothing in political behavior is "intrinsically immune to scientific analysis" and that there are no "natural limits" to the use of scientific methods and techniques in political science. To be sure, the catch phrase is "scientific analysis." By scientific analysis, however, Eulau does not mean any and every objective and rigorous analysis, but scientific analysis in a positivistic sense, that is, political analysis taken according to the positivist conception of science. Eulau, I think, fails to demonstrate in what way the qualitative difference between human and natural phenomena can be reconciled with his vision of scientific technology, however perfect it may become in the future for the analysis of political data.[19] In the final analysis, Eulau chooses to opt for what is external rather than what is intended as the only legitimate universe of scientific discourse and observation. To put it more bluntly, Eulau has yet to show how a John Watson can be reconciled with a Max Weber.

The phenomenological approach, on the other hand, is consistent with its own basic recognition of the radical differences between what is human and what is merely natural. Because political events have meanings for political actors, the observation of political scientists must be founded upon the meanings of political events interpreted by political actors themselves. Phenomenology, therefore, focuses on the intentional dimensions of human action and the social world. Because it is intentional, human action strictly speaking is neither exclusively external nor exclusively internal: it is both. Phenomenology insists that scientific methods and techniques that are appropriate only for the investigation of natural phenomena are inadequate for the investigation of the intentional structure of human action. Since political science, in common with the other behavioral sciences, presupposes a theory of action, I will next present the essentials of the phenomenological exposition of human action.

V. The Meaning of Human Action

Action is human conduct as an ongoing process based upon a preconceived project. Action has temporal, intentional, motivational, and bodily dimensions.[20] Human beings are responsible agents who know that they are the authors of their acts. They are aware of what is to be done. The presence of the project (in action) makes our action meaningful, rational, and purposive. Insofar as we have internal time-consciousness or the inner flow of duration, we have our lived experience (*Erlebnis*). However, our lived experience acquires an explicit sense or meaning only when it is grasped by the act of attention (reflectively), which is called meaningful experience (*Erfahrung*). The meaningfulness of our experience thus refers to "having experienced" and never to the ongoing process of experiencing.

The project is the purposive basis of performing an action. It is the practical determination of what is to be done and is geared toward achieving a practical goal. It is not a mere fancying, precisely because it is formulated in terms of what I *can* do within my power to reach a desired goal. Since it is only a blueprint for action, the project is independent of the actual execution of action. It refers to the action not yet executed. Because the project is the rehearsing of the course of action yet to take place, it can be modified or cancelled at will. But whereas the project is reversible and revocable, the executed action is not. The project has no practical consequences unless it is fulfilled by the act of working. For instance, a person decides to run for a public office to bring about some desirable change in government. Presumably s/he reaches this decision after a careful consideration of such factors as his/her "availability" and physical and financial capabilities. In order to win an election, which is the immediate goal, the candidate must plan ahead the course of action to take in the campaign. But the nature of a project being what it is, this does not mean that such plans are fixed once and for all. On the contrary, the candidate may change plans as the occasion demands.

In essence the project is a deliberation, a thought in the process of making a decision. Since thought always relates itself to an object, the project is that which I decide (that is, the object of my decision). By decision I commit and bind myself to my project. Decision thus involves my personal action: it is always *I* who decides what is to be done. "I involve myself in the project," Paul Ricoeur declares, "I impute to myself the action which is to be done. This is what distinguishes decision from a wish or a command in which the thing to be done is not my personal action but the course of things or the action of another, more often expressed by the conditional or the imperative."[21]

Action is motivated behavior. For instance, I decide to close the window because I have a chill. In action the project and the motive are correlative, since to understand a project is to understand it in terms of reasons for it. Behind the deliberation of a project there is a basic dimension called motivation that provides an impetus for action or sets it in motion. The motive implies both the idea of a meaning and the idea of a force. It is a meaning insofar as it is a reason for doing something and a force to the extent that it starts a bodily movement.

The phenomenological analysis of motivation endeavors to integrate the psychology and the ethics of action. Since actors are neither agnostics nor disbelievers of values, in action there is no separation between what is and what ought to be. Indeed, fact and value are cooperative in action. As actors, we encounter values in motivating a project. What motivates our action is not only such material values as needs and desires, but also such formal values as duty, loyalty, or obligation. The motive for running for a public office may be a search for deference, an addiction to playing the game of politics, a sense of duty, etc., or any combination of these. Even our needs and desires, it must be stressed, cannot simply be treated as physical magnitudes, for they are also meanings and valuations that enter into our motivational field in interaction with other meanings and valuations.

In every theory of politics there are certain explicit or implicit assumptions about human nature, and there are those who tend to oversimplify the nature of political humankind and the motivational factors of our political action. They introduce a one-sided, hence false, image of the human being and reality. Anthony Downs, for example, contends that the people who involve themselves in party politics are motivated by "their personal desire for the income, prestige, and power which come from holding office."[22] He defines human beings as consumers who maximize their own utilities. In his view, human beings seek to maximize their self-interest, and their behavior is "rational" insofar as it is directed primarily towards selfish ends. Thus Downs reduces the image of political humankind to that of economic humankind and, for allegedly analytical reasons, all political motivation to the economic motivation of pecuniary gains in market relations.[23] Downs is guilty of unduly simplifying the image of the human being by assuming that every motive, or at least every significant motive, in human conduct is reducible to the maximization of individual utilities. A corollary of this is the reduction also of the notion of rationality (or political rationality) to the categories of economic rationality in the study of human behavior in society. By so doing, Downs obliterates the distinction between the political and the economic and narrows the vision of what is distinctively political.[24] This economic reductionism of Downs, as has already been indicated in the previous section, is certainly prompted by his methodological consideration of constructing a deductive model that necessitates a conceptual simplification of "real" human beings and their motives for the sake of purportedly exact measurement and accurate prediction. As John Dewey points out in his criticism of "economic psychology," however, artificial conceptual simplifications are no substitutes for the tangles of concrete empirical facts.[25]

Human action also has a bodily dimension. As a matter of fact the body is a necessary medium for all human activity, whether doing or thinking.[26] The body is an active mode of human existence in the world. We perceive, feel, act, and think *with* our body. Thinking is no more the function of mind alone, as the rationalist has it, than acting is merely a physical event, as the behaviorist has it. As John Wild stresses:

> Human behavior is neither a series of blind reactions to external "stimuli," nor the projection of acts which are motivated by the pure ideas of a disembodied, worldless mind. It is neither exclusively subjective nor exclusively objective, but a dialectical interchange between man and the world, which cannot be adequately expressed in traditional causal terms. It is a circular dialectic in which the independent beings of the life-field, already selected by the structure of the human body, exert a further selective operation on this body's acts. It is out of this dialectical interchange that human meanings emerge.[27]

In short, I *am* my body and the body is the existing I. The body as I live it is not constituted in an objective sense. It is an active subject rather than a passive object. Were the body only an object, human beings would be nothing but pure spectators, and would thus be deprived of their status as active doers.

In social relationships, moreover, the body is the apparatus of contact (*con-tact*) with others. All interpersonal contacts require a working act of the body, whether the contact be a politician shaking hands with a voter, a gathering of legislators debating in a legislative chamber to enact a law, or a group of political campaigners working out an election strategy. By reason of having a position in the world through the apparatus of the body, a person has direct access to others. The self is incapable of having a direct relationship with real people when there is a deranged perception between ego and body in relation to other people and the external world.[28] The body, then, is a crucial locus not only for the self-interpretation of a person's own lived experience, but also for the perception and understanding of others, and ultimately for a person's social and political relationships.

VI. The Meaning of Sociality

For the acting human, to be is to be social. The human being is nothing but a nexus of relationships, and is not human without being a social being. Thus all social philosophy must begin with a clarification of this elemental problem of sociality as the relationship between the self and the other. Existential philosophy is often accused, with justification, of being a philosophy of rugged individualism.[29] Existential philosophers of past generations are to be blamed for having neglected to explore the social and political dimensions of human existence. The founder of existentialism, Kierkegaard, himself took a rather negative and conservative attitude towards politics; for him, the truth was the inward subjectivity of an existing individual and to exist meant to be as "impolitic" as possible. Yet it must not be forgotten that his insight into the ever present danger of human anonymity and alienation is prophetic. The individualism of Kierkegaard, eccentric though it may be, is a constant reminder of the importance of an individual who cannot be reduced simply to one of the faceless crowd or to the law of the statistical average. Kierkegaard decisively rejected the phenomenon of the apathetic, indolent, and formless crowd that deprives the moral character of the individual.[30]

Today, existential and phenomenological philosophers attempt in earnest to seek the roots of humankind's social existence and clarify them. In post-Husserlian phenomenology, the human lifeworld and intersubjectivity constitute two important areas of investigation. They are interrelated by the fact that the life-world is an intersubjective world given in common to all human beings.

Maurice Merleau-Ponty epitomizes the existentialist idea that human existence *is* social existence when he says:

> [Our] political task is not incompatible with any cultural value or literary task, if literature and culture are defined as the progressive awareness of our multiple relationships with other people and the world rather than as extramundane techniques. *If all the truths are told, none will have to be hidden.* In man's co-existence with man, ... morals, doctrines, thoughts and customs, laws, works and words all express each other, everything signifies everything. And outside this unique fulguration of existence there is nothing.[31]

Sociality is a multiple network of human interrelationships. It refers to the relationship between the politician and the voter, the writer and the reader, the wife and the husband, etc. Politically speaking, to be a citizen, a voter, a taxpayer, and a politician implies everywhere certain relationships. Sociality has reference both to the relationship between one individual and another and to those between the individual and a collectivity (for example, a nation or a government). Insofar as the self is a responsible agent, an individual knows not only that s/he is the author of his/her acts, but that by initiating these actions s/he also solicits and invites the responses of other agents and accepts the consequences of the actions. Thus intersubjectivity is a natural condition of the inherence of the self in the world. Because human beings are intentional, a person is not and cannot be a windowless monad. Rather, the inner and the outer are a single indivisible existence. Human beings are capable both of internalizing the external and of externalizing the internal, the dialectical process of which constitutes the self-making of an individual on the one hand and the history of a society or a civilization on the other. Individuation and socialization are thus not expressions of two incompatible opposites, but complementary expressions of this single process.

Moreover, to say that humankind is social is not to include only harmony and cooperation to the exclusion of conflict and competition. To be social also involves a tension between harmony and conflict, accord and antagonism, cooperation and competition. In politics, too, they are two inseparable faces of Janus. Politics as the process of "conflict resolutions," as it is often called, makes sense only if we take into account these two complementary tendencies of social process. Unfortunately, however, there is a pervasive tendency in contemporary American political theory to polarize conflict and cooperation in order to place a one-sided premium on conflict and competition as the essence of politics. For too many the political system is synonymous with a system of conflict. Robert A. Dahl considers politics and conflict as "inseparable twins."[32] Similarly, for E. E. Schattschneider, the language of conflict is at the root of all politics. According to him, the socialization of conflict means an expansion of the scope and scale of conflict, and the nature of conflict determines the nature of the public involvement in the American polity whose democratic government is the greatest single instrument for the contagion and nationalization of conflict.[33]

It is important that sociality be described in terms of mutuality between the self and the other (or the world). By mutuality I mean the idea that without the world there is no authentic selfhood, and without selfhood there is no world. The self and the other are reciprocal, and their reciprocity is based on the heterogeneity of the two, that is, they are differentiated, for to exist is to "stand out from" each other. The idea of mutuality preserves the identity of the self as a unique individual who can exercise autonomy without either rejecting or being engulfed by society. In mutuality there is no place for imposition and enslavement, but only for the free unfolding and the responsible execution of relationships. The individual is *in* society, but not *of* it as a part in an organic whole. As a balanced view of the self and society, therefore, the idea of mutuality rejects both the egocentric and the sociocentric interpretations of the individual and society. The absolute sovereignty of the individual over society is as unreal as the affirmation of a collective consciousness independent of and transcending individuals. In the final analysis, the extreme views of both atomistic individualism and totalitarian collectivism vastly misunderstand the nature of sociality.

The concept of mutuality also defines the meaning of human freedom and responsibility in society. Since the human being is an active and social being, freedom and responsibility are two interlocking modalities of action in the social world. Because action is the radical transition from what we *are* to what we *intend to be,* the human being is a task to be accomplished rather than a set of fixed and predetermined properties. By the exercise of our freedom, we are able to refuse to be what we are. To be is in part to be free, and the logic of action requires freedom. Freedom is our capacity to make ourselves, to transform ourselves, and to choose our own future. Action, however, is sheer freedom only in reference to the absolute possibility of the self alone, whereas it entails responsibility in the presence of others. Freedom is a necessary quality that human action requires, whereas responsibility is a moral, social, and political relationship in the meeting of the self and the other. Practical freedom is finite and conditional not only because humans exist with other humans, but also because in the field of action or interaction, others, too, assert their own freedom. Absolute and unconditional freedom is an abstraction, as is an isolated individual, because the self exists only in the midst of and in relation to others. The human being may be free without being responsible, but cannot be responsible without first being free. To be responsible is to be free. From the viewpoint of the human being as a social being, to be is to be responsible. Responsibility is of a higher order than freedom simply because it is the beginning of self-transcendence, whereas freedom is necessary only for self-realization. In the community of active human beings, responsibility is both the capacity and the demand to respond to the call of others. As a demand, it is a moral obligation. If sociality is a fact of human existence, responsibility is the moral fulfillment of this social factualness. Only through the fulfillment of responsibility can we hope to establish the linkage between the fact and the value of our existence. In essence, then, responsibility consummates all of what is in human being-in-the-world with others and hence our very humanity. In the end, the authenticity of being human must be sought in responsibility—moral, social, and political—which lies at the root of genuine reciprocity.

VII. Conclusion

In recent years many have spoken of the decline, if not the death, of the theory of politics. The chief reasons to which this alleged decline is attributed are historicism, lack of normative concern resulting from the positivist doctrine of ethical neutrality, excessive preoccupation with methodology by neglecting the substantive issues of politics, and, not least, inattention to matters political in philosophical inquiry. Whatever the reasons for the decline of political theory may be, the most pressing question is how to revive it if indeed it is in decline. This essay is written with the conviction that substantive political theory is worthy of our intellectual endeavor and deserves our serious attention. I have attempted to indicate the direction of substantive political theory based on the findings of existential phenomenology. To summarize, the basic contributions of existential phenomenology to the philosophy of politics are first of all, a clarification of the meaning of theory for human existence, and second, a descriptive disclosure of the intentional meaning of human action and sociality.

Phenomenology insists on the relevance of the all-encompassing horizon of meaning called the life-world to theoretical activity in philosophy and science. From beginning to end, phenomenology is a descriptive analysis of the meaning of that which is lived or directly experienced. The life-world refers to the complex living relationships of human being to human being in culture, in society, in history, and in politics. As a philosophy, phenomenology is concerned with the meaning of theoretical inquiry into human existence and thus with the union of theory and practice, a problem of great importance to the theory of politics. To insist, as does phenomenology, on the primacy of lived reality, and to insist that the construction of objective thought is derivative, does not downgrade theoretical activity but places it in a proper perspective. The philosopher, and particularly the political philosopher, ought not to be the person who takes delight in the "empty kisses of abstraction," but ought to be the one who is ready to speak, for the philosopher exists in the world and his/her thinking is a special way of existing in the world. Nor is the philosopher an acosmic spirit who can transcend in a single breath the vicissitudes of politics and history and indulge in the eternal secrecy of private thought. After all, philosophers exist in the world, and when they think they think always of this mundane world that is pervaded by meaning and value and from which their knowledge originates.

In addition to elucidating the meaning of theoretical activity for human existence, phenomenology also contributes in substance and method to the behavioral sciences in that it describes the meaning-structure of human action and social reality. By recognizing the qualitative difference between human and natural phenomena, phenomenology attempts to focus on and capture the meaning of action as the actor lives through it and to avoid conceptual reductionism, which encapsulates the lived in a conceptual cocoon and sacrifices it to conceptual neatness and contrivance. Phenomenology does not deny, however, the importance of what is observable from outside, but instead emphasizes the idea that what is observable from without must also be considered in relation to what is lived from within. In this way phenomenology dissolves, as it were, the dichotomy between subjectivity and objectivity, because what is lived itself precedes all such dichotomies and distinctions. Moreover, when the action of one individual takes into account that of another, there arises the question of social action and ultimately of social reality. By virtue of intentionality, human beings are relational through and through: we are nothing but a nexus of relationships in the atmosphere of humanity. Social reality is indeed the total horizon of human beings' everyday relationships with their fellow human beings in society.

In conclusion, it must be stressed that politics and philosophy are intertwined. The underlying basis of political philosophy is the idea that philosophy cannot exclude politics from the legitimate domain of human rationality and thus from its inquiry. Political philosophy is not only a philosophical treatment of politics, but is equally a political introduction to philosophy. Although political existence is by no means the whole of human reality, any philosophy that abandons politics is unquestionably less than reasonable and complete, for the rationality of politics sustains in part the rationality of philosophy. For this reason, existential phenomenology, like every great philosophy, endeavors to understand political rationality in order to understand its own rationality fully. Its philosophical insights into political matters in the human life-world help us to gain a sense of direction and to open up a new perspective in political theorizing. In seeking the meaning of theory for human existence, Husserl rightly spoke of the philosopher as the "civil servant of humanity." Inspired by this humanist vision, political philosophy hopes to define its true vocation and to integrate the two inseparable realms of theory and practice on the one hand and of values and facts in political life on the other.

Where empiricism was deficient was in any internal
connection between the object and the act which it
triggers off. What intellectualism lacks is contingency
in the occasions of thought. In the first case
consciousness is too poor, in the second too rich for
any phenomenon to appeal compellingly to it.
Empiricism cannot see that we need to know what we
are looking for, otherwise we would not be looking
for it, and intellectualism fails to see that we need to
be ignorant of what we are looking for, or equally
again we should not be searching.
—Maurice Merleau-Ponty,
Phenomenology of Perception

Common sense [*sensus communis*] is judgment
without reflection, shared by an entire class, an entire
people, an entire nation, or the entire human race.
—Giambattista Vico,
The New Science

TWO

PHENOMENOLOGY AS A CRITIQUE
OF POLITICS

I

PHENOMENOLOGY BEGAN TO EXERT its influence in earnest on
American political science only in the late 1960s and early 1970s. It
therefore coincided with the decades of political unrest and turmoil
in the midst of the Vietnam quagmire, and was only a short-lived
insurgence of a new political consciousness with the intent of
"greening" America. This new political awakening in the face of
crisis was reflected and echoed in redefining the responsibility
of the political science profession itself in the name of the "Credo of

Relevance" that challenged the moral somnambulism of the established practices of the "mainstream" political science called *behavioralism*. In his Presidential Address at the 1969 Annual Meeting of the American Political Science Association, held in New York City, David Easton crystallized the already existing mood of many American political scientists when in echoing Thomas S. Kuhn's theory of scientific paradigms, he spoke of the new "post-behavioral revolution" in political science as the most recent contribution to the profession's collective heritage that represented an opportunity for needed change. By evoking the familiar traditions of pragmatism, existentialism, and Marxism, Easton insisted that this "post-behavioral revolution" could no longer be ignored in re-examining the direction of political research and the mission of the profession to make it "relevant" to the practical world of politics.[1]

The term "post-behavioral revolution," which refers to the debut of phenomenology on the stage of American political science, may be historically accurate since it came after political behavioralism. However, it is nonetheless conceptually misleading, because phenomenology is a radical challenge to the theory of politics—a challenge that is meant to uproot the existing sedimentations of scientific practices. Therefore, the conceptual challenges of phenomenology must be understood correctly as *discontinuous* rather than continuous with the scientific tradition of political behavioralism. Or are continuity and discontinuity the two complementary aspects of a single reality called history? Or is revolution meant to be a circular motion that has no beginning, middle, or ending? As a challenge of paradigms, phenomenology's contribution to political science can most clearly be understood if it is considered as a radical alternative or counterproposal to the two influential and strategic schools of thinking in American political science: (1) political behavioralism and (2) the "classical" school of political science propounded by Leo Strauss.

The scientific practitioners of politics prefer to use the term "behavioralism" in order for them to emphasize their alleged differences from "behaviorism" in psychology. They contend that political behavioralism, unlike psychological behaviorism, is "dynamic" because it takes into account the inner processes of cognition, affectivity, and evaluation for which the term "political culture," for example, was fashioned in comparative political analysis. However, this is only a sectarian difference in the ongoing movement to scientize the human, social sciences. Like behaviorism in psychology, political behavioralism is a species of scientism. For it aims to emulate the model of the natural sciences as the only *exact, rigorous,* and *empirical* method for the study of political behavior, whether it is translated in terms of quantitative statistics, game theory, or the model of artificial intelligence.

No doubt logical positivism is the philosophical godfather of political behavioralism. However, although this is seldom noticed by political behavioralists themselves, the intellectual heritage of behavioralist scientism is rooted in John Stuart Mill's *A System of Logic* (1843),[2] Book VI of which is "On the Logic of Moral Sciences," which happened to be translated into German as *Geisteswissenschaften*, and in which the study of politics is often mentioned. However, Mill's emphasis was on "logic" rather than on the "moral." In the first place, the basic position he sought to uphold in this work was that the laws of Mind are no exceptions to the general certainty and uniformity of the laws of Nature, though they may not be exactly isomorphic to them; moreover, the laws of Nature can be made "instrumental" in accordance with the formation of the laws of Mind. Such a scientific logic inflicts, according to Mill, no humiliation on our pride as human beings. Central to Mill's theses in the scientific formulation of moral sciences is "ethology," which is the study of "human nature" or the "formation of character." Here enters Pirandello: the "characters" of moral sciences in search of an "author." For Mill, ethology is such a Pirandellonian "author" in moral sciences.

Ethology is to be made "exact" and "deductive." It is called by Mill "the Exact Science of Human Nature." For the reason of being "deductive," however, ethology is not psychology that is empirical or inductive, although it is the study of the formation of human character (characterology). Unlike psychology, ethology is governed by the "middle principles" (*axiomata media*), which lie, as the name indicates, in the middle way between the highest generalities and the empirical laws emanating from simple observation. In this connection, mention should be made of David Easton's *The Political System: An Inquiry into the State of Political Science*[3]— the influential book for the development of "systematic political theory," which, in contradistinction to "political philosophy," is meant to be "causal" rather than "moral." The work was meant to be a conceptual housecleaning in defining the scope and method of political science. True to the spirit of Mill, it set out to formulate the "conceptual framework" (a set of *axiomata*) by which political data might be organized. It deplored, for example, the condition of American political science as a kind of "hyperfactual" son who abandoned his conceptual parents.

In the second place, Mill's ethology was meant to be the anti-Durkheimian science of individual character as the foundation of the study of the collective phenomena of society and politics, although it antedated Durkheim's "sociologism" by many decades. Basic to all phenomena of society and politics, Mill insisted, is ethology, because they are "obedient" to the laws of human nature and individual character: without understanding individual character, we do not understand the collective phenomena of society and politics. Therefore, there are no "social facts" in a Durkheimian sense as the subject *sui generis* of sociology. Mill emphasized that even when they are brought together into some collectivity, human beings will never change into another compound like water. This Millian "methodological individualism" was one of the battle cries of the "Young Turks" of political behavioralism in their revolt against the dominance of "institutionalism." For political behavioralism, "human nature" has become the cornerstone or pillar of the study of political behavior.[4]

II

Leo Strauss was trained in philosophy in the 1920s in Germany, and he was well acquainted with Max Weber's sociology, Husserl's phenomenology (as a "rigorous science"), and Heidegger's "existentialized" phenomenology. As a young scholar, he was very much impressed with Heidegger's meticulous textual analysis of Aristotle's *Metaphysics*, although he vehemently opposed Heidegger's politics in later years.[5] Immersed in the classical philosophy of Plato and Aristotle, the battle that Strauss launched against modern philosophy is a replay of the seventeenth-century French "quarrel between the Ancients and the Moderns." The revival of classical philosophy is for Strauss the launching platform of a critique of modernity. He must have also been acclimated to the studies of Plato in post-World War I Germany—especially of Ulrich von Wilamowitz—that emphasized the "political Plato."[6]

Classical philosophy is the standard bearer for Strauss, for whom the modern philosophical temper represented in "positivism" and "historicism" must be rejected *in toto* as anti- or non-philosophical.[7] He was determined to wage a "classical" war against these two schools of thought. Despite his conviction that historicism is the worse of the two, his critique of historicism has been far less noticed than that of positivism in the circle of political scientists for the reason that attention has been focused on the pros and cons of political behavioralism.[8] For Strauss, the Diltheyan suggestion that interpreters can understand authors better than the authors understood themselves epitomizes the presumptuous height of historicism that eludes forever our search for truth, absolute truth—the tribunal before which modernity is on trial and to be judged.

For Strauss, political philosophy is radically "unscientific" and "unhistorical"—a judgment derived from his interpretation of the classical political tradition that seeks knowledge of the good or political good. As such, he opposed positivism and historicism as the enemies of political philosophy today. The very *crisis* of contemporary thought is a direct result of the denial of philosophy as a search for timeless truth. Strauss's mood of crisis is reminiscent of that of Husserl, who was also critical of the "fact-minded" positivism that decapitates philosophy. While for Husserl it is positivism that is the enemy of philosophical thought, for Strauss it is historicism. For, according to Strauss, historicism is *the spirit of our time*, and positivism is necessarily transformed into historicism when the understanding of the latter becomes the necessary basis of an empirical science of society.

As Strauss interprets the classical tradition, particularly that of Plato and Aristotle, the question of knowledge of the good society is central to political philosophy, which is merely a political introduction to philosophy. For Strauss, political science is the moral science *par excellence*, since it seeks the most complete good (i.e., the political good). All political action, he emphasizes, aims for either preservation or change. When desiring to preserve, we wish to prevent a change for the worse; when desiring to change, we wish to bring about something better. The idea of the better or worse implies thought of *the good*. Insofar as political philosophy aims to replace political opinion (*doxa*) with political knowledge (*epistēmē*), knowledge of the political good becomes its guiding question. Strauss contends that neither positivism nor historicism is capable of answering the question of the good society: the "value-neutralism" of positivism ignores and subverts the question, and the "value-relativism" of historicism is incapable of answering it. So the target of Strauss's attack on positivism, and thus political behavioralism as an offspring of positivism, is the formula of value-neutrality or the conception of science as "value-free," to which Strauss also attributes Weber's methodological credo of "objectivity" in the social sciences. This formula became the guidepost for the detailed criticism of behavioralism in a collection of *Essays on the Scientific Study of Politics*[9] that Strauss himself sealed with an "epilogue." He spoke disdainfully of the value-neutral doctrine of political behavioralism when he wrote:

> Only a great fool would call the new political science diabolic: it has no attributes peculiar to fallen angels. It is not even Machiavellian, for Machiavelli's teaching was graceful, subtle, and colorful. Nor is it Neronian. Nevertheless, one may say of it that it fiddles while Rome burns. It is excused by two facts: it does not know that it fiddles, and it does not know that Rome burns.[10]

As a critique of politics, phenomenology inaugurates a new way of conceptualizing political reality—one of the multiple regions of what Alfred Schutz calls "social reality," or the workaday reality of human beings in manifold relationships with other human beings in society. One of the fruitful ways of defining the role of phenomenology in relation to political science is as "metascientific," that is, as a way of examining the nature of political *science* as theoretical constructs of the common-sense constructs of political actors themselves. For the purpose of this essay, therefore, I am not concerned with the development of phenomenology as a sort of cookbook recipe for political research, although the possibility of *doing* a phenomenology of politics or of treating political science as a branch of "applied phenomenology" (e.g., ethnomethodology in sociology) is neither precluded nor denied. On the other hand, however, I insist that conceptualization not be separated from reality in defining the nature of the social sciences. For, phenomenologically defined, reality itself is nothing but the multiple structures of meaning that are the very product of a combined interplay between the conscious act (*noesis*) and the world of reality as "object" (*noema*); and, moreover, the very objects of the social sciences themselves are the common-sense constructs of actors themselves on the social scene.

As a critique, phenomenology meets the following conditions. First, it is related to the world of immediate experience. In other words, phenomenology is a *radical empiricism*. In a very important sense, therefore, *the philosophy of political science is also a philosophy of political reality.* Second, the world in its broadest sense is both constructed and given. Philosophy as conceptualization contributes actively or directly to the construction of reality itself, even though it assumes no position of superiority over common-sense rationality. For conceptualization is a special way of being or existing in the world. Third, to be critical, philosophy demands the *rigor* of self-examination as reflection. Rigor is the essence of phenomenology as a critique. To paraphrase Maurice Merleau-Ponty slightly, *the end of phenomenology as a philosophy is the account of its beginning,* and he accordingly spoke of a phenomenology of phenomenology. Phenomenology is the philosophy that is eminently conscious of the *origin* of its own activity—its origin in the everyday life-world as the all-encompassing horizon of meaning, and thus as the founding and funding matrix of all conceptualization. It is, in short, an *archaeology,* and a phenomenologist is a philosopher of "infinite tasks" in the spirit of Husserl. In the end, critical remarks on political behavioralism and on Strauss's conception of political philosophy from the perspective of phenomenology as a critique of politics parallel Merleau-Ponty's phenomenological critique of "empiricism" on the one hand and of "intellectualism" on the other for their failure to take into account the role of philosophy as an active participation in the creation of meaning or the construction of reality; that is, both are incapable of explaining adequately, albeit in different ways, the *diatactics* of the (noetic) act and the (noematic) object.[11]

Paul Valéry made the simple but profound observation that all politics involve explicitly or implicitly some general idea of the human being (or "human nature").[12] This is certainly explicit in the case of Strauss. He contends, as we have already noted, that political philosophy is both "unscientific" and "unhistorical." Philosophy is unscientific and unhistorical because it is concerned with the question of *the good political society*. Positivism and historicism are equally incapable of arriving at *objective* and *universal* knowledge of the good. One advocates value-neutralism and the other value-relativism. For Strauss, philosophy is the quest for eternal truth, and political philosophy is the quest for eternal truth about political things that are neither divine nor beastly. Philosophy is prior to political philosophy as nature is to natural right. The possibility of objective and universal knowledge depends on the ontological presupposition that "to be" is "always and everywhere to be" (i.e., "human nature"). In essence, Strauss asserts that precisely because human nature is or is assumed to be unchanging, that is, transhistorical and transcultural, truth as epistemological correctness must be accordingly timeless. Thus for him, the distinction between good and evil cannot be made if the nature of the human being is viewed as historically or culturally conditioned or changeable. Because of "human nature," the quest for objective and universal knowledge of the good or political good is as unhistorical as it is unscientific. This position may be called *ontological determinism*.

Besides the value-neutralism that is the main target of his attack on political behavioralism, Strauss further contends that political behavioralism is ridden with technical vocabulary or jargon that necessarily impairs and disregards the prescientific, common-sense understanding of political humankind or of the citizen him/herself. For the valid criteria of truth claimed by the new science of politics are derived from the formalistic canons set forth by the new science of physics or the natural sciences, rather than from common-sense knowledge of citizens. The importance of the notion of prescientific understanding originating from the interpretation of Aristotle—presumably *phronēsis*—lies for Strauss in the fact that political science itself stands or falls by the truth of the prescientific understanding of political things: "Classical political philosophy is the primary form of political science because the commonsense understanding of political things is primary."[13] For Strauss, this by no means implies that opinion is identical with, or cannot be superceded by, knowledge. On the contrary, according to him, the aim of science or philosophy is to elevate opinion to the status of theoretical knowledge: the aim of philosophy as the quest for objective and universal knowledge is to replace opinion. This is necessary because, as Strauss contends, within prescientific political thought, genuine knowledge is mixed with or inseparable from prejudices or superstitions. Classical political science was eminently aware of the imperfections of political opinion. Unlike the new science of politics (i.e., political behavioralism), however, it does not consider the remedy for the imperfection of political opinion to lie in the total rejection of common-sense understanding as such.

From the perspective of phenomenology, what must be challenged in Strauss's conception of political philosophy is its ontological determinism: the idea that "to be" is "always and everywhere to be"—the formula that what is once gained as true is and will forever be true. Hans-Georg Gadamer contends that Strauss stresses the unity of classical philosophy so much so that he fails to notice the existence of the extreme contrast between Plato and Aristotle, e.g., between the former's *eidos* and the latter's *phronēsis*.[14] Moreover, Gadamer is correct in intimating that to be rigorous, true thinking must take into account its own historical consciousness—this Strauss ignores. To be sure, historicism must be overcome historically. Gadamer contends that Strauss only points out that the classical philosopher thought "unhistorically"—that is, the ancients thought differently from the moderns—but says nothing about the possibility of thinking "unhistorically" today, since any *rethinking* of classical philosophy is necessarily a historical thinking.[15] Insofar as time itself is ineradicable, the question of what is "transhistorical" must be sought within, rather than without, the concept of history, that is, within the frame of time. Human reality understood as a historical project is the affirmation of the essence of the human being against both the naturalistic interpretation of humanity simply as part of nature and the conception of the human being as a permanently fixed set of qualities. To say that the human being is absolutely time-bound is to say that our being is not only finite, but also contingent. This contingency is denied by Strauss's ontological determinism (or essentialism) based on the permanence of human nature as the necessary ground and precondition for determining objective and universal knowledge. Precisely because the human being is a project or task to be accomplished, human beings are indeed incomplete beings in an incomplete world. Ultimately, this affirmation of human finitude and contingency is not a denial of meaning or purpose in life, but rather what makes possible an ethics in which human culpability is no longer reduced to error and in which the good is by no means preordained by something that is more or less human. The ethical becomes meaningful precisely because there is an *ambiguity* (ambi-guity) between good and evil. The good is not what is given as "human nature," but what we make of it. To say that the human condition is ambiguous is to assert that its meaning is never fixed, but constantly won by choice.[16]

"A Conquest by Method" by Paul Valéry, though written in 1897 in a somewhat different context and with a different target in mind, describes the tone and mood of what I have in mind in a phenomenological critique of political behavioralism.[17] He criticized the idea that there is in life nothing beyond the *disciplined* calculation of science and technology that greatly reduces the human ingenuity to invent and innovate. Whereas intellectualism (the thought of Strauss) is conceptually overdetermined (i.e., hypotactical), empiricism (political behavioralism) is conceptually underdetermined (i.e., paratactical). In empiricism or political behavioralism, the aim of conceptualization or the cognitive act is reduced to registering what is given as "facts" that are predetermined by the adoption of a particular type of methodology.[18] The arrogance of science and technology lies in their purported monopoly of the realm of the empirical and thus truth by means of allegedly exact, mathematizable, and quantifiable measurement, often leaving us with the foolish impression that if one woman can have a baby in nine months, then nine women can have a baby in one month. It is, in fact, an "empiricide" because the empirical is already predetermined or enframed by the techniques of the natural sciences. In essence, political behavioralism may be characterized as *methodological determinism:* to paraphrase the Biblical expression, in the beginning was Scientific Method. As an eschatology of techniques, political behavioralism is nothing but an *aspect* of modern metaphysics as technology. Heidegger uses the term "enframing" (*Gestell*) to describe the modern age as the age of technology. Technology as enframing is no longer simply a means of human activity in the traditional sense of technology as instrumental facilitation (*instrumentum*). Rather, it has become an autonomous *praxis* in itself—a type of transformation that demands the employment of mathematical and physical science.[19] *Rigor* as the battle cry or *modus operandi* of political behavioralism is nothing but the rigor of methodology itself by which truth is unreflectively or unwittingly determined beforehand. The methodological "framework" of political behavioralism works in such a way that the value of a painting is determined by its frame. In political behavioralism as a form of scientism, in short, *methodology presupposes ontology,* i.e., methodolatry.

There is no one who described the *origin* of scientism in a more penetrating way than Husserl, who traces it back to Galilean physics—the mathematization of nature, which is transformed now into the mathematization of humanity itself.[20] Husserl finds that the stupendous success of modern science begins with Galileo's mathematization of nature, which is echoed in Descartes, Hobbes, and positivism in the twentieth century. It was Galileo who mathematized nature and formulated the idea of mathematics as a universal science (*mathesis unversalis*), which also became the

foundation of Descartes's "first philosophy" (*prima philosophia*).
For Galileo and his heirs, the certainty of knowledge, scientific or
otherwise, depends on the conceptualization or idealization of nature as a *mathematical manifold*—the ideal reduction of nature to
the geometric boxes of triangles, circles, and squares. This indeed
goes back to the spirit of Plato's philosophy, but with a significant
difference in that the ancients—including Plato—intended to solve
the problem of (mathematical) method on the basis of an ontology
of (mathematical) objects, whereas the moderns since the sixteenth
and seventeenth centuries turned their attention *first* and *last* to
method as such. In modern science, the generality of method (methodology) replaced the generality of the object (ontology): modern
mathematics determines its objects by reflecting on the way in
which mathematical objects become accessible only through a general method.[21] In his conscious effort to create a new science of
politics, Hobbes emulates Galileo's geometry and mechanics and
Descartes's "first philosophy." Hobbes's ambition was to create a
theory of politics equal to Galileo's theory of physical bodies. It is
clear in Hobbes's formulation that *external nature* finds its mechanistic or physicalistic analogue in the *internal nature* of the human
being—that is, naturalistic or scientific psychology. "The naturalism of a Hobbes," Husserl notes, "wants to be physicalism, and like
all physicalism it follows the model of physical rationality."[22]

Insofar as mathematical and scientific construction is a product
of the human mind and a sociocultural object, the function of phenomenology is to clarify the conditions under which scientism
actually depends upon the life-world as the preconceptual infra-
structure of all meaning—that is, to show how scientism is indeed
the "garb of ideas" (*Ideenkleid*). Scientism, according to Husserl, is
fallacious because it is foremost a conceptual garb whereby what
once was (or was intended to be) true in the mathematical formalization of nature as a *method* has gradually been taken or mistaken
for reality itself: "What in truth is a method and the result of that
method comes to be taken for reality"—that is, the conceptual sedimentation of mathematics has concealed the reality of the life-
world to the extent that the former has replaced the latter. Husserl
further writes:

> Mathematics and mathematical science, as a garb of
> ideas, or the garb of symbols of the symbolic mathemat-
> ical theories, encompasses everything which, for scien-
> tists and the educated generally, *represents* the life-
> world, *dresses it up* as "objectively actual and true"
> nature. It is through the garb of ideas that we take for
> *true being* what is actually a *method*—a method which
> is designed for the purpose of progressively improving,
> *in infinitum,* through "scientific" predictions, those

rough predictions which are the only ones originally possible within the sphere of what is actually experienced and experienceable in the life-world.[23]

Scientism in the social sciences today is the blind transference of this methodolatry to the study of social reality: social reality has turned into a captive of scientific methodology. As an *archaeology,* phenomenology is capable of disclosing or undressing the cloak of scientism in which, unaware of its origin, methodology replaces ontology or the truth of reality. However, scientism is mistaken because, as Schutz puts it succinctly, "The concept of Nature . . . with which the natural sciences have to deal is, as Husserl has shown, an idealizing abstraction from the *Lebenswelt,* an abstraction which, on principle and of course legitimately, excludes persons with their personal life and all objects of culture which originate as such in practical human activity. Exactly this layer of the *Lebenswelt,* however, from which the natural sciences have to abstract, is the social reality which the social sciences have to investigate."[24] In short, phenomenology—unlike political behavioralism as a form of scientism—attempts to develop the methodology of political science on the basis of its ontological insight that the world of politics, unlike the world of physical objects, is constructed as the world of meaning whose *subject* is political humankind—the human being as actor on the social scene.

III

Thus far, we have discussed the metascientific contribution of phenomenology to the philosophy of political science as a critique of the prevailing conceptualizations formulated by Leo Strauss and by political behavioralists. In the remaining pages of this essay, I shall focus on the contribution of political science to phenomenology. My focus will shift from the "scientific" to the "political." The central issue in question is the confluence of the philosophy of politics and the politics of philosophy as the theory of knowledge. Here I am concerned with the issue of the authoritative structure of philosophy and science as *institutions.*

In his *Radical Reflection and the Origin of the Human Sciences,*[25] Calvin O. Schrag—a philosopher who is extremely sensitive to the crucial issues of the social sciences—landscapes judiciously a niche of phenomenology in the philosophy of the social sciences, particularly in relation to structuralism and Marxism. It is, *inter alia,* a sober reminder and warning against the often imprudent arrogance of philosophy over the empirical human sciences, i.e., what he calls the "Greyhound syndrome" (i.e., "leave the driving to us") of philosophy as the science of science (or superscience). At one point,

Schrag is critical even of the "foundation metaphor" of Husserl's transcendental phenomenology—a verdict, I am sure, that some would object to as too harsh or unfounded. No matter. Schrag's point on philosophy's "Greyhound syndrome" is well taken. In speaking of the confluence of the knowledge of politics and the politics of knowledge, I do not need to remind anyone that "politics" is not a tetragrammaton. I consider neither philosophy as *ancilla politicum*, nor politics as *ancilla philosophicum*, although the idea of the politics of knowledge has a salutary effect on demythologizing or deconstructing philosophy as the science of science.[26] One does not need to be a Baconian to appreciate the idea that *scientia est potestas*.

Gadamer emphatically denies that his *Truth and Method* is a treatise on the methodology of the human or historical sciences. Without doubt, however, it is a seminal contribution to the philosophy of the human sciences. In his denial, Gadamer means to affirm the primacy of hermeneutical ontology over any methodology whatsoever. For him, what truth means in the human sciences has grave consequences for philosophical hermeneutics, and it is in them that an answer to the question of truth must be found. The model of his hermeneutical method is the human sciences rather than the natural sciences, the modern origin of which can be traced back to the Neapolitan philosopher Giambattista Vico, who clearly saw science as a human invention, an institution, or an "academy" that has its own history.[27] It is in Gadamer's emphasis on historical consciousness or efficacy that we find the impact of the human sciences (especially history) on his philosophical hermeneutics. Its radicality lies in the assertion that the human sciences contribute to the self-understanding of philosophy itself—an unusual and rare admission from a philosopher. Thus the two complementary aspects of a single issue are (1) the relevance of hermeneutics to the conduct of social inquiry and (2) the relevance of social inquiry to the self-understanding of philosophy.[28] In this way, hermeneutical phenomenology, with an emphasis on language as an institution, envisions the ultimate unity of philosophy and the social sciences (and the humanities).

A similar point was suggested by Schutz in the concluding remarks of his phenomenological critique of the positivist "unity of science" movement in a paper entitled "Concept and Theory Formation in the Social Sciences" (1954). As far as I am aware, this revisionary suggestion has unfortunately escaped our serious attention. Let me quote Schutz himself fully on this point:

> It seems to me that the social scientist can agree with the statement that the principal differences between the social and the natural sciences do not have to be looked

for in a different logic governing each branch of knowledge. But this does not involve the admission that the social sciences have to abandon the particular devices they use for exploring social reality for the sake of an ideal unit of methods which is founded on the entirely unwarranted assumption that only methods used by the natural sciences, especially by physics, are scientific ones. So far as I know, no serious attention has been made by the proponents of the "unity of science" movement to answer or even to ask the question whether the methodological problem of the natural sciences in their present state is not merely a special case of the more general, still unexplored, problem [of] how scientific knowledge is possible at all and what its logical and methodological presuppositions are. It is my personal conviction that phenomenological philosophy has prepared the ground for such an investigation. Its outcome might quite possibly show that the particular methodological devices developed by the social sciences in order to grasp social reality are better suited than those of the natural sciences to lead to the discovery of the general principles which govern all human knowledge.[29]

I shall call this proposal of Schutz a *social critique of knowledge* for the sake of at least not confusing it with the sociology of knowledge or the critique of ideology.[30] The social critique of knowledge is much more than the sociology of knowledge or the critique of ideology. For the former insists on the acquisition of knowledge as an intrinsically social process, whereas the latter tends to treat all knowledge simply as the superstructure of the existing social conditions, i.e., knowledge as epiphenomenal. The social critique of knowledge, therefore, considers scientific knowledge as a social product by focusing on the context of an intersubjective community of investigators as scientific *practitioners*. As such, scientific activity partakes of the *social a priori* of the life-world as *social reality*.

There is no single work in the philosophy of science that has aroused more controversy in the recent years than Thomas S. Kuhn's *The Structure of Scientific Revolutions*.[31] His theory of scientific paradigms based on the social-scientific model of political institutions is at odds with the positivist aspiration to establish a unified theory of knowledge based on the model of the natural sciences, particularly that of physics to which Schutz's aforementioned suggestion is a phenomenological counterproposal. More important, Kuhn later explicitly acknowledged the role of hermeneutics or of the hermeneutical method in the interpretation of the natural sciences.[32] He puts sociohistorical consciousness back into the philosophy of science. Kuhn's analysis of science is *intrinsically* historical and psychosociological: the structure of scientific knowledge is sought from the historical development of science and in the context of an existing community of scientific *practitioners*. While Kuhn acknowledges the role of hermeneutics in the interpretation of science, Gadamer acknowledges the role of history or historical consciousness in philosophical hermeneutics. In both instances, the centerpiece is history or historical consciousness, which provides a point of intersection between philosophical hermeneutics (Gadamer) and the philosophy of science (Kuhn). It comes as no surprise, therefore, to hear that at the symposium held at Boston College in April of 1974 on the topic of hermeneutics and social science, Gadamer mentioned that Kuhn's aforementioned work supports his view, and Gadamer regarded it as further evidence of the "universality" of the hermeneutical method or the universal applicability of the hermeneutical method to the human and natural sciences.[33] We can only conjecture that the one who mediates the convergence of the views between Kuhn's philosophy of science and (hermeneutical) phenomenology appears to be Alexandre Koyré, who was influenced by Husserl's phenomenology and whom Kuhn acknowledges as his *"maître."*[34]

In an attempt to clarify his position in response to his critics, Kuhn wrote a postscript to *The Structure of Scientific Revolutions* in 1969. In its concluding remarks, there is a revealing passage whose idea has repeatedly been emphasized in his later writings: "Scientific knowledge, like language, is intrinsically the common property of a group or else nothing at all. To understand it we shall need to know the special characteristics of the groups that create and use it."[35] For Kuhn, therefore, science is an *institution* whose essence, just as much as that of language is the medium of communication, lies in its sociopolitical dimension. Like language, science is a communicative act among its practitioners, and the acquisition of scientific knowledge is the product of this intercommunication. The importance of viewing science as an institution is, in short, essentially twofold. First, scientific knowledge is the product of a sociopolitical process, or what Kuhn calls a "group" activity. Second, like language as the instrument of communication, scientific truth is not "value-free," or devoid of normative judgments in the way that the positivistic philosophers of science understand the term with their focus on the ahistorical "logic of explanation." On the contrary, Kuhn insists that scientific theorizing always involves "an inextricable mixture" of descriptive or explanatory and normative judgments.

We are all Vichian to the extent to which we hold the view that the philosophy of science is instituted in its history. Like Vico, we are concerned with the sociohistorical teleology of science as a human and political institution.[36] In this sense, the science of politics is a towering discipline—the architectonic science. Here science is viewed from a *"praxis"*-oriented rather than an "object"-oriented perspective. From the perspective of phenomenology, it is well to recognize the qualitative difference in the nature of the *objects* we investigate in the social and natural sciences. To accentuate this difference, we can speak—as does Don Ihde—of the natural sciences as "noematic sciences" and the social sciences as "noetic sciences."[37] Nevertheless, there is a unifying theme that weaves the warp and woof of the social and the natural sciences, interweaving all theorizing activity into the fabric of a social *praxis*. Just as there is the intentional unity of the noetic and the noematic in consciousness mediated by language (i.e., a "social" or "institutional" process), there is an "institutional" unity between the social and the natural sciences. All science is a "republic" (*res publica*). If such is the case, we are now in the position of *going beyond* disparate truth claims between the natural and the social sciences. To do so, we need to have the *"praxis"*-oriented view of all knowledge— social-scientific and natural-scientific; that is, we need to understand *doing* science as a communal or intersubjective project and achievement—the vision of which was hinted at by Husserl in his discussion of "the crisis of European sciences," and on which Schutz elaborated in his social phenomenology and in his treatment of the life-world *as social reality*. The life-world as social reality is a kind of "mandarin" that can make comprehensible the two incomprehensible *dialects* of the natural and the social sciences.

Nature on the one hand and humankind or the historical order we ourselves make on the other are two ontological orders of radically different magnitude. Nonetheless, conceptualization, whether it be of nature or history, mathematical or historical, is always the invented (*factum*) on which truth (*verum*) rests. The essential but not exclusive fabric of truth in conceptualization as well as mundane social life is *sociality*, which may be the "master key" for a unifying philosophy of the sciences. The verification of all truth, or the epistemological unity of the sciences, rests on the "social matrix" of communication. Of course, there are differences in the motives of conceptualization and mundane social existence. The direct motive for the latter is "pragmatic," i.e., the production of social action, whereas the predominant motive for the former is epistemic or cognitive, i.e., the production of knowledge. However, human action as project is in part cognitive, just as the production of knowledge in terms of its relevance or application in the world of social action is in part pragmatic. In this sense, Husserl speaks of theorizing—scientific or otherwise—as a special mode of *praxis* or social *praxis*. For him, science is fundamentally and foremost a human project and cultural accomplishment; as such, it is a human invention and institution. Both the world of science, as a network of interactions among *knowing subjects* in pursuit of knowledge, and social reality, as a network of transactions among *acting subjects,* partake of the same matrix: *sociality.* Epistemic claims for science are grounded in the "academy" of science as the institution of its practitioners, which, like the political community of a nation, has the structure of authority through which the value of truth is judged and allocated. In this sense, "doing science" or the acquisition of (tacit) knowledge is a kind of pedagogical training: learning and mastering the "trade" of science involves the tradition and authority of science as an institution that allocates truth-values for a given community of scientists both actual and potential. For Vico, the sciences are institutions just as are languages—and both are historical or developmental. The sciences have their histories just as words or languages do. It is most instructive to take notice of Vico's scrupulous registration of complaint in *On the Study Methods of Our Time* (1709)[38] against the prevailing pedagogic methods of scientific epistemology in his own time. This complaint is very contemporary in its message and thus relevant to that moral education of public conduct which he boldly called the "science of politics." Vico tells us that

> the greatest drawback of our educational methods is that we pay an excessive amount of attention to the natural sciences and not enough to ethics. Our chief fault is that we disregard that part of ethics which treats of human character, of its dispositions, its passions, and of the manner of adjusting these factors to public life and eloquence. We neglect that discipline which deals with the differential feature of virtues and vices, with good and bad behavior-patterns, with the typical characteristics of the various ages of man, of the two sexes, of social and economic class, race and nation, and with the art of seemly conduct in life, the most difficult of all arts. As a consequence of this neglect, a noble and important branch of studies, i.e., the science of politics, lies almost abandoned and untended.[39]

In conclusion, to link the knowledge of politics and the politics of knowledge together is perhaps to open Pandora's box. However, I think it is worth taking the risk in the *interest* (*inter-esse*) of developing what Ihde calls an "interdisciplinary phenomenology," or what I would be tempted to call a "global phenomenology." To accentuate the unity of social-scientific and natural-scientific knowledge is for me not so much to ignore the essential difference between the two as to test the durability of how the two notes sound as a chord rather than as separate notes.[40] Unlike two colors occupying the same space that produce another color, the simultaneous sound of two tones is not one mixed tone, not another tone but a chord. As there is one common humanity, the chord of the human and the natural sciences as human inventions and institutions echoes the sound of this common humanity. When we cannot speak of this universal chord, we might as well consign ourselves to silence. Musically defined, the world—scientific or otherwise—is an "auditorium" rather than a "theatre"—a community of active hearers or participants rather than a community of passive onlookers or spectators. Let me summarize my conclusion by way of Vico's "political" thought. Trained in rhetoric, philology, and jurisprudence, Vico understood well the *origin* (*archē*) of humanity in common sense (*sensus communis*)—origin as something "archaic" or primordial that cannot be deduced from something else, or the "birthplace" from which everything else may be deduced, including the "criticism" of scientific concepts.[41] Interpreted in the spirit of Vico's "new science," scientific laws may be regarded as the codified sediments of science as an institution. They may be understood as *lex* in a jurisprudential or political sense: they are not "causal" but "legal." A nation is the "birthplace" of a people held together by "common sense," and it is a common system of institutions. Science, too, is a microcosm of a nation: it is a political institution.[42]

41

Phenomenology as a Critique of Politics

Part II
Phenomenology and the Methodology of the Human Sciences

Two roads diverged in a wood, and I—
I took the one less traveled by,
And that has made all the difference.

—Robert Frost,
"The Road Not Taken"

Three

A CRITIQUE OF THE BEHAVIORAL
PERSUASION IN POLITICS:
A PHENOMENOLOGICAL VIEW

I. Introduction

THE AIM OF THIS ESSAY is not so much to show how, as Ludwig
Wittgenstein once described his mission of philosophizing, the fly
can get out of the bottle, as to show, hopefully, that it is indeed
caught in a bottle. The title is taken from Heinz Eulau's book *The
Behavioral Persuasion in Politics*,[1] in which, even though political
behavioralism is a protean movement, he attempts to spell out the
overall family resemblance of its various aspects and to formulate
the general principles of the behavioralist approach to political science and his own philosophy of humanity (that is, to define the behavioralist "paradigm"). A true critique, to be sure, is not and
ought not to be merely a negative enterprise of mere faultfinding.
Its aim should be "to sort out" or assess the scope and boundaries
of the conceptual framework under consideration. As a critique
this essay has a twofold purpose: on the one hand, it attempts to
define the limitations of political behavioralism, and on the other,
it suggests an alternative, phenomenological way of coping with
those limitations. In so doing, both political behavioralism and
phenomenology are treated as philosophies of political science.

By phenomenology, I mean the philosophical movement that was developed in Europe by Husserl and that by now represents a far broader geographical and ideological spectrum than when it was first initiated. In this essay, I rely heavily on what is known as the "second school" of phenomenology, "existential phenomenology," which attempts to synthesize the philosophical insights of Søren Kierkegaard and those of Husserl.[2] For existential phenomenologists, phenomenology is a descriptive enterprise that explores the different regions of human existence, the meaning of the human being's placement in the world. "Existential phenomenology," Paul Ricoeur concisely states, "makes the transition between transcendental phenomenology, born of the reduction of everything to its appearing to me, and ontology, which restores the question of the sense of being for all that is said to 'exist.' "[3]

In discussing political behavioralism and its critics, Eulau studies three fundamental questions: (1) the nature of the knowledge of political things, (2) the basic unit of political analysis, and (3) the nature of value in the theory of politics.[4] So far, the center of the controversy between the supporters and the opponents of political behavioralism has focused on the third issue. I shall, however, shift the center of this inquiry to the first issue. Indeed, the first issue encompasses the second and the third, for the most basic ingredient in politics is the "political *behavior*" of humankind, since politics is a system of behavior and "value," in turn, is a political thing.[5] The focal point of the issue involved in this essay thus belongs to the philosophy of political science, which reaches beyond a narrow identification with the analysis and justification of its logic and language.

The three aspects of Eulau's inquiry are not, strictly speaking, scientific questions: they are questions of philosophy, of which epistemology is only a part. Those political scientists who *talk about* these issues, regardless of their persuasion, are in fact turning to philosophy. For political science as a purely empirical discipline cannot deal with these questions. Strictly speaking, phenomenology is a philosophy, whereas political behavioralism claims to be a science. Nevertheless, political behavioralism, as the suffix "ism" suggests, is a philosophical approach to the study of politics. To talk about the nature of political behavioralism is not "doing science" but "doing philosophy," or else (to use a term fashionable in modern philosophy) it is engaging in "metaempirical" or "metascientific" activity. Curiously enough, however, political behavioralists (including Eulau) are rarely willing to admit that they are engaged in philosophical discourse, for the reason, I suspect, that they regard philosophy as an exclusively normative discipline. As Stanley Cavell rightly observes, philosophy is shunned or is considered esoteric not because a few people guard its knowledge, but because most people (including, I might add, political behavioralists) guard themselves against it.[6] On the other hand, phenomenology is not simply a methodology: it is also a complete philosophy of the human being and of social reality. Phenomenologically speaking, moreover, philosophy is not so much a particular body of knowledge as it is "the vigilance which does not let us forget *the source of all knowledge*."[7] By the same token, the philosopher is not a possessor of knowledge but rather a perpetual beginner, taking nothing for granted; for the philosopher, everything is in principle questionable.

Eulau has recently been called a "revisionist" in the behavioralist camp.[8] Perhaps he is a revisionist when he avows that there is a continuity between the "tradition" and political behavioralism. He is "more cautious in his claims and more aware of the difficulties than are most behavioralist political scientists,"[9] but his modest claims, of course, make him no less a crusader for political behavioralism.

First, unlike David Truman, Gabriel Almond, Robert Dahl, and David Easton, Eulau claims neither "revolution" nor total victory for recent political behavioralism; nor does he write a tearless eulogy for the death of the old science of politics. Instead, without fanfare, he uses the modest terms "renaissance" and "innovation." For him, political behavioralism represents a mixture of continuity with and discontinuity from the tradition; the tension between the two is symptomatic of scientific growth. Since "renaissance" means to "look both forward and backward," Eulau claims to leave the door open for "the dialogue between the hinterland of tradition and the frontiers of innovation in the study of politics."[10] Unlike Dahl, who confidently wrote an "epitaph for a monument to a successful protest" (that is, the behavioralist approach),[11] Eulau believes that "the behavioral approaches in politics will continue as separate and distinct—unless, of course, there is an unpredictable failure of nerve."[12]

Second, Eulau views science as an additive body of knowledge that is based on "the canons of scientific method" and has an infinitely open future. The growth or progress of science is made by increment rather than, as Thomas Kuhn suggests,[13] by revolution. So the scientific spirit corresponds to the "progressive" spirit of liberalism. Eulau's caution against "reified" conceptualizations (for example, Easton's and Morton Kaplan's "general systems theory") favors the Baconian inductive view of science, since Eulau is inclined to believe that in scientific endeavor, there is no real substitute for the painstaking, piecemeal "crucible of empirical research." The aim of theory is to provide analytical tools that facilitate empirical research.

Third, Eulau is methodologically self-conscious. But although his "personal document" about the "Young Turks" is a very unscientific account of that scientific movement, it must not be overlooked: there is always an autobiographical element in every intellectual journey, scientific or otherwise. Eulau means to be "persuasive." By definition, persuasion *(per-suadere)* is an emotive appeal to induce a person or a group of persons to admire one set of qualities rather than another.[14]

Fourth, Eulau explicitly acknowledges the *differentia* between what is human and what is merely natural when he says: "The behavioral persuasion in politics is concerned with what man does politically and the meaning he attaches to his behavior."[15] For both phenomenology and political behavioralism, then, the starting point of the analysis of human behavior is the *meaning* (or a set of meanings) that the actor attaches to his/her action. For every thinking and acting has a meaning for the human subject: we are condemned to meaning in politics, society, and history. This thesis of Eulau's is the essence of the phenomenological approach to the human and social sciences. One of the main criticisms made by this essay, however, will be to show that the *a priori* method and the presuppositions of political behavioralism that are based on the philosophy of the natural sciences are incompatible with, and do injustice to, the understanding of the meaning-structure of human behavior and social reality. Unlike the logical and behavioral positivists, who define scientific or empirical knowledge according to the procedures of the natural sciences, especially physics, Alfred Schutz proposes a challenging idea that "the particular methodological devices developed by the social sciences in order to grasp social reality are better suited than those of the natural sciences to lead to the discovery of the general principles which govern all human knowledge."[16]

In phenomenology and political behavioralism, the psychological view of the human being has led to an emphasis on individual behavior as the basic unit of analysis. Both approaches start from the method of individualism rather than from that of sociologism. However, like psychological behaviorism, political behavioralism as a philosophy opts for what is externally observable or what is "public" by rejecting the intended meaning (usually labeled as "private") that the actor attaches to his/her action, including value as an existential norm. Although it is extremely rare to find reference to phenomenology in the literature of political behavioralism, Eulau mentions the term "phenomenological" once, very vaguely, as he juxtaposes the public, accurate, and firsthand observation of political behavioralism with the private, inaccurate, and secondhand observation of phenomenology.[17] Political behavioralism as a scientific method abandons the relevance of the vast universe of experiential data of everyday life as being simply "subjective" or "private" and thus unscientific and unempirical. On the other hand, phenomenology is a philosophy that justifies the raw, original data of experiential meaning as the foundation of all theoretical activity. To be meaningful, the models of political humankind as abstract constructs cannot ignore the meaningful world of political actors. Phenomenology denies neither the concept of "objectivity" nor that of "science." It denies only scientism, the doctrine that insists that the only valid methods of science are those of the natural sciences, and "methodolatry," the prior requirement that scientific investigation must first start with a methodology that tends to tailor facts to fit method. The real question is not whether the science of politics is possible, but only in which direction it must move. Running counter to the facts of human experience, scientism and methodolatry commit themselves to too narrow a view of the human sciences, which must take account of the human being (including the scientist) as a unity of complementary poles of subject and object.

In the following pages, I propose first of all to describe the structure of human behavior and, in so doing, to assess critically the behavioralist conception in terms of the intentional framework of phenomenology. Second, I shall attempt to show that, in its effort to build the exact, rigorous science of politics, political behavioralism breeds conceptual reductionism. In contrast, the rigor of phenomenology as a philosophy consists in showing that objective knowledge presupposes the preobjective life-world. Insofar as the political theorizers themselves are active participants in, rather than merely passive spectators of, this life-world, political theory is to be regarded as a human project and an intersubjective enterprise. In this sense, a philosophy of political science is and must be also a philosophy of the political world. Third, I shall argue that political behavioralism is unaware of the body as the subject of both knowing and acting (that is, both the knower and the actor as embodied being). As mind is to body, so is conceptual knowledge (or symbolic meaning) to preconceptual knowledge (or felt meaning). And since mind and body are inseparable, so are thought and feeling. Moreover, the phenomenology of the body is a critique of artificial reason, and points to the inherent limitation of political behavioralism as a scientific analysis of human behavior.

II. The Structure of Human Behavior

An understanding of what political things are must precede a possibility of the knowledge of them. What, then, are political things? The answer to this question cannot just be taken for granted. For Martin Heidegger, the question, "What is a thing?"[18] is bound up with a series of metaphysical questions. What complicates the matter further in our inquiry is the adjective "political." Since the political thing is nonetheless a thing, we ought first to ask: What are things? There are both natural and human things. Natural things are flowers, trees rocks, mountains, water, air, earth, etc., things of nature, free from the handiwork or cultivation of human beings. Human things are cultural artifacts, including tools or instruments and other products of human labor, such as pipes, bells, hammers, abaci, computers, schools, highways, natural languages, mathematical and logical symbols, government, etc. To use a phrase of Marshall McLuhan's, they are all "extensions of man." Thus the question, "What is a human thing?" leads to the most fundamental question: "What is a human being?" or, to put it more existentially, "Who is the human being?" For the lack of a better term, I shall call the total being of humanity the "ontology of humankind," or, as Heidegger describes it, the human being as "being-in-the-world" (*in-der-Welt-sein*).[19]

Paul Valéry pointed out that all politics, even the most simple and crude, implies an idea of humankind and of the world.[20] Eulau's political behavioralism also raises the basic question of the human being, beginning with the idea that "the root is man" and ending with the idea that "the goal is man." The behavioral persuasion in politics considers the "analysis" of the human being and human behavior as its central theme of investigation. Its aim is not to formulate a normative philosophy of humanity, which Eulau explicitly rejects, but rather to shift the focus of political research toward psychological humankind and human behavior and away from the institutionalist approach. The behavior of a person or a group of persons rather than "events, structures, institutions, or ideologies"[21] has become the center of attention in behavioralist political research.

Eulau rejects early psychological behavioralism (that is, "the physiological stimulus-response psychology of behaviorism") as having "little in common with" modern behavioral inquiry. Whereas early reflexology exorcised mental phenomena from the social sciences, modern behavioral science

> is eminently concerned not only with the acts of man but also with his cognitive, affective, and evaluating processes. "Behavior" in political behavior, then, refers not simply to directly or indirectly observable political action but also to those perceptual, motivational, and attitudinal components of behavior which make for man's political beliefs, values, and goals. "Behavioral" is, therefore, preferable to "behavioristic," and I shall use it in the dynamic sense.[22]

Political behavioralism, then, as Eulau depicts it, rejects nothing out of hand. If it rejects nothing, it is a ubiquitous technique, which seems to be the reason why Eulau uses the term "political behavioralism" synonymously with "political behavior." However, the term is rather misleading, because political behavioralism as a scientific method is only one way, not the all-encompassing way, of analyzing political behavior. There are ways of treating political behavior either "behaviorally" (scientifically) or "non-behaviorally" (nonscientifically)—for example, phenomenologically. In order to keep their scientific method intact, behavioralists must identify their notion of behavior and overt behavior. Specifically, in order to conserve quantitative measurement, observation, and empirical testability, covert phenomena (what Eulau calls "mental" phenomena), such as intentions, beliefs, motives, feelings, and values, must be either translated into the "observable contexts" or inferred from overt behavior or from what Felix Oppenheim calls the "behavior event."[23] Thus behavior *is* really overt behavior or only the external indications of action. So-called "private" and motivational phenomena are reduced to "public" and observable events or the external components of action.

It is no mere accident that "consciousness" is a forbidden word for political behavioralists as well as for psychological behaviorists. But consciousness ought not to be treated as if it were a philosopher's myth or fable. Is consciousness just "a ghost in a machine"? Robert Lane and Karl Deutsch are two eminent political behavioralists who are willing to use the term "consciousness."[24] Lane uses consciousness in the narrowly defined sense of "sensitivity," "awareness," and "discernment," in contradistinction to "knowledge" or "intelligence." Though Deutsch criticizes mechanism for leaving no room for consciousness (or will), in mapping out his cybernetic geography of the human being he treats consciousness as an analogue to the purely internal processes of any electronic network: it is "a collection of internal feedbacks of secondary messages. *Secondary messages* are messages about changes in the state of parts of the system, that is, about primary messages. *Primary messages* are those that move through the system in consequence of its interaction with the outside world."[25] Both Lane and Deutsch agree that consciousness is something internal; it is sensitivity or the internal feedback of secondary messages. Thus they are unaware of the intentional structure of consciousness as the meeting of the internal and the external, and of the dynamic relatedness between thought and affectivity in intellectual activity as well as in the everyday life of action.

Not unlike the phenomenologist, as I have suggested above, Eulau defines the basic stuff of politics in terms of the conditions and consequences of individual action and the roles that the political actor plays in the social, cultural, and personal milieu. Most significantly, he has emphasized the importance of the meaning the actor attaches to his/her action. The presence of meaning, Eulau insists, makes the study of human behavior different from the study of natural phenomena. For this reason, the distinct merit of the behavioral approach to the study of politics lies in its focus on the meaning of human behavior. Moreover, Eulau holds that the observation of political behavior must meet the test of an intersubjective agreement between observer and observed. There must be an agreement between the meaning given to behavior by the observer and that given by the actor him/herself. This, however, requires not that the observational language of political science should be the same as the language of the political actor, but rather that their meanings must be compatible with each other.

However, because of its physicalist view of human conduct (accepting only that which is "public" or "observable"), political behavioralism, despite its claim to the contrary, is impervious to the intentional meaning-structure of human conduct. The intentional meaning-structure of human conduct is completely alien to political behavioralism in both theory and technique. The phenomenological criticism of political behavioralism is that it is attentive to (1) the intentional meaning-structure of human conduct and (2) the body as lived rather than as a merely physical thing, an inert object.

By virtue of our action, we are called active beings, and our essence is our existence. Gabriel Marcel's idea of the human being as *homo viator* dramatizes the idea that the human being is active and that, being active, we are always in the making or becoming (that is, a being-on-the-way). To express it in a slightly different way, human beings are the only beings who refuse to accept what they are[26] or, as Jean-Paul Sartre puts it, the human being is a "being which is what it is not, and which is not what it is."[27] By virtue of our action, we may be more or less an animal, but we are *never* simply an animal.[28] This is not meant so much to deny the common characteristics shared by both humans and other animals as to emphasize the uniqueness of humankind as human.

By action, human beings "extend" (in McLuhan's sense) themselves, remold their own image, and determine their own destiny. Unlike traditional natural law theory, the existentialist theory of humanity stresses that being human is not an eternally fixed property like a thing—although in no way is there a denial of biological and social constants.[29] In existential philosophy, the human being is described as a "project" or a "possibility." As a project, human existence is neither in full possession of itself nor entirely estranged from itself "because it is action or doing, and because action is, by definition, the violent transition from what I have to what I aim to have, from what I am to what I intend to be."[30] And because the human being is a possibility, we are open to the "invisible" future, that is, our future is in no sense predetermined. In his psychohistorical theory, Robert Lifton similarly characterizes twentieth-century humanity on a global scale as protean.[31] Amitai Etzioni has also proposed a sociological theory of "the active society," a theory of society based on the idea of the human being as a dynamic actor rather than a passive spectator.[32]

Phenomenology aims to describe the meaning-structure of human action from the standpoint of the human being as actor (that is, as attaching meaning to his/her action) rather than spectator. As an intentional analysis of meaningful action, phenomenology is not a psychology of introspection; it is not the opposite of behaviorism. For intentionality is neither entirely internal nor entirely external. By focusing on the essential structure of meaningful action, phenomenology attempts to avoid altogether a "psychologism" that reduces meaning (or everything) simply to psychological components. Only when the meaning of action is regarded as the simultaneous process of the internalization of the external and the externalization of the internal does one come to grips with the idea that we are our action.

In *The Structure of Behavior,* Merleau-Ponty repudiates the mechanical and causal explanation of human behavior (*comportement*). The human organism or the body (*organon*) cannot be understood in terms of physiology and/or biology alone, for the body is an active mode of being-in-the-world. In order to avoid "mentalism" (subjectivism) on the one hand and "behaviorism" (objectivism) on the other, Merleau-Ponty describes the structure of behavior as meaning (*signification*), the idea of which is to integrate the "dialectics" of the physical (physiology), the vital (biology), and the mental (psychology). The human behavioral order is not reducible to any one of these "three orders of Being" alone. Insofar as behavior represents the human order, it is a field or a structure of meaning. Thus the human order as it is presented to a "normal human being" exhibits no unequivocal distinction between the mental and the somatic. Rather, the body is a unified field, an alert, sentient "phenomenal field," not an inert, physical object. To characterize the human order as either a physical object or a mental faculty is to confuse the part with the whole. Rationalism is as false as mechanism, inasmuch as each depicts the image of the human being in a partial way. Humans act neither like a machine nor with mind alone, since the body (or the "flesh") is never solely a sum of "material" facts, or a substance, or a representation of the mind as idea. Through the body as a phenomenal field, as the root of an active mode of being-in-the-world, the world also becomes a phenomenal field. For the player in action, for example, the football field is not just an object to gaze at, but a reality that summons a certain mode of action. By the same token, perception, whose *subject* is the body, "opens on a reality which solicits our action rather than on a truth, an object of knowledge."[33]

Human beings can have a project because they are active. Insofar as action is a structure of meaning, it is an ongoing process based on a preconceived plan. Without analyzing in detail a complex network of unconscious drives, desires, motives, feelings, choices, efforts, decisions, and consents, it can summarily be stated that what characterizes the essence of meaningful action is the presence of a project. A resolution, the counterthrust of a hesitation, is the final decision to act out the project. The project is indeed an insight (insight), an "internal plan of operations." In the executing of a project, there is a fulfillment, the terminus of an action. By the very presence of a project, human action is radically distinguished from the behavior of animals. For example, the chimpanzee can move, but only the human being is capable of moving with a preconceived plan. In short, the presence of a project makes human action "meaningful," "purposive," and "rational." Moreover, facts and values on the one hand and ends and means on the other enter into the planning of an action in a complex way. In the project, the importance of valuing can scarcely be overstressed. For Sartre, who defines the task of "existential psychoanalysis" as the conscious understanding of the human being as project, human reality is identified with and defined by the polyvalent *ends* humans pursue.[34] As a matter of fact, valuing, according to Rollo May, is not only an act but *is* a project itself: "It is in the act of valuing that consciousness and behavior become united."[35]

The project as a preconceived plan temporally precedes the actual performance or execution of action. Insofar as the actor has internal time-consciousness or inner flow of duration, action is not yet "meaningful." It is merely presignifying or prerational, for lived experience in the stream of consciousness acquires explicit sense or meaning only when it is grasped by the act of attention, that is, reflectively. Just as the project is the purposive basis of action, to have a project means to have a purpose or a goal. Thus Erwin Straus writes:

> Purposive movements are directed toward a goal. A change is anticipated and realized through movements subserving a plan. In action, we reach beyond a given situation into the realm of possibilities; within a temporal horizon, open to the future, we busy ourselves producing a new situation. We do not simply react to things as they are, but we act on them—i.e., we move with the intention of modifying things from an actual to a desired condition.[36]

In the fulfillment of an action through a project, then, the possibility is realized. Fulfilled or achieved action through a project is a transcending act, that is, it transcends what is now in favor of possibility. The human being is a "multitude of possibilities," which underscores the existential meaning of the human being as *homo viator*. Herein lies the convergence between phenomenology as a descriptive method and the existential ontology of humankind.

The upright posture of the human body is, according to Straus, a uniquely human mode of being-in-the-world.[37] Human uprightness has a moral as well as a factual connotation. It means not only to stand up perpendicularly to the ground, but also to be just, honest, and right. The moral quality of rectitude, standing up for one's own conviction or righteousness, is admired by others. Thus upright posture is a truly human trait that no other animal species has. It is a specific placement of human being-in-the-world. As a spatial concept, this upright posture determines one's place, factual and moral, in relation to one's natural, social, and cultural environment. Like psychological behaviorism, political behavioralism may know a "physics" of the mind or the body, but knows nothing of the human body as an active *subject* of perception, feeling, and cognition. Without the body as an active mode of existence, the human being would be just an "absentee landlord" in the world. By means of the body as an instrument, we relate ourselves to the world and to other people, and we "extend" ourselves to the making of cultural objects. It is not only as a rational animal but as a creature of flesh, blood, and bone that humans distinguish themselves from other animals. The nonverbal forms of bodily expression, like laughing and crying,[38] are unique to humankind. The tools or instruments we make, for example, are referred to as *handi*works or *handi*crafts. In a rudimentary sense the idea of *homo faber* indicates the human ability to tame, modify, and change our environment through the manipulation of the body. And a person also mediates between him/herself and the Other through the body. The space defined by one's body becomes a precondition for communication between oneself and the social world as a whole. Only by recognizing that "I am *here*" am I able to determine that "they are *there*." By means of our spatial position, we have direct access to things and people. One's own body is an indispensable medium, not only for the self-interpretation of one's own lived experience, but also for the perception and understanding of others and thus ultimately for one's political and social relationships. Ronald Laing shows that the self "is precluded from having a direct relationship with real things and real people" when there is a derangement of perception between ego and the body in relation to the external world, that is, when the situation is "self ⇌ (body/other)" instead of "(self/body) ⇌ other."[39]

The human body is not just a physical object to be *had*. One does not own one's body as one owns an object or a thing. It is an organ, the vehicle of action or *praxis*. There is, according to Marcel, a radical difference between "being" (*être*) a body—so that bodilihood is a mode of being-in-the-world—and "having" (*avoir*) it as a mere object. For one *is* his/her body. "I *am* my body," declares Marcel, "in so far as I succeed in recognizing that this body of mine *cannot*, in the last analysis, be brought down to the level of being this object, *an* object, a something or other. It is at this point that we have to bring in the idea of the body not as an object but as a subject."[40]

The human being is a unique being who is able to reconcile the physical body (*Körper*), the impersonal and outside, with the lived body (*Leib*), the personal and inside. To distinguish between "being" and "having" in our discussion of the human body is not an idle exercise in abstract speculation; it has an import for the social sciences, whose basic area of investigation is human social action, which involves the mobility of a body that is simultaneously both a subject and an object. In sum, as John Wild stresses:

> Human behavior is neither a series of blind reactions to external "stimuli," nor the project of acts which are motivated by the pure ideas of disembodied, worldless mind. It is neither exclusively subjective nor exclusively objective, but a dialectical interchange between man and the world, which cannot be adequately expressed in traditional causal terms. It is a circular dialectic in which the independent beings of the life-field, already selected by the structure of the human body, exert a further selective operation on this body's acts. It is out of this dialectical interchange that human meanings emerge.[41]

III. The Meaning of Conceptual Rigor

Phenomenology is concerned with a systematic analysis of meanings that are actively constituted by consciousness. As a meaning-endowing act, consciousness, whether naive or theoretical, is always intentional, in thinking, imagining, feeling, perceiving, or willing. The intentionality of consciousness suggests that in every form or act of consciousness, there is always a tripartite unity of the *subject* who is *conscious* of an *object* that may be ideal or real (*ego-cogito-cogitatum*). Meaning is then constituted in the encounter between the object and the person who thinks, feels, imagines, perceives, and wills. In this sense, it is neither entirely subjective nor entirely objective. This meaning-endowing act is a uniquely human trait that characterizes both thinking and acting. And the relevance of phenomenological thought to the empirical human sciences (for example, psychology, sociology, political science, anthropology, history, and linguistics) lies in its explicit recognition of, and insistence on, the radical *differentia* between what is merely natural (or physical) and what is genuinely human in terms of this meaning-creation. If this phenomenological view is correct, then a methodology of political science as an empirical human science must be radically different from that of the natural sciences and thus must free itself from any preconceived, derivative conceptual boxes.

Since Galileo, as Husserl shows,[42] nature has been idealized or mathematized from the life-world (*Lebenswelt*). The idealized and mathematical nature in physics has gradually but decisively replaced the original nature accessible to sensibility (e.g., perception). This abstract, scientific attitude has now permeated the human life-pattern and has gained significance for modern science (human as well as natural), modern philosophy, and modern humanity. Now the ideal of *mathesis universalis* has more than ever before become a reality for human thought—in the social sciences in general and in the use of game theory, statistical techniques, cybernetics, and the "sciences of the artificial" in particular. Thus the idealized mode of thought embodied in physics has now become a model for all forms of knowledge. In this historical sedimentation of mathematized abstraction, the life-world, the source of all knowledge and action, has been forever reduced to oblivion and has become the hidden and forgotten background.

The garb of mathematized nature has replaced prescientific nature. Considered as a part of nature, the human being also partakes of the character of a mathematical manifold that, like nature, is subject to exact and precise measurement. Psychological data are being treated like natural or physical phenomena and reduced to the physical or, as Herbert Simon calls it, the artificial.[43] The philosophical justification for the behavioral approach in political science as a *predictive* science, with an emphasis on artificial model building, is embedded in the spirit and language of logical empiricism, naturalism, and operationalism. The concept of power, for example, has been central to political thought. However, "power is rapidly losing ground from the point of view of its operational, if not analytical, utility."[44] From the standpoint of exact measurement, power has become a concept difficult to define.

The methodological isomorphism of the human sciences and the natural sciences has been motivated by the phenomenal success of modern (or post-Galilean) physics in predicting. This has been accompanied by technological innovations and breakthroughs, as well as by mathematical precision and exactitude. Thus for Eulau, the possibility of further progress in behavioral research is simply a question of technology. However, because the human order is radically or qualitatively different from the natural order, it may not be isomorphically amenable to the techniques of the natural sciences. The *scientific* character of the human sciences should not be prejudged by the ready-made conceptual and methodological framework of the natural sciences. It must not be judged by how much physics, mathematics, and mechanics are found in it. To be sure, the scientific approach to human behavior is a recent event, still in its infancy. The science of politics, however, is as old as the sciences of nature. Certainly its slow or retarded development toward an exact, measurable, and predictive science is due, one begins to suspect, to something endemic to the nature of *human* behavior, which, unlike natural phenomena, defies the ideal order of regularities and uniformities.[45]

Physicalism (the positivist doctrine that holds physics as paradigmatic to all sciences, natural and social) attempts to create "a self-consistent system of unified science capable of being utilized for successful prediction."[46] Sociology (or physicalistic sociology) is for Otto Neurath the way to discover sociological laws that are congruent with the laws of physics and can be utilized for prediction. For the positivist doctrine of science, theories and laws are formulated for the sake of prediction, which is the essence of scientific explanation. Brian Barry criticizes T. D. Weldon's *The Vocabulary of Politics* (1953) as being "an application of unreconstructed logical positivist criteria of meaning to traditional political thought rather than a detailed analysis of concepts"; and he defines "analytical politics" as "the attempt to simplify the complex reality of a situation by picking out certain aspects of it and then building a model relating to these aspects."[47] It seems that Barry is critical not so much of Weldon's logical positivism as of the absence in his work of a constructive, detailed analysis of political concepts themselves.

For many practitioners of analytical politics—among others, Anthony Downs and Herbert Simon—theorizing is equated with abstract model building. In this sense, rigor becomes a declared trademark of political behavioralism as scientific analysis.[48] For Downs, as for other analytical practitioners, rigor is a methodological principle for building theoretical models used ultimately for the sake of prediction or in order to increase the liability of predictive knowledge. He postulates that according to the model of "economic humankind," human beings seek to maximize their own self-interest, and their behavior is "rational" insofar as it is directed primarily toward selfish ends.[49] Thus the model of "positive politics" as both a methodology and a theory of humanity is constructed from that of "positive economics." In the positivist model, theory is treated as "a body of substantive hypotheses" and is judged by "its predictive power for the class of phenomena which it is intended to 'explain.' "[50] For the exponent of positive economics, Milton Friedman, the notion of prediction is not limited only to the forecasting of future events (that is, saying beforehand what will happen on the basis of theory and evidence); it is also extended to the causal explanation of "phenomena that have occurred but . . . on which [observations] have not yet been made or are not known to the person making the prediction."[51] Like the methodology of positive economics, the model of positive politics, too, aims at accurate prediction, which Downs himself insists, has very little to do with the real world of political humankind. Unlike the classical and conventional meaning of *theōria*, theory (or model) is now "a filing system" (Friedman's phrase) that facilitates prediction. Downs's model building is a methodolatry in the extreme, where conceptual clarity is likened to the rigid formulation of logical axioms and physical and mathematical theories. Analytical politics is eminently nomothetic in seeking political knowledge that is completely impersonal, generalizing, uniform, and lawlike and discrediting the factual description of unique and individual events, that is, the ideographic understanding of political things.

From a phenomenological point of view of thought and action, the idea of rigor in political behavioralism is exclusively a methodological principle, but it ignores another level of rigor that clarifies the nature of the knowing subject—the scientist as a knower. Science is a human activity that is founded upon the human life-world; there is no science without scientists, and thus scientists cannot ignore their rootedness in the life-world. The rigor of phenomenology lies in its search for the presupposition or source of theoretical knowledge and activity, scientific or otherwise. It turns to the known subject as the locus of investigation and thus to science as a human project, *praxis*, and achievement—that is, the human being as the subject of the human sciences. If "objectivity" entails an anonymous epistemological subject or a nameless thinker, then it is a scandal to science as well as to philosophy. Objectivity is "nothing but the expectation of a reality which was at once susceptible by appearing while affecting me in my receptivity and of letting itself be determined by articulate speech."[52] More important, however, all theoretical knowledge and activity presupposes the ultimate and all-encompassing system of meanings called the pretheoretical or preconceptual life-world. "Straightforward experience, in which the life-world is given," writes Husserl, "is the ultimate foundation of all objective knowledge. Correlatively, this world itself, as existing prescientifically for us (originally) purely through experience, furnishes us in advance, through its invariant set of essential types, with all possible scientific topics."[53] The "phenomenological battle cry," in calling for a return "to the things themselves," is an urge to return to this everyday, preconceptual life-world as the world of "things" (*Sachen*) that is the genesis of all theoretical *praxis*. The life-world is the horizon of meanings grasped by our original, straightforward, immediate, and sensuous experience. In this life-world, there are natural and cultural objects and human beings who are its subjects, all of which together constitute our environment or "surrounding world" (*Lebensumwelt*). In it we see, perceive, and know, for example, natural objects in terms of their color, shape, size, and weight. Husserl writes that "the contrast between the subjectivity of the life-world and the 'objective,' the 'true' world, lies in the fact that the latter is a theoretical-logical substruction, the substruction of something that is in principle not perceivable, in principle not experienceable in its own proper being, whereas the subjective, in the life-world, is distinguished in all respects precisely by its being actually experienceable."[54] Phenomenology, which is concerned with "things" experienced and experiential, is a radical empiricism, and Merleau-Ponty thus speaks of "phenomenological positivism." What is empirical or factual must not, therefore, be determined by any prior methodological commitment. When every fact is reduced to method and when science is judged merely on *how* it does rather than on *what* it does, then there is methodolatry and the birth of technological rationality, where the medium becomes the message and what is important is not *what* is done or said but *how*.

Phenomenologically speaking, all objective knowledge—especially the objective knowledge of the human and social sciences—is a second-degree abstraction from the original experience in the life-world, just as geography presupposes the existence of the natural landscape. Such geometrical concepts as "straight line," "triangle," "circle," and "pentagon" have their "original" counterparts in nature itself. "The whole universe of science," as Merleau-Ponty puts it, "is built upon the world as directly experienced, and if we want to subject science itself to *rigorous scrutiny* and arrive at a precise assessment of its meaning and scope, we must begin by reawakening the basic experience of the world of which science is the second-order expression."[55] The natural scientists can abstract nature, discovering the ideal order of regularities and uniformities and excluding in principle their personal and cultural concerns from their research. Unlike their colleagues in the natural sciences, however, the social scientists cannot exclude what Schutz calls "social reality,"[56] the very reality that they are to investigate and whose subjects they are.

Phenomenology, then, seeks the radical root of theoretical knowledge in the pretheoretical understanding of the everyday life-world. To return to the life-world as "the locus of man's construction of reality and the point of access to his comprehension of all knowledge,"[57] particularly in the human sciences, is in no way a denial of the authenticity and objectivity of scientific knowledge. Such a return seeks its genetic source in the infrascientific reality of the life-world upon which all sciences are founded.[58] In criticizing behaviorism (objectivist psychology) as practicing a "psychological

Averroism," Erwin Straus comments that "objective psychology cannot exist without a black market furnished with contraband from the psychology of living experience. For by its observations, descriptions, and communications it belongs to the human world. The scholar acts and talks, he is pleased or he suffers, he is a man like all other men."[59] Thus phenomenology is critical of the methodological Averroism in which the construction of the "artificial puppet" has nothing to do with "real people." In the name of precision, exactness, and clarity, methodological Averroists treat the "operational language" of theory as if it were independent of the "natural language" of political humankind, instead of viewing the former as theoretical constructs based upon the pretheoretical construct of this very political humankind. Far more important than this is the phenomenological insistence that artificial constructionism or formalism cannot do away with the experiential knowledge of politics in the everyday life-world from which scientific constructs are abstracted.

The phenomenological posture implies more than a criticism of political behavioralism for inventing "a jargon that impedes communication and renders prose tortuous and full" (that is, for an esoteric scholasticism) or for discounting "the utility and validity of impressionist accounts of political phenomena"[60]—although no doubt these criticisms are justified and, for that matter, might well be directed toward some thinkers of the phenomenological persuasion too. All philosophical and scientific terminology is more or less esoteric jargon to ordinary people. Phenomenology is not demanding that the language of a theoretical enterprise ought to correspond to the language of ordinary people, a feat that has been mastered by only a few thinkers in the history of Western philosophy since Socrates.[61] Nor is it true that the investigation of how the everyday language of political humankind is used would dissolve all philosophical problems, or, for that matter, that a "journalistic style" is necessarily shallow, any more than a scientific style is *ipso facto* profound and elucidating.

The life-world is also a social reality, a network of interactions among human beings who are its subjects. Intersubjectivity is the "original datum" of the life-world itself. Value, that of which we approve or disapprove, is the central and integral force of this social and cultural world of action. The "republic of science," or the community of scientists, also partakes of this characteristic of the everyday life of human beings as actors. As Husserl states, "If we cease being immersed in our scientific thinking, we become aware that we scientists are, after all, human beings and as such are among the components of the life-world which always exists for us, ever pregiven; and thus all of science is pulled, along with us, into the—merely 'subjective-relative'—life-world."[62] Like every other life-style, science itself is a human project and *praxis*. The life-world is relative in the sense that its "Heraclitean flow" is relative to the perspectives of individuals, societies, and cultures, which constitute a variety of its versions. In their respective ways, these different versions of the life-world have their own invariant structures, which are open to the theoretical formulation of the life-world as a universal system of meanings.

Thomas Kuhn, whose philosophy of science has been criticized as subjective and as relativizing science,[63] supports some of he phenomenological theses. Like Husserl's teleology of scientific history, Kuhn's analysis of science is historical and psychosociological, that is to say, the structure of scientific knowledge is sought from the historical development of science and in the context of an existing community of scientists.[64] In the first place, the change of a scientific paradigm is an alteration of perspective, a new *Weltanschauung,* as it were: "When paradigms change, the world itself changes with them," and "the scientist who embraces a new paradigm is like the man wearing inverting lenses."[65] To discover a new paradigm is, then, to turn on the switch of a new *Gestalt,* which influences or colors a scientist's own perception and experience. An example of this, among many, is the Aristotelian perspective of the "constrained fall" and the Galilean perspective of the "pendulum," which perceive the same phenomenon with equally true, though different, observations. In the second place, for Kuhn, scientific theorizing involves "an inextricable mixture" of the descriptive and the normative, the thesis of which challenges the hard core of the behavioralist doctrine of value-neutrality as the essence of scientific activity. A scientific paradigm on which the puzzle-solving of normal science depends requires the total commitment of a particular scientific community, as does the acceptance of a new paradigm rising out of an anomaly or the failure in puzzle-solving of an old paradigm. In recent years, the increasing challenge to the behavioralist "paradigm" is largely directed to and based on its unsatisfactory formulation of value or its relation of fact and value to the world of political action. A scientific revolution is brought about not merely by the objective evidence it presents, but also by the normative judgment of a scientific community.[66] It is not accidental that for Kuhn, a scientific revolution resembles a political revolution and a fight for the ruling paradigm is a political fight. In conclusion, Kuhn writes that since there can be "no scientifically or empirically neutral system of language or concepts, . . . scientific knowledge, like language, is intrinsically the common property of a group or else nothing at all. To understand it we shall need to know the special characteristics of the groups that create and use it."[67]

Political behavioralism, like logical empiricism, maintains the dualism of fact and value: in the name of "the norm of value judiciousness," they are kept apart and considered to be (logically) heterogeneous. According to Eulau, political science as "a behavioral science" has not attempted to make "the world a better place to live in. But it has given new hope that it might be a better place if political ignorance can someday yield to political knowledge."[68] So the aim of political science behavioralistically viewed is to increase the knowledge of political facts instead of creating political values, for values evince emotions, which are irrational and therefore have no cognitive value. The emotive or noncognitivist view of value or ethics maintains that all meaningful statements are descriptive, that is, they report or describe the state of affairs—and that to be meaningful, all scientific statements must be descriptive. In contrast to value judgments that are "instrumental" or "extrinsic" and belong legitimately to the domain of scientific activity, value judgments that are "categorical" or "intrinsic" are not empirically verifiable. They cannot be validated as "true" or "false."[69]

The British analytical philosopher J. L. Austin, however, contends that this emotive theory of value commits what he calls "the descriptive fallacy"; that is, not all statements are necessarily reporting the state of affairs. There are statements that are "performative utterances." Performative utterances are "perfectly straightforward utterances, with ordinary verbs in the first person singular present indicative active, and yet we shall see at once that they couldn't possible be true or false. Furthermore, if a person makes an utterance of this sort we should say that he is *doing* something rather than merely *saying* something"[70] ("I do," "I apologize," "I promise," etc.). For example, when I say "I promise that . . . ," I am performing an act; I am *doing* something rather than reporting something, or someone's act of promising, or someone's saying "I promise." I think political language, the language of political humankind, is largely of a "performative" nature. If Austin's view is right, then the noncognitivist theory of value based on the heterogeneity of value and fact is misleading. For there are indicative statements that are outside its "verifiability" criterion of truth or falsity, validity or invalidity, and the heterogeneous purity of fact and value is no longer the logical question, the logic of the "is" and the "ought," but is the question of an *attitude*. Not only evaluations but perhaps all statements, both descriptive and normative, are expressions of attitudes, and "attitudes are in general but tenuously connected with emotion, since thoughts, words and deeds are much more central manifestations of them."[71] All knowledge is more or less personal or, better, *inter*personal.[72] Since political science as a theoretical activity is one of many human life-projects, its language cannot escape the ambiguous character of the language of political humankind in the life-world, in which thoughts, words, and deeds are all mixed with "emotion" as well as "reason." Thus Austin's view refuses to accept the watertight containers of fact and value as something separable. Political science in pursuit of political knowledge is, to paraphrase Alvin Gouldner, a parcel of the political world as well as a conception of it.[73] Thus political scientists themselves are part of the common society and history from and in which they construct their knowledge. We change the political world by changing our conception of it.

Thus theory and practice are two moments of human being-in-the-world. The human being is both knower and actor. Every civilization is both a civilization of *theōria* and a civilization of *praxis*.[74] The world, however, cannot be reduced to the "I think," for one cannot theorize without first participating in the life-world that constitutes the background of all theorizing activity. Theoretical knowledge is a special, though important, way of existing in the world. T. D. Weldon's conception of political philosophy as a therapy of political words or linguistic confusions is ill-conceived, for it ignores the basic fact that language has no independent existence of its own apart from humans who exist in the world. It should be remembered that words themselves do not lie; it is human beings as the users of words who lie: a lie without the liar is a scandalous abstraction.[75] Therefore, it seems more correct to say that words do not need therapy; it is the speaking person who needs it. By the same token, the function of the philosophy of political science cannot be narrowly conceived as a logical and linguistic analysis of theory construction and validation. For neither philosophy nor science can bypass the reality it purports to investigate directly or indirectly. From a phenomenological point of view, a philosophy of political science is also a philosophy of the political world. In political behavioralism, as I have stated above, rigor is an analytical and operational ideal that is identified largely with the procedures of model construction and exact quantitative measurement, which aim at prediction. I have also said, however, that there is another kind of rigor in describing and interpreting, as does phenomenology, the "sloppy data" of the human life-world without rigid conceptual castle-building. There is a kind of philosophical rigor that attempts to excavate, as it were, the existential foundation of theory as an activity. In order to seek a rigorous "archaeology" of the knowing subject, of the scientist as a knower, we need to introduce hermeneutics. Broadly speaking, hermeneutics is an existential analysis interpreting humankind's placement in the social and historical world. Thus it is applicable to all intellectual endeavors related to the human sciences: political theory (especially the history of political thought as an "exegetical" exercise), literary criticism, history, art, and psychoanalysis, as well as theology. The applicability of hermeneutics to the human sciences presupposes the idea that the human being is radically different from mere nature: both humanity and nature have a history, but only humans know that they have a history.[76] We are conscious of the past (that is, of a present that has passed) as a product of our own doing that in turn influences us, and of a future that, as a possibility, will again be of our own making. Hermeneutics is the way of integrating thoughts and actions, in particular a thinker's own thoughts and actions, in order to reveal through "a *creative interpretation*" the meaning of the human life-world as temporal and historical.[77]

In *Being and Time*, Heidegger singles out the importance of "historicality" (*Geschichtlichkeit*) in human existence in the world. For our present purpose, it is sufficient to note that such historicity leads to the notion that knowing as a special way of existing in the world is not just "the observer's observation of the observed," as the behavioralist posture has it, where the knower's subjectivity becomes anonymous, the phenomenon that Heidegger calls "they" (*das Man*). Rather, it is a participating event or happening, the participation of the knowers in the reality of things they observe: the knower is an observing *participant* in the ambient world.[78]

Take the simple example of a so-called "fact." It is like "a sack—it won't stand up till you've put something in it."[79] A fact is not "something out there," independent of an observer, but the result of an interpretation or interpolation, a comprehension of a thing or an event by a conscious, knowing subject. Michael Oakeshott thus declares:

> Fact, whatever else it may be, is experience; without thought there can be no fact. Even a view which separates ideas from things must recognize that facts are ideas. Fact is what has been made or achieved; it is the product of judgment. And if there be an unalterable datum in experience, it certainly cannot consist of fact. Fact, then, is not what is given, it is what is achieved in experience. Facts are never merely observed, remembered, or combined; they are always made. We cannot "take" facts, because there are none to take until we have constructed them. And until a fact is established, that is, until it has achieved a place in a coherent world, it is no more than an hypothesis or a fiction.[80]

Facts are no more to be taken as "givens" than are values. A *factum* is a thing done, made, or experienced, and as such it reveals the accomplished performance of one who experiences in relation to an event, i.e., an interpretative participation of the knowing subject. The criterion of relevance always and decisively enters into the determination of a fact. By stressing the interrelatedness of "facts," "observation," and "theory" in scientific discovery, Norwood Hanson regards "facts" as not being "picturable, observable entities."[81] Facts in relation to theory, and in turn theory in relation to facts, are really hermeneutical events. Kuhn also shows that in scientific discovery, which is "a complex event" that "involves recognizing both *that* something is and *what* it is," both theory and fact, both conceptualization and observation, are "inseparably linked."[82] For Merleau-Ponty, similarly, Husserl's *Wesensschau* (intuition of essence) is the mental operation that consists of reading of the essential meaning structure of a multiplicity of facts. In theorizing, the factual and the essential are mutually related.[83] Therefore, there are no facts that are raw and crude. Needless to say, moreover, the language of statistics without interpolation is a disjointed, meaningless collection of dots, numbers, lines, and graphs. I am inclined to agree with Sheldon Wolin when he says that "facts are more multi-faceted than a rigid conception of empirical theory would allow" and that "nothing . . . is more necessary as a condition for theorizing than the facts not be univocal."[84]

IV. Embodiment and Artificial Reasoning

Eulau uses the phrase "logic of science" as the key device in separating the inner (subjective) from the outer (objective) and taking one side, the outer, as the only valid domain of scientific discourse. As has been indicated in Lane's and Deutsch's conceptions of consciousness, political behavioralism is unwilling to recognize a complicity between outer expression and inner thought, cognition and affectivity (or feeling), and mind and body, as illustrated particularly in Lane's divisive conception of "consciousness" and "intelligence."

It is in *The Principles of Psychology* (1890) that the radical empiricist William James distinguishes between "knowledge-about" (conceptual knowledge) and "knowledge by acquaintance" (preconceptual knowledge) and attempts to show their mutual relatedness. To the extent that pure experience is feeling, knowledge by acquaintance is felt knowledge, whereas knowledge-about is thought knowledge: "Through feelings we become acquainted with things, but only by our thoughts do we know about them. Feelings are the germ and starting point of cognition, thoughts the developed tree."[85] Thus there is a mutual dependency between feeling and symbolization. As for feeling or felt meaning, it is "an inward sensing" that is definitely there inside us as "a concrete mass"; nevertheless, it is hard to specify what it *is*.[86] Like thinking or any other form of consciousness, feeling is intentional (that is, feeling is always feeling *of* something). But unlike thinking, which has a sharp cleavage between subject and object, feeling is "the manifestation of a relation to the world which constantly restores our complicity with it, our inherence and belonging in it, something more profound than all polarity and duality."[87] Feeling as some "non-mediatizable immediate" is, therefore, an embodied mode of participation in the world.[88] To introduce feeling in our discussion, it is worth realizing, is not to slight conceptual knowledge but to insist stubbornly on the inseparability of the two and on the unity of mind and body.[89]

Felt meaning is a presymbolic, ongoing flow of experiencing. It has an important function in what we think, observe, and perceive and in how we behave. Although it is yet to be articulated fully in symbols, this felt, flowing mass of human experience is richer and broader than thought, observation, speech, and action. It makes sense to say that "we can know more than we can tell" and that "we mean (or 'sense') more than we can say."[90] Broadly speaking, meaning is not limited to what is symbolically expressive, that is, it is not concerned merely with the logical, syntactical, and semantic structures of symbols. If it were, human thought processes would be like the working of programmed computers and human speech would be like playing a record on a phonograph. Yet since feeling and symbolizing go hand in hand, one is capable of symbolizing one's felt meaning or expressing it in words or speech. Our thought is the mediation between felt meaning and symbols, and the latter have a direct and selective reference to the former.

Furthermore, the phenomenological notion of the human being as an embodied agent offers a tentative, negative answer to Eulau's claim that no segments of political behavior are "intrinsically immune to scientific analysis,"[91] since there are no *a priori* or inherent limits to scientific techniques. According to Eulau, since scientific creativity "knows of no predetermined limitations," all segments of political behavior can in principle, or potentially, be treated "behaviorally," for "the future is always contingent, and contingencies are difficult to foresee."[92] The scientific analysis of political behavior is then posed as potentially a technological question. It seems that the possible perfection of computer technology or artificial intelligence is what Eulau has in mind. He believes that the progress of science, like the "progressive" spirit of liberalism in which he has faith, has no *a priori* or inherent limitations. Eulau's scientific faith may be challenged by the phenomenological consideration that the human being is an embodied agent, an idea that seems to point to the absolute limit of simulation as applied to the understanding of human behavior. The obvious fact that computers are not human, that human beings are not machines because they are embodied agents, ought to be elaborated. The technological limitation or possible perfection Eulau speaks of here is ultimately the question whether the computer simulation of human intelligence is limited or possible perfectible.

In recent years there have been attempts to justify the science of politics in terms of the models of artificial intelligence or cybernetics. Herbert Simon, for example, attempts to make psychology a science of the artificial and goes as far as to say that the proper study of humankind is not the human being, but the science of the artificial design[93]—a claim that indeed exceeds the initial vision of Norbert Wiener for the possibilities of an exact science of humanity and society.[94]

Karl Deutsch's cybernetic model is one of the philosophically most sophisticated justifications in political behavioralism for the use of artificial intelligence or cybernetics in the investigation of the functions of a political system. For him, a model is any "physical device" that, under a set of operating rules, can process a set of symbols: "The set of symbols and the set of operating rules form a *symbol system* or a *model*" (for example, a language, a system of geometry, a logical calculus, chess, or poker).[95] As an intellectual device for the understanding of reality, it is necessarily simplified, rather than a "complete replica." For Deutsch the shortcomings of both classical mechanism and organism are that the quantitative approach of the former excludes the qualitative categories of change, growth, novelty, and purpose, and that the qualitative approach of the latter lacks the details of quantitative measurement. The cybernetic model he proposes, then, is supposed to be an alternative model to accommodate the shortcomings of these two models, in that it is "applicable to problems involving both quantity and quality . . . [by] facilitating the recognition of patterns, together with measurement and verifiable predictions."[96] In seeking an essential unity between the mental and the physical, Deutsch claims that his model is strikingly different from the Cartesian mode of thought, which makes "a sharp division between the process of mind and the physical world accessible to science."[97] Although Deutsch acknowledges the complexity of human information processing, the present technological impossibility of building a complex machine that can adequately perform the functions of human thought processes, and the dynamic quality of human mind (that is, mind as "a single run pattern of information flow"), his cybernetic model nonetheless succumbs to physicalism as it paves the way toward rigorous and quantitative measurement and prediction. Human mind, for example, is held to be an analogue to the information process of artificial intelligence. Information is defined as "a patterned relationship between events" that is physical, being "carried by matter-energy processes"; and because it is different from "form," it is analyzable into *"discrete units"* that can be quantitatively measured. Subsequently, mind is "any self-sustaining physical process which includes the seven operations of abstracting, communicating, storing, subdividing, recalling, re-combining and reapplying [discrete] items of information."[98] And just as a symbol is "an order to recall from memory a particular thing or event, or a particular set of things or events," meaning is by the same token a "physical position in a sequence of events."[99]

The optimism expressed by researchers in cognitive simulation or artificial intelligence is now being challenged by the findings of existential phenomenology.[100] According to the phenomenological tradition of Husserl, Heidegger, and Merleau-Ponty, researchers in artificial reason are necessarily committed to the following two assumptions: (1) an epistemological assumption that all intelligent behavior can be simulated by a device whose only mode of information processing is that of a detached disembodied, objective observer; and (2) the ontological assumption, related to logical atomism, that everything essential to intelligent behavior can in principle be understood in terms of a determinate set of independent elements.[101]

Proceeding from these two assumptions, researchers in artificial intelligence believe that human intelligence can essentially be simulated or formalized, or that psychology is a science of the artificial. According to this thesis, the acquisition of knowledge is viewed as the function peculiar to the disembodied mind as a rational faculty or, in the cybernetic model of Deutsch, as the function of an electronic network. "Machines," Hubert Dreyfus declares, "are perfect Cartesians. They are able to deal only with the determinate and *discrete bits of information* which Descartes called 'clear and distinct ideas'."[102]

Although they may reject the "metaphysical cargo" of Descartes, theorists of artificial intelligence rely on the Cartesian idea of mind as a thinking substance or thing, a necessary corollary of psychophysical parallelism (mind and body both as substances or *res cogitantes* and *res extensae*).[103] By replacing the *res cogitans* with artificial rationality and rationalism with artificialism, they accept the idea of the human being as a disembodied mind. Humans and their behavior can be understood without understanding their physiology or biology,[104] just as the computer can be understood without understanding the physical properties of its hardware. So human language itself is an artificial design, and the acquisition of language is regarded as a purely intellectual or cognitive operation. Speaking of the relation of language and thinking, Simon is willing to say that "only the thinkable is expressible,"[105] and the signified is identified with the signifiable. But in fact the contrary is true: the acquisition of language involves a kind of *habituation,* a use of language as a tool or instrument. The employment of language, which is an effect and also one of the most active stimuli of intellectual development, does not appear to be founded on the exercise of pure intelligence but instead on a more obscure operation—namely, the child's assimilation of the linguistic system of his environment in a way that is comparable to the acquisition of any habit whatever; the learning of a structure of conduct.[106]

I see no reason why the same process may not be assumed for any human learning, for the adult and the child equally, unless one believes in two ontological orders of a different sort, one for the child and another for the adult.

Phenomenology has now shown conclusively, I think, the qualitative differences between the information processing of a computer (which, by the way, must have a "body" in order to "think") and the intelligence of a fully embodied agent in (1) pattern recognition, (2) problem solving, and (3) bodily skills.[107] The existence of this difference does not overlook the fact that some *specific* intelligent human performances can be simulated by a computer. But it does mean that "*fully* intelligent behavior would be impossible in principle for a digital machine."[108] Human behavior, individual or social, cannot be fully predicted by simulation. Because it is capable of handling only "unambiguous, completely structured information," the machine is incapable of handling the ambiguous and "ill-structured data" of the human daily life-world.[109]

It may be concluded, therefore, that the basic and radical difference between the human and the machine is that the human being is a fully embodied agent, an agent with the living body necessary for both thinking and acting, whereas the machine is only a thing with an artificial body, which, when not out of order, may be faster, more efficient, and more error-free than a human being. But at best it can be only a replica of a human being. It is not because of "human pride," as Simon suggests, that an objection is raised here against the identification of the human and the artificial. It is indeed feasible to produce servomechanisms that will surpass the human intelligence in speed and accuracy. The objection raised here is based not on the human pride of superiority, but on the way in which embodied human beings think and behave qualitatively *differently* from any other organism or any mechanism. By proposing to reduce human thought to a "program" or "information flow" and the human body to an information container or hardware, Deutsch's cybernetic model and particularly Simon's science of artificial intelligence—both of which focus solely on the clear "thinking" or "intellective" component of the human being—help us to understand human beings as a "cyborgs" but fail to understand them as natural and embodied beings. Herein lies, perhaps, an answer to Eulau's faith that all segments of political behavior are accessible in principle to behavioralist techniques and that the progress of scientific analysis is just a question of technology. The behavioralist philosophy of humanity and human behavior fails in the end to take into account the dialectic of thought and feeling (or of symbolic and felt meaning) on the one hand and the body as an active mode of being-in-the-world on the other. Above all, it suspends or leaves out the theorizers themselves as the *subjects* of their own thought and action in the everyday social and historical life-world.

V. Conclusion

The phenomenological critique of the epistemology of political behavioralism in this essay is based on the ideas, first, that the question of the nature of political knowledge cannot ignore the question of political science as a human project, *praxis,* and achievement; and, second, that the methodology of political science must be consonant with the nature of political things, the most basic component of which, as Eulau would agree, is the *behavior* of humankind, political humankind. Political behavioralism shows indifference to, and intolerance of, the living, and often ambiguous dialectic of the "visible" ("outer") and the "invisible" ("inner") by bifurcating the objective and the subjective, science and the life-world, cognition and affectivity, value and fact, and finally action and thought. The behavioralist methodological ideal of rigor, scientific objectivity, operational exactitude, quantitative measurement, and finally prediction, in order to build the citadel of an exact science after the model of the natural and mathematical sciences, especially physics, points to its indifference to science as a human project and the scientist as a human being. Insofar as it touches on the visible or outer perimeter of the human being, behavioralist philosophy provides an incomplete image of humanity and science. If the incomparable gadfly of ancient civilization, Socrates, is forthright in professing that the unexamined life is not worth living, then the foremost duty of scientific life is to examine and reflect on itself as a human *praxis,* which is the first order of rigor and magnitude. Conceptual parsimony, or rather operational stricture, short-circuits the profusion of human experience and is insensitive to the agility, elasticity, and ephemeral quality of human thought, ignoring the experiential knowledge of political things in the everyday life-world as the source of scientific knowledge. The political behavioralist who refuses to recognize him/herself as the knowing *subject* in the life-world, or who thinks of him/herself as an anonymous epistemological subject, may be likened to the philosophical solipsism

Wittgenstein once professed: to paraphrase Wittgenstein's passage, the behavioralist self is not the human being, not the human body or the human soul, but rather the scientific subject, the limit of the world—not a part of it.[110] A way to overcome this scientific solipsism is the phenomenological archaeology of the political scientist as a knowing subject in relation to the life-world. The historicity of the political theorizer suggests the idea that political theory as a human activity is a hermeneutical event.

Political behavioralism as a scientific technique necessarily reduces the inner to the outer and takes the latter as the only legitimate domain of scientific enterprise. This physicalist view regards human consciousness as an epiphenomenon of the physical and is incapable of understanding the intentional structure of human behavior as a structure of meaning that is neither entirely subjective nor entirely objective in the traditional sense of these terms. Moreover, it ignores the notion of embodiment (*Subjektleib* or *sujet incarné*)—the idea that the body is not a mere physical object, but is essentially the *subject* of consciousness and behavior. Human beings may no longer be the physical center of the universe, just as the geocentrism of Ptolemy is replaced by the heliocentrism of Copernicus, but they are still the *meta*-physical center of the world.

Phenomenologically speaking, the philosophy of political science *is* at the same time the philosophy of the political world. Theoretical activity, scientific or philosophical, is a special way of existing in the world, and political knowledge is a part of the political world as well as a conception of it, for the world is an active synthesis of what is given and what is constructed. Like action, thought itself is an active mode of participation in the world. Theory thus conceived is no longer a formalistic enterprise, for example, a logical and linguistic analysis. A phenomenology of politics—or, better, the hermeneutics of politics—suggests a new perspective or "paradigm" in political theory that is capable of synthesizing philosophy and science, fact and value, and knowledge and action. In other words, it is capable of synthesizing *theōria* and *praxis*, the tension of which has been the twilight zone of Western political theorizing since its inception in ancient Greece. If "the goal is man," in the final analysis this goal cannot merely be a methodological credo. It is ultimately an ethical one. The theorizer, the scientist as well as the philosopher, is the "servant of humanity," and it is this phrase that defines his/her true *vocation*. She/he can no longer remain an ethical amnesiac.[111]

Natura enim incerta est.
—Giambattista Vico,
De Studiorum Ratione

Just as there is sleepwalking, there is also
sleepthinking.
—José Ortega y Gasset,
Historical Reason

The solution to the problem of identity: Get lost.
—Norman O. Brown,
Closing Time

Four

The Genealogy
of Technological Rationality
in the Human Sciences

I. Introduction

THERE IS NO NEED to emphasize that the fundamental project of
technology threatens to create a vast necropolis from two converg-
ing fronts; the macro-behemoth (a gigantic pile of nuclear arsenals)
and the micro-monolith (a high stack of computer chips). We are
coming very close to the realization of that ancient prophetic warning of a Hindu scared scripture: *I am my death*. The phenomenological sociologist John O'Neill puts the same idea differently: "We
may well be the first human society to think of itself as the last."[1]
    In this essay, however, I am concerned only with the potential of
technology to destroy our inner human landscape in the philosophy
of the social sciences. It is a critique of technological rationality,
both instrumental and autonomous, directly or indirectly in terms
of Heidegger's "fundamental ontology" and critique of technology

73

(*Technik*), Husserl's phenomenology of embodiment, and Ortega y Gasset's "circumstantial" anthropology. My argument is that all the calculative models of cognition are incapable of rendering *sociality*—the most fundamental concept of the social sciences—as the diatactics of the self and the other. The basis of my contention is not that technological rationality obliterates the inner soul, but that it overlooks and is incapable of understanding the body as the active and synergistic mode of existing in the world.

By "genealogy," I mean the critical analysis of genesis, meaning-genesis. It implies the fecundity as well as the quintessence of phenomenological thinking. The founder of phenomenology, Husserl, often used the term *introduction* to characterize a new investigation in the existing body of phenomenological knowledge; Heidegger spoke of *questioning* as the "piety of thinking" and never abandoned the conception of phenomenology as the open-ended, infinite *possibility* of thinking; and above all, Merleau-Ponty was fond of using the term *interrogation* for his philosophical research to insist that the questioner him/herself is already implicated in the questions she/he raises. To paraphrase Merleau-Ponty slightly in order to accent this genealogical spirit in phenomenological thinking, the end of phenomenological philosophy is the account of its beginning. In essence, the true phenomenologist is necessarily and always a perpetual beginner, returning to genesis.

Before Husserl, Heidegger, and Merleau-Ponty Nietzsche pioneered genealogy as a mode of philosophical inquiry based primarily on the "dithyrambic" aesthetics of music. In Nietzsche's genealogy, there is the ineluctable enmeshing of origin and value, that is, the chiasmic reversibility of the value of *origin* and the origin of *value* that implies the eternal returning of the values. Genealogy embedded in the aesthetic purports to break the iron grip of established reality and demands the transformation of the given toward a new discovery of reality—the vital upsurge that Nietzsche called the transvaluation of all values. Here, however, genealogy is simply meant to be both "destructive" and "constructive" at the same time, i.e., deconstruction as a double. In *The Basic Problems of Phenomenology,* Heidegger defines deconstruction as a "critical process in which the traditional concepts, which at first must necessarily be employed, are de-constructed down to the sources from which they were drawn."[2] From this, construction or reconstruction naturally follows.

As mentioned above, sociality may be defined as the "diatactics" of the self and the other. The neologism *diatactics* is coined by Hayden White in order to replace the term dialectics, and avoids certain ideological overtones of Marx, on the one hand, and the transcendental overtones of Hegel, on the other; diatactics is neither "paratactical" (conceptually underdetermined) nor "hypotactical" (conceptually overdetermined).[3] As applied to the conceptualization of sociality, diatactics is neither overdetermination nor underdetermination of the self by the other, or of the other by the self. Sociality may be said to have two sides: sociability and asociability, e.g., cooperation and conflict, war and peace. For purposes of the present exposition, the term *diatactics* is appropriated in two additional ways. In the first place, the logic of diatactics connotes historical movement or change without entailing any teleological progression as in Hegel and Marx. This is the essence of "historical reason" in Ortega.[4] In rejecting monism, dualism, and reductionism, diatactics is further embedded in the sense of *ambiguity*. For the *etyma "ambi"* means "bothness" as in "ambivalence" and "aroundness" as in "ambiance." Ambiance, milieu, circumstance, and environment are all familial or neighboring concepts.[5] Consider sociality or human plurality as a diatactical complicity (or "correlation") of distinction and equality. The existential condition of human plurality requires living as a distinct and unique being among equals.[6] If humans were not equal, there would be no common ground for communicating or acting. As "earthy creatures" or creatures of *terra*, humans all together represent a "solid *ground*" for an egalitarian principle. The principle of equality is exemplified in the conception of the human as the *language animal*—the equality of humans everywhere who are distinct from other living beings and nonliving things. At the same time, if humans were not distinct, there would again be no need to communicate or act. Distinction—individual differences—thickens the density of human plurality. It assumes a radical alterity of the other person.[7] Again, there are many different languages—according to one estimate, about 3000— in the history of human civilization. Not only is each language distinct, but since each individual appropriates a given language uniquely, all linguistic communication or understanding within the same linguistic system is indeed some sort of translation.[8]

In the second place, diatactics implies sense perception or the sensorium. More specifically, it alludes not only to the intimate sense of touch insofar as it is tactile, but also the organizing capacity of tactility as the synaesthesia or synergy of the entire sensorium.[9] Insofar as it rejects the separatist or dualist approach to mind and body, diatactics incorporates *conception* with *perception:* there is no disembodied rationality, and human reason is never disembodied. For too long, unfortunately, the body has been unemployed in the agora of philosophical conceptualization. Merleau-Ponty insists that as consciousness is to the body, so "I think" (*cogito*) is to the "I perceive" (*percipio*). His emphasis on the corporeality of the body as the subject of perception is an urge to return to perception as the natural landscape on which the geography of conception is mapped out. This is the meaning of the "primacy of perception" in Merleau-Ponty's phenomenology.[10] So he insists that perception *per se* is a nascent *logos*. The notion of corporeal intentionality, or the body as capable of conferring meaning, is truly his seminal contribution to phenomenology and also

the philosophy of the social sciences. As our body fertilizes our mind, so does our perception cultivate our conception. In fact, etymologically speaking, con-ception implies "togetherness," whereas perception implies the opposite: "separateness." Here it is significant that the verb "to conceive" is associated with the "fertility" (or fecundity) of the body in the process of thinking (with language). Elizabeth Sewell bemoans the fact that conception has become an intellectual (i.e., disembodied) term. She writes that "the human organism thinks as a whole, and our division of it into mind and body is the result of overemphasis on logic and intellect in near isolation which has led us into so one-sided a view of the activity of thought, so gross an underestimation of the body's forms of thought and knowledge."[11] In brief, conception is viewed undiatactically or unambiguously. The separation of conception and perception as well as that of mind and body is arbitrary or, better, artificial.

II. *The Cartesian Genesis*

Since genealogy implies genesis, meaning-genesis, we should trace the modern technological rationality to its origins in Descartes.[12] With him, certainty, or a true and certain "vision of the world," resides in the conceptualization of philosophy or *prima philosophia* as *mathesis universalis*. Descartes is substantiating the view of Galileo, who wrote in *II Saggiatore*:

> Philosophy is written in that vast book which stands forever open before our eyes, I mean the universe; but it cannot be read until we have learned the language and become familiar with the characters in which it was written. It is written in mathematical language, and the letters are triangles, circles, and other geometrical figures, without which means it is humanly impossible to comprehend a single word.[13]

Not only is this visual language revealing, but it shows the infatuation with typographic culture. The mathematical "measuring" (the musical sense of *metron*) of the universe, however, is nothing new; it goes back to Pythagoras and his followers, including Plato, in ancient Greece. What is new with the modern conception of mathematics, however, is that it attends first and last to method as such, whereas the ancients intended to solve the problem of method on the basis of an ontology of objects. As Jacob Klein argues, in modern science the "generality of the method" (methodology) replaced the "generality of the object" (ontology).[14] Descartes sets "methodism" in motion in modern intellectual thought, the methodological monism predicated on mathematics as paradigmatic of "clear thinking"—against which, it is worth noting here, the Neapolitan philosopher Giambattista Vico disputed so strenuously and counteracted with his own proposal called the "New Science" of humanity or "humanities" (*studia humanitatis*) with an emphasis on rhetoric, philology, and jurisprudence.[15]

Of the body, Descartes wrote:

> Nature also teaches me by these sensings of pain, hunger, thirst, etc., that I am not lodged in my body merely as a pilot in a ship, but so intimately conjoined, as it were intermingled with it, that with it I form a unitary whole. Were not this the case, I should not sense pain when my body is hurt, being, as I should then be, merely a thinking thing, but should apprehend by sight any damage to his ship; and when my body has need of food and drink I should apprehend this expressly, and not be made aware of it by confused sensings of hunger, thirst, pain, etc. For these sensings of hunger, thirst, pain, etc., are in truth merely confused modes of thinking, arising from and dependent on the union, and, as it were, the intermingling of mind and body.[16]

However valid or invalid the analogy of "a pilot in a vessel" (*un pilote en son navire*), and even if Descartes is not a thoroughgoing dualist,[17] there is the problem of characterizing the mind as a "thinking substance," because to be a substance, the mind is not *indigens*, i.e., it needs nothing more than itself to exist.[18] That is to say, insofar as it is not *indigens*, it must be independent of the body as well as of other minds. If there is a union between mind and body, it is a weak or loose union, that is, it is a "confederation" rather than a "federation"—to use the analogy of the American Republic in its formative years.

Philosophical certainty for Descartes lodges in the *cogito* or the mind as a "thinking substance" (*res cogitans*). The problem of the Cartesian *Cogito*, or the mind as the basis of explaining sociality is at least threefold. First, the *cogito* is inherently egocentric because it is always and necessarily *ego cogito* (the "I think")—the epitome of an "inner person" in isolation from others.[19] Second, to say that mind is a thinking substance (*res*) is, following the Greek and scholastic tradition, to say that it needs nothing more than itself to exist, that is, it is in no need of the body (*res extensa*). Once the self and the other are viewed as two separate substances, egocentrism or even solipsism is inevitable. Third and most important, sociality is not merely the meeting of minds, disembodied minds, alone, but is first and foremost intercorporeal. For there is no "invisible person"; insofar as a person is his/her body, she/he is visible. R. D. Laing, for example, shows that the self is precluded from engaging in a direct relationship with real things and real people when there is a derangement of perception between the ego and the body in relation to the external world, that is, when the situation is "self $\rightleftharpoons$ (body/other)" instead of "(self/body) $\rightleftharpoons$ other."[20]

The seminal contribution of phenomenology to the human sciences or behavioral sciences is the notion of embodiment, whose basic thesis is that our body is not an object, but is primarily a subject. The body is not an object to be had in the sense of possession, but is an active mode of existing in the world. "I *am* my body," declares Gabriel Marcel, "in so far as I succeed in recognizing that this body of mine *cannot*, in the last analysis, be brought down to the level of being this object, *an* object, a something or other. It is at this point that we have to bring in the idea of the body not as an object but as a subject."[21] This phenomenological notion of the body rejects the Cartesian analogy of mind and body as a "pilot in a vessel." Since it is neither pure materiality nor pure spirituality, the body is capable of acting as an ontological hinge between the self and the other. In essence, the body *inhabits* the world. Describing the acquisition of language as the primordial form of socialization or the diatactical process of internalizing the external and externalizing the internal, Merleau-Ponty provides us with the true sense of the body as habituation when he declares that

> the acquisition of language is a kind of *habituation*, a use of language as a tool or instrument. The employment of language, which is an effect and also one of the most active stimuli of intellectual development, does not appear to be founded on the exercise of pure intelligence but instead on a more obscure operation—namely, the child's assimilation of the linguistic system of his environment in a way that is comparable to the acquisition of any habit whatever: the learning of a structure of conduct.[22]

For Descartes, thinking is a weighty matter of ideas—"clear and distinct ideas" at that. Philosophy as *mathesis universalis* is thoroughly compatible with a visual metaphysics or metaphysical cinematics. For him, clarity means that objects are present to the mind's eye without mistakes. The idea of distinction simply enhances the notion of clarity in that to be distinct, an object must be precise and different from other objects, that is, it contains nothing but what is clear in itself, i.e., distinction is a function of clarity. Therefore, Cartesian metaphysics based on the *Cogito* is identifiable with, and epitomizes, the aristocracy of vision or sight as unambiguous. As a matter of fact, visual metaphysics goes hand in hand with the egocentrism of the *Cogito,* because unlike the other forms of the human sensorium (e.g., hearing), vision is not only isolating or distancing, but also anaesthetic in denying the sociability of the senses. There is a fundamental narcissism and social amnesia of and in all vision.[23] Sounds tend to socialize, unify, and synthesize, whereas sight tends to isolate, divide, and analyze. In other words, in visual metaphysics there is an identity or isomorphism between the "eye" and the "I." Just as vision demotes the other senses, so does the *Cogito* as visual thinking "overlook" and "theorize" away the other person. Heidegger maintains that the "I" (or the "eye") of the *Cogito* as thinking sub/stance (*res cotigans*) becomes the center of thought from which the "I-viewpoint" and the subjectivism of modern thought originate. In this Cartesian pro/position, the one who posits and thinks is the "I": "the subjectivity of the subject is determined by the 'I-ness' (*Ichheit*) of the 'I think.' "[24] For Heidegger, in other words, the "I-viewpoint" of the Cartesian *Cogito* coincides with the modern age as "the age of the world picture" (*Weltbild*). Visual metaphysics and subjectivism are one and the same process, a process that constitutes the problematic of modern epistemology in relation to the human sciences—whose epicenter is, in contrast, the concept of sociality.

In this connection, Jeremy Bentham's meticulous architectural plan in the last quarter of the eighteenth century for the Panopticon or the Inspection House should not be overlooked. For it is a Cartesian plot. The Panopticon is literally the prison-house of visualism. Its prisoners, who live in perpetual solitude in the "islands" of cells partitioned by impregnable walls, may be likened to the solitary confinement of the *Cogito* or epistemological subject as bodiless substance. Moreover, the Panopticon epitomizes the inextricable link between visualism and the ironclad *network* of what Michel Foucault calls "disciplinary technologies."[25] It is, as the term itself implies, the all-encompassing or all-encircling prison-house of visualism whose surveillance mechanism or "discipline principle" puts to use the Cartesian oracle of *clarity* and *certainty:* it is the interlocking of the life in perpetual solitude of the "hypnotized" and incarcerated prisoner and the mechanism of total control. Inspection *is* control. In the very words of Bentham himself: "Solitude thus applied, especially if accompanied with darkness and low diet, is torture in effect, without being obnoxious to the name."[26] The grand design of the Cartesian *Cogito* intends to make philosophy or the *prima philosophia* a peculiarly panoptic institution. Indeed, Cartesianism is the panopticism *par excellence* in which absolute knowledge or knowledge with absolute certainty is a private possession *of* and *by* vision or sight. Perhaps it is no coincidence that in French "knowing" (*sa/voir*), "having" (*a/voir*), and "power" (*pou/voir*), all appear to have "seeing" in common (*voir*, "to see") as their suffix. Indeed, knowing as visual produces the physics of power and makes the human being the "master and possessor of Nature."

The keyword of the Panopticon principle is *inspection*—the double idea of perpetual vision and vigilance in which the prisoner is never out of the inspector's sight. The idea of inspection is regarded as control by the omnipotent vigilance of "seeing without being seen." To put it slightly differently, the inspector who controls has "the unbounded faculty [and physical facility] of seeing without being seen" and the prisoner is "awed to silence by an invisible eye."[27] Without doubt there is in the Panopticon the dialectical welding of visibility and invisibility, for, as Foucault puts it, it is "a machine for dissociating the see/being seen dyad: in the peripheric ring, one is totally seen, without ever seeing; in the central tower, one sees everything without ever being seen."[28] Moreover, panopticism is a network of the spectacular manifestation of discipline as the coercive exercise of power in which "the vigilance of intersecting gazes was soon to render useless both the eagle and the sun."[29] In essence, visibility is a technocratic "trap," whereas invisibility is "a guarantee of order." The seeing inspector and the seen prisoner form a complementary pair; one cannot function without the other. As an interplay of the force of light and the force of darkness, the invisible eye of the inspector is the visible "I" of the prisoner. The "optic/ized" or "objectiv/ized" prisoner in the Panopticon is a passive and powerless onlooker who is the desubjectivized object of towering observation. No wonder, etymologically speaking, there is a filiation between the "optical" and the "objective." In sum, Bentham's Panopticon is the architectural parable of modern humanity as the passive "functionary" of the technocratic network. It is also a reminder that we are prisoners of our own *making*. In its brightest moment, the Enlightenment is at best a Pyrrhic victory because, as Foucault points out, it invented the disenchanting system of discipline while discovering the brilliant principle of liberty.[30]

III. Cartesianism Today

Let me now turn to four contemporary theories of human behavior that reflect Cartesianism: (1) B. F. Skinner's behaviorism, (2) Edward O. Wilson's sociobiology, (3) Herbert A. Simon's "sciences of the artificial," and (4) Marshall McLuhan's autonomous technological media. In one way or another, each has the environment to "overdetermine" the self. For purposes of critique, let me adopt Ortega's "circumstantial" anthropology, for several reasons. First, it was Ortega who recognized the Cartesian principle of "clear and distinct ideas" as philosophical harbinger of modern technological rationality, which is grounded in the idea of "repose" (*repos*) as the method of purging ourselves of passion. Second, Ortega's formulation of primordial reality as the *duplexity* of the "I" and "circumstance(s)" (*circum-stantia*) in *Meditations on Quixote* (1914) not only antedated Merleau-Ponty's phenomenology of perception as the primordial contact between the self and the world that rejects the clear dichotomization of *res cogitans* (*pour-soi*) and *res ecxtensa* (*en-soi*), but also anticipated Heidegger's formulation of human reality (*Dasein*) as being-in-the-world (*In-der-Welt-sein*) and Husserl's formulation of the life-world (*Lebenswelt*) as sociocultural reality.[31] For Ortega, reality is the diatactical correlation of the I and circumstances. As a condition of human life, circumstance is "the other half" of reality. He rejects the Cartesian formulation of the *Cogito*, which reduces the world to the I or makes the I *independent* of the world. And he treats Husserl's "reduction" in the same way: it is "clearly and simply impossible." Ortega writes:

> The realism of antiquity held that the reality of the world was independent of human thought. Modern idealism holds that thought is independent of the world. I say: an *independent world* or *independent thought* do [*sic*] not exist.[32]

Reality, in other words, is the diatactics of the "I" and "circumstances": human beings are creatures of circumstances and circumstances are also the creation of human beings. Third, Ortega's concept of *circumstance* is related to the English *environment*. There are three kinds of environment that surround humanity: social, natural (both physical and biological), and technological or artificial. In the explanatory models of human behavior, these correspond to the theories advanced by Skinner, Wilson, Simon, and McLuhan. Moreover, these three models share something in common: the overdetermination of the self by the environment— social, biological, or technological.

(1) It is no accident that in *Beyond Freedom and Dignity*, Skinner points to Descartes as the first who envisioned the environment as playing an active role in the mechanism of human behavior. (Parenthetically, it was Auguste Comte who translated the biological *milieu* into the social *environment* in the formation of his "positive philosophy.") Skinner contends that the "technology of behavior" fills an important niche in remedying current and future social problems. It complements physical and biological technology with social engineering. The science of humanity, according to Skinner, covers two basic areas: genetic endowments and environment. He

relegates the former and the latter to biology and psychology, respectively. The boundary between the two disciplines, however, is crossed when Skinner declares without equivocation:

> The environment not only prods or lashes, it *selects*. Its role is similar to that in natural selection, though on a very different time scale, and was overlooked for the same reason. It is now clear that we must take into account what the environment does to an organism not only before but after it responds. Behavior is shaped and maintained by its consequences.[33]

He cringes at the slightest hint of "mentalism" (the mind as an autonomous substance), "uncaused" behavior, or an inner life (*homunculus*): there is no "autonomous human being." His is the thoroughgoing determination of the self by the environment. Skinner even rejects the explanatory model of humanity based on information theory or cybernetics as inappropriate because it is predicated on the existence of an "inner processor." He insists, therefore, that science—that is, the science of human behavior—is nothing but the effort not to dehumanize, but only to "de-homunculize" the human.

The genesis of this "environmentalism" or the determination of the self by the environment in Skinner can be traced most clearly, I believe, to Descartes's theory of music in *Abrégé de la Musique* (1618), which was written under the influence of his friend and musical theorist Marin Mersenne. Descartes was driven to the examination of all objects, including aesthetic objects, from the perspective of the certitude that is demonstrable in geometric theorems.[34] Music, too, is likened to mathematics. In the aesthetic theory of music, as in philosophy, we strive for a "clear and distinct" principle by controlling passions or emotions whose value is translated into "simplicity" or "elegance." The idea that truth is beauty means that the "beauty" of an aesthetic principle is as simple or elegant as an arithmetic or geometric figure. Following mathematical theorists of his time, Descartes "rationalized" musical harmony as a matter of mathematical equations and diagrams. For him, musical harmony symbolizes clear and distinct thinking.

Consistent with his scientific and technological rationality, what is most interesting about Descartes' theory of music is the theory of sound or acoustics. For him, the *object* of music is *sound*. "For him," John Hollander writes, "the essence of music is instrumental sound, or the vocal intonation of sound modeled on the former, the voice being treated as merely another instrument. For him, in short, the effects of music upon feelings are purely matters of acoustics and physiology."[35] With Descartes, even the human voice becomes "instrumentalized."

(2) Sociobiology is an interface of biology and sociology. It attempts to generalize about human social behavior from the vantage point of biology. As such it fills the gap of what Skinner calls "genetic endowments," and then spills over into psychology and the other social sciences. Sociobiology is envisioned as "a new human science." According to Charles J. Lumsden and Edward O. Wilson, "Defined as the study of the biological basis of social behavior, it [sociobiology] carries evolutionary theory into the previously un-Darwinized fields of psychology and the social sciences."[36] Sociobiology as a new paradigm of the social sciences is a form of scientism in its basic assumption that "all domains of human life, including ethics, have a physical basis in the brain and are part of human biology; none is exempt from analysis in the mode of the natural sciences."[37] Sociobiology is a reductionistic discipline in that it does not pretend to examine only the biological basis of human social behavior, but is meant to be the whole theory of it. Lumsden and Wilson admit that sociobiology is reductionistic to the extent that it decomposes complicated systems into manageable components for scientific analysis, but it is also synthetic (i.e., nonreductionistic) in that the analyzable parts are reassembled so that their validity can be tested by experimentation or mathematical formulation. On the question of purpose in human behavior, sociobiology adopts a mechanistic model with the assumption that moral judgment, too, is a physiological product of the brain and as such it can be simulated by computer science or cybernetics: "Sophisticated goals," Lumsden and Wilson insist, "can be built into machines."[38] In this respect, sociobiology advocates social engineering or what Skinner calls the "technology of behavior" to alter every part of human behavior, including the deepest levels of human motivation and moral reasoning.

Despite the similarity in the "Darwinized" language between Skinner's behaviorism and Wilson's sociobiology, Wilson contends that Skinner's behaviorist theory is "a severe form of scientific reductionism," because it rejects conceptions of mental phenomena that cannot be tested experimentally.[39] Sociobiology is Cartesian to the extent that the reality of mental phenomena (e.g., thinking and moral reasoning) can be *computed* or *calculated* experimentally or mathematically in alliance with "cognitive psychology." Insofar as all mental phenomena are assumed to be products of the physiological mechanism of the brain, the rationality of sociobiology may be likened to the Cartesian disembodied *Cogito*. In this sense, it may be concluded that, the denial of Lumsden and Wilson notwithstanding, sociobiology is more—doubly more—reductionistic than Skinner's behavioristic technology of behavior because while Skinner's behaviorism stops at the language of Darwinian biology in refuting information theory or cybernetics as believing in the ghost in a machine, sociobiology reduces not only the human to the biological but also the biological to the mechanism of the brain, and openly avows its alliance with cybernetics.[40] It would indeed be foolhardy to deny that biological conditions are necessary to the shaping of human behavior, but sociobiology confuses necessary conditions with sufficient ones.[41] In other words, it is reductionistic.

Let me elaborate my criticism of sociobiology as reductionistic in terms of Ortega's notion of *circumstances*, which is related to the biological notion of the *Umwelt* (the "surrounding world"). Ortega acknowledges his indebtedness in formulating his conception of the human as a "circumstantial" being to the German biologist Jakob von Uexküll, who published in 1909 the book *Umwelt und Innenwelt der Tiere*. Uexküll's work is the beginning of the biological known as *ethology*—the science that attempts to study animal behavior in the natural habitat rather than in laboratories, with the hopes of ridding the work of anthropocentric or anthropomorphic prejudices. It should be noted here that for Lumsden and Wilson, sociobiology is related to ethology insofar as both disciplines are interested in the investigation of an organism's adaptation to its environment. Lumsden and Wilson, however, insist that while ethology focuses on the details of individual behavior, sociobiology concentrates on "the most complex forms of social behavior and the organization of entire societies" and "is grounded in population biology: in the genetics, ecology, age structure, and other biological traits of whole aggregates of individuals."[42] Like cybernetics or the study of artificial intelligence, sociobiology focuses on the *structural* analysis of a system. At the same time, it is different from Skinner's behaviorism, which, like ethology, is the study of the adaptation of individual human behavior to the environment.

Ortega's "circumstance," however, is *not* the biological *Umwelt*. Ortega's formulation—"I am I and my circumstance"—requires a radical distinction between the "I" and "circumstance," where one is never reducible to the other. Otherwise, he would commit the fallacy of both anthropomorphism (reducing animal behavior to human forms) and theriomorphism (reducing human behavior to animal forms, e.g., the popular theory of the "territorial imperatives"). "The distinction between men and animals," Alfred North Whitehead asserts, "is in one sense only a difference in degree. But the extent of the degree makes all the difference."[43] While from the standpoint of the biological *Umwelt,* on the one hand, the human is a *function* of the environment, that is, the environment by and large determines human behavior, Ortega, on the other hand, wishes to affirm the existential or ecstatic character of human reality. Circumstance is circumstance for a person precisely because we are capable of "interpreting" and appropriating our environment for ourselves. In this sense, Ortega's formulation of "I and my circumstance" is close to Heidegger's definition of human reality as being-in-the-world, in which the phrase "being-in" should not be likened to the mere location of an object "in" space, but connotes the *active* way in which humankind creates a world for itself. Nature has a history but it does not know that it has a history. Thus Ortega declares that humanity has no nature but only history. The human is the only being that is capable of bringing about *changes*. Life (or history) itself is not a *factum* (a substantive) but *faciendum* (a gerund), i.e., something that has to be accomplished.[44]

(3) The "high" rationality of artificial intelligence is the apex of technological rationality. Today it surpasses the original vision of its founder, Norbert Wiener himself, in its claims if not in its realization. The pursuit of an artificial matter of ideas, the philosophy of artificial intelligence is a matter not so much of creating "the second self"—to use the title of Sherry Turkle's study on the subject—as of replacing the thinking self with an artificial one. Like Descartes, researchers in artificial intelligence regard thinking as the most important thing in the world. Unlike Descartes, however, such researchers reduce the *Cogito* to the formal sense of abstraction; thought or what is thinkable is bereft of the thinker or thinking agent. Researchers in artificial intelligence respond to their critics by saying that the idea that there must be an agent who does thinking is "a modern echo of the [Cartesian] idea that there must be a 'soul' in the pineal gland."[45] Nonetheless, the post-Cartesianism of artificial intelligence preserves the physicalist legacy of Descartes—of course, the physics of the mind without physicists themselves. In essence, it both disembodies and despiritualizes humanity, in that there is an isomorphism between the human and the machine.

In his 1983 work, *Reason in Human Affairs*, Herbert A. Simon touches on the issues of Edward O Wilson's sociobiology. For Simon, rationality, when broadly defined, is the way of an organism's survival-oriented adaptation to its environment (the idea of human rationality adapted to the evolutionary biology of natural selection). He affirms the *instrumental* nature of science and technology for solving the problems of contemporary society and political institutions. As a matter of fact, he views reason itself as "wholly instrumental." While rejecting the "Olympian model" of "subjective expected utility theory" as "a beautiful object deserving a prominent place in Plato's heaven of ideas,"[46] he deems the central thesis of sociobiology compatible with the "behavioral model" based on "bounded rationality." The evolutionary theory of sociobiology is, in other words, compatible with the behavioral model because both envision rationality as evolutionary adaptation. The behavioral mode assumes that in the process of social and cultural evolution, human thinking and problem solving—including its computational aspects—can be "factorable" into various separate condominia in choosing good or better alternatives for improvement and amelioration. Like the theory of biological evolution, it is "anti-utopian." Simon's behavioral model also favors "weak altruism" or enlightened self-interest, that is, the situation where "an individual sacrifices fitness in the short-run but receives indirect long-run rewards that more than compensate for the immediate sacrifice."[47] However, according to Simon, there is a radical difference between the mechanism of cultural inheritance and that of biological inheritance: the former, but not the latter, is "distinctly Lamarckian," that is, acquired cultural traits can be transmitted. The acquisition of (scientific) knowledge, too, is a vital component of the total process of evolution. Scientific knowledge is not only instrumental, but also incremental—presumably as opposed to "paradigmatic" in the Kuhnian sense. Simon notes that

> the teleology of the evolutionary process is of a rather peculiar sort. There is no goal, only a process of searching and ameliorating. Searching is the end. I suggested earlier that evolution is sometimes regarded as a detailed explanation for rationality precisely because it doesn't require a detailed explanation of process; the important thing is adaptation, however the adaptation is brought about. Evolution permits one to postulate the ends without specifying the means. Now we see that the matter is really the other way around. Evolution, at least in a complex world, specifies means (the process of variation and selection) that do not lead to any predictable end. From ends without means, we have come full circle to means without ends.[48]

What is most interesting in Simon's behavioral model is that it is piggybacked on the "sciences of the artificial" or artificial designs. It is for this reason that I have elsewhere treated the cybernetic model as the apotheosis of behavioralism.[49] Simon's earlier *The Sciences of the Artificial* represents in an important way the most abstract strain of technological rationality and, at the same time, the highest overdetermination of the self by the environment, especially the artificial environment. For him the artificial is identical with the adaptive. In *Reason in Human Affairs*, it is called "docility," which may be defined as the propensity to behave in the adaptive socially approved ways and to refrain from behaving in socially disapproved ways. Simon's notion of docility is comparable to a combination of Skinner's positive and negative reinforcement of behavior, i.e., of reward and punishment. Interestingly, docility is also called "programmability," which is the conduciveness in, for example, thinking and learning to accept "programs" under social pressure.

For Simon, the science of the human *is* the science of the artificial, which is no longer cheap rhetoric. To "operationalize" human thinking, it must be reduced to the formal, mathematical model of artificial intelligence. For the study of artificial intelligence is necessarily mathematical, that is, the mathematization of the human is the model of the human in artificial intelligence. Insofar as psychology is a science of the artificial, the computer simulation of human thinking is also the mathematization of thinking. To render any concept "operational" is to reduce it to discrete bits of information or "atomic facts." The acquisition of language itself, when operationalized, is the process of artificialization. Simon thus declares that "there is no contradiction, then, between the thesis that a human being possesses, at birth, a competence of acquiring and using language and the thesis that language is the most artificial, hence also the most human of all human constructions."[50] Here Simon grafts Chomsky's "Cartesian linguistics" onto the rationality of artificial intelligence.

By "artificial," Simon means "human-made" or "designed" as opposed to "natural." The synonyms for artificial intelligence are "complex information processing" and "the simulation of cognitive processes." He asserts that "the world we live in today is much more a man-made, or artificial, world than it is a natural world."[51] And the most significant parts of our environment are strings of artifacts called "symbols." For Simon, the behavioral sciences can be divided into two important fields: "cognitive psychology" and "engineering design" (or engineering logistics). For him, the Cartesian dualism of the inner and the outer disappears when the former is submerged in the latter or when the inner environment becomes simply a function of the outer environment. Since simulation is a way both to understand and to predict the behavior of any system, it also becomes a technique of understanding and predicting the organization of the human mind (or the process of thinking), which can be known without knowing the physiological structure of the brain. Just as physiology or neurophysiology is not necessary to understand the process of thinking, knowledge of the body is not necessary to understand the way the mind functions, that is, the inner environment of the "adaptive system" called *homo sapiens*. Simon argues for—to use his own term—"*the disembodiment of mind.*" Similarly, when "*only the thinkable is expressible* and *vice versa*"—which he considers to be a Kantian formulation—then the inner environment of thinking is determined by the outer environment of symbolic expression, verbal or otherwise (i.e., "behavioral"). To understand and/or predict it, human behavior must be formalized into causal "laws" and formal "rules."

(4) Since, for Simon, science and technology epitomize human rationality, reason itself is nothing but *instrumental*. Scientific knowledge is as morally neutral as technology: we cannot, he insists, derive the "ought" from the "is." Nevertheless, he is critical of the failure of the media to go beyond "the news and the fads of the present moment," beyond "the newsworthy, the sensational, the novel." He comes to the conclusion that "TV is perhaps even a worse offender that the older media on this dimension because it can create not only a local trend, but a national or international focus of attention."[52] In this regard, Simon stands in stark contrast to Marshall McLuhan's euphoria concerning electronic technology (e.g., TV), which both ecumenicizes the senses and globalizes humankind. What is interesting about McLuhan for our discussion here is twofold. First, the Cartesian saga of technological rationality has an unexpected twist in McLuhanism. Second, McLuhanism is the edifice of "autonomous technology," of the idea that technology is no mere *instrumentum* or means to an end, but an end in itself, that is, technological rationality indeed becomes a teleology.

McLuhan, too, celebrates cybernation because it is the ultimate source of making the tactile contact between humanity and technology, allowing us to return once again to a synaesthetic interplay of the senses. For him, Descartes' notion of "clear and distinct ideas" reflects the highly visible order of typographic culture that began with the Gutenberg revolution. Unlike Descartes, McLuhan is concerned primarily with the sensorial workings of the body and particularly with the tactility of electronic technology, which is markedly different from machine technology. To use his hyperbolic and flippant expression: "The electric light is pure information."[53]

More important, McLuhan expresses the essence of autonomous technology in his celebrated slogan: *the medium is the message*. For him, "The 'content' of any medium is like the juicy piece of meat carried by the burglar to distract the watchdog of the mind."[54] The "content" of any medium is always another medium: for example, according to him, the content of writing is the medium of speech; the content of print is the medium of the written word; and the content of the telegraph is the medium of print. What would be, we might ask, the content of the human mind if it were not stuffed with enframed images "processed" by technology?[55]

It is the allegedly anti-Cartesian McLuhan who actually extends Simon's Cartesian theory of artificial intelligence. Simon is ignorant of the "categorical imperative" of autonomous technology as the reversal of the traditional end-means continuum: *means has now become end and the ultimate environmental determinant of* the self.[56] To recognize this we can be guided by Heidegger's seminal reflection on the question of technology, where he contends that we have not yet fully understood the nature of technology in which humanity itself has become "functionary." What has to be understood is the idea that the *essence (Wesen)* of modern technology is nothing technological, that is, modern technology has ceased to be just *instrumental*. It is no longer simply a means to human activity or the human *telos*. For it is not merely the application of mathematical and physical sciences to *praxis*, but is a *praxis* itself. In brief, the rationale of traditional technology as *instrumentum* is obsolete and anachronistic. Nonetheless, we continue to justify, as does Simon, the "end of technology" in terms of this outmoded idea of *instrumentum*. In so doing, we still view technology as morally neutral and forget that in technology, end has already been subverted by means. Today, this forgetting—the forgetting of the true being of technology as the "ontological fix" of contemporary humanity everywhere—constitutes the poverty of moral thinking *par excellence*.

IV. Conclusion

At the beginning of this essay, I proposed that the Cartesian *Cogito* with its visual metaphysics is incapable of justifying sociality as the diatactics of the self and the other (environment). On the one hand, the *Cogito* (the "I think") is inherently egocentric because it incarcerates the self in the prison-house of thought. It is consistent with Descartes' metaphysical cinematics that is driven to "clarity." To wit or pun: the "I-viewpoint" is the "eye-viewpoint." On the other hand, the human being also becomes the *manipulandum* of the environment. There is no contradiction here because once the body becomes soulless, it is like an *instrument* in the exact sense in which Descartes theorizes about the human voice in his instrumental acoustics. The body is necessary in order to make our presence visible in the world while our thoughts remain *in/visible*. As the active mode of being-in-the-world, the body mediates the contact between the "I" and "circumstance." Ortega revealed the genesis of technological rationality in Descartes' *Cogito*, which turns philosophy into a *mathesis universalis*. Skinner's "technology of behavior," the physicalism of Wilson's sociobiology, and Simon's behavioral or cybernetic model are all *extensions* of the Cartesian disembodied *Cogito* with a radical difference: disembodied thought has now been transformed into anonymous thought in artificial intelligence, because the *Cogito* is not only disembodied, but also bereft of the subject or agent who thinks. In order to justify sociality—the quintessence of the social sciences—we need the conception of the body as an active mode of being-in-the-world, that is, the active mediator of the "I" and "circumstance." Both the *Cogito* and artificial intelligence are, to put it another way, undiatactical because one is "undersocialized" and the other is "oversocialized." The model of "oversocialized humanity" in artificial intelligence is incapable of explaining social change—and even if it could do so, it would explain it only fortuitously or by fiat, because the idea of any meaningful social change assumes the *initium* of the individual, or what Vico calls the "heroic mind" that every individual possesses. Moreover, the political implication of artificial intelligence as anonymous is enormous: the birth of a mass society or totalitarianism in which society is a *mass* of anonymous individuals as *manipulanda*.[57] Merleau-Ponty attacks the heart of artificialism when he observes that as "man really becomes the *manipulandum* he takes himself to be, we enter into a cultural regimen where there is neither truth nor falsity concerning man and history, into a sleep, or a nightmare, from which there is no awakening."[58]

Five

THE SPECTRE OF ETHNOCENTRISM AND THE PRODUCTION OF INTERCULTURAL TEXTS

I. Prologue

THE COMPARATIVE STUDY OF POLITICAL CULTURES would be a
good testing ground for the universal applicability of phenomenology to the methodology of the cultural sciences (e.g., linguistics and
anthropology) for no other reason than that the life-world as
historico-sociocultural reality is claimed to have a set of *invariant*
structures presumably siphoned out of *variant* cultural life-forms.[1]
Phenomenology is and will always remain a conceptual watchdog
for the empirical sciences such as comparative politics and culture.
This essay is an exercise in phenomenology as conceptual "fieldwork." What is required of it is a conceptual housecleaning in
comparative politics and culture.[2] There is one work with a phenomenological orientation that deals directly with the comparative
study of political cultures: *The Homeless Mind: Modernization
and Consciousness*, by Peter Berger, Brigitte Berger, and Hansfried

Kellner.[3] It brings phenomenological insights to bear on the phenomenon called *modernization*—the enormously popular password for those political scientists who are interested in studying "political development" in the non-Western world—in terms of two key categories: technology and bureaucratization. From the side of recent developments in "deep anthropology," phenomenology has sympathetic ears from Mary Douglas[4] and Clifford Geertz,[5] whose calls for "thick description" (Geertz's term) in anthropological studies have a familiar phenomenological ring. Douglas's description of how to decipher a meal and Geertz's discussion of the Balinese cockfight, for example, are phenomenological descriptions *par excellence*. While Douglas speaks of "implicit meanings" and "the active voice language" as appropriate for phenomenological anthropology, Geertz pleads for the respect for "local knowledge" or "a local turn of mind" as a theoretical prerequisite for ethnographic studies. Geertz's call for the respect for "local knowledge" echoes Alfred Schutz's insistence that the sociologist must base his/her scientific knowledge on the common-sense constructs of acting agents on the social scene. In the case of anthropology or ethnography, scientific investigation or conceptualization is more complex than the study of the investigator's indigenous culture itself, simply because these layers of common-sense knowledge happen to be those of "alien" actors in an "alien" culture.

II. Phenomenological Beginnings for Comparative Culture

The topical focus of phenomenology most relevant to the comparative study of cultures is "anthropology" as defined in the philosophical tradition of Husserl, Heidegger, Scheler, and Merleau-Ponty. In *Being and Time*, Heidegger already spoke of primitive *Dasein* as an enlightening guide for the construction of "fundamental ontology." He writes:

> To orient the analysis of Dasein towards the "life of primitive peoples" can have positive significance as a method because "primitive phenomena" are often less concealed and less complicated by extensive self-interpretation on the part of the Dasein in question. Primitive Dasein often speaks to us more directly in terms of a primordial absorption in "phenomena" (taken in a pre-phenomenological sense). A way of conceiving things which seems, perhaps, rather clumsy and crude from our standpoint, can be positively helpful in bringing out the ontological structures of phenomena in a genuine way.[6]

In this essay, however, I will focus on the following two aspects of Husserl's phenomenology: philosophical anthropology, and the phenomenology of the life-world, which also contains quite logically a critique of scientism as decapitating philosophy or human thought.

In his 1931 lecture on "Phenomenology and Anthropology," Husserl set the tone for developing *philosophical anthropology* based on his phenomenological insights.[7] In it he recognizes the inherent tension between the "transcendental" and the "anthropological." One is concerned with "essential" or invariant structures, and the other with variant "facts." For Husserl, phenomenological apodicticity requires philosophical anthropology to transcend all relativity without ignoring or destroying empirical integrity. This is, of course, the familiar tension within the history of phenomenology as a philosophical movement: the "transcendental" and the "existential" approach. The first refers to Husserl's emphasis on the constitution of the transcendental ego as the prerequisite for radical and rational reflection on human existence and the world. That is to say, we must first learn to disengage our consciousness to a transcendental level in order to illuminate our existence and world. The second is the claim that we can directly describe our consciousness, engaged consciousness, without keeping it at bay in a separate, theoretical chamber. Husserl himself explained that when we turn away from the naive exploration of the world to the exploration of transcendental consciousness, we do not turn our back on the world and retreat into the uninterested, monastic field of theoretical contemplation. On the contrary, he insists, this transcendental approach is the only way that makes possible the scientific exploration of the world.

The importance of the phenomenology of the life-world as historico-sociocultural reality lies in the fact that it is not only methodological, but also substantive for the comparative study of cultures. To discuss its relevance to comparative culture, we must speak of the life-world not in the singular, but in the plural, i.e., a plurality of life-worlds as empirical worlds. Of course, one can attempt to reconcile phenomenology as a search for invariance with a plurality of life-worlds by focusing on the life-world as *perceptual* rather than a sociocultural world. It is Merleau-Ponty who takes up the challenging theme of Husserl's life-world and develops it fully into a phenomenology of perception. For Merleau-Ponty, the perceived world (the "prelinguistic" and "precultural" world) is the presupposed matrix of all cultural rationality—the rationality of everyday *praxis* as well as that of *theōria*. It is an institution inasmuch as it is an *initiating* act and it is the sedimented repository of meanings. In *The Visible and the Invisible,* Merleau-Ponty was concerned with the "diacritical" dimension of perception and culture. Neither is totally independent of the other. Perception itself is a "learning," or is "always already" informed, of the cultural or ecological milieu. Just as unspoken language is silence, so is perception bereft of culture, that is, "wild perception," *imperception*.[8] Following Merleau-Ponty's insights, the historian Donald M. Lowe contends that the history of perception is the intermediary like between the content of thought and the structure of society. He argues, in other words, that there is no invariant ideality of perception.[9] Speaking about the understanding of the physical world, Patrick A. Heelan too rejects the idea that we can see the world with an "innocent eye." Following the fundamental philosophical insights of Heidegger and Merleau-Ponty, he argues—convincingly, I might add—that perception is *already* a "hermeneutical act."[10]

III. The Spectre of Ethnocentrism

Husserl, of course, was concerned with the crisis of *European* sciences and *European* humanity. Unlike Hegel, however, he is by no means an ethnocentrist. What I have in mind here is Hegel's "Orientalism" or teleological philosophy of history and culture, which, as we will later see, is also found in the conceptual prejudice of the so-called "behavioral" or "scientific" study of comparative politics or "political development." For Hegel, the East—China and India—represented the childhood of history. For him, Chinese history, like the rhythm of nature, repeats itself endlessly and becomes an unhistorical history—a historical infantilism or paleography in the progression of world history. Chinese history is the static and seamless flow of the eternal yesterday. In the modern European philosophy of history since Hegel, the tendency is to assume, explicitly or implicitly, the spiritual and moral superiority of Western culture to non-Western culture, and this tendency is being carried over by Western specialists and observers on modernization. In the familiar terminology of modernization, the scientific, technological, and industrial civilization of the West is held to be superior to the nonscientific, nontechnological, and nonindustrial culture of the non-Western world. Although it is an ideological phantom, the so-called "Third World" is more than a numerical designation: it does indeed represent a moral ordering.

Though it has its epistemological problems, the so-called "cultural relativism" of such anthropologists as Benjamin L. Whorf and Ruth Benedict has been most instrumental to the overcoming, in contemporary anthropology, of Western ethnocentrism—the unwarranted assumption that the Western system of knowledge or truth has the privileged guardianship of all rationality.[11] Against Hegel's ethnocentrism, Merleau-Ponty advances both hermeneutical autonomy and the possibility of discovering the universal *essences* of human culture beyond objectivism and relativism. He spoke well of ethnological findings from Marcel Mauss to Claude Lévi-Strauss. Their ethnological findings open up the "*lateral universal*," which is "no longer the overarching universal of a strictly objective method," but which is acquired

> through ethnological experience and its incessant testing of the self through the other person and the other person through the self. It is a question of constructing a general system of reference in which the point of view of the native, the point of view of the civilized man, and the mistaken views each has of the other can all find a place—that is, of constituting a more comprehensive experience which becomes in principle accessible to men of a different time and country.[12]

Unlike Hegel, who viewed Oriental thought in a cavalier fashion, it is for Merleau-Ponty immensely interesting, suggestive, and instructive. Philosophical truth as absolute and universal knowledge is for Merleau-Ponty not certified by the Occidental seal of approval alone. For him, all thought is part of the life-world as the total meaning horizon of a historico-sociocultural world; each philosophy is a sort of anthropological type and none has any special birthright to a monopoly of truth. "If Western thought is what it claims to be," Merleau-Ponty stresses, "it must prove it by understanding all 'life-worlds.' "[13]

For Merleau-Ponty, the arrogant path of Hegel that excludes Oriental thought from absolute and universal knowledge and draws "a geographical frontier between philosophy and non-philosophy" also excludes a good part of the Western past. Philosophy as a perpetual beginning is destined to examine its own idea of truth again and again because truth is not divided among doctrines, but is a treasure scattered about in human life before philosophical formulation. If so, Western philosophy too is destined to reexamine not only its own idea of truth, but also related matters and institutions such as science, economics, and politics. Merleau-Ponty thus declares:

> From this angle, civilizations lacking our philosophical or economic equipment take on an instructive value. It is not a matter of going in search of truth or salvation in what falls short of science or philosophical awareness, or of dragging chunks of mythology as such into our philosophy, but of acquiring—in the presence of these variants of humanity that we are so far from—a sense of the theoretical and practical problems our institutions are faced with, and of rediscovering the existential

field that they were born in and that their long success
has led us to forget. The Oriental "childishness" has
something to teach us, if it were nothing more than the
narrowness of our adult ideas. The relationship between
Orient and Occident, like that between child and adult,
is not that of ignorance to knowledge or non-philosophy
to philosophy; it is much more subtle, making room on
the part of the Orient for all anticipations and "premat-
urations." Simply rallying and subordinating "non-
philosophy" to true philosophy will not create the unity
of the human spirit. It already exists in each culture's
lateral relationships to the others, in the echoes one
awakes in the other.[14]

IV. Scientism: Conceptual Reification and Empiricide

For the purpose of my analysis here, I will take as my major
theme the *diatactics* of "essence" and "fact" within the phenomenological context of the life-world as historico-sociocultural reality,
the importance of which, as I have already pointed out, is both
methodological and substantive. By *diatactics*, I mean the nonreductive, reciprocal relation between any two (or more) given disparate phenomena. The term is borrowed from Hayden White,
who employs it in order to avoid the *hypotactics* (conceptual overdetermination) of Hegel on the one hand and the *paratactics* (conceptual underdetermination) of Marx on the other.[15]

The nonreductive interlocking of the "essential" and the "factual" is not a simply matter of the judicious balancing of the "conceptual" and the "factual" (as nonconceptual), precisely because
there is no fact that is simply "given," that is to say, because they
are equally conceptual *praxis* (i.e., *factum* in the Vichian sense of
the term). As such, in interpretation there is indeed a thin boundary
between "essence" and "fact." Fact is something never "given" but
always "made": it is the product of experience, thought, or judgment. Therefore, diatactically speaking, it is wrong to identify "essence" with the product of philosophical activity on the one hand
and "fact" with the product of scientific activity on the other. *Science focuses on the factual with its peripheral vision fixed on the
essential, while philosophy focuses on the essential with its peripheral vision fixed on the factual.* To put the same idea in the language of Merleau-Ponty:

> We need neither tear down the behavioral sciences to
> lay the foundations of philosophy, nor tear down phi-
> losophy to lay the foundations of behavioral sciences.
> Every science secretes an ontology; every ontology an-

ticipates a body of knowledge. It is up to us to come to terms with this situation and see to it that both philosophy and science are possible.[16]

We are quite familiar with the old problem of misunderstanding the Husserlian phenomenological operation called *Wesensshau* (the "intuiting of essence") as if it were a magical mental gymnastic rather than a reading of the essential structures of meaning based on a multiplicity of facts. Thus, as I have already stressed, we must speak of the life-world not in the singular but in the plural, i.e., a plurality of life-worlds—or else the essential would be bereft of empirical content. In that case, the phenomenologists already prejudiced in favor of the conceptual, would be in no better position than their counterparts, the scientific empiricists, with their prejudice in favor of the factual. The phenomenological position propounded here may be likened to Goethe's "tender empiricism" in which theorizing lends a "musical" ear to the empirical. In this connection, it is worth noting that in his *Introduction to Political Analysis*, David E. Apter, who was originally trained as an Africanist, describes his approach as "hermeneutic," which is offered as an alternative to the "behavioral" and the "paradigmatic." "In my view," Apter suggests, "the danger of the behavioral position, with its emphasis on quantitative detail, specialization, and fine application, is that it will engage small minds on small issues, while the paradigmatist position with its emphasis on grand solutions will engineer empty architectural plans for buildings that can never be built."[17] Apter's "hermeneutic" position parallels what I call the phenomenological diatactics of the "essential" and the "factual": the judicious avoidance of conceptual overdetermination in terms of essence and conceptual underdetermination in terms of fact. The so-called "scientific" or "empiricist" approach to comparative politics falls into—paradoxical though it may sound—both *conceptual reification* (e.g., often ethnocentrism) and *empiricide*, which are really two sides of the same coin in that they both ignore the phenomenological diatactics of "essence" and "fact."

In his celebrated and often anthologized article "Interpretation and the Sciences of Man," Charles Taylor contends that Western comparative analysts may very well conceal their ethnocentric bias of an ideological kind in the allegedly objectivist language of their methodology. In warning of the hidden ideological prejudice of a scientific empiricist, Taylor notes that

> the result of ignoring the difference in intersubjective meanings can be disastrous to a science of comparative politics, viz., that we interpret all other societies in the categories of our own. Ironically, this is what seems to have happened to American political science. Having

strongly criticized the old institution-focused comparative politics for its ethnocentricity (or Western bias), it proposed to understand the politics of all society in terms of such functions, for instance, as "interest articulation" and "interest aggregation" whose definition is strongly influenced by the bargaining culture of our civilization, but which is far from being guaranteed appropriateness elsewhere. The not surprising result is a theory of political development which places the Atlantic type polity at the summit of human political development.[18]

I would suggest that the reason for the ideological, technocentric bias in Western comparative politics is due, by and large, to conceptual reification in what Husserl called "scientism," or methodolatry as a false and unexamined eschatology of (scientific) techniques. Conceptual reification and empiricide are packaged as one in the cargo cult of scientific methodology.[19] By conceptual reification, I mean here the unexamined or unconscious imposition of one set of concepts on the understanding of an "alien" culture. Empiricide is only the reverse side of this conceptual reification that ignores "a local turn of mind" or the "ontological difference" of a culture alien to the analyst's own. The essential organization of culture consists of the interlockings of significance values: it is therefore both subjective, individually or collectively, in that they are experienced internally and objective, in that they are embodied in external manifestations.

Scientism, according to Husserl, originates in the Galilean mathematization of nature into geometric boxes of triangles, circles, and squares.[20] It is fallacious because it is foremost a conceptual garb whereby what once was, or was intended to be, true in the mathematical formalization of nature *as a method* has gradually been taken or indeed mistaken for reality itself. Moreover, scientism practiced in the cultural sciences is doubly removed from sociocultural reality because a methodology that may be valid for the investigation of natural phenomena is blindly or naively accepted as true in the investigation of human phenomena. In short, methodolatry bypasses or overlooks the common-sense or experiential understanding of "local" or "alien" actors on the social scene: therefore, it packages together conceptual reification and empiricide. To use the very explicit language of Alfred North Whitehead, it is the "fallacy of misplaced concreteness." Empiricide is the inevitable result of taking for granted "fact'—scientific or otherwise—as something already "made" or "achieved" (*factum* in the Vichian sense of the term), i.e., the result of ignoring the mak*ing* of "fact" as a "hermeneutical act." Because the "scientific" study of comparative culture is *assumed* to be just "factual" or "given" rather than "made" or interpretive, abstract ideas in scientific methodology are taken for granted or unexamined in relation to experiential evidence. What has to be done properly from the outset is to avoid "categorial mistakes" by examining on a conceptual level the two layers of translatability: (1) the language of natural-scientific methodology into the language of social-scientific methodology and (2) one set of concepts into that of another "alien" culture.

V. *Textualizing Japan:*
The Case of Roland Barthes's Empire of Signs

This section is concerned with Barthes's "cultural criticism" of Japan in terms of his deconstructive semiology.[21] It attempts to show the importance of "local knowledge" or "a local turn of mind" as absolute prerequisite for comparative culture.

(1) Barthes's *Empire of Signs* describes Japan as a vast network of signs or a galaxy of signifiers. It is, as Susan Sontag puts it, "the ultimate accolade" of semiology.[22] Just as fashion is the language of fashion and the city is an ideogram, the country Japan is an "empire of signs" or an ideographic "city." *Empire of Signs* is in itself the mosaic scanning by an itinerant eye of a tantalizing parade of signs, each of which counts and falls in its proper place; its ordered randomness accentuates the carefree and spontaneous sense of natural balance and unity with no privileged center. It is called a "luxurious and eclectic album."[23] *Empire of Signs* is the cultural landscape or, better, the geography, of itinerant cultural topics. It is inevitably an intellectual autobiography as well as *Gedankenexperiment* of Barthes's deconstructive semiology as a universal science in which Japan is one of its laboratories. In this regard, *Empire of Signs* is an exotic subtext of or a "supplement" to his semiology: at least it adds colors and flavors to the texture and fabric of his written corpus as a whole. It would be wrong to say, however, that Barthes intended to write a scholarly text on Japan and make a scholarly contribution to Oriental studies in the tradition of his countrymen Paul Masson-Oursel, Marcel Granet, Henri Maspero, and René Sieffert. Rather, he is an enthusiastic and observant amateur. Precisely because he is an amateur, he is able to pump in an air of fresh insight. Barthes's *Empire of Signs,* as Jonathan Culler characterizes it judiciously, is a combination of "touristic commentary on Japan with a reflection on signs in everyday life and their ethical implication."[24] It is indeed a discerning, abecedarian account of Japanese culture as a system of signs.

(2) The title of Barthes's work is, as it were, the wrapper of the content of Japanese culture as a system of signs. To decipher or zero in on the content, we must unwrap the wrapper. The content

is packaged with a decorous plethora of cultural *bonsai* cultivated as miniaturized texts. If, however, the wrapper were the gift itself, the title would be the content: there would be no inner soul separate from the textual flesh. For Barthes, Japan displays an epicurean menu of exotic icons: Zen, *satori, mu, haiku, sumotori, pachinko, ikebana, Kabuki, Bunraku, Zengakuren, hashi, miso, sashimi, sukiyaki, tempura,* etc. It would be wrong to conclude that Barthes attends only to the "wrapping" of Japanese culture while dispensing with its "contents." What is to be recognized here is the need to deconstruct the all-too-commonplace dichotomy between the visible and the invisible, outside and inside, appearance and reality, wrapping and content, surface and depth, manifest and latent, concrete and abstract, ritual and choice, text and intention, style and form, deed and word, etc. Where there is no dichotomizing doublet, there is indeed "sincerity." Since the visible body initiates the rite of passage to the invisible soul of an alien culture by a foreign observer or tourist, let us look more closely at the outer appearance. It is doubly important in understanding Japanese culture and Barthes's Japan because of the extraordinary attention paid to it by the Japanese themselves, and consequently for Barthes himself in *Empire of Signs.* From a semiological perspective, too, the outer is as important as, if not more than, the inner.

What is a sign? It is, according to Barthes, the union of the signifier and the signified. The term is translated in Japanese as *shirushi* (or *kigo*), which means any visible *marking*—particularly nonlinguistic marking. It is interesting to see the unusual Japanese deference to the content is indicated immediately in the outer appearance of the translated copy of Barthes's *Empire of Signs.* In addition to its addenda inside (more pictures, extra explanatory notes, and the translator's introduction), the translation is boxed and wrapped with wax paper. The cover of the book is clothed with printing paper of excellent quality. Whether or not one can read Japanese, the external appearance gives one the impression that this is an important work indeed. If Barthes's work is to be judged by its cover, we would attend to it. The outer box has a separate wrapper with the photograph of a traditional, aristocratic, anonymous courtly woman that could easily depict a scene from the *Genji monogatari.* The picture is explained in the French original simply as *"Fragment d'une carte postale,"* reminding us of Jacques Derrida's recent work on Freud. Without doubt the woman *is* the sur/facial *centerfold* of *Empire of Signs,* which is consonant with Barthes's own semiological approach. As a picture is worth a thousand words, the woman is the "studium" where Barthes displays the multicolored galaxy of signifiers in Japanese culture. First, it is a picture. As such it *de/sign/ates* the presence of Japan in absence. In photography, according to Barthes, form and content coincide. The literal message of the woman (denotation) is not clear, but its symbolic message (connotation) is worth exploring. Clearly, Barthes is interested in signifying the traditional depth of Japanese culture. Second, the courtly woman is wearing a colorful, long garment that befits her long black hair. This ferment is ingrained, as it were, in the fabric of Barthes's text. Interestingly enough, Barthes in *The Fashion System* discusses clothing as protecting, covering, and masking. He quotes Hegel's aesthetic approvingly: "As pure sentience, the body cannot signify; clothing guarantees the passage from sentience to meaning; it is, we might say, *the signified* par excellence."[25] What then does the garment of the courtly woman signify in relation to her pure sentience? The absolute privacy of sex? Speaking about the absence of sex in *pachinko*, Barthes observes that in Japan "sex is in sexuality, not elsewhere," whereas in the United States, on the contrary, "sex is everywhere, except in sexuality."[26] So much for the outer cover.

Zen is the inner soul of Japanese culture, and writing is for Barthes Zen's *satori*—an inner awakening or enlightenment. He is fascinated with and celebrates the graphism of all things Japanese. As a nation of ideograms or pictograms, Japan is a graphic bliss or *nirvana*. Barthes has a tremendous proclivity to describe nonlinguistic signs in linguistic terms: every human face—including his own shown in the Kobe *Shinbun* during his tour in Japan and that of a corpulent *sumotori*—as a written text, an inscription, or a citation; *miso* as adding "a touch of clarity"; *sukiyaki* as becoming "decentered, like an uninterrupted text"; *tempura* as a "grammar" or visibly graphic; the city as an "ideogram"; *Zengakuren* as "a syntax of actions"; the stationery store as an "ideographic marquetry," etc. In the context of his deconstructive grammatology, in short, Barthes's discovery of Japan as a nation of ideographic inscriptions may be likened to the famous wooden statue in Kyoto of the enlightened Zen monk Hoshi where the visage of divinity is emerging through a crevice of his face.

Barthes declares that writing is a *satori:* Zen and *satori* are signified by the void or empty (*le vide*). There is the *kanji* (ideogram) "void" calligraphed for Barthes by a female student. Underneath the *kanji* is the Japanese pronunciation *mu* and *le vide*. In Japan, in the country of writing whose inner soul coincides with Zen, *mu* is the abyssal "ground" or *Urgrund* of everything or everything is a metaphor of *mu*. Barthes writes:

> Writing is after all, in its way, a *satori; satori* (the Zen occurrence) is a more or less powerful (though in no way formal) seism which causes knowledge or the subject to vacillate: it creates an emptiness of language. And it is also an *emptiness of language* which constitutes writing; it is from this emptiness that derive the

features with which Zen, in the exemption from all meaning, writes gardens, gestures, houses, flower arrangements, faces, violence.[27]

The key expression to understand Barthes's Japan—and his deconstructive semiology—is "an emptiness of language." In the first place, however, there is an ambiguity in Barthes's own description of the *kanji "mu"* as *le vide*. *Mu* is *sunyata* in Sanskrit. When a Mahayana text was introduced to the Chinese in the second century, they were not able to grasp with ease the idea of *sunyata* (emptiness, *kung* [Chinese] and *ku* [Japanese] as they did many other "abstract" Buddhist concepts, although they found it akin to the Taoist idea of *wu* (nothingness) as in the famous *wu-wei* (no-action) in the *Tao Te Ching*. Ideogrammatically, *mu* and *ku* are two different characters. *Mu* (Japanese) or *wu* (Chinese) is *le néant*, whereas *ku* is *le vide*. The Japanese translation clearly indicates this difference.

In the second place, the expression "an emptiness of language" is "*un vide de parole*" in Barthes's original French text. Therefore, the English translation of *parole* as "language" is rather misleading, inasmuch as it makes little sense to speak of writing as an emptiness of language itself. In the tradition of Saussurean linguistics, *langage* consists of *parole* and *langue*. If writing is "*un vide de parole*," it is contrasted with speech as event within the (Japanese) language as a system. For it, too, is an integral part of language (*langage*). The passage cannot be understood otherwise. Writing as a *satori* is anti-phonocentric resonating with the general aim of deconstructive grammatology. The dialectical opposite of writing is not language but speech. The Japanese translation of *parole* as *kotoba* (spoken word[s]) is aware of this fundamental distinction between language as speech and language as writing. Moreover, deeply rooted in Chinese and Japanese thought is the tradition that the dialectical opposite of speech is not writing, but rather silence or the "unsayable." There is, however, no glaring contradiction here because writing is always a silent transgression of verbal acts. In the Zen tradition, here is a diatactics of speech and silence: speech is the *yang* of silence and silence the *yin* of speech. Just as in John Cage's compositional techniques sound and silence are posed as complementary, Sontag considers silence not as an "incineration of consciousness" but, on the contrary, as a *pharmakon* for the pollution of language.[28] Silence may be invoked as a copula, hyphen, punctuation, or even rupture in the dialectical flow of human communication. As such its communicative value exceeds and surpasses that of "empty talk" (*parole vide*). To Zen, as the tradition goes, silence is more suitable than eloquence.

According to D. T. Suzuki, whose name in the West is synonymous with Zen, Zen's *satori* is realized in *performance* which may be (a) verbal (speaking) or (b) actional.[29] First, since Zen is an everyday occurrence in our social life, we need to communicate with one another through the medium of language. Unlike the rules of linguistics as the science of language (presumably including semiology), however, Suzuki insists that Zen verbalism is intuitive and experiential, that is, nonconceptual and lived. Cutting through the conceptual or intellectual sedimentations, Zen attempts to reach directly or im-mediately *konomama* (thisness) or *sonomama* (thatness)—i.e., "isness," the attainment of which is called *satori*. Thus the attainment of *satori* avoids conceptual detours. According to Barthes:

> If this state of *a-language* is a liberation, it is because, for the Buddhist experiment, the proliferation of sec-ondary thoughts (the thought of thought), or what might be called the infinite supplement of supernumer-ary signifieds—a circle of which language itself is the depository and the model—appears as a jamming: it is on the contrary the abolition of secondary thought which breaks the vicious infinity of language. In all these experiments, apparently, it is not a matter of crushing language beneath the mystic silence of the in-effable, but of *measuring* it, of halting that verbal top which sweeps into the gyration the obsessional play of symbolic substitutions. In short, it is the symbol as semantic operation which is attacked.[30]

Second, *satori* is a *moral* emancipation, that is, moral fulfillment *by doing*, which is deeply Sinitic (i.e., both Confucian and Taoist). Consider the famous Confucian idea of the "rectification of names" (*cheng ming*) that is addressed to the performative power of speech in human conduct *qua moral*. The only way to bridge ver-balism with moral fulfillment by doing is to regard speaking it-self as the act of doing (i.e., the theory of language both as speech acts and as moral acts). The Japanese as well as the Chinese con-sider "sincerity"—literally meaning the "completion" of "spoken words"—as the acme of moral virtue. Nishida Kitarō—the greatest Japanese philosopher of the twentieth century—regards intuition as the basis of artistic creativity as well as of moral conduct. Intu-ition rather than the intellect is the *élan vital* of artistic and moral creativity. Mencius, too, considered "intuitive knowledge" (*liang chih* or, literally, "good knowledge") as the basis of everyday moral conduct. Culler is right, as noted earlier, that Barthes's commen-tary on Japan as empire of signs *is* also an ethical one.

(3) *Empire of Signs* is the testimonial of an itinerant pilgrim—not unlike the Zen monk Hoshi who, too, travelled to China in the beginning of the T'ang period in search of Zen (*satori*)—in search of semiological markings (*shirushi*) in all things Japanese whose

epicenter is writing (*écriture*). For Barthes, we may say, Japan was a semiological *geisha* house where the free play (*asobi*) of signs takes place.[31] Although Barthes succeeds in "intellectual deprovincialization" and thus must be applauded for his intention and effort to overcome the conceptual "sound barriers" of Western narcissism, we cannot answer with certainty whether or not he succeeds in instituting an exogamous link between semiology and Japanese culture. To be universally valid, his semiology as the *science of all* signs must encompass different galaxies of markings of which Japan is only one.

To discover Japan as the country of writing is not at all contrary to the affluent exhibition of the Japanese photocracy we have all come to know so very well in recent years—the photocracy that in an extended sense of the term could include photography, painting, dramaturgy, fashions, packaging, gastronomy, and above all calligraphy. *Empire of Signs* is a belles-lettrism of Japan at its best: as Barthes himself admitted, he enjoyed writing it more than any other book. No doubt the most revealing and original formulation of Barthes's work is: writing is a *satori*. And since Zen is the inner soul of Japanese culture, there is all the more reason why the *écrivain* Barthes is interested in *haiku*, which he views as the privileged monument of Zen. The most significant question is not how many cultural trophies Barthes gathered, but whether or not *Empire of Signs*—the "ultimate accolade" of Japanese culture in the eye of a semiologist—is the insemination and dissemination of his semiology. Although every intellectual endeavor for a *savant* is, to some extent, autobiographical (and Barthes's *Empire of Signs* is no exception to this rule), one hopes that it is ideally a reciprocation, as in the spirit of exchanging gifts, of the *insemination* (taking) of Zen and the *dissemination* (giving) of his semiology.

The idea of writing as *satori* already involves a semiological strategy. By strategy I mean a chosen set of calculated moves in order to "win" a conceptual game. Part of this strategy is the very selection of what signs are to be taken as significant indicators of Japanese culture. There is, however, a serious problem in relating Zen and *satori* to semiology. It is in essence the problem of reconciling the French cult of writing (*écriture*) and the Japanese cult of inner tranquility, unless, of course, writing like Zen calligraphy is the carnal "enjoyment" (*jouissance* or *asobi*) of a person as a non-utilitarian activity undertaken solely for serenity or what Martin Heidegger calls *Gelassenheit*, which has been identified as a common denominator identified by such Zen specialists as Suzuki, Eugen Herrigel, and Karl von Dürckheim. It is also the clash between semiology as a conceptual, linguistic system and Zen as intuitive, actional experience, which is correlated with the question of the unity or duality of the inner and the outer, depth and surface, the content and the wrapping, gastronomic look and actual taste, and meaning and sign. The conception of writing as *satori* raises the unresolved paradox of Zen as an *inner* awakening and writing as *outer* ex/pression. This paradox is accentuated in Barthes's Japan because structural semiology as a method of cultural interpretation has a built-in conceptual propensity to disregard the inner in favor of the outer, or, in the case of Japan, to wrap Zen with semiology. Barthes is certainly not unaware of the problem when he defines the sign as the union of the signifier and the signified, and when he acknowledges that Zen wages a war against the prevarication of meaning (*sens*) and that the meaning of a sign is polygamous, not monogamous. John Sturrock thus observes that "in Japanese culture, or at any rate Barthes's version of it, the exterior of a thing *is* the thing, there is no informing but invisible agency within. Japan is a country full of rich and intriguing signifiers whose charm is that they have no signifieds."[32]

For Barthes, there is no inner soul or privileged center in Zen's *satori* because it is *mu* or the void, which is contradictory to dominant Western metaphysics. The denial of the inner or depth in favor of the outer or surface may well be a conceptual trapping of structural semiology rather than the understanding of Zen from *within*. Thus Sturrock speculates that "the opposition deep-set/flush is itself a Western not a Japanese one, and the Japanese might very well employ a different code in order to locate the Oriental soul."[33] There is always the latent danger of catching Zen with a semiological net. It is for this reason that in his important article the Chinese philosopher Chang Tung-sun identifies Western reasoning with the *logic of identity,* while identifying Eastern reasoning with the *logic of correlation,* which is neither monistic, nor dualistic, nor reductionistic.[34] As clothing is to the body, so is the sign to culture. Since without clothing it is pure sentience, the body too cannot signify, or at least cannot signify sufficiently. By the same logic, culture cannot signify without signs as external indication. There is a famous saying by the Chinese Taoist Chuang Tzu that words exist for meaning and once the meaning has been gotten, the words can be forgotten. Culture or language is not like a white onion—a subject of Basho's *haiku* of which Barthes seems fond—every layer of which is a surface without an inner core or center. Even in Zen there is mention of "the mind of no-mind" (*mushin no shin*). It may very well be true that surface is as telling as depth, but in language the signifier without the signified is "babbling" or "doodling." Culture is like language: to understand it, we must understand the diatactics of the subjective and the objective without a facile reductionism. Cultural interpretation is the navigation of the stormy channel between the Scylla of subjectivity and the Charybdis of objectivity.

What is lacking in Barthes's structural semiology as a method of cultural interpretation, therefore, is, and is compensated for by, a phenomenology of lived experience (*l'expérience vécu*) or the life-world (*le monde vécu; Lebenswelt*). In Barthes's case of Japan as the country of writing as well as Zen, we need to *hear* Zen's *voice* of invisibility as a prerequisite to *see* its visible surface. There is a lesson to be learned from Ralph Ellison's "invisible man" who struggles for his visibility by lighting up his basement with 1369 light bulbs. The message to be gotten here is not to disregard the outer, but rather to encourage the dialectical coupling of the inner and the outer or the invisible and the visible, that is, to abandon any facile monism, dualism, or reductionism.

Without the benefit of a phenomenology of lived experience as the founding and funding matrix of *all* conceptualization, there is in cultural interpretation the ever present danger of conceptual "entrapment" or the prevarication of meaning—especially in the interpretation of a culture, including its own linguistic system, that is unfamiliar or dissimilar to the observer's own. This is not to suggest "Go native" or "Think Japanese" here, but only to intimate that a phenomenology of lived experience is the prerequisite for any cultural interpretation. Cultural interpretation is necessarily an echo of the original voice of culture as a network of intersubjective meanings—those meanings that are not just in the minds of the individual actors, but are rooted in their social and institutional practices, including their language, i.e., what Michel Foucault calls, "discursive practices." More significantly, to ignore a network of intersubjective meanings is to open—often inadvertently—the safety valve, as it were, that prevents the spillage of ethnocentrism or, as Barthes himself calls it, "Western narcissism." To attend to intersubjective meanings is to respect "a local turn of mind" and not to miss the cultural contextualization of indigenous signifiers. Barthes himself observes that in the Occident the mirror is a narcissistic object for people to look at themselves, whereas in the Orient it is *empty* and symbolizes the *emptiness* (*ku* or *le vide*) of all symbols. To be "enlightened" or to attain a *satori*, Barthes's writing on Japan must be *emptied* of the perceptive strategies of his semiology. To deconstruct (phenomenologically) Barthes's *Empire of Signs* is simply to trace the *presence* of semiological reflection in the mirror of his Japan.

There is no intimation here that Barthes is an ethnocentrist. Nor is it implied that his understanding of Japanese culture is shallow, superficial, or surfacial. What is pointed out is simply the potential danger of the categorial grid of structural semiology or, for that matter, of any conceptual system that ignores, consciously or unconsciously, a system of intersubjective meanings. Barthes himself noted that in Japan sex is in sexuality, not anywhere else. This observation assumes, to be sure, the knowledge of the *inner* working of sexuality in Japan. Parallel to the problematic of the content of wrapping is *Kabuki*'s *onnagata*, which is in actuality the male actor playing the staged role of the female (i.e., the transvestite actor). Without knowing the *inner* working of *Kabuki*, here again, he might be easily mistaken for an actress. Let us make no mistake: a mask is *never* a real face, although the former tells on occasion a lot about the latter. Moreover, there is nothing wrong with the good looks of often decorative gastronomic Japanese dishes pleasing to our (hungry) eye, but they do not always or necessarily guarantee good taste. Taste, good or bad, is to be known only in the eating.[35] In brief, when chained to the categorial grid of structural semiology, cultural interpretation courts conceptual reification, that is to say, falsification. Just as, in Zen, the written is only a copy or translation of something original or real, to *textualize* the real is to *fabricate* it or, at best, to reduce it to a confessional autobiography or a cultural narcissism.

VI. Coda

True to its name, ethnography is concerned with the *ethics* of *writing* about another (foreign, exotic) culture. The ethics of producing the intercultural text must meet at least the following twofold requirement.

First, the intercultural text is the product of "translating" lived experience into textuality, a *reportage*, as it were, which must at all cost avoid abstraction, since abstraction is a way of producing a text, any text, with no or very little respect for everyday, lived experience. Thus Steven Feld, who considers ethnography not only as fieldwork but also as detective work after the fashion of Geertz, warns of the armchair speculation in formal analysis that has "a tendency to trivialize interpretations from direct experience."[36] Abstraction ultimately ends in superimposing preconceived categories on experience. It is conceptual raping, so to speak. Although hermeneutical distancing can never be totally complete—that is, the total elimination of "prejudgment" in translation is impossible because the intercultural text is inevitably a fusion of two different cultural horizons—the intellectual obligation in the first magnitude of the ethnographer is to minimize abstraction. To put it in the language of hermeneutical phenomenology, the ethnographer must bracket or suspend categorial judgment on the phenomena under observation. Scientism or the positivist conception of science, for instance, is abstraction and conceptual imposition for the simple reason that what is defined as *rational* or *objective* is already predetermined by the particular, Western standards of science and truth-claims. *Ab initio*, therefore, scientism is Eurocentric. In it rationality and ethnocentricity are coeval and imply each other. The post-positivist or post-analytical philosophers of science such as Gaston Bachelard, Thomas Kuhn, Stephen Toulmin, Mary Hesse, and Paul Feyerabend have already shown that all scientific theories—or, as Kuhn prefers to call them, scientific paradigms—are nothing but truth-claims established by the existing authority of a scientific community in a given society (or culture) in a given period of time.

Second, there is the interrelated question of *reflexivity* in ethnography or the study of comparative culture. Certainly the question of ethnocentrism, be it "Orientalism" or "Occidentalism," is linked closely to the lack of reflexivity. The uncritical and unreflexive attitude of an inquirer in the production of an intercultural text breeds ethnocentrism, albeit often incipiently. Reflexivity is nothing more than a way of instructing ourselves about how to be critically and explicitly conscious of what we are doing as intellectuals.[37] Since the inquirers are themselves implicated in the very activity of inquiry in which they are engaged, reflexivity is a way of making the inquirers "defamiliarize" themselves with the phenomena under investigation. In brief, it intends to overcome the conceptual naiveté of an ethnographer or a foreign observer and thus to fend off the slippage of ethnocentric overtures and prejudices. It must be pointed out that reflexivity is already an integral and indispensable part of phenomenology as philosophical criticism: as Richard Zaner puts it succinctly, "I disengage from myself in order to engage myself in myself critically."[38]

Ethnography is basically a variation in the theory of intersubjectivity, of the self and the other as foreign.[39] To avoid ethnocentrism, the production of an intercultural text as a theory of intersubjectivity must be based on "lateral thinking" in a twofold sense. First, "lateral thinking" differs from "vertical thinking" in that the former digs a new hole in another place while the latter digs the same hole deeper and deeper.[40] Second, lateral thinking presumes the multiversity of different cultural realities. The intercultural world is a world of "multiple realities." Thus lateral thinking contains a *logic of correlation*. It epitomizes what Jean-François Lyotard calls the "postmodern condition" of knowledge in that it not only is sensitive to differences, but also tolerates the incommensurable.[41] To translate lateral thinking ethnographically, it is an acknowledgment of what David B. Wong calls "moral relativity."[42] Lateral thinking as a logic of correlation is evident in our preceding exposition of Merleau-Ponty's approach to comparative philosophy. A close colleague of Merleau-Ponty, Claude Lévi-Strauss, too, was sensitive to lateral thinking when he paid homage to the "primitive" or "savage" mind in his Inaugural Lecture at the Collège de France—the homage paid to the preservation of the *lateral continuity* of humanity in the same spirit as Merleau-Ponty.[43]

To follow the instruction of Lévi-Strauss for reading the meaning of the myth, lateral thinking is like reading "an orchestral score," that is, the nonsequential (i.e., correlative) reading of ethnographic events (myths) as "bundles"—"we have to read not only from left to right, but at the same time vertically, from top to bottom."[44] More important, the ancient Chinese logic of *yin* and *yang* is lateral thinking *par excellence* since it seeks archetypical differences of *yin* and *yang* as complementary. Unlike the dialectical logic of Hegel or Marx, the *yin-yang* logic of correlation knows no final synthesis or *telos* of all syntheses, but only the eternal flow of the differences (opposites) as complementary. Even Marx, who called himself "a citizen of the world," succumbed to Eurocentrism in the footsteps of his mentor, Hegel.

Anthropology, according to its very name, is supposedly the "science of humankind" in general. From its very inception, however, it was invented and practiced to be the study of the "primitive" peoples and their cultures, that is, it was invented ethnocentrically. Lateral thinking can reinvent anthropology by broadening its intellectual horizons so as to correlate the benefits of one for the others, including of course the benefits of the "primitive" for the "civilized." The "experimental" formulation by George E. Marcus and Michael M. J. Fischer of "anthropology as cultural critique" incorporates lateral thinking.[45]

The world in which we live today is the marketplace of ideas. To put it differently with an allusion to Edward W. Said's rendition of "travelling theory," ideas *do travel*. For him, the movement of ideas from one place to another and from one period of time to another is the "enabling condition of intellectual activity."[46] The history of ideas is indeed an intellectual travelogue. Ideas, however, travel not in one direction alone, but in many directions—to use an acoustic expression, they travel in all directions. In the final analysis, an intercultural text is born out of the diatactical confluence of "travelling" ideas based on the principle of difference, not of identity. It is an orchestration of the differentiated many. For this reason alone, we should defenestrate the visualist term *identity* from intercultural discourses and the production of intercultural texts and replace it with the musical term *harmony* as polyphonic—the harmony of the many in which the difference of each from the rest does not disappear, but is heard. Harmony is the result of making music together, whereas there is no single, all-encompassing perspective of all perspectives to be had—except the Idea in heaven—in the production of intercultural texts.[47]

Writing for *Esprit* in 1961, Paul Ricoeur addressed himself to the perennial question of the One and the Many—the connection between the dawn of "universal civilization" and the waning of "national cultures" in which he urged us to abandon "the dogmatism of a single truth."[48] The emergence of a single world civilization signifies for Ricoeur the fact that we have reached the crossroad between "the twilight of dogmatism" and "the dawn of real dialogues." It would be premature, however, to announce the death of national cultures. In the end, whatever the future shape of universal civilization may take, it will be orchestrated by an "anthropology of the life-world" (life-worlds).[49] In the production of intercultural texts, we can no longer treat truth dogmatically and complacently—with the Western censor presiding over the procession of universal ideas. We cannot divide humanity into two separate ontological camps in a hierarchical order, one as the superior or privileged master and the other as the inferior or unprivileged slave. On the contrary, an integral humanism or humanitarianism as the opposite of ethnocentrism can exist only in the lateral relationships of all cultures in which the echoes of each awaken and are resonant with the others. For—to repeat Merleau-Ponty and paraphrase the medieval description of God—truth's center is everywhere and its circumference nowhere.[50]

Part III
Phenomenological Ontology and the Study of Politics

This task of describing the human life-world has been neglected in the West since the time of Plato, who called it a cave of fleeting shadows, and now faces serious difficulties and possible aberrations.

—John Wild,
"The Interrogation of John Wild"
(interview)

Six

LEO STRAUSS'S CONCEPTION OF
POLITICAL PHILOSOPHY

I

THE POLITICAL THOUGHT OF LEO STRAUSS commands the respect and admiration of even his critics. His critical intellectual carpentry is sharp, cutting, and often rebuking. His criticism of modernity, whether it be that of Machiavelli, Max Weber, an existentialist, or a scientific political scientist, is inspired by and deeply rooted in the Greek intellectualist essentialism, particularly that of Aristotle, and the age-old tradition of nature and natural right, as is shown in his work, *Natural Right and History.*[1]

Strauss's intellectual urgency is matched by the mission Plato envisioned when he wrote the *Republic* while lamenting the decline of the Athenian polity. As Strauss himself confesses, Strauss's undertaking is neither "self-forgetting and pain-loving antiquarianism nor self-forgetting and intoxicating romanticism"; the urge that led him to revive classical political thought is stirred by the crisis of the West in our time.[2] This alleged Western crisis is, as Strauss sees it, reflected in two philosophical doctrines: (1) positivism and (2) historicism. Sharing the opinion of many of our contemporaries, Strauss bemoans the fact that they are the causes of the "decay" and perhaps "putrefaction" of political philosophy. At the very bottom of his criticism of modernity based on the classical pattern lies the impending philosophical premise that the truth is an expression of eternity that is valid for all time and unconditioned by the "historicity" of human existence in the world. "Truth the eternal" knows surrender neither to the historical circumstances nor to the existential conditions of the thinker him/herself. The high tribunal in which modernity, positivism, and historicism in particular are on trial is classical political thought, which was, according to Strauss, initiated by Socrates and continued by Plato, Aristotle, Cicero, and St. Thomas Aquinas, coming to an end with Machiavelli, the founder of modern political philosophy. Strauss writes:

> The meaning of political philosophy and its meaningful character is as evident today as it always has been since the time when political philosophy came to light in Athens. All political action aims at either preservation or change. When desiring to preserve, we wish to prevent a change to the worse; when desiring to change, we wish to bring about something better. All political action is then guided by some thought of better or worse. But thought of better or worse implies thought of the good. The awareness of the good which guides all our action has the character of opinion: it is no longer questioned but, on reflection, it proves to be questionable. The very fact that we can question it directs us towards such a thought which is no longer opinion but knowledge. All political action has then in itself a directedness towards knowledge of the good: of the good life, or the good society. For the good society is the completest political good.[3]

To Strauss, philosophy is the quest for eternal truth, and political philosophy is the quest for the eternal truth about political things. Political philosophy is, to be sure, a philosophical discipline, for it is a branch of philosophy. Philosophy is prior to political philosophy, as nature is to natural right. "The discovery of nature," writes Strauss, "necessarily precedes the discovery of natural right. Philosophy is older than political philosophy."[4] Nature is certainly a key term in Aristotle's philosophy, including his theory of value. Classical political philosophy is in essence a philosophy of "natural right," just as philosophy is necessarily a philosophy of "nature." Consequently, Strauss judges and criticizes both positivism and historicism in terms of the principles of nature and natural right.

According to Strauss, there are the following four characteristics embodied in classical political philosophy: first and foremost, political philosophy as a philosophical discipline was predicated on the idea that contemplation (*theōria*) is prior and superior to action (*praxis*); second, theoretical knowledge is derived from the primary common-sense understanding of political humankind; third, political philosophy was directly related to political life itself; and fourth, it was concerned with the idea of the best political regime or constitution (*politeia*).[5] This essay is a critique of Strauss's conception of political philosophy in light of existential philosophy and phenomenology. The philosophical approach that attempts to synthesize the existential thought initiated by Søren Kierkegaard and the phenomenological thought initiated by Edmund Husserl has become known as "existential phenomenology" (or "phenomenological existentialism"), and its representatives are Martin Heidegger in Germany; Jean-Paul Sartre, Maurice Merleau-Ponty, and Paul Ricoeur in France; and John Wild in this country.[6] In Section II, I shall examine especially the first principle that is cardinal in the essentialist position of Strauss and show the inadequacy of his conception of political philosophy by pointing out that (1) it creates an "egocentric" dualism that is inimical to political or social philosophy in any meaningful way and (2) because of its theory-centered and dualistic character, the second and third principles are self-refuting. In Section III, I shall point out that, despite some fundamental differences, the existential and phenomenological approach is in agreement with Strauss's criticism of positivism that separated "value" from "fact." In Section IV, I shall clarify Strauss's description regarding the relationship between theoretical (reflexive) understanding and pretheoretical understanding in light of the phenomenology of the life-world. In Section V, I shall critically examine Strauss's charge that existentialism is "radical historicism"; in so doing, I shall elucidate the meaning of "historicity" and argue that the substantive issue involved is one of ontological determinism and indeterminism.

II

The philosophical position of Strauss is, as has been briefly indicated, one of "essentialism" as opposed to "existentialism." By essentialism I mean simply the philosophical doctrine that asserts the primacy of thought (whatness) over action (thatness). It includes existence in essence, whereas existentialism reflects essence in terms of existence. In this sense, essentialism is diametrically opposed to existentialism (or the philosophy of human action).

Essentialism has become the dominant Western tradition since Plato and Aristotle. The primacy of *theōria* over *praxis* is advocated in Plato's *Republic* and Aristotle's *Politics* and *Ethics*. "[T]he enormous superiority of contemplation over activity of any kind, action not excluded . . . ," writes Hannah Arendt, "[is found] in Plato's political philosophy, where the whole utopian reorganization of *polis* life is not only directed by the superior insight of the philosopher but has no aim other than to make possible the philosopher's way of life."[7] Strauss himself writes of Plato that "the ultimate aim of political life cannot be reached by political life, but only by a life devoted to contemplation, to philosophy. This finding is of crucial importance for political philosophy, since it determines the limits set to political life, to all political action, and all political planning. Moreover, it implies that the highest subject of political philosophy is the philosophic life; philosophy . . . offers, as it were, the solution to the problem that keeps political life in motion."[8]

To philosophize for Strauss essentially "means to ascend from the cave to the light of the sun, that is, to the truth" where lies " 'the island of the blessed'—contemplation of the truth."[9] We must understand his criticism of Machiavelli in terms of his position. For Strauss the cardinal sin committed by Machiavelli is not so much that he created the immoral world of power politics as that he committed an intellectual profanity. That is to say, Machiavelli lowered the classical standard of philosophic life, thereby changing its very conception of philosophy. Strauss would say that in the *Prince* political philosophy becomes merely a "policy science" or statecraft and "wisdom" becomes "craftiness." "Wisdom," he writes, "was not a great theme for Machiavelli because justice is not a great theme for him."[10] "Instead of saying," he continues, "that the status of philosophy becomes obscured in Machiavelli's thought, it is perhaps better to say that in his thought the meaning of philosophy is undergoing a change. The classics understood the moral-political phenomena in the light of man's highest virtue of perfection, the life of the philosopher or the contemplative life. The superiority of peace to war or of leisure to business is a reflection of the superiority of thinking to doing or making."[11]

Contemplation or knowledge (*epistēmē*) is the pure thinking of thought. It is concerned with, as Aristotle says, "thoughts with no object beyond themselves."[12] Knowledge contemplates "being as being and that which belongs to it per se."[13] The *noesis* is the "active possession of thought as thought which is called *theōria*."[14] This noetic activity is truth (*alētheia*), which is necessary, eternal, and universal. Therefore, as Werner Marx says, philosophical knowledge (or *noesis*) for Aristotle is "a 'possessing' of subject-matters of thought, *noeta*, in the realization that they are thought by thought or grasped through intuition. It is an unconcealing of these *noeta* which occurs beyond chronological time."[15] *Physis* for Aristotle meant the principle of "natureness" of particular natures,[16] which is also beyond time. Philosophical knowledge seeks "the principles and ultimate causes," and the relationship between *epistēmē* and *physis* is that the former must necessarily belong to the latter.[17] The philosopher is one who " 'sees' the unity of *physis*" in his/her activity.[18] One sees the unity of *physis* only in the "philosophical attitude." This "seer" is no one but the philosopher. Thus the *philosophos* ("lover of wisdom") seeks nature, to which philosophical knowledge or the principles and ultimate causes of things must belong. The life of *theōria* is separated from the life of *empeiria*. The activity of the philosopher who thinks pure thought is set apart from the activities of the other people, that is, the "philosophical attitude" is separated from the "natural attitude."[19] In Aristotle and also in Strauss, the "philosophical attitude" is not only different from, but also—as the logical corollary of the primacy of thought entails—superior to the "natural attitude."

Now for Strauss as well as for Aristotle, the human being is by nature a social and political animal, or else either a god or a beast. In his *Politics*, Aristotle intimates that only in political association do human beings reach the height of perfect self-sufficiency (*autarkeia*). In his *Ethics* he defines self-sufficiency as "that which when isolated makes life desirable and lacking in nothing."[20] For Strauss, "the philosopher has the greatest self-sufficiency which is humanly possible."[21] There is a dilemma here in the effort to reconcile the "philosopher's attachment to the eternal beings" with "the natural attachment of human being." Who is more sufficient, the philosopher or the person who engaged in politics? In the *Republic*, Plato resolves this question in the idea of the "philosopher-king." Aristotle also deals with the question of "the good man" and the "the good citizen," and the latter is a relative concept, that is, relative to a particular political regime. Like Plato, Aristotle comes to the conclusion that "the excellence of the good citizen is identical with that of the good man" only in the ruler.[22] However, the dilemma still remains because not every philosopher is or can become a ruler. For Aristotle, the ultimate answer to this dilemma is clear: since perfect felicity, which is something final and self-sufficient, is the end of activity, contemplative activity is perfect felicity. As Strauss says of Aristotle, "The difficulty arises from the fact that the highest end of the individual is contemplation. He seems to solve the difficulty by asserting that the city is as capable of the contemplative as is the individual. Yet it is obvious that the city is capable at best only of an analogue of the contemplative life. . . . [He reaches the conclusion that] man is more than the citizen or the city. Man transcends the city only by what is best in him."[23] Aristotle further holds that the life of leisure or contemplation is not only more felicitous, but also no less active than the life of work or action. "Well-*doing*," he writes, "need not be . . . a life which involves relations to others. Nor should our thoughts be held to be active only when they are directed to objects which have to be achieved by action. . . . [S]peculations and trains of reflection followed purely for their own sake are far more deserving the name of active."[24]

The essentialist position of Strauss culminates in the view that political philosophy is not the philosophic treatment of politics, but the popular political treatment of philosophy, and that its aim is to transform the political life to the philosophic life.[25] For him, what is truly human is contemplation or wisdom that is "divine"; it is not "work but thinking that constitutes the humanity of man" and wisdom is "the end of man."[26]

Having examined Strauss, who accepts the classical essentialist doctrine of the primacy of theory over practice, a few critical remarks are now in order from the standpoint of the philosophy of human action. (1) Classical essentialism separates thought from action and creates a dualism, and (2) it is a nonrelational (that is, nonsocial) philosophy and, for this reason, is opposed materially to *political* or *social* philosophy in a very basic sense, because what is political or social must always be relational.

First, Plato and Aristotle established the long cherished tradition of the idea that the only good life is the theoretical life, and Strauss is an adherent of this tradition. It is quite clear that an intellectualistic persuasion led Aristotle to claim that thought is no less active than action on the one hand and that active doing does not necessarily involve a relation to others on the other. "The history of Greek philosophy," Martin Buber points out, "is that of an opticizing of thought, fully clarified in Plato and perfected in Plotinus. The object of this visual thought is the universal existence or as a reality higher than existence."[27] Similarly, John Macmurray calls the theory-centered philosophy without reference to action "the speculative metaphysical conundrum."[28] His is reminiscent of Kierkegaard, who criticized as "a chimera of abstraction" the doctrine in which the truth is the identification of being with thought.[29] For the unity of thought and action is achieved only when we consider action as primary and prior to thought. Theoretical activity is carried out or done *in* this world and it is *of* this world. Abraham J. Heschel says that "no thought is an island. . . . Authentic thinking originates in an encounter with the world. We think not only in concepts; we think *in* the world. Thinking echoes man's total relationship to the world."[30] "Theoretical knowing and speaking," Wild also writes, "presupposes this world. They are themselves special ways of being in the world."[31] The truth that philosophy seeks is nothing but the dialectic mediation between self and world through action. Only in this way is the unity between theory and practice achieved: as Robert O. Johann, S.J., writes, "In place of the divorce between theory and practice, the two will fuse in a genuine whole. Philosophy will not merely explain life, but help constitute it. Its role is to contribute to the realization of a level and mode of experience that cannot be had without it, a level where thought and action, knowledge and reality are one."[32] On the contrary, classical essentialism ultimately makes thought irrelevant to the reality of life by creating the dualism between thought and action. This dualism results from the "exaggerated intellectualism" that thought is prior and superior to action. Properly speaking, however, it is life that is greater and more inclusive than thought, and thought constitutes a part of the whole called life.

Second, theory-oriented classical philosophy is "monological" or "egocentric." It is egocentric (or monological) for the reason that theoretical activity is by its very nature a solitary and nonpartici-pant game in which the thinker is a "disinterested spectator" de-tached from the world of action. The thinker *qua* thinker does not participate in the world in relation to other actors. As contrasted to theoretical activity, however, action is "dialogical" or "hetero-centric."[33] Only action is heterocentric, because it is the active en-counter of the self (as actor) with other actors. In short, it *is* "an instantiation of the 'I and You' " both as actors.[34] Therefore, the philosophy of action is necessarily dialogical or heterocentric. Max Weber delineates what is social from what is nonsocial. As he de-scribes it, action is not social "if it is oriented solely to the behav-iour of inanimate objects"; it is social only if it is oriented to the behavior of other actors. Like "solitary prayer," "contemplation" (thought) is nonsocial, for it involves no actual relation to other actors,[35] and we might say that philosophical reflection is the thinking subject's relation only to the *object* of thought and that therefore it is not social.

III

For Strauss, positivism, including the "new science of politics," is the doctrine that defines truth and the empirical exclusively in terms of the procedure of the natural sciences.[36] Judging from the classical standard of natural right, the principal error that this doc-trine commits is the separation between "value" (the Ought) and "fact" (the Is), that is, ethical neutralism, which, according to Strauss, Weber also advocates. Therefore, the new science of poli-tics does not and cannot ask the question of the best political order.

In positivism, value is drowned—to use the expression of Eric Voegelin—"in the ocean of fact."[37] Strauss would criticize the pos-itivist view that evaluation (that is, the judgment of value) has no objective, and thus epistemological, validity (or "meaning") be-cause it is simply an ejaculation of subjective feeling and thus is "empirically unverifiable." The issue in question is really one of methodology, that is, it is the question of the way in which the em-pirical is validated. Strauss objects to the sort of scientific imperi-alism that brackets or ignores the importance of the Ought and, as a result, encourages an ethical neutralism. He maintains that social scientists are not totally immune from values simply because they are also members of society. Likewise, many existential and phenomenological analyses show that values and norms are the constitutive elements of the life-world.[38] Wild holds that "in the *Lebenswelt* value is not a later addition. It is constitutive of the thing. . . . A human culture is not a neutral structure with approvals and disapprovals added on. It *is* a structure of approvals and disapprovals."[39]

It must be stressed, however, that there is an irreducible difference between the existentialist and the Aristotelian (thus Straussian) analysis of human values and, consequently, between their critical attitude toward the ethical neutrality of positivism. The existentialist critique of positivism is more radical than that of Strauss, because it gets to the *ontological,* not just the *methodological,* root of the problem of value. In the existentialist analysis, there is an ontological distinction on the one hand, and a methodological distinction on the other, between what is human and what is natural, and the latter is rooted in the recognition of the former. It is both anti-Aristotelian and anti-positivistic.

In the Aristotelian analysis, the ontological unity of human (that is, the human being as a rational animal) and natural things means that they belong to the universal scheme of the same *physis* and *cosmos;* nature as pertaining to the human order is essentially normative, that is, the Ought or goodness is that which conforms to nature, whereas its opposite is the perversion of it.[40] The existential position, however, is anti-Aristotelian in accepting the modern (that is, Cartesian) distinction between nature and history and subsequently between the natural sciences (*Naturwissenschaften*) and the humanities (*Kulturwissenschaften*), and it insists that a radically different approach is needed for the investigation of what is human. Moreover, Heidegger maintains that the analysis of human existence (*Dasein*), that is, *Fundamentalontologie,* is the starting point of general ontology. As Karl Löwith puts it, human existence for Heidegger is "the ultimate *source* and also *end* of the ontological interest."[41]

The existential analysis is anti-positivistic, for positivism stresses the methodological unity between the natural and the social (or human) sciences by urging that the same methods employed in the former can be used with equal validity in the latter. Wild, for instance, distinguishes between "scientific facts" and "world facts," and holds that objective science is incapable of grasping adequately "world facts," that is, what is essentially human and the things that belong to the human realm. The analysis of human facts requires "phenomenological method," which attempts to describe the intentional and relational structure of human existence in the world as it is lived from within.[42] It does not mean, however, that the existential and phenomenological analysis abandons nature; on the contrary, the world includes nature among its aspects insofar as nature is brought into relation with human existence.[43]

IV

Strauss furthermore criticizes the new science of politics because, contrary to the classical science of politics, it overlooks the importance of the language and common-sense understanding of political humankind. He contends that "the language of Aristotelian political science is identical with the language of political man,"[44] whereas the new science of politics rejects the language of the marketplace as ambiguous and imprecise. Thus this notable insight of Strauss consists in giving a new meaning to the Aristotelian notion of the natural world as the common-sense world or ordinary political humankind. He writes that "political science stands or falls by the truth of pre-scientific awareness of political things. . . . Our perceiving things and people is more manifest and more reliable than any 'theory of knowledge'—any explanation of how our perceiving things and people is possible—can be; the truth of any 'theory of knowledge' depends on its ability to give an adequate account of this fundamental reliance."[45] Moreover, in reference to Aristotle, Strauss writes that "the *Politics* contains the original form of political science: that form in which political science is nothing other than the fully conscious form of the common sense understanding of political things. Classical political philosophy is the primary form of political science because the common sense understanding of political things is primary."[46]

In the phenomenological movement, too, an intensive search has been made to bring philosophical reflection close to the life-world.[47] Phenomenology attempts to uncover and elucidate the meaning of immediate lived experience and to relate it to human being-in-the-world as it is nakedly given.[48] Alfred Schutz stresses the intersubjective (or social) character of the life-world when he calls it "social reality," which is "the sum total of objects and occurrences within the social cultural world as experienced by the common-sense thinking of men living their daily lives among their fellow-men, connected with them in manifold relations of interaction."[49] It is Husserl who at the end of his philosophical career first discusses the *Lebenswelt* as the pretheoretical world that is the material for philosophizing.[50] As early as 1927, Heidegger also introduced the idea of "being-in-the-world" (*In-der-Welt-sein*) in his phenomenological analysis of human existence.[51] His revolutionary originality in his *Being and Time*, as Löwith judiciously notes, "consists above all in making the words of ordinary speech a philosophical terminology,"[52] and for Heidegger language is the dwelling place of Being whose shepherd is the human being.[53] John Wild, furthermore, argues for the structure of this preconceptual knowing and experience as "an existential *a priori*" and writes that "there is a world of perception marked by stable structures which meet our three criteria for the *a priori*. They hold universally and necessarily for all men. They condition particular experiences, and are presupposed by ordinary language and science. Finally, they are normally hidden in the fringes of the objects of our attention, and require disciplined, phenomenological methods to be clearly focused."[54]

In the above light, we are in a position to say that what Strauss has said of the natural world and Aristotle is quite "phenomenological," and this does not seem entirely accidental, because Strauss recognized Husserl and Heidegger among "the four greatest philosophers of the last forty years"—the other two are Henri Bergson and Alfred North Whitehead—although he is somewhat critical of all the four for having had no concern for political philosophy.[55] The phenomenological analysis of the life-world is related to Strauss's theses that (1) scientific or philosophic knowledge (*epistēmē*) presupposes the prescientific or prephilosophic (*doxa*), which is the common-sense understanding of political (that is, natural) humankind, and (2) the former is dependent on or derived from the latter. By describing the phenomenology of the life-world, and especially the constitutive phenomenology of the "natural attitude" (*natürliche Einstellung*) expounded by Schutz, I hope to clarify Strauss and also to pinpoint the weakness of his essentialist conception of philosophy.

Exactly what, for Strauss, is this "prescientific" or "natural" world? It is, as he describes it, "the world in which we live and act," and it is "not the object at which we detachedly look but of 'things' or 'affairs' which we handle."[56] It is the world in which political things "present themselves in political life, in action."[57] Strauss is critical of Weber for the error of not having attempted "a coherent analysis of the social world as it is known to 'common sense,' or of social reality as it is known in social life or in action."[58] According to Strauss, we cannot identify the prescientific world with the world in which we *now* live because the latter "is already a product of science. To say nothing of technology, the world in which we live is free from ghosts, witches, and so on, with which, but for the existence of science, it would abound."[59] Therefore, "to grasp the natural world as a world that is radically prescientific or prephilosophic, one has to go back behind the first emergence of science or philosophy. It is not necessary for this purpose to engage in extensive and necessarily hypothetical anthropological studies."[60] Perhaps this suggests that we must return to the unadulterated form of nature and natural right. However, here is the difficulty: if, as

Strauss says, philosophy and political philosophy are coeval with the discovery of nature and natural right, how are we able to distinguish the natural world from the philosophic world?

This difficulty can be resolved, as phenomenology does, only if the life-world as "prescientific world" (*vorwissenschaftliche Welt*) is understood essentially as a nonhistoric concept. That is to say, one does not have to go back to the world prior to the rise of science or philosophy to understand this prescientific world. Thus there is no "post-scientific" knowledge. "By *world*," Wild explains, "Husserl meant not a thing, not any set of objects, but rather an ultimate horizon within which all such objects and the individual person are actually understood in the 'natural attitude' of everyday life. This horizon of concrete experience is sharply contrasted with the objective horizons of science which attend exclusively to objects via perspectives that are partial and abstract."[61] Therefore, the term "prereflective" or "prepredicative" world conveys its meaning more adequately than the term "prescientific world": it is "preconceptual," "prelogical," and "prephilosophical" in the sense that conceptualization, logic, and philosophy are all reflective activities; and this prereflective knowledge is the "matrix" of reflective knowledge (*Wissenschaft*). By the same token, the life-world is the world "which precedes knowledge, of which knowledge always *speaks*, and in relation to which every scientific schematization is an abstract and derivation sign-language, as is geography in relation to the country-side in which we have learnt beforehand what a forest, a prairie or a river is."[62] If, then, we regard the prescientific world as a historic concept, there is indeed the difficulty of determining and understanding it as "the world in which we live." Stephen Strasser suggests that the term "prescientific" refers to "a certain level of our personal cognitive life"; it refers to "man's perceptive and apperceptive life."[63] As Wild elucidates further:

> Pre-conceptual experience is not a chaotic manifold of discrete impressions, but a vast world horizon including many sub-worlds and regions. I believe that phenomenology has now shown that such basic characteristics of linguistic consciousness as intentionality, meaning, temporality, retention, protention, understanding in a broad sense of this term, and purposive striving are all present to us in their original bodily presence. This world is pervaded by ambiguity, for perception is dominated by its object, and the fringes are always vague. But similarities and differences are recognized. Order and meaning are present in a confused way, and are ready to be linguistically clarified, fixed, and communicated. Hence reason does not appeal on the scene as a completely alien intruder into an empirical chaos where

order must be created *ex nihilo*. The way for clarification, completion of meaning, and communication has already been prepared.[64]

Like Strauss, Schutz insists that the constructs and models of the social sciences are "founded on the prescientific common-sense experience of social reality."[65] Positivism and naturalism, Schutz contends, fail to take this social reality into account. However, unlike Strauss, Schutz maintains that the analysis of social reality is accessible only from the "subjective point of view," that is, "the interpretation of the action and its settings in terms of the actor."[66] His "subjective analysis" of action means that action must be understood from the standpoint of the actor's "whole system of projects and motives," rather than that of the observer or disinterested spectator. When, therefore, action is defined "subjectively," it is "human conduct as an ongoing process which is devised by the actor in advance, that is, which is based upon a preconceived project."[67] In this respect, Schutz's phenomenological analysis of social reality comes together with the sociological method of Weber.[68] For Weber, "subjective understanding is the specific characteristic of sociological knowledge."[69] Although Strauss is critical of him for separating the Ought from the Is, Weber is not in any sense a positivist. For as Weber says, "We can accomplish something which is never attainable in the natural sciences, namely, the subjective understanding of the action of the component individuals."[70]

The scientist *qua* scientist or the philosopher *qua* philosopher, that is, theorizer, does not participate directly in the life-world as an actor. The life-world is primordial and primary because the world of theorizing necessarily presupposes it: it is "pregiven to both the man in the world of working and to the theorizing thinker."[71] Because it is the world of "I live through" in contrast to the world of "I think," distinctively theoretical problems do not arise in it, even though they are posterior to it. "The importance of this 'life-world,' " as Maurice Natanson puts it, "is not its status as knowledge but its focus as the meaningful ground of human action."[72]

The life-world is a distinctively historical and cultural world. In it human beings are born, live, and die. It is the world not only of love and joy, but one of hate and sorrow as well. It is the world in which we find "roads, plantations, villages, streets, churches, implements, a bell, a spoon, a pipe. Each of these objects is moulded to the human action which it serves."[73] Prereflective knowledge included in the life-world is essentially pragmatic and utilitarian because knowledge exists for the sake of doing rather than for the sake of knowing. On this level, knowledge is immediate rather than mediate, as it is in reflection. It is "knowledge in action," that is, knowledge with a view of action.

Emotion, moreover, is an important element of action and thus of the life-world in which action is performed. In recognizing this fundamental fact, the ethics of action differs from an intellectualistic ethics and the emotive theory of ethics. The philosopher of action, however, does not maintain that action is completely irrational, for the simple reason that action implies human rationality. Instead of saying that intellect is what makes the human being different from other beings, the philosopher of action would say that the true human *differentia* is action, for human beings alone can perform action. In the past, an intellectualistic prejudice has misled us to identify reason or rationality with intellect[74] and eventually to make a genuine ethics of action meaningless because it ferments only the ethics of intellect or contemplation. When rationality is identified with intellect, the only reasonable action is an intellectual activity, that is, the supremacy of thinking. But it is a mistake to say that the world of action is a blind, chaotic, and impulsive world, although because of its very nature it is a more ambiguous and emotive world than that of thought. In all fairness, we must say that emotion has its own rationality, and thus we can talk not only about the rationality of intellect alone, but also about the rationality of emotion as well. The shortcoming of a rationalist argument is the identification of reason with intellect whereby the life-world is regarded necessarily as a cave world, and thus the rationalist has neglected the investigation of the rich field of human emotion and its role in the life-world. It is no coincidence that existentialism as a philosophy of human action has seriously been concerned with the problem of emotion, which in integral to human action and living.

V

Although it can be said, as the preceding pages have shown, that there is at least an area of mutual concern in their respective emphasis on value and the priority of the common-sense understanding of ordinary people to philosophical activity, what makes the existentialist mode of thinking so radically different from the essentialist thought of Strauss is that the former is concerned with historicity as an inseparable dimension of human existence, whereas, I shall show, the latter ignores it completely. In criticizing historicism, Strauss lists two types: "theoretical historicism" and "existentialist historicism," which is "radical" or perhaps more radical than the first, although it is not clear as to exactly what Strauss means by the term "radical." Similarly, Emil L. Fackenheim, who is also critical of historicism as a self-contradictory doctrine, considers Heidegger as a more revolutionary thinker than Colling-wood.[75] First, Strauss contends that all forms of historicism are at fault because they explicitly or implicitly deny the "possibility of historical objectivity," that is, the understanding of truth established by a past thinker as this thinker him/herself understood it. They deny the "experience of history" exactly as it is. Second, Strauss's more serious objection to historicism is that it denies the eternal truth rooted in nature and natural right. Historicism, he writes, "either ignores or else distorts" the experiences regarding "right and wrong which are at the bottom of the philosophic contention that there is a natural right."[76]

Therefore, the question of historicism for Strauss is integral to that of the possibility of truth beyond historical time. As he contends, historicism rejects the idea of the good society "because of the essentially historical character of society and of human thought," while positivism does not ask questions about the good society.[77] To Strauss philosophy is not just an expression of the *Zeitgeist*, but is something that transcends the historical conditions of an age; it is both transhistorical and transsocial. Thus historicism is criticized not only for obfuscating, but also for rejecting "the fundamental distinction between philosophic and historical questions," thereby affirming that "human thought is historical and hence unable to grasp anything eternal."[78] The crucial point of Strauss's argument is directed against the claim of the relativity of philosophical truth. He would therefore reject Collingwood, who asserted not only that "metaphysical presuppositions are unprovable," but also, more radically, that "the validity of metaphysical presuppositions depends on their historical setting."[79] If, then, by historicism Strauss means just a historical relativism (as I think he does), the existentialist concern with human historicity is by no means a historical relativism. Heidegger, for example, "achieved the self-redemption of modern historicism . . . only through absolutizing historicity itself."[80]

The essentialist posture of Strauss may be summarized in the following two principles. First, human being is a complete whole and has a permanent structure; our having a permanent structure means that being human is and will remain always the same so that, as Strauss says, "to be" is "always to be." Second, this human whole—including its future as the object of thought—is completely knowable or intelligible, that is, the future of humanity can be anticipated and predicted by thought.[81] This view is what I would call an ontological determinism. Strauss views philosophy or the theory of knowledge from the vantage point of the essence of nature, which is eternal. The essence of nature includes the existence of the human being, who is called a rational animal—an existence that also has an *essential form* like all other nonhuman beings and things. As Aristotle says, to be a philosopher is to know the unity of this nature. In contrast, existentialism is an ontological indeterminism: human *being* is incomplete primarily because our future is yet to be achieved, and human thought, as a constitutive part of human existence, is limited because it cannot determine or predict the future. From an existentialist and phenomenological standpoint, therefore, what humans *think* and what they *do* (in action) must be distinguished in order to clarify the issue of historicity. There is history (*Historie*) or, to be more exact, the science of history, which is a recorded investigation of the human past, that is, "objective" history (*Geschichtswissenschaft*); and radically different from this scientific study of history is history (*Geschichte*), which is what is actually lived by human beings as actors, that is, "subjective" historicality (*Geschichtlichkeit*). The former always presupposed the latter, never *vice versa*, in the sense that "subjective" history becomes the material or object of history. This view is truly the existential radicalization of history and justifies historiography in terms of humankind's historically rooted being: such historicity presupposes the ultimate existential thesis that human beings *are* what they do, that is, the idea of active self-making or of the human being as history-maker. As Sartre says, the fundamental principle of existentialism is the notion that "man is nothing else but what he makes of himself."[82]

The fundamental opposition between the essentialist and the existentialist position is clear. The essentialist position of Aristotle that Strauss avows to follow considers that nature (and human nature) is universal, determinate, and fixed, whereas the existentialist stand, on the contrary, views human existence as something particular, contingent (that is, subject to chance and accident), and active.[83] The former, from the point of view of universal, determinate, and fixed essence, passes over not only history (*Historie*), but also historicity, and thus the idea of human self-making. Like his predecessor Aristotle, Strauss ignores the importance of time, especially the future, in the constitution of human existence. It is not accidental, as Löwith observes, that Aristotle, who examined almost everything under the sun, did not write a single treatise on history.[84] The Greeks in general ignored the significance of the future as a dimension of human temporality for the deterministic reason that "even future events would submit to the same laws as past events."[85] In *Poetics*, Aristotle states that poetry is more philosophical than history because poetry is of its very nature an expression of "universals," whereas history is the presentation of "singulars."[86]

To say that human existence is contingent means that its future is not predictable. The Greeks failed to see that the human being is always a possibility. For to say that human nature is eternal (that is, "to be" is "always to be") is tantamount to saying that it is "always present," that is, it is fundamentally constant and is merely reiterated in a series of nows. On the contrary, to say that humanity is not fixed or is contingent means that the human being is "a constant possibility" or has an indeterminable future.[87] Thus the basic insight of existentialism, as Robert O. Johann, S.J., declares, is the view that, in rejecting conventional natural law theory, the human being is a *project;* this view affirms the idea that human nature is not fixed by universal essence, but is always "a task to be accomplished."[88] This is the crucial difference between human affairs and nonhuman matters. The organic analogy of the human self always entails a determinism. Its difficulty is lack of the ontological distinction between the organic world and the human world. Max Scheler opposes the zoomorphic view of humankind when he writes that "man can be either more or less than an animal, but never *an animal.*"[89]

From the standpoint of the philosophy of action, moreover, the ontological determinism that Strauss advocates loses its ground before it starts. The historicity of human existence is the historicity of action, for to exist means to act. Action implies that distinction not only between good and bad, but also between right and wrong, for it refers to the self's involvement in the world, which is nothing but a nexus of relationships. What determines human historicity is temporality. Human existence is ecstatic. In self-making, a human being who is situated in the present captures the past and then projects him/herself into the future. Temporality is a constitutive element of action, that is, time is determined by action. The past is what has already been done and the future is whatever may yet be done (that is, possibility), while the present is "the point of action" (that is, actuality). Not only is action irreversible—that is, what is done cannot be undone—but determinism is also an impossibility, because it amounts to saying that the future is already done. Moreover, the *raison d'être* of action as choice is "the actualizing of a possibility." What "stands out" about action is its possibility; the world is nothing but the possible field of action; and history is "a continuum of action."[90] And since action makes humans what they are, to be human is to be free and, correlatively and primarily, responsible, because human beings act only in relation to others. In the final analysis, "historicity" pertains to reality: as Alexandre Kojève says, "Reality (at least *human* reality) is not given once and for all, but created itself in the course of time. . . ."[91]

VI

Leo Strauss's conception of political philosophy, following the classical tradition, is one of essentialism, which rests on the primacy of theory over practice. In the final analysis, my critique of his essentialist persuasion can be summarized as follows. His basic difficulties, as I see them, are endemic to his essentialist injunction that thought (whatness) is prior and superior to the real world of action (thatness). The negative corollaries of this essentialist position are a lack of appreciation for human historicity and a rejection of the emotive level of human action as something "irrational," because essentialism is preoccupied with what humans think rather than with what they do. Especially its ontological determinism— that is, human events are predictable on account of essence, which is universal, determinate, and fixed—has led to discounting the future as an ecstatic dimension of existence. However, as has been suggested in the beginning of this essay, the most serious consequences of this essentialist conception of political philosophy are that (1) it is egocentric and thus self-refuting as a political philosophy and (2) it is too scholastic a quietism to be directly relevant to political life, despite Strauss's own claim to the contrary.

In the first place, Strauss's conception of political philosophy is self-refuting; it ends up with denying *ab initio* the very idea of political reality, which is relational, because, as John Macmurray so effectively argues, intellectual activity (or thought) is by its very nature egocentric (or nonsocial) as contrasted to the heterocentricity (or sociality) of action. In a very rudimentary sense, therefore, essentialism is inimical to a genuine philosophy of politics or social philosophy. The thinking self as Strauss conceives it is nothing but an "enclosed monad" and an "insufficient" being, because thinking as regarded in this way is the withdrawal from the existential world of practice. It is thus not existential philosophy but the traditional essentialism of Strauss that has "a kernel of subjectivism" at its very root.[92] Strauss himself admits that philosophizing is the ascendance from what he calls "public dogma" to "private knowledge."[93] Truth, however, is not "private knowledge" accessible to the divinely inspired elite but, as Karl Jaspers says, is communicability.[94] Even the "private knowledge" (or "autobiography") such as *Natural Right and History* is published to be read by others. If truth is related in any way to reality, it must be said at once, with Martin Buber, that where there is no reciprocity there is no reality.[95] Contrary to the existential and phenomenological attitude, to consider philosophy as the ascendance from the cave world to the world of the sun is to flee from the real human world, which is always finite and historical, to the imaginary world of ideas. However, we are all condemned to the meaning of history, and "the philosopher is not an acosmic spirit, hovering above the course of history and raised above social reality, who is capable of comprehending the universe of being in a single glance."[96] Philosophy is more, not less, elevated by the consecration of the life-world rather than abasing it as something low. Although we cannot discredit Strauss's originality in an attempt to restore, as it were, the status of the "forgotten person" in the street and of his/her immediate understanding of political things as the necessary presupposition of all theoretical—both philosophical and scientific—investigations, his essentialism is far short of justifying theoretical activity as a superstructure of the pretheoretical world of everyday life. While, as Strauss agrees, positivism takes the naive life-world too lightly and, for this very reason, may be charged with negligence, his essentialism is guilty of self-contradiction.

In the second place, political philosophy cannot remain simply an alibi for intellectual purity and lethargy. I claim neither that existentialism has worked out a satisfactory political philosophy of its own nor that the disinterested pursuit of truth should be identified with political ideology. As Maurice Merleau-Ponty says of the philosopher of action, s/he "is perhaps the farthest removed from action, for to speak of action with depth and rigor is to say that one does not desire to act."[97] The only point I insist on here is that philosophy must somehow come to the aid of a rationally formulated system of ideas relevant to real political situations. To this very end existentialism as a philosophy remains favorably open. Noting the fact that recent academic philosophy has become "a barren wasteland" to cultural life, John Wild comments that "nothing more terrible can happen to a human culture than the breakdown of its ideology."[98] Only by bringing together academic philosophy and culture can the philosopher proudly think of him/herself as the "civil servant of humanity" in the Husserlian spirit.[99] Contrary to Strauss's belief that "philosophic ideas alone have had significant political effect,"[100] thought alone is not sufficient to transform the world and, instead, ideas must be translated into action to affect the world and history. For only action is creative and effective. It alone can achieve "the violent transition from what I have to what I aim to have, from what I am to what I intend to be."[101] What, we may ask Strauss, is the value of asking purely scholastic questions about the good society unless they guide the course of political action? All value judgments do have certain existential consequences even if, to the author's own displeasure, they are misconstrued or abused. Political philosophy, exactly as Strauss views it, is impotent unless it guides political action on the basis of a sound philosophical analysis of the political world. Precisely on these grounds, existential philosophy is adequate because not only it is the *de*scription of existential values, but is committed to the *pre*scription of existential norms as well.[102]

At best the Straussian way—to quote Martin Heidegger, who speaks here of Aristotle's philosophy—"can by no means be the only answer to our question. To state if favorably, it is *one* answer among many others."[103] Yet what is the fate of a philosophy that reifies concrete reality into mere abstract essence? The ultimate merit of the philosophy of human action is that it calls for constant vigilance to the limitation of thought: the real world is not what we think, but what we do. The real is not identical with the mere thought about it, but it is proper to say that thought (or philosophy) is only an intellectual component of reality. Political philosophy may be difficult because it aims at reflection with a view to action as well as with a view of knowledge. It can hope to be the complete philosophy of the whole person only when it links the self as thinker with the self as actor. It may be difficult, but it is too important to be ignored.

Appendix

In "Positivism, Historicism, and Political Inquiry," *American Political Science Review*, 66 (September 1972): 796–817, Professor Eugene F. Miller discusses (pp. 812–14) my views on the relevance of existential phenomenology to the philosophical foundation of political inquiry and comes to the conclusion that "there is much to be learned from Jung's reexamination of the philosophical foundations of political inquiry, but he does not provide us with a genuine alternative to an historical relativism" (p. 814). Here I shall limit my present comments to a clarification of a few crucial points and postpone what I hope will be a fuller dialogue to another occasion.

Since I take Miller to be essentially a Straussian or belonging to the school of contemporary political thought whose spiritual guru is Leo Strauss, I ought to mention the essay in which I have presented an explicit critique of Strauss's "essentialism."[1] In this essay, I agreed with Strauss that positivism has created a moral vacuum in contemporary political thought. Yet I asserted that "while, as Strauss agrees, positivism takes the naive life-world for granted and, for this very reason, may be charged with negligence, his essentialism is guilty of self-contradiction."[2] Strauss tends to reject all modern thought, by which he means thought that does not conform to the classical standards as he interprets them: thus, for him, the history of modern thought is a history of nonphilosophy. His essentialism must be understood in terms of his ontological supposition that "to be" is "always to be," that is, there is *physis*, which is unchanging, permanent, and universal. Without *physis* there can be no ethics, metaphysics, and epistemology. For Miller, too, without *physis* there is no valid ground for both "evaluation" and "explanation"; to use the language of Stanley Rosen, who is critical of both Heidegger and Wittgenstein and whom Miller often cites with approval, there is only "nihilism." It must be pointed out, however, that Miller, unlike Strauss and Rosen, has not reduced positivism to a form of historicism, nor has he considered historicism as worse than positivism.

The word *historicism* has a controversial history in contemporary thought from Karl Popper to Strauss, whose respective conceptions of it are diametrically opposed. Is existential phenomenology a form of historicism or historical relativism? Miller seems to think that it is. The belief that existential phenomenology is a historical relativism stems from a misunderstanding of the notion of the life-world (*Lebenswelt*). Inasmuch as the phenomenology of the life-world is a hermeneutics of social existence, so is Miller's epistemology a hermeneutics of *physis*. Take the example of Heidegger, whose philosophy I learned from the late John Wild (along with Edmund Husserl's and Maurice Merleau-Ponty's phenomenology, William James's radical empiricism, and John Macmurray's philosophy of action). For Heidegger, the "world" is the most inclusive horizon of meaning, and it is radically historical (or temporal). To acknowledge human historicality (*Geschichtlichkeit*) is not to commit one to historicism (*Historismus*). To say that human beings are temporal is, for example, simply to affirm that we are finite beings—we "die," and only human beings can "die." Upon a close examination, Heidegger's thought does not reject *physis* as *logos* or *alētheia*. Whereas Miller, like Strauss, wishes to defend the notion of *physis* understood by post-Socratics, Heidegger goes back to the primeval notion of *physis* in pre-Socratics. Further, Miller seems to be suggesting that phenomenological thought is merely an extension of the *Lebensphilosophie* of Wilhelm Dilthey. It is well known that in defending the notion of philosophy as a "rigorous science" (*strenge Wissenschaft*), Husserl was critical of Dilthey's historicism.

Then the real question is not simply an affirmation or a denial of "human nature" as such—with a denial being called "historicism." Rather, Miller is interested in defending that version of human nature which is unchanging and universal and without which, according to him, there is no possibility of knowledge or intelligibility. Even if there is a constant and universal human nature, the question of how conflicting theories about the permanent structure or content of human nature can be resolved remains to be answered. Miller's version of human nature is the one that is claimed to have a set of predetermined characteristics, whereas for the existentialist view, the essence of humankind is open and indeterminate. Temporally speaking, the former is a fidelity to the past, whereas the latter is an affirmation of the open future in the passage of time. "For human reality," Simone de Beauvoir writes in *The Coming of Age*, "existing means existing in time: in the present we look towards the future by means of plans that go beyond our past, in which our activities fall lifeless, frozen and loaded with passive demands."[3]

Like Strauss, Miller holds that the world of common-sense understanding (or, as Strauss calls it, the "natural world" of human beings) is the presupposed foundation of the scientific or philosophical conceptualization of political things. However, essentialism, Miller's notwithstanding, reduces the world of lived experience (existence) to the world of pre-fixed essence (*physis*). It is tantamount to a claim for the primacy of *theōria* over *praxis*. According to Miller, "To know *that* a man is presupposes already some knowledge of *what* man is."[4] Here "existence" presupposes "essence." For him, therefore, without *physis* or in historicism "there is no possibility of obtaining knowledge that is objective, final, or absolute."[5] In contrast to essentialism, however, in phenomenology the relevance of the life-world does not lie in its status as knowledge, but instead lies in its status as the meaningful ground for human action, that is, as the original source of knowledge. So the geography of conceptual knowledge presupposes the natural landscape of preconceptual understanding. By exalting *theōria* at the expense of *praxis*, humanity itself is reduced to "a little abstract effigy."[6] By "opticizing" thought[7] or conceptual knowledge, essentialism loses sight of the life-world and of its importance. It is then the quest for epistemological certainty or absoluteness that constitutes the central concern for Miller, insofar as he holds that "the distinguishing characteristic of human nature is man's desire and capacity to know."[8] The same temperament is shared, though strangely enough, by scientific objectivism, whose slogans are, among others, conceptual rigor and predicative certainty.[9] By intending to elevate the intelligible, essentialism regards conceptual thinking as the activity of a disembodied and worldless mind. Whereas Husserl speaks of theoretical *praxis,* essentialism treats philosophy as if it is a lifeless activity.

Human dignity, which both Miller and I cherish, is not served or preserved by postulating a pre-fixed human nature. On the contrary, it is elevated by affirming freedom, the denial of a pre-fixed human nature, in a world whose meaning is not fixed but must be constantly won. As John Wild once said, freedom is not a natural but an existential norm. For a predetermined human nature (and a predetermined history, too, for that matter) is the death of human freedom and dignity or, as B. F. Skinner has it, the triumph of the reinforced human being "beyond freedom and dignity"—or, more appropriately, "*against* freedom and dignity." The existentialist thesis that the meaning of existence is not fixed but is constantly won is not an acknowledgment of nihilism in which everything is permitted. According to Simone de Beauvoir, existential philosophy not only permits an elaboration of ethics, but also is the only philosophy in which ethics has its place. It makes possible a genuine ethical theory precisely because it focuses on *how* human beings *act* rather than *what* they *are*. This is why I called the essentialism of Strauss "an ontological determinism." The structure of good and evil is not of God-given nature, but is a human gift that has to be worked by *us all* in coexistence or transaction. As Martin Buber puts it, only where there is mutual sharing is there reality or responsibility—including the reality or responsibility of thinking. Humankind ought to be distinguished from God, as time is from eternity. In conclusion: it may be said that the differences between Miller's views and mine stem from two fundamentally different styles of philosophy and ultimately views on life itself. Perhaps one is "priestly" and the other "jesterly." Be that as it may, if I were to call a standoff between our styles or views and to refuse to acknowledge the superiority of mine over his, I would be a "historicist," and that would make my contention superfluous.

Seven

BEING, PRAXIS, AND TRUTH: TOWARD A DIALOGUE BETWEEN PHENOMENOLOGY AND MARXISM

I. Introduction

THE MOST INTELLECTUALLY EXCITING HAPPENING TODAY is the flow or whirlpool of crosscurrents in phenomenology, Marxism, structuralism, and psychoanalysis. My purpose here is to cultivate a dialogue between phenomenology and Marxism. On the one hand, phenomenology has already been organized into a tripartite movement in a span of three or four intellectual generations: (1) transcendental, (2) existential, and (3) hermeneutical. On the other hand, Marxism too has developed into a complex, variegated, and changing system of thought over its one hundred years of history with three main areas of focus: (1) philosophical anthropology, (2) economic analysis, and (3) socialist doctrine.[1] In this light, therefore, my aim in this essay is neither to homogenize nor to miscegenate the two. For the moment anyway, a synthesis is premature and undesirable.[2] If premature, it will result in a homogenization or a miscegenation and, worse, in an obfuscation or obliteration of inherent differences between the two movements—one *as* phenomenology and the other *as* Marxism. Eclecticism, as a natural product of synthesis, arises our of intellectual laziness, which is contrary to both "rigorous" and "dialectical" thought—the respective aims of phenomenology and Marxism. Nonetheless, my aim here is to attempt to go beyond the claustrophilia of purists from both camps—phenomenological and Marxian—who, afraid of contamination, sneer from the outset at any attempt at a dialogue as abortive and anathema. In short, the aim of my essay is "diacritical"—to use Maurice Merleau-Ponty's term—in seeing as mutually valuable what is alien to Marxism in phenomenology and what is alien to phenomenology in Marxism, and thus in seeing them as complementary to each other.[3]

II. The Primacy of Ontology

Ontology questions the nature of reality (as Being), whereas epistemology is the conception of knowledge or epistemic truth. Ontology and epistemology imply each other: as Merleau-Ponty points out, "Every science secretes an ontology; every ontology anticipates a body of knowledge."[4] *How to know* something presupposes *what* that something *is*. By the primacy of ontology—the organizing theme in this effort toward a dialogue between phenomenology and Marxism—I mean to emphasize that epistemology is grounded in ontology. Without ontological grounding, epistemology is an empty abstraction that degenerates into scientism or even results in the hegemony of scientism.[5]

Marxism is primarily an ontology that questions and organizes human reality in such categories as *praxis,* labor, and sociality. Strictly speaking, phenomenology is a philosophy of meaning based on the definition of consciousness as intentionality. Since different realities correspond to different structures of meaning, meaning is the phenomenological conception of reality that is to be described. However, the emphasis of the term "consciousness" (*Bewusstsein*) itself is on "being" (*Sein*): it is "being-conscious" or "conscious-ness." Phenomenological reduction (*epochē*) too is the philosophical act that allows "the birth of a being for meaning."[6] The theme of ontological primacy envisions humankind as unified, which was also the vision of Marx's philosophical anthropology. Max Scheler was indeed prophetic when he said in *Man's Place in Nature* in 1928 that in our age, human beings have become more problematic to themselves than in any other age in recorded history, and he bemoaned the dismal state in which the study of humankind finds itself.[7] Today, the fragmented image of the human being in the human sciences into "political humankind," "economic humankind," "sociological humankind," "psychological humankind," "religious humankind," "symbolic humankind," etc., mirrors the fragmentation of humankind itself. The specialized division of academic labor is more a curse than a blessing in understanding humankind fully. When the study of the human being becomes fragmented, the unified vision of humanity necessarily suffers and is likely to fall into oblivion. What we need urgently, therefore, is a *philosophical anthropology* that can provide us with a unified vision of the human being in nature and society in a time of crisis.

Martin Heidegger's primary aim is to awaken our thought from the "forgottenness of Being" (*Seinsvergessenheit*) that constitutes the history of Western philosophy since the time of Plato. Heidegger's "ontological homecoming" calls for the restoration of the historical in Being and understands Being as historical. After Hegel's philosophy of history, the history of Western philosophy has never been the same. For Marx as for Hegel, the "real" and "rational"—albeit in different patterns and sizes—are cut out of the same fabric called "historical existence."[8] In fact, it is by way of the theme of the historical existence of humankind that Alexandre Kojève and Jean Hyppolite brought Hegel close to French existential phenomenology, just as it is through the interpretation of Hegel that Georg Lukács, Karl Korsch, and Antonio Gramsci "westernized" the Marxist movement. Merleau-Ponty noted in 1947 that Marxism as a philosophy of history lay the basic conditions for humanism:

> The decline of proletarian humanism is not a crucial experience which invalidates the whole of Marxism. It is still valid as a critique of the present world and alternative humanisms. In this respect, at least, *it cannot be surpassed*. Even if it is incapable of shaping world history, it remains powerful enough to discredit other solutions. On close consideration, Marxism is not just any hypothesis that might be replaced tomorrow by some other. It is the simple statement of those conditions without which there would be neither any humanism, in the sense of mutual relation between men, nor any rationality in history. In this sense Marxism is not a philosophy of history, it is *the* philosophy of history and to renounce it is to dig the grave of Reason in history. After that there can be no more dreams or adventures.[9]

In his famous "Letter on Humanism" in 1947, Heidegger refers to the idea of "homelessness" (*Heimatlosigkeit*) of the modern world whose destiny is tied to the historical character of Being. According to him, Marx's view of history is superior to other historical accounts because of its fundamental insight, inspired by Hegel, into alienation (*Entfremdung*) as having its roots in the homelessness of modern humanity.[10] He judged, albeit somewhat hastily, that because Edmund Husserl's phenomenology and Jean-Paul Sartre's existentialism fail to recognize the importance of the historical in Being, they are incapable of entering a productive dialogue with Marxism. And despite Heidegger's suggestive utterance, his knowledge of Marx, and their being both *revisionary* philosophers proclaiming the "end of philosophy" in one and "end of history" in the other, most Marxists are reluctant to engage in a dialogue with Heidegger, a circumstance that unfortunately is in large measure due to purely political rather than philosophical considerations.[11]

From our perspective, the common thread between phenomenological ontology and Marxism goes back to the philosophical principle Giambattista Vico enunciated: *verum ipsum factum*. For all Viconians, historical consciousness is an ontological precondition for epistemology. What Enzo Paci said about phenomenology in the established tradition of Vico is equally applicable to Marxism as "a new science": "It is demanded by the necessity of basing the sciences on the operations that we perform in time. We can know these operations in temporal reflection which is both history and the foundation of its meaning in truth."[12] For Vico as for Marx and Heidegger, the historical is characteristic of *human specificity* or *eccentricity*. The Vichian principle says that how to know presupposes what there is to know, that is, the knowledge of human history depends on understanding that it is human-made. Only because human history is an order of *factum* is it *verum* for us. The order of *verum* follows the order of *factum;* but for the latter there would be no former. We have the certainty of historical knowledge because we make our own history, that is, human history is human-made, whereas we have no certainty of the knowledge of nature because it is God-made. To be sure, there is also a history of nature (or "natural history"), but it is only human beings who recognize that we have a history or make history. However, Marx questions Vico's formulation as to whether "natural history" itself is not human-made rather than God-made. For as Marx contends, "Technology discloses man's mode of dealing with Nature, the process of production by which he sustains his life, and of the mental conceptions that flow from them."[13] Marx seems to think that humans make not only their own history, but external nature as well (i.e., nature mastered in and by technology is also human-made).

The ontology of humankind attempts to define human specificity: the specific nature of *being* human or what makes human beings human. This is the common framework in both Heidegger's *Being and Time* (1927)[14] and Marx's *The Economic and Philosophic Manuscripts of 1844,*[15] from which—in the name of philosophical anthropology—there emerge structural similarities with thematic differences. Heidegger's description of the eccentricity of *Dasein* as "care" (*Sorge*), "project" (*Entwurf*), and "being-in-the-world" (*In-der-Welt-sein*) parallels Marx's description of human specificity in terms of *praxis*, labor, and sociality. While Heidegger began with the ontology of humankind and "turned" to the thinking of Being in general from the specific analysis of *Dasein* as such without ever abandoning the fundamental issues raised in *Being and Time*, Marx, "turned" to specific economic analysis in *Capital* without ever losing sight of the basic concern and issues raised in *The Economic and Philosophic Manuscripts,* which questions a philosophy of humanity. Marx's critique of capitalist political economy as dehumanizing ("careless" in Heidegger's language) is predicated on his definition of human essence and humanity. In this sense, there can be no radical break in Marx between the "philosophy" of humanity and the "science" of the economic.[16] Rather, the latter explicitly or implicitly presupposes the former. In Marx not only does "science" never abandon "philosophy," but also the economic assumes and retains an ontological status.

For Heidegger, the question of human reality is posed as that of *Dasein.* It is called "fundamental ontology" (*Fundamentalontologie*) because the human being has a *privileged* position in the order of things. Although the term *Dasein* evokes an ambiguous sense of generality, it has at least the following three advantages in defining human specificity that should be noted for this discussion: (1) it clarifies the fundamentals of human specificity in the general framework of Being as totality; (2) with its emphasis on historicality (*Geschichtlichkeit*), it avoids the traditional, logocentric definition of the human being as *animal rationale* with a fixed set of immutable properties; and (3) it removes both subjectivist and objectivist implications from the language of philosophical anthropology. What is the essence of the human being called *Dasein* for Heidegger? It is defined as being-in-the-world, with care as its *radical* center connecting humankind uniquely with the world: the hyphenated phrase is meant to pinpoint human specificity in an inseparable relatedness of human beings and the world. Unlike Husserl's phenomenology, which is consciousness-centered, Heidegger views phenomenology as the *disclosure of that which is as it is in itself:* "Only as phenomenology, is ontology possible."[17] The analysis of *Dasein* as being-in-the-world not only rejects the Scylla of the subjectless world and the Charybdis of the worldless subject, but also affirms thinking or knowing as an existential mode of *Dasein.* Since the essence of *Dasein* is its existence, both thinking and doing are different but integral modes of existing in the world. Moreover, the existential structure of *Dasein* as care determines the structure of time and project as the *radically human* mode of understanding the world. In project there is the temporal primacy of the future over the past and present. All in all, the existential mode of *Dasein* as care, project, and being-in-the-world is radically different from the way a thing or an object simply *is* in its *natural environment (Umwelt).*

For Heidegger, the world is the inseparable correlate of human-kind's being and is divided into three distinguishable regions: (1) "being-with" others (*Mitsein*) or the social world (*Mitwelt*), (2) the world of natural things, and (3) the world of human-made objects or artifacts, whose purpose is determined by their serviceability, usability, and manipulability. The existential character of *Dasein* indicates that not only is the generic "human being" distinguished from other things both natural and artificial, but also each human being is distinguished from another. *Dasein* has in each case its own sphere (i.e., *Jemeinigkeit*), a personal domain called "I," "you," "he," or "she." This "mineness" defines the eccentricity of each person: every human being *ex-ists*, that is, *stands out from* every other. Therefore, for Heidegger, what is each person's "own" (*eigen*) makes him/her "authentic" (*eigentlich*). The opposite of the "authentic" human being is the "inauthentic" human being: the "One" (*das Man*) who has nothing of its "own" and lives in anonymity (i.e., "Nobody").

Just as Heidegger replaced Husserl's transcendental "consciousness" with everyday care, so did Marx replace Hegel's Idea or Concept with *praxis* and labor. The most *existential* dimension of Marx's thought lies in his criticism of Hegel's idealism, which has its parallel in his Danish contemporary Søren Kierkegaard—who like Marx, was critical of Hegel for reducing concrete existence to abstract thought. Let us recapture Marx's famous polemic against Hegel in his preface to the second edition of *Capital,* written in London in 1873. Although he admitted being a pupil of the "mighty thinker" Hegel and recognized him as the first thinker to present the general form of the dialectic in a comprehensive manner, Marx contended that his own *dialectical method* is directly opposed to Hegel's, insofar as the latter reduces our historical existence to the processual matter of thinking under the name of the Idea or Concept. For Marx, Hegel's dialectic transforms the real world into the "phenomenal" form of the Idea, that is, reality into the predicate of the Idea. So for Marx, the aim of "materialism" is to find the rational kernel within the mystical shell of the idea; it is to demystify the "mystification" of concrete reality by conceptual thought, since "the ideal is nothing else than the material world reflected by the human mind, and translated into forms of thought."[18] With Hegel, Marx contends, the dialectic stands on its head. The task of Marx is to turn it right side up again. It is only in this spirit that we must also understand Marx, who says: "Life is not determined by consciousness, but consciousness by life"[19] and "Consciousness can never be anything else than conscious existence, and the existence of men is their actual life-process."[20] So Marx's "life" parallels Heidegger's "existence" defined as the essence of *Dasein*. It is quite clear that Marx's objection to "idealism" in the name of "materialism" is no denial of "consciousness" as such. What he is objecting to, instead, is Hegel's "pure" transcendental consciousness associated with intellectual thought and "theoretical bubble-blowing": he is objecting only against the *idealization* of consciousness apart from "life-process." For Marx as for Kierkegaard, to identify thought with existence is an *abstraction* in the etymological sense of the word. In this sense, too, Communism for Marx is not an *ideal* but meant to be a *real* movement of history.

As care is to Heidegger's fundamental ontology, so is *praxis* to Marx's philosophy of humanity. For Heidegger, the world is precisely a world because of *Dasein's* care. For Marx, too, the world is a world (or a human world) because of *praxis*. In terms of *praxis* Marx defines human specificity as a whole. The essence of the human being as species-being (*Gattungswesen*) is realized in *praxis*, which is social through and through. As Karel Kosík observes, *praxis* is one of the most important concepts in Marxian, "materialist" philosophy. And insofar as "praxis *is the sphere of human being*,"[21] Marx's "humanism" is a philosophy of *praxis par excellence*. *Praxis* is what defines humankind in its comprehensive totality. It is the "project" of human beings in making history and nature. First of all, *praxis* is not practical activity as opposed to thinking or knowing, but is the determination of human specificity in its totality.[22] For Marx as for Heidegger, thinking itself is an active mode of existing in the world. Ontologically, *praxis* is not a correlate of cognition or an epistemological category, that is, the former is not a product of the latter. Rather, cognition is a form of *praxis* or theoretical *praxis*. Second, *praxis* is the activity that transforms humankind and society as well as nature. As humans transform nature by *praxis*, it becomes *technē* or the activity of "making." This aspect of *praxis* is what Heidegger refers to as the world of artifacts. Third, *praxis* as social corresponds to Heidegger's social world, which is a network of human beings' relationships with other human beings. The concept of sociality with its normative implications is the most distinguishing characteristic of Marxism as a philosophy of humanity.

If Marxism is a philosophy of *praxis*, a question arises from it concerning the relationship between philosophy and *praxis*. In this regard, most instructive is Merleau-Ponty's "last lecture" at the Collège de France, entitled "Philosophy and Non-Philosophy since Hegel" in which, parenthetically speaking, he refuses to dissociate philosophical questions from all works of Marx—including *Capital*.[23] Central to any interrogation of Marxism concerning philosophy and *praxis* is the question of how one is transformed into the other. It is for Hegel a question of *praxis* becoming philosophy, whereas it is for Marx the question of philosophy becoming *praxis* (i.e., of the abolition of philosophy). In Marx, philosophy is abolished only if it is realized in *praxis*. "Practice," Merleau-Ponty notes, "will be that which implies the true realization of philosophy (a theory that is the true destruction of itself as a separate theory) where the light of philosophy is rediscovered. This practice therefore incorporates philosophy in its entirety, and, in this sense, destroys it, truly surpasses it, because it contains it."[24] In this process of philosophy becoming *praxis,* the proletariat as a carrier of the universal becomes both the head and heart of the Revolution: it realizes philosophy as its embodiment and thus becomes "the philosophical god." As the agent of philosophy, the proletariat transforms the world: the "word" of philosophy is realized in the "action" of the proletariat. As a carrier of the universal, the proletariat in its action is the realization of humanity claiming to be the *movement* of history—the *Weltgeist.*

What makes Marxism unique as a philosophy of *praxis* is its focus on labor as a producing, economic activity that is embodied in the activity of the proletariat. As the whole is to the part, so is *praxis* to labor. As a form of *praxis,* labor partakes of all of the characteristics—the transformative and social attributes—of *praxis* itself. By their labor, human beings transform nature into use-objects and commodities, a process that involves the *relations* as well as the *forces* of production. Labor is the appropriation of nature by and for human beings. Because of labor, according to Marx, nature itself appears to human beings to be *their* work and *their* reality. Broadly conceived, labor *is* characteristic of human specificity. Thus Marx declares in a famous passage in *Capital:*

> We pre-suppose labour in a form that stamps it as exclusively human. A spider puts to shame many architects in the construction of her cells. But what distinguishes the worst architect from the best bees is this, that the architect raises his structure in imagination before he erects it in reality. At the end of every labour-process, we get a result that already existed in the imagination of the labourer at its commencement. He not only effects a change of form in the material on which he works, but he also realizes a purpose of his own that gives the law to his modus operandi, and to which he must subordinate his will.[25]

What Marx calls "imagination" at work in labor and work has the structure of "project" in the phenomenological discussion of humankind, whether this "project" is understood broadly as humanity's mode of understanding the world in Heidegger's fundamental ontology or narrowly as the "planning" of action in Alfred Schutz's social phenomenology.

Moreover, Marx's labor-oriented analysis of the human being as species-being has another important implication that has so often been forgotten and unnoticed—namely, that it is conceived in Marx's revisionary way of defining humankind as opposed to the Hegelian or idealist view of the human being defined in terms of the abstract "rationality" of thought. For Marx, therefore, defining human beings *concretely* in terms of labor is an extension of his conception of the human being as "a natural, embodied, sentient, objective being." The aim of Marx's emphasis on the human being as a sensuous and embodied being is to offer a new view of humankind in opposition to the logocentric conception of the human being as "rational animal." This is why Merleau-Ponty is right in observing that Marx's philosophy of humanity is not primarily a philosophy of consciousness, but a philosophy of humankind "incarnate."[26] And since, according to Marx, imagination or project makes human beings human, radically distinguished from animality, so is labor not simply a biological phenomenon. He contends that while animals reproduce only themselves, humans reproduce "the whole of nature." As we can infer from Marx's insistence that there is a radical distinction between the merely "natural" and the "humanly natural," human sexuality as sensuous activity has for human beings more than a "reproductive" function.

Whether the conception of human beings as labor reduces them and their total activity to *homo oeconomicus* and economic activity (i.e., "economism") is a serious question concerning the Marxist movement as well as Marx's own thought. It is one thing to emphasize the importance of the economic in human life; it is quite another, however, to reduce human *praxis* to the economic. There seems to be a double reason for Marx's focus on labor and the economic: one has already been mentioned as a challenge to the "rationalist" view of the human being and the other is the basis of challenging capitalist political economy as dehumanizing. As the old Chinese saying goes, "to catch a tiger one has first to enter its den"; that is, to challenge capitalist political economy, Marx must deal with it in its own terms—the economic.

To be sure, Marx's concrete analysis of humankind with an emphasis on labor and the economic in terms of basic human needs and requirements has a definite advantage over Heidegger's general conception of the human being as *Dasein*. From Marx's perspective, Heidegger's manner of "ontologizing" may be too abstract. In this respect, what the phenomenologist Emmanuel Levinas says of Heidegger is instructive and worth noting: "*Dasein* in Heidegger is never hungry. Food can be interpreted as an implement only in a world of exploitation."[27] However, Heidegger is no ontological obscurantist if by an "obscurantist" we mean, as Thomas Mann once observed, one who sacrifices generalities and forgets larger implications by attending to minute details. On the other hand, Marx's labor-oriented analysis is not an unmixed blessing. It has a "reductive" tendency—which is not to say that Marx's thought is a reductionism. Even Kosík, whose focus on Marxism is a focus on *praxis* as totality, insists that *"the economic structure will continue to maintain its primacy as the fundamental basis of social relations."*[28] So for one thing, at least Heidegger's care does not convey the sense of exploitation in humanity's dealings with nature, whereas Marx's labor does because it is basically the activity of exploiting nature by and for human beings as an essential dimension of human specificity.[29]

Economism or economic reductionism is a result of identifying labor with *praxis*, which constitutes the norm of understanding Marx's thought by his orthodox followers as well as his severest critics. The reduction of Marx's thought to the economic and his conception of the human being as *homo oeconomicus* betrays his own dialectical thought. There are different aspects of economism. First, it means that the economic determines the totality of human activities rather than being merely one primary activity. Second, in determining human history, the economic is subject to causal determination. Third, economic "structures" as the objectified dimensions of labor determine labor considered as labor of an active and creative subject or agent. However, one thing is certain in this analysis. If Marxism is regarded as an economic reductionism in one or all of its forms, it appears incompatible with the phenomenological conception of humankind. Therefore, Merleau-Ponty contends that it is wrong to say that in Marxism economics determines the totality of the social world, just as it is equally wrong to reduce Freudianism to a theory of human sexuality as a biological phenomenon. Instead, he suggests that the significance of the economic lies in that the problems of human beings are reflected in it, that is to say, there is a human significance in the economic. In an important but rarely noticed lengthy footnote in his *Phenomenology of Perception*, Merleau-Ponty declares:

> When "materialist" history identifies democracy as a "formal" régime, and describes the conflicts with which such a régime is torn, the real subject of history, which is trying to extract from beneath the juridical abstraction called the citizen, is not only the economic subject, man as a factor in production, but in more general terms the living subject, man as creativity, as a person trying to endow his life with form, loving, hating, creating or not creating works of art, having or not having children. Historical materialism is not causality exclu-

sive to economics. One is tempted to say that it does not base history and ways of thinking on production and ways of working, but more generally on ways of existing and co-existing, on human relationships. It does not bring the history of ideas down to economic history, but replaces these ideas in the one history which they both express, and which is that of social existence. Solipsism as a philosophical doctrine is not the result of a system of private property; nevertheless into economic institutions as into conceptions of the world is projected the same existential prejudice in favour of isolation and mistrust.[30]

It is this stretching in the manner of Merleau-Ponty rather than shrinking the meaning of the economic in Marx that there can be a dialogue between phenomenology and Marxism.

The idea of social existence occupies the centrality of Marx's "humanism." The human being as species-being is social through and through in producing, making, and doing. Marx's concern for alienation is focused on the social alienation of human beings from their fellow human beings, although he also spoke of alienation involving that of humans from nature, from their activity, from their products, and finally from themselves. Thus the ultimate *telos* of *praxis*, which is the creation of Communism, is to produce a community of human beings, not a pile of goods and commodities. Human reality *is* an orchestration of social relationships. Although Marx objected to the conceptual reification of Hegel's rationalism and offered the alternative conception of the human being as *praxis* and as a sensuous and embodied being, he was unaware of the subjective egocentricism inherent in rationalism or thought-centered philosophy.[31] On a similar ground, Schutz contended that Husserl's transcendental phenomenology is incapable of justifying intersubjectivity. Despite his alleged "individualism" based on phenomenological ontology, which has become the prime target of attack by Marxists like Adam Schaff, Sartre is one of the first who observed that Cartesian rationalism is incapable of rendering a philosophically consistent justification for intersubjectivity or sociality that is also intercorporeal. For as Sartre rightly pointed out, once the self and the other are regarded as disembodied substances (*res*), which is to say two separate substances, solipsism is inescapable.[32] It is quite clear that modern rationalism or thought-centered philosophy embedded in the Cartesian formula, "*Cogito, ergo sum,*" which continues today in cyberneticism, is inherently egocentric or solipsistic, that is, *anti-social*.

Sociality as dialectical implies the simultaneous process of the internalization of the external and the externalization of the internal—the conception of sociality that is at once neither "individualistic" nor "sociologistic."[33]I will explicate this dialectic of sociality by examining in Marxism the structure of language as a *social* form of *praxis*. For Marx, social intercourse is the genesis of language. He wrote:

> Language is as old as consciousness, language is practical consciousness, as it exists for other men, and for that reason is really beginning to exist for me personally as well; for language, like consciousness, only rises from the need, the necessity, of intercourse with other men. Where there exists a relationship, it exists for men: the animal has no "relations" with anything, cannot have any. For the animal, its relation to others does not exist as a relation. Consciousness is therefore from the very beginning a social product, and remains so as long as men exist at all.[34]

However, it is fair to say that Marx developed no systematic philosophy of language as we know it today. Because Marx emphasized language as the medium of social intercourse or regarded the basic function of language as communication, he failed to conceive directly language as intrinsic to humankind's very humanity. Particularly lacking from his thought is the consideration of language as the *mediation* between human thought and the world, which helps further to unlock the mystery of language as a direct linkage between the subject and the object.[35] To emphasize consciousness or linguistic consciousness simply as a social product is to invite the sociologization of the *Cogito*. Language is not a closed system of signs, words, and symbols. The use of language is not simply "reproductive," but is "productive" as well. Language is an open system that is both inwardly and outwardly "porous."[36] After all this is said, however, we do not mean to say that a philosophy of language cannot be developed on the basis of the initial insights of Marx.

One of the most comprehensive developments of the Marxist philosophy of language is found in V. N. Voloshinov.[37] His *social* conception of language is most relevant to our discussion here. Phenomenologically put, it treats language as the simultaneous birth of the *signified* being of the world and the *signifying* being of humankind.[38] As a pre-Lacanian Marxist, Voloshinov is understandably critical of Freudianism as biologism. He contends that the "biological individual" that has become "the alpha and omega of modern ideology" is an improper abstraction. Outside society, that is, outside socioeconomic conditions, the human creature is not a *human being*. Animals, too, are biological; but what makes human beings human is our "second birth" or "social birth." The acquisition of language as a social phenomenon signifies for Voloshinov humanity's second birth. By social he means to emphasize language as an "interindividual territory." Thus what is most interesting in Voloshinov is his conception of language as embodying the dialectical conception of sociality. On the one hand, he is opposed to subjective "psychologism," and cites approvingly the early argument of Husserl against Wilhelm Dilthey. Like linguistic phenomenology as developed by Husserl, Heidegger, Hans-Georg Gadamer, and Paul Ricoeur, Voloshinov too contends that "ideology" is a system of ideas—apart from the system of material production—that requires first a linguistic system of signs (e.g., the hammer and sickle). In his context, the term "ideology" has an unusual meaning in that it is a linguistic system of signs, wherein the human sciences (*Geisteswissenschaften*) themselves are called the "ideological sciences." For Voloshinov, language as a linguistic system of signs is not the subjective property of "consciousness." Rather, following Marx, "*consciousness itself can arise and become a viable fact only in the material embodiment of signs.*"[39]

On the other hand, however, Voloshinov is equally critical of "abstract objectivism" (e.g., Ferdinand de Saussure's structuralism and Emile Durkheim's sociologism), which dissolves the inner dimension of the human being as a linguistic *subject*. Therefore, his anti-psychologism does not result in "structuralism" or "sociologism." For language is the dialectic of diachrony and synchrony where one is not reduced to the other and neither has primacy over the other. Voloshinov's anti-sociologism seems to be a result of taking seriously Wilhelm von Humboldt's notion of the "inner form of language" (*innere Sprachform*)—that is, the "generative and transformative" aspect of language. One of the main points in Voloshinov's criticism of "abstract objectivism" is that it is incapable of explaining "the inner generative process of a language." For him, therefore, language is not just a static "structure," a ready-made artifact handed down from generation to generation. Rather, it is a historical, dynamic, and living phenomenon. Following Marx's philosophy of *praxis* as concrete in opposition to abstract activity, Voloshinov finds his proof of language as a dynamic social phenomenon in what he calls the "utterance" (or the speech act) or "verbal interaction," which constitutes "the basic reality of language." The utterance is a social relationship by means of words. By the same token, the word itself implies both the carrier of inner meaning and the medium of outer expression. As such it is a two-sided act involving a reciprocity between the speaker and the listener. Language as utterance is a moment of communication. Thus it is not a monologue but intrinsically a dialogue. It is the meeting of the inner and the outer in the act of communication between two persons—the speaker and the listener, where one is "reversible" to the other. That is to say, inner meaning and outer expression in language are created out of "one and the same material." In the end, for Voloshinov, to reject the dualism between the inner and the outer is to overcome individualism and sociologism, both of which betray the dialectic of sociality or humankind's social existence.

III. Epistemological Excursions

In the preceding pages I have contended that Marx's primary concern was the nature of human social reality in its broadest sense rather than questions of conceptual knowledge or epistemology. Marxism is primarily an ontology of humankind; it is not a philosophy of the *Cogito*. "Scientific" Marxism must presuppose or ignore Marx's "humanistic" construction of reality. If the former ignores the latter, that is, if science ignores ontology, Marxism risks a conceptual reification (i.e., conceptualization without being grounded in ontology) as objectified conceptual structures dissolve or suffocate the human being as the subject or agent of *praxis*. To say that Marxism is primarily an ontology of humankind, however, is not to mean that there are no epistemological elements in it. To reject the identification of reality with conceptual thought, too, is not to denigrate epistemology or the role of thought and rationality in human life. What we are insisting on here is simply that conceptual rationality, however important it may be, is only one form of rationality. After all, its aim is to clarify *what we are*. Also, the Marxian dialectic at work is the conceptual category whose purpose is to describe the *real* movement of history as *praxis* rather than to produce knowledge. It is a category of relations: between the different stages of historical development as a whole, between the whole and the part, and between different parts in a whole. The internal relation between ontology and epistemology is that of the whole and the part, just as there is a relation between *praxis* and labor or economic activity. In the end, the inflation of or misguided emphasis on conceptual thought results inevitably in what we might call the *fallacy of misplaced ontology*.

In 1979, the anthropologist Marvin Harris proposed a research strategy to build "a science of culture" in the name of materialism.[40] However, what he intends to replace with "cultural materialism" is "dialectical materialism," which, he contends, is of Hegelian origin and is consummated in Lenin, who made "the dialectical tail" wag "the materialist dog." Harris aims to replace nonscientific and nonempirical "dialectics" with "the objective and empirical aspects of Marx's scientific materialism." However, his cultural materialism is at best a limping Marxism. He transplants the Marxian body under the head of David Hume and then makes

Marxism walk on its Humean head. What is wrong with Harris's cultural materialism is that it regards Marxism merely as an epistemological, scientific strategy. As he emphasizes, "The epistemological points that Marx and Engels were trying to establish cannot be made by means of the concept of 'reality.' For scientific materialists, the issues of what is real or unreal is subsumed entirely by the epistemological generalities of the scientific method, . . . Materialists need only insist that material entities exist apart from ideas, that thought about things and events are separable from things and events."[41] Thus the knowledge-centered materialism of Harris called "cultural materialism"—in which the adjective "cultural" is a spurious adornment—is at best an epistemological reification that loses the fundamental insights of Marx on the nature of reality.

A similar attempt has been made by David-Hillel Ruben.[42] One main difference between Harris and Ruben is that the one rejects the "dialectical" Lenin and the other defends Lenin's "reflection" theory of knowledge or scientific materialism in *Materialism and Empirio-Criticism*. Moreover, Ruben is willing to grant to materialism an ontology or an ontological theory about the nature of reality, whereas Harris reduces materialism to an anthropological research strategy. However, Ruben insists that in order for it not to be a blind act of faith, materialism is in need of a theory of knowledge that "underpins" it. He claims that the only true materialist theory of knowledge is the "reflection" theory of truth, which Lenin saw more clearly than any other Marxist before or since. "Materialism," Ruben says, "asserts the essential independence of reality from all thought"[43] in which the function of thought is to reflect independent reality: "What materialism needs, epistemologically speaking, is a correspondence or reflection theory of knowledge on which the relationship between a belief or a thought and the objects or real states of affairs which the beliefs are about is a contingent relationship."[44] In brief, materialism asserts the existence of *something* other than the mind or its content. On the other hand, according to Ruben, the reflection theory of knowledge is in need of materialism as an ontology, but the converse is not true. Epistemology is a necessary but not a sufficient condition for ontology. Nonetheless, it becomes quite clear in his critique of Lukács, Gramsci, Korsch, Leszek Kolakowski, and Alfred Schmidt that the version of Marxism Ruben wishes to defend is monistic naturalism. For in it thought, ontologically speaking, is a part of the overall system of nature; and to prevent an "ontological duality" between consciousness and nature, consciousness must be dependent on nature. The inconsistency of Ruben's analysis lies in an ontological monism on the one hand and an epistemological dualism on the other insofar as he maintains that thought is a part of the reality of nature yet reality is independent of thought. For him, any dialectical mediation—the hallmark of Marxism—is incompatible with his "materialist epistemology." Any dialectical mediation between the act of consciousness and a real object is for Ruben an "idealist" inflation of materialism (or naturalism), even if he wished to reject the "dark night" of the Second International or "reductive materialism." He wishes to affirm—absurdly, I think—nature independent of mind or humankind and "a world which would exist . . . even if every kind of sentient being in the universe were to be eliminated tomorrow, or indeed had never even come into existence."[45] First and worst of all, the reflection theory of knowledge stifles the creative power of thought and robs philosophy of its power to transform and emancipate the world. In it thought or the mind is a *camera obscura* whose "reflected" product is only an upside-down image of the external world. Second, Ruben misplaces his emphasis—though far less than Harris—on epistemology over ontology and misguides Marx's materialism into monistic naturalism. Third, Ruben profoundly misunderstands the role of the dialectic in Marx: the dialectics of human and nature, subject and object, consciousness and reality, thought and action. It should be remembered that the opposite of the dialectic is not duality, but dualism. The dialectic is a double-edged sword. It rejects dualism on the one hand and reductionism on the other. It is a theory of reality in which the two opposites are interdependent, whether they be thought and action, the master and the slave, or the capitalist and the proletariat. Furthermore, the question of whether nature or world is human-dependent or human-independent (*praxis*-dependent or *praxis*-independent) in Marxism as a philosophy of *praxis* is a meaningless one or, at best, one of secondary importance. From the standpoint of *praxis*, what really matters is the interaction between human beings and the external world or the appropriation of nature by the human species.

In his *Adventures of the Dialectic,* Merleau-Ponty calls Leninism a "gnosticism" because in *Materialism and Empirio-Criticism,* for example, Lenin adds a heavy dose of "materialistic metaphysics" to the dialectic. The diagram of Lenin's Bolshevism places the knowing subject outside the fabric of history, releases it from self-criticism, inserts the subjective into the objective, and reduces the order of possibility to that of fact. On the epistemological plane, Lenin's gnosticism shuts itself off from philosophical challenges concerning humankind and history. On the practical plane of translating epistemology into the order of action, Lenin's Bolshevism "means replacing total praxis by a technician-made action, replacing the proletariat by the professional revolutionary. It means concentrating the movement of history, as well as that of knowledge, in an apparatus."[46] The Party elitism and bureaucratism of Lenin is a *natural* result of his epistemological gnosticism. In short, Lenin's Bolshevism is an insertion of the *movement* of both historical knowledge and action into an institutionalized and regimented apparatus, that is to say, both *theōria* and *praxis* are functions or instruments reduced solely to the "matters" of the *apparatchiks* or "produced" and "administered" by the Party machines. Ultimately, his epistemological and practical bureaucratism is a result of treating the "iron law" of the dialectic as identities: the unequivocal identity of the Soviets with the people, the Party with the Revolution, the professional revolutionaries with the Party, the Party with the dictatorship of the proletariat, and finally the Party with the State itself, which is Hegelian rather than Marxian.

All in all, it is only as phenomenology that Marx's epistemology can be understood. Phenomenology provides a better approach here than does the reflection theory of knowledge due to the way phenomenology rejects "idealist" subjectivism on the one hand and "scientific" or positivist objectivism on the other. Marx's epistemology is neither "empiricism" nor "intellectualism" in the sense that Merleau-Ponty understands them and is critical of them for the following reasons:

> Where empiricism was deficient was in any internal connection between the object and the act which it triggers off. What intellectualism lacks is contingency in the occasions of thought. In the first case consciousness is too poor, in the second too rich for any phenomenon to appeal compelling to it. Empiricism cannot see that we need to know what we are looking for, otherwise we would not be looking for it, and intellectualism fails to see that we need to be ignorant of what we are looking for, or equally again we should not be searching.[47]

Phenomenologically understood, Marx's thought is neither "idealistic" (*intellectualist*) nor "reflective" (*empiricist*) as in Lenin's epistemology *à la* Ruben.

The "critique of ideology" (*Ideologiekritik*) has been the most productive and prominent aspect of the Marxian theory of knowledge *founded on* or *grounded in* materialist ontology. Despite its tendency to sociologize or oversociologize the *Cogito,* it has been useful in unveiling the socioeconomic sediments hidden in all thought. Marx's critique of ideology is an archaeology of a "false consciousness" or of the "hidden," "unconscious," or "sedimented" dimension of reality. Its tradition has now been continued with the critical theory of the Frankfurt School in alliance with new developments in psychoanalysis. Marx's critique of ideology is rooted in the idea that consciousness, both theoretical and practical, is determined by social existence. Consistent with Marx's emphasis on labor and economic activity in social existence, ideas have their socioeconomic contents and serve the domination of one class over the other. Crudely put, all ideas are the manifestations of class consciousness and interests. As Kosík says, "Marxist critique detects social and economic content in *every* philosophy, including the most abstract, because the subject who elaborates a philosophy is no abstract 'spirit' but a concrete historical person whose reasoning reflects the totality of reality, complete with his own social position."[48]

A reductive tendency in Marxism lies in its emphasis on the economic as the primary ontological category and the basic foundation of all other social relationships. It should be mentioned here that Jürgen Habermas's critique of Gadamer's hermeneutics has its basis in Marx's philosophy of *praxis*. With Heidegger's inspiration, Gadamer, in his *Truth and Method* (1960), proposes that because language is a privileged medium between human beings and the world, truth can be defined in terms of "linguisticality" (*Sprachlichkeit*).[49] In turn Habermas accuses Gadamer of committing the "idealism of linguisticality." [50] For, according to Habermas, language itself is ideological in that it is a medium of social relationships (power, domination, work, or life-practice). Thus for Habermas, hermeneutical reflection must give way to the critique of ideology. In reply to Habermas, however, Gadamer asserts that Habermas's theory of interests is itself an aspect of hermeneutical reflection. As he contends, it is absurd to suggest that the concrete factors of work and politics (the material being of life-practice) have nothing to do with the hermeneutical reflection of language. For one thing, a critique of ideology that intends to unmask the "deceptions of language" is, of course, also a linguistic act of reflection. What hermeneutical reflection as "effective reflection" insists here is not that linguisticality determines all *praxis*, but rather that there is no practical, social reality that is represented in consciousness without ever being formulated and articulated linguistically: all reality, Gadamer rightly insists, happens *within* language. A critique of ideology, however critical and effective it may be in unmasking the material, practical, or societal "prejudices" behind the veil of language, is a particular form of hermeneutical reflection on "prejudices" because nothing is "prejudice" without being unveiled in language or articulated linguistically. This is indeed the efficacy of Gadamer's hermeneutical awareness (*wirkungsgeschichtliches Bewusstsein*) as a linguistic critique (*Sprachkritik*).[51]

Furthermore, another resonance with the Marxist critique of ideology might be discerned in Husserl's attempt to disclose the meaning-genesis of science in the life-world (*Lebenswelt*), for the aim of Husserl's critique of scientism is to show the way in which the life-world may be *occluded* in science. Thus the Marxist critique of ideology and Husserl's critique of scientism would seem to reciprocally echo one another. In this respect, Enzo Paci discovers phenomenology in Marxism and Marxism in phenomenology, with each augmenting or complementing what is lacking in the other. The increasing awareness of the problem of scientism within the Marxist movement and its own self-criticism is due undoubtedly to Husserl's influence.

In *The Crisis of European Sciences and Transcendental Phenomenology,*[52] Husserl defines the life-world as the most comprehensive horizon of meaning structures in everything we think and do. Thus the discovery of the phenomenology of the life-world has been heralded as one of "the most momentous accomplishments of contemporary philosophical thought."[53] In his seminal work, Husserl aims to establish the sociocultural life-world as the *"founding matrix"* of all theorizing in both science and philosophy. Echoing Husserl, Merleau-Ponty emphasizes the natural landscape of the life-world as the foundation of the conceptual geography of science when he says:

> The whole universe of science is built upon the world as directly experienced, and if we want to subject science itself to rigorous scrutiny and arrive at a precise assessment of its meaning and scope, we must begin by reawakening the basic experience of the world of which science is the second-order expression. Science has not and never will have, by its nature, the same significance *qua* form of being as the world which we perceive, for the simple reason that it is a rationale or explanation of the world.[54]

According to Husserl, modern science begins with Galileo's mathematization of nature. It was Galileo who mathematized nature and formulated the idea of mathematics as a universal language of science. For Galileo and his heirs, the certainty of knowledge, scientific or otherwise, depends on the idealization of nature as a mathematical manifold—the ideal reduction of nature to the geometric boxes of triangles, circles, and squares. Husserl's important insight is the notion of "a garb of ideas" (*Ideenkleid*) in which what is concealed or veiled in the mathematization of nature is in fact the prescientific world called the life-world whose perceptual and cognitive style is presupposed in all conceptualization. From Husserl's notion of the *Ideenkleid* there emerges a critique of scientism that exposes the taken-for-granted conceptual garb whereby what once was, or was intended to be, true in the mathematical idealization of nature *as a method* has gradually been taken or indeed mistaken for reality itself (i.e., conceptual reification). According to Husserl,

Mathematics and mathematical science, as a garb of ideas, or the garb of symbols of the symbolic mathematical theories, encompasses everything which, for scientists and the educated generally, *represents* the life-world, *dresses it up* as "objectively actual and true" nature. It is through the garb of ideas that we take for *true being* what is actually a *method*—a method which is designed for the purpose of progressively improving, *in infinitum*, through "scientific" predictions, those rough predictions which are the only ones originally possible within the sphere of what is actually experienced and experienceable in the life-world.[55]

Thus it is very tempting to compare Husserl's critique of scientism as the *Ideenkleid* that occludes the life-world in science with Marx's critique of ideology. If we regard the life-world as the meaning horizon of quotidian sociocultural relationships, then it is the base, whereas science is a "superstructure." Paci claims that "[what] Husserl did not know is that the crisis of the sciences, as the occluded use of the sciences that negate the subject, is the crisis of the capitalist use of the sciences, and, therefore, the crisis of human existence in capitalist society."[56] In grafting phenomenology onto Marxism, the phenomenologist Paci does not suggest naively that by occluding the life-world, scientism reflects the capitalist economic or class structure. Rather, he suggests that this occlusion basically involves the negation or "forgetting" of the human being as the subject of thought and action. Nor is it suggested uncritically and crudely, as some Marxists do, that the bourgeois mind is apt to be a mathematical mind, and *vice versa*.[57]

Marcuse also correctly sees that Husserl's archaeology of scientism, represented in Galilean physics or the Galilean style of science, is not a sociology of knowledge. However, Marcuse interprets Husserl's critique of science in the direction of the technological mastery of nature, since geometry is the measuring and quantifiable discipline of space that is a prerequisite for the domination of nature. Therefore, for Marcuse, the fundamental insight of Husserl's critique of science based on the phenomenology of the life-world lies in its discovery of the hidden, unexamined, and "irrational" core of scientific rationality, for "pure science has an inherently instrumental character prior to all specific application; the Logos of pure science is technology and is thus essentially dependent on external ends."[58] Thus for Marcuse, Husserl's demystification of science by phenomenological reduction (*epoché*) is "a therapeutic method" that parallels the aim of Marx's critique of ideology and, for that matter, Marcuse's own critique of technological rationality in advanced industrial societies today.

However, Marcuse is critical of Husserl's critique of science at several crucial points. Like Paci, Marcuse regards Husserl's reduction (*epochē*) as going *behind* the problem of reification. Unlike Paci, however, Marcuse is critical of Husserl's "conceptual meta-language" for failing to come to grips with "the constituent subjectivity" for the critical analysis of the "empirical reality" that is the life-world itself. In essence, for Marcuse, Husserl's transcendental subjectivity couched in a conceptual metalanguage is unable to explain and overcome the crisis of European science and thus of European humanity. For Husserl's transcendental subjectivity is "a pure cognitive subjectivity." Thus Marcuse contends that "one does not have to be a Marxist in order to insist that the empirical reality is constituted by the subject of thought *and of action*, theory and practice."[59] Marcuse's ultimate contention is that although Husserl recognizes the "fetishism" (Marcuse's term) of scientific rationality, he fails to come to terms with the realization of *humanitas*, simply because he replaces the hubris of pure science with that of pure philosophy, thus concealing its own "ideological veil"— which, according to Marcuse, is inherent in all transcendentalism since Kant. To rephrase it simply, Marcuse's contention is this: Husserl's transcendental phenomenology is a philosophy of *theōria*, not of *praxis*, although what the "ideological veil" of Husserl's philosophy might be is left unexplained.

Marcuse, I think, misunderstands the intention and execution of Husserl's critique of science. Husserl is not directly concerned with a critique of the "instrumental rationality" of science, although he recognizes the use of science for the technical control of nature.[60] Instead, his critique of scientism as conceptual reification aims to ground scientific epistemology in the ontology of the life-world, that is, to disclose its ontological presuppositions. To be sure, no one—including Marcuse himself—is prevented from "extending" Husserl's critique of science to a critique of technological rationality—a critique that is neither unimportant nor undesirable. For the development of modern technology such as nuclear technology and genetic engineering is inconceivable without the development of pure sciences such as nuclear physics and genetic biology. Thus a critique of technology presupposes a critique of science, that is, the latter precedes the former. Contrary to Marcuse, the point is simply that science turns into technology but *is not* technology itself, that is, the theoretical knowledge of nature is not the same as the practical mastery of it. At this point one might be critical of Husserl's lack of serious concern for technology as an extension of science. However, Marcuse has no need to criticize Husserl on this point precisely because Marcuse saw—that is, misunderstood—technology as the *logos* of science itself.

Husserl's critique of science, as Marcuse himself rightly points out, is a *philosophical* analysis, which by its very nature distanciates itself from science or the life-world. As a philosophical analysis, Husserl's critique discloses the "hidden" meaning-genesis of

155

Being, Praxis, and Truth

science (or for that matter, of all forms of conceptualization) in the everyday life-world. Like Heidegger, he reminds science of its "forgotten" origin in life-worldly being. Conceptual reification arises in science from the forgetting of the life-world as the origin of its meaning. By this ontological rehabilitation Husserl aims to establish the "forgotten" life-world as "the universal medium of access" to the world of all conceptualization. Aron Gurwitsch points out:

> As a product of the mind, science of the Galilean style requires phenomenological clarification. Because of the role of the life-world as the presupposition of scientific construction, the problems which (if one is to be systematic) must be attacked first are those related to the life-world itself and the experience through which it presents itself, i.e., perceptual experience. Subsequently, a phenomenological account must be given of the higher intellectual processes which, like idealization, formalization, and so on, are basic to the construction of the pure mathematics and the mathematization of nature.[61]

So, contrary to Marcuse's criticism, *conceptual distanciation* in Husserl's transcendental phenomenology is a matter of philosophy's integral requirement but expresses no hubris or contempt for the "empirical reality" of the life-world as Marcuse alleges. Nor is it a claim for the superiority of *theōria* over *praxis*. In no way does the conceptual metalanguage of phenomenology in the name of reduction (*epochē*) imply its superiority over the ordinary discourse of common people. Even Gurwitsch's insistence on the "higher intellectual" account of phenomenology over science is a matter of defining the former's priority rather than superiority over the latter. What is so ironical in Marcuse's criticism of Husserl's alleged hubris of cognitive subjectivity is that in criticizing "positive thinking" as an attempt to validate cognitive thought by experience of facts, Marcuse himself disdainfully speaks of Ludwig Wittgenstein's and John Austin's "ordinary language philosophy" as engaging in "baby talk."[62] Marcuse too wished to *distanciate* cognition from fact, philosophy from ordinary existence, *theōria* from *praxis*—legitimately so, because to function effectively, a philosophy of *praxis* is always nothing but conceptualization *about praxis*, from which it must assume its proper distanciation. The real difficulty of Husserl's transcendental phenomenology, which Marcuse forgets to mention or explore, is not just that it is purely cognitive but that, as Schutz noted, it is incapable of justifying intersubjectivity as crucial to social and political theorizing, which is in itself a *philosophical* problem. Furthermore, one of the main aims of philosophy is to question the presuppositions of the empirical sciences and the meaning they have for universal humanity. For

Husserl, therefore, the philosopher's ultimate aim as "civil servant"—of course, without the ideological trappings of being a technocrat or bureaucrat—through the "heroism of reason" is nothing more than to *aid* the preservation of European humanity and civilization.

IV. Conclusion

Thus far we have emphasized the possibility of a *dialectical coupling* of phenomenological ontology and Marxism, that is, we have explored their *convergences and divergences*. The very possibility of a dialogue between these two philosophical movements centers around the grand theme of philosophical anthropology, which attempts to specify what is distinctively human or define human specificity. However, there is a "reductive" and "dogmatic" tendency in the movement of Marxism: a tendency to reduce theory to the instrument of action, philosophy or epistemology to a critique of ideology, the human to the economic, *praxis* to labor (producing) and work (making), alienation to capitalism, consciousness to the "reflection" of matter, humanity to the proletariat, politics to the Party, freedom to necessity, and sociality to collectivity. From the standpoint of phenomenology, the failing of Marxism is its tendency to *identify* the whole *with* one of its parts. Having surveyed critically the original contributions of Marx's materialism and the Marxist movement to the understanding of humankind and history, Leszek Kolakowski comes to the conclusion that "Marx at times enunciated his theory in extreme, dogmatic, and unacceptable forms. If his views had been hedged round with all the restrictions and reservations that are usual in rational thought, they would have had less influence and might have gone unnoticed altogether."[63] This is indeed the true hallmark of the great thinkers from Plato to Heidegger. They are the "hedgehogs" of human thought who, according to the Greek poet Archilochus, know only one big thing.[64] Paradoxically, however, any great thinking has a price to pay. We shall conclude our analysis with a critical note on the price Marx's "humanism" has to pay for its greatness.

As Kierkegaard observed, concepts have their histories and they, just like individuals, cannot withstand the ravages of time.[65] If we are to be true to the logic of Marx's own thought as dialectical, we should think of it in terms of *doing* Marxism, just as we speak of *doing* phenomenology. Thus in doing philosophy, Marxism as a *movement*—for that matter, every philosophical movement—needs continual interpretation in order to preserve and transmit its tradition and to renew it at the same time. For interpretation is the dialectical appropriation of the past tradition for the sake of both the present and the future. As Ricoeur emphasizes, "tradition . . . , even understood as the transmission of a *depositum,* remains dead tradition if it is not the continual interpretation of this deposit: our 'heritage' is not a sealed package we pass from hand to hand, without ever opening, but rather a treasure from which we draw by the handful and which by this very act is replenished. Every tradition lives by grace of interpretation, and it is at this price that it continues, that is, remains living."[66] Thus interpretation as the dialectic of transmission and renewal is both unavoidable and necessary to "living Marxism." Despite what Marx said about "interpretation" in favor of "transformation," the spirit of hermeneutics and that of living Marxism are in this light not incompatible. The creative interpretation of Marx's thought seems needed now more than ever before, if Kolakowski's concluding remarks in his study of Marxism as a movement are correct: "At present Marxism neither interprets the world nor changes it: it is merely a repertoire of slogans serving to organize various interests, most of them completely remote from those with which Marxism originally identified itself."[67] Inasmuch as phenomenology cannot ignore Marxism, phenomenological ontology can have an instructive place in living Marxism. After all, they are both revisionary philosophies whose aim is to establish the foundations of humankind and the earth.

Technology is one of the most important issues of our time. Human emancipation as the *telos* of *praxis* is unthinkable without relating it to the prevailing issues of technology, which controls the destiny of humanity today. In a letter written on April 9, 1976, to the participants in a colloquium on his thought at De Paul University in Chicago, Heidegger urged them to look into the issue of an interface between modern science and technology because "the rapidly increasing efficiency of these drives the forgottenness of Being to the extreme and thus makes the question of Being appear irrelevant and superfluous."[68] For him, the question of technology is bound up with the entire tradition of Western metaphysics from Plato to Nietzsche. The question of Being cannot escape the question of technology. For they together open up the possibility of a "transformed abode" of the human being in the world, which has become universally technologized. Michael E. Zimmerman goes directly to the heart of Heidegger's thought when he says: "Heidegger's most important legacy will be his fundamental insights into the nature and problem of technology."[69] Husserl too, as I have discussed above, explored the meaning-genesis of modern science based on Galileo's mathematization of nature, which made possible humanity's technical control of nature. Despite the seminal contribution of Marx to many human issues, his weakness emerges from the forgetting in his later thought of the "initial question" he raised concerning the inseparable relation between the humanization of nature and the naturalization of humankind in *The*

Economic and Philosophic Manuscripts. Although the question of humanizing nature preoccupied his later thought, the question of naturalizing humankind had fell into oblivion. Today, however, it is worthwhile to recall his "initial question."[70] The tendency of Marx's materialistic "humanism" to exploit nature or the earth based on labor and work as the "producing" and "making" capacities of the human being prompted Heidegger to conclude that "the essence of materialism is concealed in the essence of technology, about which much has been written but little has been thought."[71]

The development of Marx's thought as a whole is no doubt anthropocentric. In so concluding, however, I do not mean to underestimate or reject his fundamental insights into human specificity or eccentricity in opposition to both logocentrism and biologism, which reduce the human to conceptual thought in the first case and the human to the nonhuman in the second. Anthropocentrism, which may or may not be logocentric but is never biocentric, ignores the nonhuman or assimilates it into the human (e.g., nature becomes "a social category").[72] Marx's "economic analysis" based on labor and work is meant to emphasize the value of appropriating nature for humankind. By means of our labor and work we make nature instrumental to our needs and ends. What Heidegger said about Marx's fundamental insight into alienation refers to the alienation of human being from human being. However, human beings have now become "homeless" in separating themselves, with the aid of technology, from the earth that is their natural habitat or household (*oikos*). For Marx, the species-nature of humankind as social being whose opposite is alienated humanity (in capitalist society) refers to the relation only between human being and human being, but not between humankind and nature and earth. In the tradition of Hegel, Marx affirms nature (*an-sich*) as the "negation" of the human being (*für-sich*). Material scarcity itself is viewed as the negation within humankind of humankind by matter or external nature. In Marx's "humanism," as we have already mentioned, the idea of the human being as a natural, sensuous, and embodied being has a twofold purpose: first, it is to oppose the logocentrism of Hegel; second, by incorporating it into a philosophy of labor (producing), work (making), and *praxis* as *technē*, Marx opened up the way to justify the endless appropriation and exploitation of nature for human desires, needs, and demands.[73] Although Heidegger's care, unlike Marx's labor, lacks specificity, the advantage the former has over the latter is that, as I have already intimated in passing, it has no exploitative connotation. In short, Marx's "humanism" became preoccupied with the humanization of nature at the expense of the naturalization of humankind. In it the question of technology is assumed to be one of use and misuse to meet human requirements.

In conclusion, we propose the idea of a "new humanism" or a new philosophy of humanity in the ontological tradition of Heidegger and Merleau-Ponty—a philosophy that is able to reconcile the human being with nature without abolishing human specificity. This may require an "archaeology"—in Michel Foucault's sense of tracing backward rather than tracing forward as in "history"—of Marx's thought for the purpose of reopening and reevaluating the "forgotten" dimension of his "initial question." This new humanism is a philosophy of planetary humankind that is *not* anthropocentric. In *expanding* the idea of "sociality" to the relation of humanity and nature, it envisions truth as vision at work and vision as nature at work. The *Tao* of the dialectic is a "coupling" or an "intertwining" of the human and the natural and its talisman is the "synergic body" or "flesh" (Merleau-Ponty's terms), which is a bi-dimensional and bi-directional phenomenon: the idea of "two in one" and "one in two." This new humanism is an ontology of de-centered humankind with a vision of truth that is neither entirely "spiritual" nor entirely "material," but is capable of sustaining a "chiasm"—not a chasm—between the two.[74]

The essence of truth is freedom.

—Martin Heidegger,
On the Essence of Truth

Eight

THE QUESTION OF THE MORAL SUBJECT IN FOUCAULT'S ANALYTICS OF POWER

THE QUESTION OF ETHICS has preoccupied Michel Foucault throughout the different stages of his thought. Ethics and politics are for him inseparable. In his early major work, *The Order of Things,* he asserted that "[the] knowledge of man unlike the sciences of nature is always linked, even its vaguest form, to ethics or politics."[1] In his 1983 interview in Berkeley he reiterated his interest in "politics as an ethics."[2]

There is one phrase that marks the distinguishing characteristics of Foucault's thought: the ubiquity of power. "A society without power relations," he declares, "can only be an abstraction."[3] In Foucault's thought, power may be said to be the linchpin of all social relations in connecting everything to everything else. It is embedded in all human events and institutions, not just in what has traditionally been called "government," the "state," or political institutions. From beginning to end, the thematics of power have been the *leitmotif* of Foucault's investigation of differing topics. By its ubiquity, power attains an ontological status, as it were, in Foucault's thought. It is everywhere and comes from everywhere: it is "always already" here and there. The most seminal insight of Foucault is the idea that power exists *as relations,* and this relational mode of investigating power is called by him the *analytics of power.* For power is regarded not as a static substance (*res*) in the Cartesian tradition, but as an ensemble of dynamic relations. Foucault writes:

> Power in the substantive sense, *"le" pouvoir,* doesn't exist. What I mean is this. The idea that there is either located at—or emanating from—a given point something which is a "power" seems to me to be based on a misguided analysis, one which at all events fails to account for a considerable number of phenomena. In reality power means relations, a more-or-less organized, hierarchical, co-ordinated cluster of relations.[4]

In confluence with the French structuralism of Claude Lévi-Strauss, Roland Barthes, Jacques Lacan, and Louis Althusser, Foucault rejected the notion of the subject. While in *The Savage Mind,*[5] which is a polemic against Jean-Paul Sartre, Lévi-Strauss enunciated the "dissolution of man," Foucault wrote the following requiem in the concluding sentence of *The Order of Things:* "Man would be erased, like a face drawn in sand at the edge of the sea."[6] It is in his introductory remarks to *The Archaeology of Knowledge* that we find the sharpest reaction to a subjectivity that could be construed narrowly as phenomenological or broadly as post-Cartesian or post-phenomenological:

> If the history of thought could remain the locus of uninterrupted continuities, if it could endlessly forge connexions that no analysis could undo without abstraction, if it could weave, around everything that men say and do, obscure synthesis that anticipate for him, prepare him, and lead him endlessly toward his future, it would provide a privileged shelter for the sovereignty of consciousness. Continuous history is the indispensable correlative of the founding function of the subject: the guarantee that everything that has eluded him may be restored to him; the certainty that time will disperse nothing without restoring it in a reconstituted unity; the promise that one day the subject—in the form of historical consciousness—will once again be able to appropriate, to bring back under his sway, all those things that are kept at a distance by difference, and find in them what might be called his abode. Making historical analysis the discourse of the continuous and making human consciousness the original subject of all historical development and all action are the two sides of the same system of thought. In this system, time is conceived in terms of totalization and revolutions are never more than moments of consciousness.[7]

It seems that what is crucial in the context of our discussion on the moral subject of power is not the question of whether Foucault is a philosopher of continuity or discontinuity, but of how the idea of continuity or discontinuity funds the movement of the historical subject.[8] Here Foucault's argument concerning the *necessary* and *sufficient* connection between the sovereignty of consciousness and historical continuity falters and is short-circuited in several ways.

First of all, a critique of phenomenological subjectivity requires the consideration of phenomenology as the constitution of meaning—including, of course, the constitution of internal time-consciousness in terms of "retention" and "protention"—by the transcendental *ego* to attain the apodicticity of knowledge. In short, it needs a critique of phenomenology as a "metaphysics of presence."

Second, Foucault fails to take into account Maurice Merleau-Ponty's phenomenological idea of the "instituting subject," so as to avoid the "egological" predicament of the "constituting subject." To quote fully Merleau-Ponty's own words:

> If the subject were taken not as a constituting but an in-stituting subject, it might be understood that the subject does not exist instantaneously and that the other person does not exist simply as a negative of myself. What I have begun at certain decisive moments would exist nei-ther far off in the past as an objective memory nor be present like a memory revived, but really between the two as the field of my becoming during that period. Likewise my relation to another person would not be re-ducible to a disjunction: an instituting subject could co-exist with another because the one instituted is not the immediate reflection of the activity of the former and can be regained by himself or by others without involv-ing anything like a total recreation. Thus the instituted subject exists between others and myself, between me and myself, like a hinge, the consequence and the guar-antee of our belonging to a common world.[9]

In addition to overcoming the impasse of conceptualizing inter-subjectivity or coexistence as the relation between the self and the other, the advantage of this ontological hinge is at least threefold. (1) It overcomes both the overdetermination and the underdeter-mination of the self over the other or, ethically speaking, the po-larization of total power and total freedom, or total submission and absolute freedom; (2) it offers a judicious balance between innova-tion and tradition as sedimented meanings; and (3) it gives us the conception of human plurality as a dialectical complicity of distinc-tion and equality. Here we are turning to the language of Hannah Arendt's *The Human Condition,* where human plurality as the ba-sic condition of both speech and action is conceived of as having the twofold character of equality and distinction. If human beings were not equal, she explains, there would be no common ground for communicating or acting; if human beings were not distinct, on the other hand, there would again be no need to communicate or act. Distinction—individual differences—thickens the density of human plurality.[10] Similarly, Emmanual Levinas maintains that pluralism is not a multiplicity of numbers, but is predicated upon "a radical alterity of the other."[11]

Third and last, if history is viewed as more or less continuous, Foucault must by *logical* necessity recognize some form of subjectivity as sovereign; that is, he harbors or shelters the privileged status of consciousness. If, on the other hand, history is viewed as discontinuous, he is compelled to abandon the sovereignty of consciousness. Contrary to Foucault's own argument, moreover, the sovereignty of consciousness becomes the *precondition* for the thesis that history is discontinuous, because history changes, that is, becomes discontinuous, only by virtue of the sovereign *agency* of consciousness itself. In the end, the question of whether history is continuous or discontinuous would be dissolved by itself if we entertain the idea of historical transformation as "transgression," in Georges Bataille's sense, or "destruction," in Heidegger's sense. Then and only then, are continuity and discontinuity two sides of the same historical process. For transgression is not only the overstepping of what is prohibited, but is also delineated precisely by what is prohibited by tradition. Similarly, by "destruction" Heidegger means "a critical process in which the traditional concepts, which at first must necessarily be employed, are deconstructed down to the sources from which they were drawn."[12]

In Foucault's later writings, the retrieval of the subject or the habilitation of a "new subject" may perhaps be seen as enhancing the tenuous links between his own thought and phenomenology or at least rendering the relation all the more ambivalent. We would be remiss if we failed to notice his 1982 discussion of "The Subject of Power" that attempts to go "beyond structuralism"—the structuralism that dissolves "man" as subject. He now attempts to habilitate subjectivity in his analytics of power, which is linked at the same time to freedom, declaring that

> [the] political, ethical, social, philosophical problem of our days is not to try to liberate the individual from the state, and from the state's institutions, but to liberate us both from the state and from the type of individualization which is linked to the state. We have to promote new forms of subjectivity through the refusal of this kind of individuality which has been imposed on us for several centuries. When one defines the exercise of power as a mode of action upon the actions of others, when one characterizes these actions by the government

of men by other men—in the broadest sense of the term—one includes an important element: freedom. Power is exercised only over free subjects, and only insofar as they are free. By this we mean individual or collective subjects who are faced with a field of possibilities in which several ways of behaving, several reactions and diverse comportments may be realized. Where the determining factors saturate the whole, there is no relationship of power; slavery is not a power relationship when man is in chains.[13]

From the perspective of phenomenology, Foucault must not go unchallenged and unanswered. Our primary contention against him is that his *architectonic* of power is built on the shaky grounding of social ontology whose pillars in different sizes and shapes are free, individual subjects. We are reminded here of Henrik Ibsen's play *The Master Builder,* whose main plot is the story of a man who, having dreamt of building a church tower that "points straight up in the free air—with the vane at a dizzy height" and "a real castle-in-the-air" on a firm foundation, plunges in the end to a ghastly death because he has built too tall a house on too shallow a foundation.[14] The phobia of the subject in Foucault's analytics of power is, unfortunately, like teaching people how to swim by continuously teaching aquaphobia.[15] Yet worse, his late addendum— "free subjects" and "new forms of subjectivity"—is like urging someone to swim on dry land! There is, however, a way of constructing social ontology that has a place for the subject but is not subjective, i.e., the conception of the *subject as relational.*

Merleau-Ponty contended that "in Sartre there is a plurality of subjects but no intersubjectivity. . . . The world and history are no longer a system with several points of entry but a sheaf of irreconcilable perspectives which never coexist and which are held together only by the hopeless heroism of the I."[16] To reject the "heroism of the I" is for Merleau-Ponty to decenter the subject toward the affirmation of intersubjectivity. In the analysis of language, the *act* of speaking (*parole*) and the *structure* of language (*langue*) are mutually dependent. For him, therefore, "language makes thought, as much as it is made by thought."[17] According to the linguist Emile Benveniste, "Language is possible only because each speaker sets himself up as a *subject* by referring to himself as *I* in his discourse."[18] Paul Ricoeur, whose hermeneutical phenomenology has been influenced by the linguistic theory of Benveniste, forces the issue against the structuralist, subjectless theory of language by formulating concisely the "habitation of the word" as "a trader between the system and the event" and by asserting that the speaking being of the human being and the spoken being of the world are two interdependent categories.[19] By the same token, all interpretation is the dialectical movement of transmission and renewal. The structure without the event is useless, while the event without the structure is powerless. In the end, the subject who is capable of asserting *I* is never absolutely sovereign and completely isolated: s/he is always already social or intersubjective.

To confirm the desubstantialized, relational analysis of power without subject-phobia, and without sacrificing the idea of novelty and "free subjects," we should resort to auditory metaphors and models against visual ones, whose chronotopical unity is arranged in terms of the primacy of time and space or the "utopia" (*ou/ topos*) of time.[20] In the first place, the auditory "tympanizes" social ontology because the ear is, as Jacques Derrida puts it, "the distinct, differentiated, articulated organ that produces the effect of proximity."[21] In the second place, it enables us to *displace* and *conceptualize* power as polyphonic. Yet the *conception* of power as polyphonic relations preserves the "otonomy"[22] of the self, which arrests hermetically sealed independence at one extreme and totalistic subjugation at the other. Musically speaking, mood as *dis/ position* is the *attunement* of an individual existence to the world as a being-in-the-world. As Heidegger observes: "Mood is never merely a way of being determined in our inner being for ourselves. It is above all a way of being attuned, and letting ourselves be attuned in this or that way in mood. Mood is precisely the basic way in which we are *outside* ourselves. But that is the way we are essentially and constantly."[23]

There is, moreover, a further analogy to be drawn between the ubiquity of power and that of sound. There is a qualitative difference in human experience between the visual and the acoustic. Color does not separate itself from the object, whereas sound separates itself from its source (e.g., voice or the sound of a musical instrument.) In other words, color is a dependent attribute of an object, sound is not. While the color we see is the property of a thing itself and we confront color in space, the tone we here is not the property of anything and we encounter it out of or from space. Color is locatable and localizable in one single position with the object, whereas sound, once separated from its source, has no definite topological property or determination, although its source is locatable. Most importantly, sound travels in no one particular direction; it travels in all directions. Musical tones have no locatable places: they are *everywhere* or *ubiquitous*.[24] The ubiquity of sound does not imply, however, that the language, message, or meaning of music as the organized movement of sound in time is inexact and imprecise. Its meaning or message is played out, just as speech is uttered or enunciated.

Ethics or the ethics of power must be grounded firmly in social ontology—the ontology of social relations.[25] To be more specific, by the basic model of social relations we mean the "neighborhood" or "gathering" in multiple forms of the I (ipseity) and the other (alterity) as equiprimordial in the shared field of time and space. We shall designate as *proximity* this chronotopically shared field of the self and the other as equiprimordial in which the sense of "otonomy" is preserved. By proximity, therefore, we refer to what the social phenomenologist Alfred Schutz calls the consociational relationship (*Umwelt*) or we-relationship (*Wirbeziehung*) in which two (or more) persons share together or simultaneously both a section of time and a sector of space, that is, chronotopical immediacy. It may be called the "paramount" relationship because it is the basic modus by which all other types of social relationship are determined and understood.[26]

Foucault's ethics of power, however, lacks an ethics of proximity or, as it were, an ethics with a human face.[27] To put it more forcefully, there *cannot be any* ethics of proximity in it. It cannot be otherwise because his thought is allergic to the subject, while the basic condition of proximity demands the *confirmation* of the self and the other as two *interdependent subjects*. In order to avoid both extremes of individualizing and totalizing tendencies, we need a third term that has primacy over both ipseity and alterity but does not exclude them as the conditions of its existence: dialogue, conversation, communication or community—that is, the *we* as the union of ipseity and alterity governed by the sense of mutual participation and attunement. It works as the maieutic between the atomization of the individual and the depersonalization of institution.

The literary theorist Denis Donoghue defines conversation as the best form of verbal and responsive communication in a circle of proximity. It may be compared to a theatrical performance before a small, friendly audience conjuring up a sonorous space in which the resonating voice becomes the epitome of human presence. Ideally, conversation is more than communication: it is no less than "communion," because what is most essential in it is the presence of the desire to be with others and to share each other's experience. What matters most, in other words, is the processual rite of giving and receiving rather than what is said and the encoding and decoding of its message. Conversation as communion may be celebrated rather than criticized for its open-endedness and incompletion: "The validity of the words in a conversation is their continuous participation in communication. In a conversation, the two voices are making a music of desire, varying its cadences, tones, intensities."[28]

The ethics of proximity is an embodied phenomenon, which Foucault's "bio-power," too, presupposes. While the Cartesian body as "substance" is the body-object, the ethics of proximity is grounded in the body-subject. The incarcerated body as the object of the Panopticon depicted so forcefully by Foucault in *Discipline and Punish* exemplifies the body-object.[29] It is the *object* of discipline and punishment. In contrast, the body-subject is an active, living agent of communication with the world of others (*Mitwelt*); "the body answers the world by authoring it."[30] Although the body seems distinctively characteristic of Foucault's new subjectivity, particularly in his historical analysis of human sexuality, he seems nonetheless unaware of, if he does not reject, the body as subject. At any rate, he fails to deal with it systematically. Thus, unfortunately, Foucault's analytics of power can offer no ethics of proximity. It was indeed a "defacement" or an "effacement" of the body-subject when he spoke poetically of the erasure of "man" as "a face drawn in sand at the edge of the sea."

The ethics of proximity as an embodied phenomenon is characteristic uniquely of Emmanuel Levinas's phenomenology of the face (*visage*), which is an ethics of the I who is capable of *facing* the other as "you." The face-to-face relation with the other may be called—following Levinas himself—an "interface."[31] To insert the name of Levinas into a phenomenological critique of Foucault's ethics of power is no accident. For Levinas is the social ontologist (or "meontologist") and ethicist *par excellence,* in whose thought "Being" and "value" are chiasmic twins. We can go even further: the primacy of the ethical constitutes a common tie between Levinas and Foucault. For Levinas, the idea of "totality" is purely theoretical, while "infinity" is an ethical category.[32] Foucault's analytics of power or power/knowledge intertwinement, with an accent on the formation of discursive practices, may be regarded as a consolidation in form, as it were, of Levinas's "theoretical" and "ethical" concerns subsumed under the category of infinity without totality.

In Levinas's social ontology, which accentuates the primacy of the ethical, subjectivity is affirmed never for itself (i.e., never monologic or egocentric) but only for another (*pour l'autre*) (i.e., dialogic or heterocentric). Subjectivity comes into being as "heteronomic": "It is my inescapable and incontrovertible answerability to the other that makes me an individual 'I'."[33] Thus the notion of responsibility or answerability that coincides with the ethical or the ethics of proximity is, first and foremost, the confirmation of the I that is what Levinas calls the "meontological version of subjectivity," based on the face as its most basic modus. He writes, therefore, that responsibility is "the essential, primary and fundamental structure of subjectivity. For I describe subjectivity in ethical terms. Ethics, here, does not supplement a preceding existential base; the very node of the subjective is knotted in ethics understood as responsibility."[34] Martin Buber, too, propounded the ethics of responsibility. According to him, there are two primary words: the "I-Thou" and the "I-It." The subject *I* must be the I of either "I-

Thou" or "I-It," or else it is nothing at all: "There is no *I* take in itself, but only the *I* of the primary word *I-Thou* and the *I* of the primary word *I-It*."[35] In either case, the I is always already *relational* or *dialogical* through and through; where there is reality, there is sociality. In responsibility lies the *we* as the midterm between the isolated *I* and the *No-body* (*das Man* or the "anonymous Other," to use Heidegger's word).[36] Only in reference to the *we* does responsibility constitute the *ethical* condition of language itself. The question of "who is speaking" is never entirely subjective. Nor is language totally a subjectless structure for the simple reason that, as Edith Wyschogrod puts it tersely, it "does not float emptily in social space."[37]

Now for Levinas, the face epitomizes the ethics of proximity. It not only establishes the direct and immediate *contact* with the other, but is also solicited by and gravitates toward the other. The face-to-face relation is, Levinas tells us, "the primordial production of being on which all the possible collocations of the terms are found."[38] The face *is* indeed an ethic, a human ethic: "the epiphany of the face is ethical."[39] And since the face speaks (in silence), speaks uniquely from and for each individual, it is an ethical discourse. By the same token, its *look* is not and cannot be determined by the objective color of an eye. In the final analysis, the face is an ethical hermeneutic of the body or the human as embodied.

What is the ultimate *telos* of human plurality or intersubjectivity as polyphonic? For Levinas, it is peace (or harmony). With the idea of peace, the question of the ethical merges with that of the political (*res publica*). In the tradition of phenomenology—including, of course, the ethical phenomenology of Levinas—Hannah Arendt[40] has developed a *public philosophy* with a focus on the *specificity of power* as political. Despite their differences, some of which separate them radically, there are parallels and intersections between Arendt's and Foucault's thought.[41]

Power is defined most generally by Foucault as "the multiplicity of force relations,"[42] which is omnipresent in, and all-pervasive to, every level and dimension of human relationship. This view, however, produces a mixed result because it *both* dismantles *and* obfuscates the established notion of power as specifically political. On the one hand, power is regarded as not being an exclusively political concept. Rather, it—like Foucault's definition of "government"—is extended to encompass a variety of nonpolitical human relationships including knowledge-claims and such institutions as the clinic, the asylum, the prison, the school, the church, and the family. Insofar as power is "decentered," everything we do is political or contains an element of politextuality. On the other hand, Foucault's view obfuscates the *specificity* of power as political, although the conceptual configuration of power as such denies no specificity.

The question of the subject is what puts Foucault and Arendt a world apart. Arendt offers an answer to Foucault's enigmatic question on the subject of power: the primary subject of power *is* the human, moral subject. Her definition of action and power based on the conception of human plurality provides us with the midworld that avoids the Scylla of individualizing and the Charybdis of totalizing tendencies without abandoning the human, moral subject.

For Arendt, the faculty of action alone—not the faculties of labor and work—makes the human being a political animal. Human plurality is the existential and ethical condition of both power and action. Above all, it is an association (*koinonia*) of equals as humans who are all capable of acting. Foremost, however, it is an association of subjects—that is, in Arendt's language, "distinct and unique persons." Human plurality defined as such polyphonically defies the "antipolitical" thought of uniting many into one (*homonoia*).

However, her defense of the human, moral subject in the context of human plurality and politics as polyphonic is not a subjectivist one, since action and isolation are antithetical or mutually exclusive terms. For Arendt, power is human potential "to act in concert" (for the common good), and as such it is impossible in isolation. Thus power is not something in the possession of an individual, a group of individuals, or an organization. True to the existential and phenomenological tradition, on the other hand, Arendt's unwavering defense of the human, moral subject, which is linked to the civility of power, is directed against the undesirable political consequences of the anonymous, faceless One (*das Man*), or "ochlocracy"—to use her own phrase.[43] The exemplar of this "anonymous One" is Adolf Eichmann—the paragon of "thoughtlessness" that appeared to be "terrifyingly normal." It is important to note that Arendt does not argue for the death penalty for Eichmann on the basis of the presence or absence of his *intention to kill*. Her argument against the "banality of evil" rests on the "desubjectivized" ethics of consequences, i.e., on the ethics of responsibility, rather than on the ethics of pure intentions. As Arendt argues, politics is not the nursery, because in it obedience and support are one and the same; and where *all* are deemed or held guilty, *nobody* is. For her, in brief, political ethics makes sense only when there is the human subject, the specific individual, who must be held responsible for the consequences of his/her "thoughtless" yet violent crimes. It was in the name of the moral solidarity of human plurality that she concluded in the last paragraph of her own "verdict" on the Eichmann trial in Jerusalem: " . . . just as you supported and carried out a policy of not wanting to share the earth with the Jewish people and the people of a number of other nations—as though you and your superiors had any right to determine who should and who should not inhabit the world—we find that no one, that is, no member of the human race, can be expected to want to share the earth with you. This is the reason, and the only reason, you must hang."[44]

Arendt's "consensualist" conception of power (and action) as human potentiality to act in concert for the common good includes the existential, Nietzschean idea of *initium* (the initiative) or, to use the phrase of Merleau-Ponty, the "instituting subject" who embarks on something new at his/her birth. Being political is metaphorically conceived of as "second birth." I say "metaphorically" because birth, as the initial insertion of the self into the world, is always already a *de facto*, if not *de jure*, political act. To be born and to act politically are two steps in the same act. What is so interesting about Arendt's discussion is the linkage between natality and (political) action. She writes that "philosophically speaking, to act is the human answer to the condition of natality. Since we all come into the world by virtue of birth, as newcomers and beginnings, we are able to start something new; without the fact of birth we would not even know what novelty is, all 'action' would be either mere behavior or preservation."[45] For Arendt, natality, freedom, and action are the inalienable *birthrights* of men and women as human. Natality is the sacrosanct occasion for a distinct subject—each in his/her own unique way—to embark on something new or novel. By virtue of it, human existence is *invested as freedom* (to use the expression of Levinas, who implicitly refutes Sartre's conception of human existence as condemned to freedom). The investiture of human existence as freedom, however, can never be absolute: there is no unconditional freedom insofar as we, the individuals, inhabit and share the same political arena or universe. "Political theory," writes Levinas, "derives justice from the undiscussed value of spontaneity; its problem is to ensure, by way of knowledge of the world, the most complete exercise of spontaneity by reconciling my freedom with the freedom of the other."[46] Nor is politics a zero-sum game between power and freedom. The dialectical complicity of power and freedom tells us that freedom is not the "end of power," and power is not the "end of freedom."

Most significantly, we should not lose sight of *initium* as the human gift in consortium with others to transform rather than just to preserve. The direction of transformation, however, is not predetermined or preordained. In other words, the future course of human action is unpredictable or—as Arendt put it—"incalculable." The reverse side of unpredictability is irreversibility. In terms of human faculties, they are called the capacity of "promising" and "forgiving," respectively, which marks off human existence from animal life. Arendt goes out of her way to emphasize the "unequaled clarity" of Nietzsche on "the connection between human sovereignty and the faculty of making promises," a point whose relation to Nietzsche's "will to power" is, according to her, often overlooked by Nietzsche scholars.[47] Be that as it may, Arendt shows the indeterminacy of power as political action in terms of its etymological derivation from Greek, Latin, and German: *dynamis, potentia,* and *Macht*—the "potential" character in particular of *Macht* being rooted in *mögen* and *möglich.*[48] The following passage from *The Human Condition* sums up the qualities and attributes of power as the essence of political action: "Power is actualized only where word and deed have not parted company, where words are not empty and deeds not brutal, where words are not used to veil intentions but to disclose realities, and deeds are not used to violate and destroy but to establish relations and create new realities."[49]

What is sadly missing from Foucault's account of power is the idea of *initium* as freedom to transform old realities and create new ones by each subject in concert with others. Being "compatriotic" to power, Foucault's formulation of resistance is ironically—I say "ironically" because his analytics of power is agonistic in form and tone—too undialectical to function effectively as the agent of historical and social change.[50] To use the existentialist language of Simone de Beauvoir, Foucault's formulation allows no genuine "ethics of ambiguity,"[51] that is, the *ambi/guity* particularly between power and resistance.

By way of conclusion, it should be emphasized that the primary subject of power is the human, moral subject who is capable of activating—and activating anew—meaning and value in words and deeds for both him/herself and others. Just as human interexistence is the existential and axiological condition of power, so is social ontology the presupposed ground for the analytics of power. There is the dialogical way of thinking human intersubjectivity that neither overdetermines nor underdetermines the power of the subject. Since we are concerned primarily with the *intelligibility* of power in history and society, there is no easy escape from the notion of subjectivity. Human subjects are called "self-interpreting animals" by virtue of which, as Foucault himself readily acknowledges, the human sciences are differentiated from the natural sciences.[52] To paraphrase the phenomenological thought of Merleau-Ponty, we might say that to be reflective, to be self-interpreting, philosophy must interrogate the set of questions wherein they who question are themselves implicated by the question. Not only would history remain unintelligible and intransigent, but also historical change would be, at best, enigmatic without the subject who triggers it. Defaced humankind at the edge of history and politics is condemned to nihilism.[53] Once power is left to itself without the subject, the moral subject, it subverts or even destroys the very ground and rationale of what defines power as an ensemble of multiple relations.[54] In the end, Foucault's analytics of power is fractured and scarred by the radical discontinuity between the end of "man" and the nascence of the (new) subject. In other words, his idea of new subjectivity is left ungrafted to the analytics of power. And yet to give credence to the idea of historical continuity is to harbor or shelter the sovereignty of consciousness. To translate the same issue into the problematic context of literary theory today: in Foucault's thought, the author dies, without the birth of the reader who is capable of fusing the horizons of the past and the future or mediating the continuity and discontinuity of the world and history as text or intertext.[55] This, I submit, is the ultimate, unresolved dilemma, if not black hole, of Foucault's analysis of knowledge, politics, and history. Yet as long as there are traces and tracks of knowledge, politics, and history, it is premature to renounce, abandon, or write a requiem for the moral subject.

Criticism . . . is the production of knowledge to the
ends of power and, maybe, of social change.
—Frank Lentricchia,
Criticism and Social Change

The rebirth of fantasy as well as of festivity is
essential to the survival of our civilization, including
its political institutions.
—Harvey Cox,
The Feast of Fools

Nine

MIKHAIL BAKHTIN'S BODY POLITIC: A PHENOMENOLOGICAL DIALOGICS

I

THE POPULARITY OF MIKHAIL BAKHTIN is soaring high in literary
circles today, though falling a little short of reaching an eponymous
status—not yet, anyway. Tzvetan Todorov is unrestrained in his enthusiasm for Bakhtin: "He is the most important Soviet thinker in
the human sciences and the greatest theoretician of literature in the
twentieth century."[1] His faithfuls notwithstanding, Bakhtin is indeed a literary "charismocrat." Our enthusiasm for him, however,
inevitably dampens when we are cautioned against enlisting the
help of his thought to justify almost anything. When the Bakhtin
scholars themselves speak unabashedly of "the Bakhtin industry"
while writing on the writings of Bakhtin, they make us awfully un-
easy about discussing him for the fear of joining his bandwagon or
intellectual fashion show, although we can dismiss that kind of talk
as oxymoronic. Bakhtin may best be characterized as a "philosophical anthropologist" in the established Continental tradition of
Heidegger, Gadamer, Scheler, Jaspers, Buber, Merleau-Ponty, and

Ricoeur, whose architectural structure is supported by the dialogical principle. After the announcement—particularly in French philosophy—of the "death of man" (*anthropos*), an announcement that made the "self" into "a cemetery sentinel," philosophical anthropology has become an endangered species. So our effort to preserve it would be a magnanimous gesture indeed. The dialogical principle will be the focus of this essay, since it is the seminal contribution of Bakhtin to the body politic and his master key to unlocking the mystery of human existence.

In Bakhtin's thought, the discovery of dialogue is the recovery of humanity. Dialogue is for him everything: "To be means to communicate dialogically. When the dialogue ends, everything ends."[2] To be human is to be interhuman. The purpose of Bakhtin's body politic based on the dialogical principle is to shape the human by the interhuman, to build a pantheon of the human on the foundation of the interhuman. Bakhtin continues and preserves—in the footsteps of Marx, William James, and Buber—the discovery by Ludwig Feuerbach of a "Thou" that has been hailed as the "Copernican revolution" of social thought.

II

By virtue of the dialogical principle, the human being may be said to be a nexus of social relations in the atmosphere of humanity. We are social through and through; where there is no sociality, there is no reality. Bakhtin sides with Marx, while opposing Freud. As Katerina Clark and Michael Holquist explain, "If in Freud self is suppressed in service of the social, in Bakhtin it is rather a function, indeed a creation of the social. In Freud, the more other, the less self; in Bakhtin, the more other, the more self."[3] It would be a mistake to assume, however, that the self defined as a function of the social in Bakhtin is a hapless homunculus manipulated at will by almighty society. Bakhtin's primacy of the social (dialogical) rejects both individualism/psychologism and sociologism/historicism: the overdetermination of the self or society is a one-sided and thus false idea, and it is detrimental to both. For both individualism and sociologism fail to understand the dialogic of the self and the other.

The prototype of dialogue is the consociational or face-to-face encounter, which has the "chronotopicity" (i.e., temporal and spatial synchronization) of *hic et nunc*. It is the way Denis Donoghue defines "epireading" as dialogical reading in contrast to "graphireading" (monological reading). Based on the Greek *epos* (word, speech, or utterance), epireading is the reading of the text as a transcription of speech in which the reader hears directly the audible voice of an author, whereas graphireading, based on the Greek *gra-*

phos (writing), sees the text as a collage of impersonal signs where the written text attempts to replace the audible voice. For Donoghue, conversation, with its own autotelic flow, is the best form of verbal communication. It may be likened to a theatrical performance before a small, friendly audience in which the resonating voice epitomizes human presence. Conversation is "communion" because what really counts in it is the presence of the desire to be with others and to share each other's experience.[4]

Dialogue is structured as the interplay of speaking and answering (responding). For speaking without the response is monologic. The primacy of the response dictates the happening of a dialogue. For Bakhtin, the matter of "addressivity" is the soul of dialogue and the essence of the logosphere. The anticipated presence of the response gives dialogue and the logosphere the assured sense of pragmaticity. Speaking of the internal dialogism of the word, Bakhtin wrote that

> every word is directed toward an *answer* and cannot escape the profound influence of the answering word that it anticipates. . . . Primacy belongs to the response, as the activating principle: it creates the ground for understanding, it prepares the ground for an active and engaged understanding. Understanding comes to fruition only in the response. Understanding and response are dialectically merged and mutually condition each other; one is impossible without the other.[5]

The idea of answerability or responsibility is endemic to the history of the dialogical principle from Feuerbach in the beginning to Buber and now Bakhtin. Let us remind the reader that the German etymology clearly shows a familial circle of "word" (*Wort*), "answer" (*Antwort*), "to answer" (*antworten*), and "to be responsible for" (*verantworten*).[6] The primacy of the response represents for Bakhtin the movement from the "Ptolemaic" to the "Copernican" mode of language, from the egocentric (monologic) to the heterocentric (dialogic) mode of communication.

The question of the subject, that is, of one *who speaks* or one *who authors* an utterance, is elemental and integral to Bakhtin's dialogism. The presence of intention is constitutive of the human subject. In his recent critique of artificial intelligence or cybernetics, John Searle, the philosopher of the speech act, insists that the presence of intention makes the human voice radically different from a talking machine.[7] However, in the post-phenomenological movement in philosophy today—particularly in France—the subject has been orphaned, exiled, or even treated (mistreated) as an illegal alien. In contrast, the phenomenologist Calvin O. Schrag has launched a heroic program to reclaim "humankind" and the "subject" in the forlorn land of philosophical discourse, that is, to reinstate "a new space for subjectivity" *in* communicative *praxis*. Schrag's reclamation of the subject signals the "homecoming" of the orphaned "subject." His program focuses on the renewed question of "the decentered subject," of the subject who occupies no primary or privileged position in the field of discourse and action.[8] Since decentering means having no privileged center, the decentered subject in the social context resembles *sukiyaki*—one of the favorite among Japanese dishes for Western diners—which is, interestingly, pictured by the semiologist Roland Barthes as "decentered, like an uninterrupted text" both in looks and in the order of ingestion.[9]

In Bakhtin, the dialogical principle, of necessity, decenters the subject. The intention or *initium* of the subject by no means leads to subjectification or subjectivism—let alone subjugation. Dialogization or personalization as opposed to reification is for Bakhtin never "subjectivation."[10] Let us take the placement of the I in Buber's basic formation of "I-Thou" and "I-It." Here the I implies no subjectification because, since it is inseparable from "Thou" or "It" and is a function only of "I-Thou" or "I-It" as a whole, the I of "I-Thou" and the I of "I-It" (whether a "Thou" or an "It" be human or nonhuman) are two radically different I's. Because of the presence of intention or *initium*, the self and, *correspondingly*, the social (dialogical) are for Bakhtin never "given" but always "conceived" or "posited":[11] the social includes the intentional insertion of the subject with no privileged center; thus it is interchangeable with intersubjectivity as viewed by Merleau-Ponty, who once contended that in Sartre's thought, there is only "a plurality of subjects" with "irreconcilable perspectives" glued together only by "the hopeless heroism of the I."[12]

Bakhtin, too, opposes the idea of both "*I* own meaning" and "*no one* owns meaning" and opts for the "middle way": "*we* own meaning." His dialogue of self and other as *we* is no insipid pluralism, because while they are coeval, they are irreducible to each other. Each is *existential* in his/her own right. For the *we* is always and indubitably inter/subjective and cannot be otherwise. It may be called inter-intentional—the meeting of two (or more) intentions. As a matter of fact, only the presence of intention in the self assures the radical alterity of the other as well. "Language," Bakhtin thus writes, "is not a neutral medium that passes freely and easily into the private property of the speaker's intentions; it is populated—overpopulated—with the intentions of others. Expropriating it, forcing it to submit to one's own intentions and accents, is a difficult and complicated process."[13] In sum: the self and the other are co-authors of, and active co-participants in, the ongoing movement of the *we*. Therefore, society as *institution*, not as constitution, has a double meaning: inauguration (instituting) and establishment (institutionalization).[14] In the same vein, we may say that Bakhtin has *instituted* a new way of conceptualizing the human condition.

Here Hannah Arendt's discussion of human plurality is extremely instructive and illuminating. In *The Human Condition*, she contends that "no human life, not even the life of the hermit in nature's wilderness, is possible without a world which directly or indirectly testifies to the presence of other human beings."[15] Human plurality is governed by the dialogic or the two interlocking principles of "distinction" and "equality." The principle of equality refers to the shared quality of human beings as human (i.e., the humanity of humankind), whereas the principle of distinction is the unique, eccentric quality of each human being as individual (*individuum*). Human plurality thus defined would produce *heterarchy*, which is a system of differences, multiple differences.[16]

The principle of distinction refers to the question of the subject as *initium*, of the "who" of speaking and acting, which is, for Arendt, deeply embedded in the existential tradition of Kierkegaard and Nietzsche. To initiate is to embark on something new, as is done by every subject at his/her birth. Here, being political is metaphorically conceived of as "a second birth"—"metaphorically" because birth, as the initial insertion of the self into the world, is always already a *de facto*, if not *de jure*, political act. Thus to be born and to act politically are two steps in the same act, and natality is indissolubly linked with action (including political action).[17] For Arendt, natality, freedom, and action are the inalienable *birthrights* of every human being *as* human. Natality, in other words, is the inviolable opportunity granted each and every individual to embark on something genuinely new or novel, each in his/her own unique way. And it is by virtue of this that human existence is—to use the expression of Emmanuel Levinas—*invested as freedom*. But the investiture of human existence as freedom can never be absolute, for there is no unconditional freedom insofar as we, the individuals, inhabit and share the same geopolitical universe.[18]

III

For Bakhtin, the dialogical principle is quintessentially a linguistic principle.[19] The human being is indeed the language animal—the speaking, talking, verbalizing, or "uttering" animal. Bakhtin's "translinguistics" (*metalingvistika*) is the pillar of his seminal contribution to the body politic. Thus we will focus on the physiognomy and anatomy of his translinguistics in which the utterance is a molecular unit, and the word is an atomic unit, of the dialogue.

Translinguistics is concerned with the *transactional effects* (*pragmata*) and thus entails an ethics. Bakhtin's translinguistics may be defined as "performative utterances" or a parley of performances in order to accentuate the sense of *doing* things with words in the presence of others. What "effective history" (*Wirkungsgeschichte*) is to Gadamer's hermeneutics, translinguistics is to Bakhtin's philosophy of dialogue.

Let us go a step further by taking a cue from Shoshana Felman, who speaks of the "speaking body" (*corps parlant*) and evokes the sense of corporeality or the carnal aspect of language when she views speech (*parole*) as "corporeal promise" (*promesse corporelle*), which beckons a conjugal relationship between Austin's philosophy of language and (Lacanian) psychoanalysis as the "talking cure."[20] Dialogue or conversation is a "parlia-ment" of men/women as "talking bodies." Speaking of Lacan's theory, Felman stresses the fact that the "true thrust" of the psychoanalytic dialogue between the therapist and the client is illocutionary: "Fundamentally, the dialogic psychoanalytic discourse is not so much informative as it is performative,"[21] and thus is unmistakably ethical as well. Because dialogue is an embodied phenomenon, that is, a tactical encounter, we can reappropriate the meaning of Hayden White's neologism called "diatactics"[22] in order to stress what is tactical in a twofold sense: first, the intimate, synaesthetic sense of touch in a circle of talking bodies, and second, the pragmatic side of language-in-use.[23] "Speech," Roland Barthes sums up, "is always tactical."[24]

Performance is already a postmodernist idea.[25] For our purpose here of discussing Bakhtin's translinguistics, the idea of performance, as in the "performing arts," accents the utterance of dialogue as the ethics of *doing* essentially in a twofold way: (1) as embodied phenomenon and (2) as play.[26] Richard Schechner holds that a linguistic model as applied to theatrical performance is suspect because language is "head learning," whereas performance is "body learning."[27]

The notion of language as performance goes back in modern Western thought to the eighteenth-century Neapolitan philosopher Giambattista Vico, for whom "a man is properly only mind, body and speech, and speech stands as it were midway between mind and body."[28] He also observed that "words are carried over from bodies and from the properties of bodies to signify the institutions of the mind and spirit."[29] As he anthropomorphized nature by means of the body in order to animate it, Vico wrote:

> It is noteworthy that in all languages the greater part of
> the expressions relating to inanimate things are formed
> by metaphor from the human body and its parts and

from the senses and passions. Thus, head for top or beginning; the brow and shoulders of a hill; the eyes of
needles and potatoes; mouth for an opening; the lip of a
cup or pitcher; the teeth of a rake, a saw, a comb; the
beard of wheat; the tongue of a shoe; the gorge of a
river; a neck of land; an arm of the sea; the hands of a
clock; heart for center (the Latins used *umbilicus*, navel,
in this sense); the belly of a sail; foot for end or bottom;
the flesh of fruits; a vein of rock or mineral; the blood
of grapes for wine; the bowels of the earth. Heaven or
the sea smiles; the wind whistles; the waves murmur; a
body groans under a great weight. The farmers of
Latium used to say the fields were thirsty, bore fruit,
were swollen with grain; and our rustics speak of plants
making love, vines going mad, resinous trees weeping.
Innumerable other examples could be collected from
all languages.[30]

Bakhtin's view of language as an embodied phenomenon is—to
use the laconic and suggestive expression of Clark and Holquist—
"a Slavic version of Tantrism."[31] It is deeply rooted in and stems
from the kenoticism of Russian Orthodoxy, i.e., the belief in the humanity of Christ and the potential spirituality of matter. The body
is not only the material condition of the soul's existence, but also
the window, as it were, through which we can peep into the condition of our soul. For this reason, the body's playtext is a "deep
play." Not only does the body "speak" and speak the "language"
of silence, but the human being speaks only by means of the body.
The utterance, for Bakhtin, synchronizes or dialogizes mind and
body: the uttered word becomes flesh.[32] There is the important expression in Japanese (Zen) Buddhism called *kufu*, which is the way
of thinking with the whole body rather than just with the head. It
is, as the Japanese would say, "thinking with the abdomen" or with
hara as "the vital center" of the human body. *Kufu* seeks to "un-
stick" the deadlock and dilemma of the intellect in the fields of
mental and spiritual discipline. Thus it is said to be "a sort of spiritual birth pang."[33] The Japanese speak gumptiously of *hara no
aru hito* or *hara no nai hito*, of "a man with or without a belly."
There are also *hara no hiroi hito* and *hara no semai hito*: "a man
with the broad belly" and "a man with the narrow belly." *Hara* or
belly signifies the integrated character or personality of a human
being in the sense of having the vital unity of mental, psychological,
and spiritual qualities.[34]

The body is an active, living agent of communication. It would
be wrong, however, to say that the body is merely the medium of
communication. For it *is* communication, expression in and for itself. Phenomenologically viewed, I *am* my body, and my body is my
way of being-in-the-world with others. To wit: the body *is* indeed

the subject. As Clark and Holquist put Bakhtin's idea of the body/ subject so poignantly and succinctly, *"the body answers the world by authoring it."*[35] This "living body" (the body/subject) is the "source " of Bakhtin's "phenomenology of the senses." In *Love's Body*, Norman O. Brown speaks eloquently of silence as the body's "language." For silence is nothing but the word becoming flesh. "To recover the world of silence, of symbolism," he asserts, "is to recover the human body."[36] To modify his formula slightly by adding two brackets around the letter *m* of the word *mother:* "Silence is the [m]other tongue."[37] We might even speculate that the unconscious is really structured like silence rather than language.[38]

Anybody who is slightly acquainted with the Chinese ideogram would recognize it as a choreography of the body whose artistic rendition, called calligraphy, is the (brush) "painting" of the body as ideogram. Calligraphy is a pantomimic art, somatography. This is the reason that calligraphy is revered by the Koreans and Japanese, as well as by the Chinese, as much as the art of painting itself. In very significant measure, Chinese ideography is a choreography of human gestures—the fact of which should be good enough to take the ideogram as more than, as Hugh Kenner has it, a sinophiliac fad.[39]

Picasso's *Swimmer* (1929) and *Acrobat* (1930) are two choreographs of the human body in fluent and rhythmic motion that approach ideography or calligraphy. They are, in short, dancing or frolicking anthropograms. With the Vichian Samuel Beckett, we can say that in language as gestures, the spoken and the written are identical. Michel Foucault, too, cashes in on the question of the calligram as he discusses René Magritte's paintings, particularly "The Use of Words I" (1928–29) and "The Art of Conversation" (1950), which have come under the influence of the calligrammic poet Guillaume Apollinaire.[40] Each painting or drawing of Magritte is structured like a Zen *koan*—the technique based on a paradox or puzzle, i.e., a surprise element, to attain *satori* (enlightenment). For it is "a systematic attempt to disrupt any dogmatic view of the physical world."[41] For example, Magritte's "The Use of Words I" is a representation of a pipe with the inscription underneath it that reads: "This is not a pipe" (*Ceci n'est pas une pipe*). For Foucault, the calligram "alphabetizes the ideogram."[42] As Magritte said, however, in writing to Foucault, "there is no reason to accord more importance to the invisible than to the visible, nor vice versa,"[43] and thus the calligram ideogrammatizes the alphabet as much as it alphabetizes the ideogram: the two processes are reversible.

The face—the aristocracy of the body, as it were—is itself a corporation of expressions as "ideograms." For Bakhtin, as we have already intimated, the primordial form of dialogue is a face-to-face encounter or "confrontation," that is, the consociation of persons dictated by the chronotopicity of "here" and "now." The face mirrors the structure of a genuine dialogue. It is the most visible and thus the most expressive part of the human body. In an interesting piece from 1939 called "Faces" (*Visages*), Jean-Paul Sartre draws our attention to the privileged and strategic place of the face in human social encounters: "In human societies, faces rule."[44] The face is a *Gestalt* in itself and its movements, like those of the body itself, are gestures. Following the long established tradition of Western thought, Sartre favors the nobility of vision, and the gaze or look points to "the nobility of faces because it holds the world at a distance and perceives things where they are."[45] The most interesting part of Sartre's discussion of the human face is the fact that since we cannot see our own faces in the original, living act of dialogue, the faces of others teach us about our own faces, that is to say, the latter mirror the former. It is the object/ive lesson of heterocentricity, the primacy of the other rather than the self, in the dialogical formulation.

The face "utters" silently, and its utterance is an ethics of silence. The face *is* indeed an ethic, a human ethic: "the epiphany of the face," Levinas declares, "is ethical."[46] As the face speaks (in silence but often elegantly), speaks uniquely from and for each individual, it is an ethical discourse or, better, utterance. The face-to-face relation with the other may be called an "interface"—to borrow the term used by Levinas[47]—where the I is capable of *facing* the other as "you." In "interface," the face not only establishes the direct and immediate *contact* with the other, but is also solicited by and gravitates to the other. The face-to-face relation is, Levinas tells us, "the primordial production of being on which all the possible collocations of the terms are found."[48] In his social ontology that accents the primacy of the ethical, therefore, subjectivity is affirmed never for itself (i.e., never monologic or egocentric) but only for another (*pour l'autre*) (i.e., dialogic or heterocentric). It comes into being as "heteronomic": "It is my inescapable and incontrovertible answerability to the other that makes me an individual 'I'."[49] In Levinas's ontology as in Bakhtin's dialogism, therefore, the affirmation of the I is hitched to the notion of responsibility or answerability. Levinas writes that responsibility is "the essential, primary and fundamental structure of subjectivity. For I describe subjectivity in ethical terms. Ethics, here, does not supplement a preceding existential base; the very node of the subjective is knotted in ethics understood as responsibility."[50] In Levinas as in Bakhtin, in sum, the ethics of "interface" only decenters but does not "deface" or "efface" the subject as the spatial and temporal locus of responsibility.

The most radical and imaginative part of Bakhtin's body politic is the *carnivalization* (dialogization) of the world.[51] Carnivalization is for Bakhtin the political embodiment of play, which, as we have already said, is a cardinal element of the aesthetic in transforming consciousness and creating a new way of conceiving the world by breaking up the colorless and prosaic monopoly of the established order.[52] Bakhtin's provocative study of Rabelais seems to disguise his own personal protest in the form of a "hidden polemic"—as he himself suggested, an engaging form of dialogue— against the oppressive, closed society in which he lived.[53] Carnival or the carnivalesque model of the world deconstructs, transgresses, and transforms the *canonical* order of truth and the *official* order of reality. It is the creation of the imagination incarnate—the regal product of *initium* or *inventio*. The dialogic of carnival intends both to *destroy* a "real" world and to *construct* a "possible" world at the same time. In carnival as deconstruction, dialogue is celebrated as the contemporization (fusion) of time as remembrance of the past and as anticipation of the future, a fusion in which transmission and renewal go hand in hand.[54] Dialogue, in essence, is a protest against the monologic "misrule" of officialdom. The Socratic dialogue, according to Bakhtin, is thoroughly "heresiarchical"—that is, it intends to dismantle the hierarchical: it "does not have to respect hierarchical distinctions; it freely blends the profane and the sacred, the lower and the higher, the spiritual and the material."[55] Above all, Rabelais's body politic breaks down the established tradition of the spiritual as "high" and the material as "low" and brings the former to the level of the latter as if they form a double helix.

Carnivalization is first and foremost the "humorous"[56] play and display of the body in revolt; it is a playtext[57] that feasts on the body politic. Carnival is a vestimentary display—always colorful and often outrageous and extravagant. It is truly a colorful parley. Transvestitism is one of the most revealing expressions of carnival life as the embodiment of the "reversible world." Vesteme points to the semantics of clothes, costumes, dresses, or fashions. The importance of vesteme is often noted by Barthes, who avowedly wears the philosophical garment of Hegel's aesthetics: it is impossible to imagine that the body can even signify anything without clothing. Here only clothing guarantees the rite of passage from pure sentience to meaning.[58] Nonetheless, we may say that for a philosophical dinner, Bakhtin wears dialogical sportswear, while Hegel dresses in a dialectical tuxedo.

So much for vestemes. But since the outside is reversible to the inside, the semantics of the body is a dialectical (or better, diatactical) interplay of clothing and eating (and drinking). It is, in brief, the intertext of vestemes and gustemes. Here Bakhtin and Mao Zedong converge. Mao was fond of using gastronomic metaphors to promote his revolution: "Revolution is not a dinner party"—a double *entendre* in that the making of the Chinese revolution may not be, but will result in, a dinner party for the deprived peasantry. Mao insisted that the mouth has two functions to perform: to speak and to eat (to feed). Bakhtin's work on Rabelais also establishes a set of protocols for the carnivalesque, including gastronomy and gustemes. Bakhtin discovers the interlocking link between the two basic human activities: eating and speaking. He speculates that "the origins of language itself may lie in the sharing of food as a primal expression of culture over nature, establishing a connection between digestion and dialogue."[59] It took the personal experience of deprivation, poverty, hunger, and above all ill health (i.e., "lean time") for Bakhtin to discover the phenomenology of eating as a celebration: "Man's encounter with the world in the act of eating is joyful, triumphant; he triumphs over the world, devours it without being devoured himself."[60]

Carnival life, whose high point in Western civilization was reached in the Renaissance, according to Bakhtin, intends to transform, transgress, and subvert the established order of history and society. He wrote that it

> is past millenia's way of sensing the world as one great communal performance. This sense of the world, liberating one from fear, bringing the world maximally close to a person and bringing one person maximally close to another (everything is drawn into the zone of free familiar contact), with its joy at change and its joyful relativity, is opposed to that one-sided and gloomy official seriousness which is dogmatic and hostile to evolution and change, which seeks to absolutize a given condition of existence or a given social order. From precisely that sort of seriousness did the carnival sense of the world liberate man. But there is not a grain of nihilism in it, nor a grain of empty frivolity or vulgar bohemian individualism.[61]

Carnival is for Bakhtin a celebration of community; it liberates people and brings them together in communal living. Revolution, too, is an act of subversion. However, it is a violent act of subversion to reverse an established social order, whereas carnival, as we have already intimated, is the playful body in rebellion or the ludic form of subversion. For Bakhtin, the most distinguishing characteristic of violence is that *it knows no laughter.*[62] Everything great, he asserts, must have an element of laughter. By laughter Bakhtin means a "laughing laugh" or "Gogolian laugh" that is joyful, open, and festive as contrasted with the laugh that is satirical, negative, and closed. Unlike seriousness, laughter is uplifting and liberating. Bakhtin speaks of the "social, choral nature of laughter, its striving to pervade all peoples and the entire world."[63] While anger, for example, divides, laughter unites. In essence, laughter lifts our barriers and clears our paths toward multilateral relationships with others, while the monologic of violence tends to foreclose the possibility of any dialogue, since it wishes instead to destroy or kill the other.[64] The act of violence is, however momentarily, a failure of nerves, a loss of the will to communicate.

There is a radical difference between revolution and rebellion. One is violent, while the other is not. In promoting dialogue actively and openly, heterarchy makes revolution both untenable and undesirable. For the very idea of revolution or the violent act of subversion puts an end to the dialogue that heterarchy wishes to promote. Violence itself often results from such nondialogical defacements as alienation and anonymity.[65] Here heterarchy decisively takes the side of Albert Camus's "rebel" (or person in rebellion) who renounces calculated violence, whether it be political murder or capital punishment. For rebellion is "a protest against death" as well as against tyranny, brutality, terror, and servitude. The rebel senses and cultivates his/her obligation to human solidarity: according to Camus, "I rebel, therefore we exist."[66] Rebellion is a "mediation" between silence and murder. It is justified by the fundamental existential imperative that "man is the only creature who refuses to be what he is."[67] Since, according to Camus, the rebel is one who says "no" and "yes" in the same breath or act, such a refusal is not a "renunciation," even less a nihilism, because whenever s/he says "no," s/he also says "yes" to something better.

Camus justifies rebellion against revolution in the name of tolerance. "Rebellion at grips with history," he asserts, "adds that instead of killing and dying in order to produce the being that we are not, we have to *live and let live* in order to create what we are."[68] The rebel readily acknowledges the dialogical interplay between the *ethical* principle of culpability and the *epistemological* principle of fallibility, whereas the (serious) revolutionary thrives on the monologic of inculpability and infallibility. While truth, Herbert Marcuse intimates,[69] is the *end* of tolerance, so also untruth licenses the withdrawal of tolerance. Nevertheless, epistemological dogmatism and moral absolutism contradict the essence of Bakhtin's dialogical principle that always and incessantly recognizes the zone of ever present, porous *ambiguity* between doubt and certainty. Most interestingly, Merleau-Ponty uncovers an inherent dilemma in the dialectic of revolutionary violence:

> There is no dialectic without opposition or freedom,
> and in a revolution opposition and freedom do not last

for long. It is no accident that all known revolutions have degenerated: it is because as established regimes they can never be what they were as movements; precisely because it succeeded and ended up as an institution, the historical movement is no longer itself: it "betrays" and "disfigures" itself in accomplishing itself. *Revolutions are true as movements and false as regimes.*[70]

In the end, revolution calls for and tolerates neither dialogue nor dialectic.

IV

Today we are living in a technometropolis. We have indeed become disenchanted with the world whose dominant prose is written in the language of technology and with the modern condition of humanity, which is enframed by the "monocentrism" of technology, including the cybernation of knowledge and the computerization of society. We are all wired to, and become hostages of, the network of technology from which there is no exit in sight. Technology has indeed become totalizing, one-dimensional, planetary, and terribly banal and normalizing, when the fundamental project of macro-technology threatens to create a vast necropolis for the entire earth and bring humankind to the brink of collective extinction or what Jonathan Schell calls "the death of death," and when micro-technology claims to have created our "second self" whose "soul" may soon become, if it has not already become, imprisoned behind the invisible walls of some gigantic technological Panopticon. In these conditions, it is inevitable that, as Merleau-Ponty pointed out, "we enter into a cultural regimen where there is neither truth nor falsity concerning man and history, into a sleep, or a nightmare, from which there is no awakening."[71] So also the Hindu scripture long, long ago had a clear warning for humankind when it said: "I *am* my death."

In the advent of technocratic monocentrism, it is inescapable that Bakhtin's heterarchy as a postmodernist idea should be extended to the deconstruction of the technological. For the technological is to the interhuman what monologue is to dialogue. Bakhtin's heterarchy is inherently heresiarchical because it intends to destroy the "real" world of technocratic monoculture and construct the "possible" world of the dialogical. In the following pages, I shall argue that Bakhtin's dialogism or Bakhtinianism, unlike McLuhanism, is really *ecotopian.*

Technology *disembodies* the human and the interhuman. The human being has now become an extension of the technological itself. Indeed, the medium is the message—to quote the popular slogan of Marshall McLuhan himself. For McLuhan, it is not the body as the subject of the sensorium that touches television, but television that "touches" the human subject, as is clear when he anthropomorphizes television—for that matter, all electronic technology including cybernetics—as tactile.

Technology has also served well the *telos* of the human being as *homo faber* or *homo oeconomicus,* particularly "possessive individualism." Because it is anthropocentric, it is contrary to *ecopiety*—a deeply abiding sense of reverence for the sacrament of coexistence, absolute reciprocity, among all living beings on earth—both human and nonhuman. Ecopiety is divided into *homopiety* and *geopiety:* reverence for interhuman relationships and for human-nature relationships. Geopiety is an extension of Bakhtin's dialogism or heterarchy based on kenosis or "the potential spirituality of matter." For kenosis is capable of transforming nature or *Gaia* from an "It" to a "Thou." Ecopiety underscores the idea that all reality—cosmic, human, and natural—is social. It is the dialogical principle that everything is connected to everything else in the universe. Thus the dialogical principle actively promotes the idea of harmony as a gathering of many as an ordered whole. Insofar as it is an orchestration of differentiated many (polyphony) based on the Arendtian notion of plurality as the dialogic of "distinction" and "equality," harmony is preeminently heterarchical.

The "self-assertiveness" of the human being is anti-dialogical. The anti-dialogical principle of humankind and nature may be called speciesism (or "humanism") and the anti-dialogical principle of human being and human being is individualism. Speciesism is prejudice of the human species against other nonhuman species. It is clearly manifested in the ruthless and rampant manipulation, exploitation, and domination of nature or *Gaia* that culminates in the technocentric *Weltanschauung* of modern humankind. By regarding it as a pile of use-objects, modern technology desacralizes nature. It aids the utilitarian man or woman of labor and work in the production, fabrication, and consumption of goods out of nature's abode.

Individualism is the anti-dialogical principle of relationships between human being and human being that destroys the atmosphere of sociality as a harmonious network of relationships. The ideology of liberalism as "possessive individualism" highlights this anti-dialogical principle of interhuman relationships, which has its modern origin in Hobbes and Locke. In Lockeanism, however, there is a conscious integration of individualism and possessiveness: Locke is the possessive individualist *par excellence,* for the concept of the human being as laborer or exploiter of nature—whose tradition, by the way, Marx inherited—is necessary for the acquisition of private property and wealth. The ideology of Locke's liberalism, with its philosophical foundation laid out by Hobbes, promotes the ethos of technological civilization, which aims to subjugate nature for the exclusive benefits of humankind. The utilitarianism of labor and industry in exploiting and dominating nature or the land, which when uncultivated by human labor is called by Locke "waste," builds the society of acquisitive individuals or "economic humankind." For Locke, things of nature are useless unless they acquire "values" on account of labor and industry. In the end, Lockean possessive individualism incorporates both anti-dialogical principles of relationships between human being and human being on the one hand and between humankind and nature on the other. The possessive individualist in the Lockean tradition, who is also the "functionary" of technology, is thoroughly "self-assertive" in any dealings with other people and with things.

In conclusion, Bakhtin considered dialogue as the contemporization of the old and the new: "There is neither a first word nor a last word. The contexts of dialogue are without limit. They extend into the deepest past and the most distant future. Even meanings born in dialogues of the remotest past will never be finally grasped once and for all, for they will always be renewed in later dialogue."[72] Dialogism is meant for Bakhtin to be an *ethical vocation* that is capable of reenchanting and reintegrating the world by first, and constantly, loosening up playfully its rigid, established structures. In Bakhtin's dialogism, every utterance in the dialogue is intrinsically ethical. This ethical vocation redefines, or gives a new, unique meaning to, the old, already severely battered word *humanism*.

Bakhtinianism is a new humanism or "post-humanist" humanism, so to speak, whose dialogical pantheon can house all beings and things not only human but also nonhuman, whose inexorable *telos* is nothing but the perpetuation of dialogue itself. Bakhtin's dialogical construction of reality works like the master key, as it were, that unlocks the mystery of all things. It is eminently *ecotopian*, not utopian, because it is "everywhere," not "nowhere." The panoptic quality of Bakhtin's dialogism may be likened to the Renaissance Italian humanist Giovanni Pico's idea of mutability explained as "the secret gate through which the universal invades the particular. Proteus persistently transforms himself because Pan is inherent in him."[73] For this if for nothing else, Bakhtinianism is a cause for celebration.

There is one particular cultural object which is
destined to play a crucial role in the perception of
other people: language.
—Maurice Merleau-Ponty,
Phenomenology of Perception

It's performance that matters—pacing, economics,
juxtapositions, aggregation of tone, the whole conduct
of the shaping presence.
—Richard Poirier,
The Performing Self

Ten

LANGUAGE, POLITICS, AND
TECHNOLOGY

I

FOR VERY GOOD REASONS, the human being is said to be *the language animal*. Language discloses the being of humanity and of our
relation to the world, and thus it is without doubt central to human
thought and conduct. The *calling* of philosophy itself is to teach
and learn to think *in* and *through* language about human attunement to the world both natural and social. By understanding the
nature of language, therefore, we hope to understand the essence of
human thought and conduct. Insofar as language is the master key
to the understanding of humankind, it is no accident that the "linguistic turn" fashions the trend of all modern philosophy—analytical philosophy, structuralism, phenomenology, etc.

Language exists for the sake of communication, and expression
is the result of humankind's imperious need and desire to communicate. There are two aspects of the "way" of language or linguistic

expression: one is *meaning* and the other the *medium*. They are inextricably linked, that is, they are *"diatactical"*—to borrow the suggestive word of Hayden White.[1] However, the contemporary discussion of language tends by and large to focus on one or the other but not both, resulting in the dichotomy of the "message" and the "medium" or the reduction of one to the other. Therefore, the following point of Martin Heidegger in *What Is Called Thinking?* is noteworthy: " 'Way' here means melody, the ring and tone, which is not just a matter of how the saying sounds. The way or how of the saying is the tone from which and to which what is said is attuned."[2] Thus language must be understood in terms of the diatactics of the *what* and the *how* of linguistic expression.

As an archaeology of language, phenomenology affirms the primacy of language as performative utterances. For Maurice Merleau-Ponty, the phenomenology of language implies an active conception of historical meaning that transcends the opposition of consciousness and things on the one hand and the individual and the collective on the other. For him, both a philosophy of consciousness (idealism) and a philosophy of things (realism or materialism) are too one-sided or half true, that is, they are false. In the former consciousness is overweighted at the expense of things, while in the latter things are overweighted at the expense of consciousness. As a consequence, they fail to see language as the active mediation between consciousness and things: the one sees language as the creation of pure consciousness, and the other sees language merely as representing things in consciousness. Not only does historical change, the living diatactics of necessity and contingency, parallel linguistic change, but also the presence of the individual in the collective and of the collective in the individual are clearly evidenced in linguistic change and innovation. To avoid the one-sidedness of either idealism or realism, the notion of both consciousness and language may be redefined as an *institution*—that is, a balance between innovation and sedimented meanings or between absolute freedom and total submission. Here we may well cite Merleau-Ponty who writes:

> If the subject were taken not as a constituting but an instituting subject, it might be understood that the subject does not exist instantaneously and that the other person does not exist simply as a negative of myself. What I have begun at certain decisive moments would exist neither far off in the past as an objective memory nor be present like a memory revived, but really between the two as the field of my becoming during that period. Likewise my relation to another person would not be reducible to a disjunction: an instituting subject could coexist with another because the one instituted is not the

immediate reflection of the activity of the former and can be regained by himself or by others without involving anything like a total recreation. Thus the instituted subject exists between others and myself, between me and myself, like a hinge, the consequence and the guarantee of our belonging to a common world.[3]

By defining language as an institution, Merleau-Ponty aims not only to overcome the opposition of consciousness and things, which both idealism and realism fail to do, but also to preserve the notion of language itself as the active synergy of event (act) and system (structure). More important, moreover, the archaeology of language as an institution is also an archaeology of social existence in a double sense: language is not only itself a social phenomenon, but is also the medium of discovering social reality as well as that which makes human communication possible. This is why language is the master key for understanding the human being as a social and political being. Just as the conception of consciousness as an institution aims to overcome the opposition between idealism and realism, so also does the conception of language as an institution attempt to overcome the opposition between the self and the other in defining the meaning of social reality in which the power of language and language of power are coeval and mutually implicated.

Speech and writing are two distinct modes of expression that can be clearly delineated in the historical development of language. There are also two major races of writing: (1) alphabetic and (2) ideographic. Biographically and historically, speech precedes writing. There is then the primacy of speech over writing in the acquisition of language. Speech is performative utterance, which demands performative competence, while writing is literary, which demands literary or grammatical competence. These two different forms of linguistic competences constitute the whole of communicative competence. Although there are certain rules for the performance of speech, stress on grammatical competence in the use of language emerged only with the invention of writing—especially the invention of printing technology or the production of printed books with and after the Gutenberg revolution in the West.

In addition to rhetoric (speech) and grammatology (writing), there is a third important factor in the communicative theory of language: it is the factor of technology or media technology. Those who have focused their attention on the technology of language and communication in recent years have made significant contributions to the theory of language as communication. They have sharpened our awareness of how the various forms of media technology shape and differently transform the patterns of the human sensorium, social relationships, and cultural patterns. However, the distinction between speech and writing is not, as some would insist, a distinction between two forms of technology. The Greek term *technē*, from which the modern use of "technology" originates, was originally meant to be "doing" (art) rather than "making" (technology). Therefore, it is proper to say that speech is an *art* of doing or performing. Although speech may use technology as its medium (e.g., a microphone), speech produces no visible artifacts or external objects. It is *the word made flesh*. It is a function of the natural body, of the bodily organ called the mouth—the tongue, teeth, palate, and lips. Thus Merleau-Ponty writes that "it is no more natural, and no less conventional, to shout in anger or to kiss in love than to call a table 'a table'. "[4] On the other hand, writing not only is a technology, but depends on technology (e.g., ink, papyrus, paper, and keyboard). Therefore, there is a radical or ontological break, if you will, between speech and writing. Keeping this in mind, our discussion based on the phenomenology of language in the following pages will be divided into three themes: (1) the nature of Homeric oral poetry, (2) a critique of Marshall McLuhan's theory of communication, and (3) the ethics of language as performance. Our focus is on the second theme; the first is its prologue and the third is its epilogue.

II

There is no better terse summary of the origin of European thinking than Bruno Snell's in *The Discovery of the Mind*, where he says: "However primitive man's understanding of himself as presented in Homer's speech may appear to us it also points far into the future: *it is first stage of European thinking*."[5] Oral poetry is indeed the beginning of European language and thought, and Homer was an "oral poet"—his poetry was "oral poetry" whose words were sung.[6] T. S. Eliot, who is extraordinarily sensitive to the acoustic effect of poetry, had in mind the speaking power of poetry as the origin of language when he declared that "the poet is *older* than the other human beings."[7] The oral poet is the "first human" and oral poetry the "first language." Although we speak loosely of "oral literature" in order to circumvent cumbersome locutions, oral poetry or "ethnopoetics" is not the same as "literature," which comes only with and after the invention of written language: strictly speaking oral poetry is *not literary*.

Hermeneutics itself was meant to honor its patron saint Hermes and his sacred or magical canon of spoken language. As the legend goes, the god Hermes was the "magician" of spoken words who was "spellbinding." According to the Homeric "Hymn to Hermes," he invented the lyre out of a tortoise shell, the meaning of whose legend is synonymous with the discovery of the universe (uni-*verse*) as the sounding orbit. He was a singer or bard (*aoidos*) as well as a player of the lyre, that is a "herald" (*keryx*): he was a virtuoso of sound-making whose *kerygma* or message was aired by, and encoded in, the sound of spoken words. The term *herald* is related to the Latin *carmen* (song) and the Sanskrit *karuh* (to sing) and *karus* (bard), and the herald's voice scales the pitch of the "signifying excellence of voice." As the "master of speech," Hermes was the messenger of Zeus; in his capacity as a herald he gave Pandora her voice. No wonder, then, this genuine Olympian was "the friendliest of the gods to men."[8]

Music as song and language as speech have the common origin: breath (*thymos*). Breath is an invisible element. It is no accident that crying, the (e-)motion of breath, is the first sign of life. In the Homeric view of humankind, the word *psychē* was affiliated with the breath of life, which departs from the mouth. "To live" is "to breathe": breath is the sign of life, and its stoppage is death. In turn, speech is the first sign of becoming fully human. Julian Jaynes notes that even such an unmetaphorically sounding English word as the verb "to be" was generated from the metaphor "to grow" or "to make grow," which is *bhu* in Sanskrit, and the English forms *am* and *is* have evolved anagrammatically from the Sanskrit *asmi,* "to breathe."[9] Because it is breath, the human voice is atmospheric. *In their origin, breath and being have, as it were, the same mother: to be is to breathe.* In Rainer Maria Rilke's *Sonnets to Orpheus,* there is a pithy line: *Gesang ist Dasein* (singing is Being or existence). And since breath begets voice, the Orphic voice was the beginning of language. As the legend goes, Orpheus—very much like Hermes—was a musician or a player of the lyre (i.e., a "lyricist"). With his music, Orpheus made not only humans, but rocks, mountains, streams, trees, forests, birds, and animals dance. "The cults we associate with his name," Ihab Hassan writes, "blend word and flesh into the dance of existence. Orpheus sings, and his song moves stones, trees, and beasts. The reason is simple: singing Orpheus restores himself to nature, and moves with the secret life of things. His lyre carries the music of universal harmony and eternal response."[10] In the person of Orpheus, therefore, music and poetry embody a promise of eternal and universal harmony.

For our discussion here, we should note three characteristics of Homeric oral poetry. First, in Homeric poetry, which is oral and auditory (i.e., acoustic), the mouth and the ear were the main organs of communication, in contrast to literate societies, which rely primarily on the eye. In oral poetry, which was sung by bards or minstrels, speech and music became inseparable. They were integrated into the acoustic culture. They had their common ancestry in songs.

Second, in oral poetry *composition is spontaneous performance.* Even the term "composition" (com-position) is, like the term "oral literature," something of a misnomer in reference to oral poetry, which is invisible or placeless and relies on auditory memory. In this sense, oral poetry is radically different from written poetry, where composition and performance are not separated, but occur simultaneously. "For the oral poet," Albert B. Lord stresses, "the moment of composition is the performance. In the case of a literary poem there is a gap in time between composition and reading or performance; in the case of the oral poem this gap does not exist, because composition and performance are two aspects of the same moment. . . . An oral poem is not composed *for* but *in* performance."[11] Composition in oral poetry, pretty much like "creative music" (jazz) today, is improvised. As performance, oral composition constitutes spontaneous communication rather than the formulation of ideas in thought. As such, there is an integration of the "word" and the "deed" in oral poetry. For Goethe, who exalted in *Faust* the Mephistophelian virtue of "greenness" of life as opposed to the "greyness" of all theory, the word "composition" in reference to the productions of art and poetry is a degrading misuse of the word. For a work of art or poetry is an organic whole, which, unlike a piece of cake or a machine, cannot be "composed": how can we therefore say, he retorted, that Mozart has *composed* his *Don Giovanni!*[12]

Third, in the Homeric culture, the "oral *technē*" of poetry was the instrument of preserving the dynamic "flow" of a tradition or a way of life (i.e., received wisdom as an institution). In the Homeric age, which was epitomized by oral poetry, the poet was a "tribal encyclopedist" as well as "encyclopedic minstrel" who preserved the *nomos* and *ethos* of culture. The edification of a way of life was "harped" by "thrilljoy mouths overstapeaking"—to use James Joyce's expression. *Poiēsis* was *technē*, and *mimēsis* was the poetic technique of communication to preserve the acoustic effects (*pragmata*) of an oral culture. Poetry was an oral performance, wherein memorization by means of reiterated recitation preserved the acoustic effects of culture. The dynamic flow of this oral culture was preserved in the cornucopia of poetry, that is, in its repetition, redundancy, and verboseness. The Homeric epic or a "river of song," as it is called metaphorically, constituted "a body of invisible writing imprinted upon the brain of the community."[13] "The poetized word," Eric A. Havelock writes, "acts as a kind of electricity in the atmosphere."[14] As the old proverb goes, *verba volant, scripta manent.* Homer spoke of "winged words": the evanescence of spoken words as sounds. To borrow the expression of Edmond Jabès: as words are to unmoving bows, spoken utterances are to moving arrows.[15]

Music (*mousikē*), too, is a *technē* that augments and amplifies the record and recall of significant speech for the transmission of a tradition or a way of life. Music is meant to "augment" (in the technical musical sense of "slow down" or "draw out") the oral transmission of the tradition in its living memory.[16] Tradition is the "concert" of the past and the present dancing together. The sung words of oral poetry are maieutic or midwifely in the transmission of culture. By "augmenting" the tempo of the oral transmission, music too facilitates the memorization or remembrance of the cultural message contained in oral verses, which are by nature formulaic. The formulaic style necessary for oral transmission appears "repetitive" and "redundant" only when the spoken is transcribed in writing. And since music facilitates the memorization of cultural messages, we now understand clearly—or, better, "loudly"—why the goddess of memory, Mnemosyne, is the supreme ruler of the Homeric oral culture and the guardian of the aesthetic delight of Homeric poetry whose words were sung. Above all, she is the mother of the Muses. Cultural messages were heard as invisible sounds in the ear rather than seen in the eye as visible objects. The acoustic world is indeed "a globe of memory" in which its tradition was transmitted as "a rain of memory."

Logos, too, originally meant the power of speech.[17] Following this tradition, Plato in the *Phaedrus* and the *Seventh Letter* was critical of writing. Akin to painting, writing implants forgetfulness at the expense of memory and the conceit of wisdom rather than wisdom itself. Speaking of the inadequacy of language in describing the essential quality of any object, Plato wrote that "no intelligent man will ever be so bold as to put into language those things which his reason has contemplated, especially not into a form that is unalterable—which must be the case with what is expressed in written symbols."[18] For Plato as for Socrates, dialogue or the dialectic was a form of con*versa*tion, the give-and-take process of oral questioning and answering. Cast in the form of dialogues, Plato's written works in the spirit of the oral thinker Socrates are meant to minimize the monologic defect of the written words.[19]

III

There is no one today who celebrates the new arrival of time-binding oral culture more enthusiastically than Marshall McLuhan. His is the new Delphic oracle of electronic technology, for it is associated with the advent of electronic technology in the twentieth century (e.g., telegraph, telephone, phonograph, radio, and above all television). The quintessential line in his "poetics" of electronic technology is "the medium *is* the message." The synaesthesia, as opposed to the Balkanization, of the human sensorium is an attunement to the "music" of electronic technology. The importance of McLuhan's thought lies in his preoccupation with technology as (the instrument of) human communication rather than as the instrument of control over nature. He is a philosopher of culture who is also one of the most outspoken apostles of our age as the age of electronic technology. McLuhan moreover embraces a purely disembodied, cybernetic formula when he declares, for example, that "the electric light is pure information."[20] "By imposing universalizable relationships that are the result of instant speed," he writes, "electronic technology dethrones the visual sense and restores us to the dominion of synesthesia, and the close interinvolvement of the other senses."[21]

The appellation "McLuhanism" is a high tribute paid by his commentators, for good or ill, in recognition of his eponymous status. Straightforward simplicity is the gist of his cultural epistolaries, which are loud and clear. He has a flair for pungent phraseology. In the unabatedly aphoristic, punnish, epigrammatic, and hyperbolic but often discerning fireworks of his highly stylized expressions, which are indicative of his training in literature, lurks a grandiose but simplified design of history that can be matched with Oswald Spengler's and Arnold Toynbee's in our age. For McLuhan, the history of the Western world is a circular movement (i.e., revolution) of the responses that the human sensorium engenders to the challenges of communication media. It is a three-stage drama from (1) tribalization in oral culture and (2) detribalization in alphabetic and typographic culture to (3) retribalization in electronic culture in the making of a "global village." In essence, the "post-literate" culture of the electronic age is a return to the "pre-literate" culture of Homer. To sum up the importance of McLuhan's theory of communication: first, it focuses on the technology of communication; second, it is a critique of the history of Western thought dominated by the model of sight; third, it stresses an interplay of the human sensorium and the cultural patterns of communication media; and fourth, it is utterly engrossed in, and impressed by, the effects of electronic technology, which is as visionary as Lenin's slogan—the "electrification" of Russia.

In *The Gutenberg Galaxy,*[22] McLuhan describes the nature of typographic culture. He writes: "The alphabet, when pushed to a high degree of abstract visual intensity, becomes typography."[23] This long typographic period is characterized by the preeminence of the space-binding power of the eye over the time-binding power of the ear. The second coming of oral culture with the advent of electronic technology that reintegrates or "etherizes" the human sensorium signals the metaphysical end of the long reign of the typographic culture of the eye. *Understanding Media* is a gay chorus to celebrate the second coming of oral culture accompanied by the "music" of electronic technology that penetrates the human senses with the intimacy of tactility. For the medium as technology is indeed the message itself.

For McLuhan, electronic technology gives organic unity. For after all, it is "handmade" or an "extension" of our organic body. The food-gatherer in the tribal culture of the ear reappears as an information-gatherer in electronic culture: "In this role, electronic man is no less nomad than his paleolithic ancestors."[24] Ultimately, electronic technology culminates in "automation" or "cybernation" in which invisible contact is made between humanity and technology. Cybernation is a retribalization and a return once again of the synaesthetic interplay of the senses. Have no fears about automation, McLuhan assures us. For "panic about automation as a threat of uniformity on a world scale is the projection into the future of mechanical standardization and specialism, which are now past."[25] In the end, electronic technology as synaesthetic tactility promises to confer upon us a "global embrace" and "a perpetuity of collective harmony and peace." "The ecumenical movement," McLuhan declares, "is synonymous with electronic technology."[26]

McLuhan's theory of communication is indebted to the work of his compatriot, Harold A. Innis. *The Gutenberg Galaxy* pays a high tribute to Innis when McLuhan himself acknowledges that it is "a footnote of explanation" to Innis's work.[27] *The Bias of Communication*[28] by Innis pertains to the theory of communication in the fast moving context of history and culture, a context in which the medium or the technology of communication itself is a determining factor. It is a calligraphy of history in broad strokes in configuration with the human sensorium. One can taste the flavor of "Inniscence" (Innis-cence)—to use McLuhan's clever and inventive phase—as an appetizer in McLuhan's highly charged idea that "the medium is the message," with its polemic style of expressions and conceptual "bulldozing." For McLuhan as for Innis, it is the medium of communication that shapes and controls the structure of the human sensorium and association. The message is contentless. "For," McLuhan explains, "the 'content' of a medium is like the juicy piece of meat carried by the burglar to distract the watchdog of the mind."[29] It is contentless in another sense as well, because the "content" of any medium is always another medium. For example, the content of writing is the medium of speech; the content of print is the medium of the written word; and the content of the telegraph is the medium of print, etc.

All electronic technology, according to McLuhan, is tactile because electricity itself is tactile: "Electricity offers a means of getting in touch with every facet of being at once, like the brain itself. Electricity is only incidentally visual and auditory; it is primarily tactile."[30] As such, electricity not only has no "point of view," but is also synaesthetic. Indeed, McLuhan claims that electronic technology, as opposed to mechanical technology, is of "organic" nature. Cybernation, whose organizing principle is electric, is also synaesthetic: "What makes a mechanism is the separation and extension of separate parts of our body as hand, arm, feet, in pen, hammer, wheel. And the mechanization of a task is done by segmentation of each part of an action in a series of uniform, repeatable, and movable parts. The exact opposite characterized cybernation (or automation), which has been described as a way of thinking, as much as a way of doing. Instead of being concerned with separate machines, cybernation looks at the production problem as an integrated system of information handling."[31] When McLuhan claims that television is tactile, he is dealing with more than an interplay of the senses themselves. The tactility of television as electric is an interplay of the sensing subject and the sensed object as the technological medium. Whatever else the message that "the medium is the message" may mean, it means that the medium replaces the message or that they are isomorphic. It is not the human subject who "touches" television, but television that "touches" the human subject. In this way, electronic technology or television in particular is anthropomorphized.

McLuhan's metaphorical invocation of tactility for television is quite consistent with his anti-visualist critique of typographic culture in favor of the flood of electronic technology in the twentieth century. For him, tactility represents the utmost intimacy of the human being with the medium as technology. Whereas sight is the least intimate, touch is the most intimate on the scale of the human sensorium. However, claiming tactility for electronic technology or television is an incredible proposition that is phenomenologically untenable and inadmissible, since there is an absolute boundary between the human (the message) and the technological (the medium). By attributing the synaesthetic intimacy of tactility to television, McLuhan replaces the primacy of the sensing subject with that of the sensed medium. Just as television replaces the tactility of the human sensorium, so typewriters, cars, phonographs, radios, and ultimately a network of electric wires called artificial intelligence replace the human hands, the human feet, the human voice and ears, and human intelligence.[32]

McLuhan's metaphorical attribution of tactility to television may be psychologically evocative and appealing, but is is conceptually uninformative and misleading. It is a con-fusion rather than a configuration that, as the proper use of metaphor demands, discloses the resemblance of dissimilars. In McLuhan's case, the use of the metaphor of "tactility" becomes a sort of conceptual "bootlegging." His psychological evocation conceals a fundamental confusion between two ontological categories: the human and the technological. He misrepresents the *diatactics* of the two, that is, the unity of the two disparate phenomena as *complementary*. With

McLuhan we agree that the sense of touch is intimate and associative and that the intensification and domination of visualism diminishes the role of hearing and touch in modern thought and culture, resulting in the production of an anaesthetic society of specialized and psychically impoverished individuals in a world of linear time and Newtonian space. McLuhan, I think, is amply justified when he thought, for the reason of synaesthesia or the ecumenical interplay of the senses, that the ideal form of *The Gutenberg Galaxy* would have been an ideogram or, better, a mosaic galaxy of ideograms. The ideographical writing of the Chinese language, unlike phonetic and syllabic writing, is originally based on human gestures: it is a choreography of gestures.[33] "In contrast to phonetic letters," McLuhan and Harley Parker write, "the ideography is a vortex that responds to lines of force. It is a mask of corporate energy."[34]

Let us pursue further this important issue of the diatactics of the human and the technological by comparing McLuhan's advocacy with Heidegger's critique of technology. McLuhan's unabated enthusiasm for electronic technology as synaesthetic leads to the conclusion that "Heidegger surfboards along on the electronic wave as triumphantly as Descartes rode the mechanical wave."[35] However, McLuhan is critical of Heidegger because he "seems to be quite unaware of the role of electronic technology in promoting his own non-literate bias in language and philosophy. An enthusiasm for Heidegger's excellent linguistics could easily stem from naive immersion in the metaphysical organicism of our electronic milieu."[36] For McLuhan, the hegemony of visualism since the invention of the phonetic alphabet culminating in the typographic culture has been overcome by the advent of electronic (i.e., nonmechanical) technology as (the medium of) communication, while for Heidegger the modern age as the age of the "world picture" (*Weltbild*) is the continuation of artificial photosynthesis. For Heidegger but not for McLuhan, the mechanical and the electronic are fundamentally the inseparable continuum of technology, although they have different wave lengths. From the perspective of Heidegger, McLuhan is an apostle or high priest of the metaphysics of our age as the age of technology whose highly charged expressed is "the medium is the message." In the context of McLuhanism, Heidegger is right when he insists that technology is no longer simply a means of human activity. For it is not merely the application of mathematical physical science to *praxis*, but is itself "an autonomous transformation of praxis, a type of transformation wherein praxis first demands the employment of mathematical physical science."[37] In this respect, technology is the essence of modern metaphysics. And insofar as technology has become an autonomous *praxis* in itself, the traditional rationale of technology as instrumental facilitation (i.e., *instrumentum*) that serves the *telos* of humankind is anachronistic. Means *has become* end. Heidegger's critique of technology as "autonomous" rather than merely an "extension" of the human being is then comparable to what Langdon Winner calls "reverse adaptation"—the phenomenon in which "technical systems become severed from the ends originally set for them and, in effect, reprogram themselves and their environments to suit the special conditions of their own operation. The artificial slave gradually subverts the rule of its master."[38] This, in fact, is the "categorical imperative" of the rationality of technology as "autonomous." From the point of view of cybernetics, the human being *is* a machine: human beings become *reified* because their essence is determined not by their unique existence, but by the objectified product of their own activity. McLuhan's metaphorical invocation of tactility for television aims to enhance the image of its anthropomorphic "intimacy" as (the medium of) communication. From the vantage point of Heidegger's thought, however, television, which is preeminently visual rather than tactile, affirms the modern age as the age of the world picture. The world viewed as picture in television is an *aspect* (*idea*) of what Heidegger calls "enframing" (*Gestell*). According to him, the *essence* of technology is *Gestell*, which, as "to set in place" (*stellen*), is eminently spatial and visual. Television too is part of this enframing in the modern age as the age of the world picture. "The fundamental event of the modern age," Heidegger writes, "is the conquest of the world as picture. The word 'picture' [*Bild*] now means the structured image [*Gebild*] that is the creature of man's producing which represents and sets before."[39] As the essence of all technology as enframing is re-presenting, television too *re-presents* as picture or structured image the original presence of the world as it *is*. Here Ludwig Wittgenstein's distinction between "seeing" and "seeing *as*," that is, seeing a real object and seeing it as a picture or an image, is instructive. For him, there is a "categorial difference" between seeing a real object and seeing a picture-object: the latter or "the flashing of an aspect on us seems half visual experience, half thought."[40] Television viewing or watching belongs to the category of "seeing as" or seeing a picture-object. Just as the confusion between seeing a real object and seeing a picture-object is a categorial mistake, so is the confusion between the human and the technological in terms of the metaphor of tactility. In short, visual images are the stuff of television as a "reproducing" medium of communication. McLuhan's metaphor of tactility for television conceals and even deceives its imagistic visualness. Were television not preeminently visual and imagistic, there would be virtually no difference between it and radio. Color television is the artificial fluorescence of light that emanates from the palette of red, blue, and green.

To capture the *eidos* or essence of reality by means of an anthology of images is forever a Sisyphean task. Here we would be remiss if we failed to mention Susan Sontag's superb account of the identity between camera and chimera (or Plato's cave) in *On Photography.*[41] In reference to photography as a visual pantheon, she speaks of image as a semblance of knowledge, a subtraction of reality, and an appearance of participation. According to Sontag, "A photograph is pseudo-presence and a token of absence."[42] The American Indians understand this well when they do not allow their kiva to be photographed because photography desacralizes it. Yet photography's immobility is its virtue, while the mobility of images is television's vice. While retaining photography's essence of visualism, television—unlike photography—is not conducive to pensiveness because in it there is no retardation of vision. As such, the assault of television's "ray gun" on the human mind is far more intense, aggressive, and thus paralyzing than that of photography.

Let us consider here Jerzy Kosinski's novel *Being There,*[43] which I take to be a satirical commentary in a Heideggeran mold on American society enframed by the network of television technology. It is a portrayal of Heidegger's anonymous "they" (*das Man*) that is the reversal of authentic existence (*Dasein* or "there-being"). The anti-hero of the novel is Chance for no other reason than that he was born by chance. Chance is an orphan who was adopted and lived the hermetic life of a gardener without having ever been outside the household until he was thrown out because of the death of the Old Man who kept no record of him as a member of his household. More importantly, Chance is a sort of simpleton whose mind has been molded or fixed by television, since he is unable to manage to read or write. Chance's comprehension of reality is filtered through the tube: he scans the world as picture. For him the world becomes an instant picture on the television screen, and television brings other people "inside his eyelids." In other words, he learned to see the world in terms of what he saw on the television screen: he is the epitome of humanity's visual addiction and fixation, i.e., an "image-junkie." According to Kosinski, "The [TV] set creates its own light, its own color, its own time. It did not follow the law of gravity that forever bent all plants downward. Everything on TV was tangled and mixed and yet smoothed out: night and day, big and small, tough and brittle, soft and rough, hot and cold, far and near. *In this colored world of television, gardening was the white cane of a blind man.*"[44] As a creature of television, Chance is unable to respond to the sexual overture of EE (Elizabeth Eve), who happens to be the wife of Benjamin Rand, Chairman of the Board of the First American Financial Corporation, which is the most important financial institution in the land. She takes him to be "a man of restraint" who does not practice "all of those American lovers'-lane tricks, all of the fingering, kissing, tickling, stroking, hugging."[45] She takes him to be "very brainy, very cerebral." In truth, however, "He wanted to tell her how much he preferred to look at her, that only by watching could he memorize her and take her and possess her. He did not know how to explain to her that he could not touch better or more fully with his hands than he could with his eyes. Seeing encompassed all at once; a touch was limited to one spot at a time. EE should no more have wanted to be touched by him than should the TV screen have wanted it."[46] While her legs and arms wrapped around him like "a web of sprawling branches" of a tree in a garden, Chance repeatedly says to her, "I like to watch you" as he likes to watch television.

American society or, for that matter, the whole world, takes seriously the *"channeled existence"* of this simpleton who has been enframed by television. He achieves instant fame and success because the society takes or mistakes what he says as a gem of "wisdom." This is a satirical and uncanny twist in the novel. When Chance introduces himself to EE as Chance and gardener, she takes him to be Chauncey Gardiner—Chance's second birth by chance. The metaphor of "gardener" impresses Benjamin because "a productive business man is indeed a laborer in his own vineyard."[47] While the President of the United States is visiting the sick Benjamin, he meets Gardiner and asks his opinion about the bad "season" on Wall Street. Bewildered by the question, Chance plainly replies after a slight hesitation: "In a garden, . . . growth has its season. There are spring and summer, but there are also fall and winter. And then spring and summer again. As long as the roots are not severed, all is well and all will be well."[48] Impressed with the "wisdom" of Gardiner as "one of the most refreshing and optimistic statements" he has heard in a very long time, the President uses in his television appearance Gardiner's "wisdom" in reassuring the public of the long-term health of the nation's economy despite another "seasonal" decline in productivity.

IV

The essence of (Homeric) oral poetry lies in the conception of language as *performance*. McLuhan's vision of the world as a "global village" in the age of electronic technology is tantamount to a celebration of the homecoming of oral culture. His contribution to the theory of communication is, as we have noted, essentially twofold: (1) a critique of the visualism that has for so long fostered the fragmentation of humankind and society and (2) the recognition of the medium rather than the message as central in human communication. Paradoxically, however, his conception of electronic technology as tactile espouses the "image" of technology without the "handle." McLuhan's formula that "the medium is the message" can be challenged by the question Rousseau raised in his treatise *On the Origin of Language:* "An orator uses ink to write out his compositions: does that mean ink is very eloquent liquid?"[49]

It seems to me that one of the challenging agenda for the construction of a new theory of politics is the ethical consideration of language as performance. "The word," Georges Gusdorf declares, "owes its efficacy to the fact that it is not an objective notation, but an *index of value.*"[50] What is so banal about McLuhanism or McLuhan's "fetishism of the medium" based on electronic technology and cybernation is that it makes impossible the ethics of language, that is, it amounts to a rejection of the possibility of performative utterance as the *intentional activation* of meaning (*Sinngebung*) in the phenomenological sense (i.e., actively conscious and meaningful). Throughout his writings, McLuhan repeatedly and emphatically disavows any espousal of moral judgments by accepting uncritically and categorically the arrival of the age of electronic technology.

Hannah Arendt was one of a few political theorists in our immediate past who was concerned with the immoral quagmire of the amoral attitude: "the banality of evil," along with lying in politics, as the result in large measure of "image-making" or the acceptance of politics as a variety of "public relations." She was concerned with the immoral consequences of human "thoughtlessness," of humankind's inability to think. Let me quote at some length what Arendt had in mind when she spoke of "the banality of evil":

> To talk about thinking seems to me so presumptuous that I feel I owe you a justification. Some years ago, reporting the trial of Eichmann in Jerusalem, I spoke of "the banality of evil" and meant with this no theory or doctrine but something quite factual, the phenomenon of evil deeds, committed on a gigantic scale, which could not be traced to any particularity of wickedness, pathology, or ideological conviction in the doer, whose only personal distinction was a perhaps extraordinary shallowness. However monstrous the deeds were, the doer was neither monstrous nor demonic, and the only specific characteristic one could detect in his past as well as in his behavior during the trial and the preceding police examination was something entirely negative: it was not stupidity but a curious, quite authentic inability to think. He functioned in the role of prominent war criminal as well as he had under the Nazi regime; he had not the slightest difficulty in accepting an entirely different set of rules. He knew that what he had once considered his duty was now called a crime, and he accepted this new code of judgment as though it were

nothing but another language rule. To his rather limited supply of stock phrases he had added a few new ones, and he was utterly helpless only when he was confronted with a situation to which none of them would apply, as in the most grotesque instance when he had to make a speech under the gallows and was forced to rely on clichés used in funeral oratory which were inapplicable in his case because he was not the survivor. Considering what his last words should be in case of a death sentence, which he had expected all along, flagrant contradictions in examination and cross-examinations during the trial had not bothered him. Clichés, stock phrases, adherence to conventional, standardized codes of expression and conduct have the socially recognized function of protecting us against reality, that is, against the claim on our thinking attention which all events and facts arouse by virtue of their existence. If we were responsive to this claim all the time, we would soon be exhausted; the difference in Eichmann was only that he clearly knew of no such claim at all.[51]

What Arendt demands here is not our ability to theorize abstractly or think in abstraction, but our ability to make moral judgments based on the *sensus communis* as a universal characteristic of humankind's very humanity affirmed by the wisdom of the oral thinker Socrates. It is thinking as a natural necessity of human life that is a faculty of every person who belongs to the species called humans. Speech is performative utterances. As such it is indeed *"prescriptive"* in the double sense of the term: it is not yet written or yet to be written and moral at the same time. It is important to distinguish in the ethics of language between the spoken (rhetoric) and the written word (grammatology).

The philosophy of language as speech acts has too often been claimed as a new revolution in modern philosophy. However, close examination shows that it goes as far back as the classics of Confucian and non-Confucian moral philosophy in ancient China. In the tradition of Sinitic thought, the concept of *performance* is what really counts in the ethics of "saying" as well as the ethics of "doing." As a matter of fact, the distinction between "saying" and "doing" disappears as soon as we consider "saying" itself as a form of "doing." In the *Analects,* Confucius said: "Without knowing *the force* of words, it is impossible to know men."[52] This affirms the following: the centrality of language to human conduct, the ethics of language embodying the humanity of humankind, and the spoken word as "pre-scriptive." Take the following examples of what Confucius said about the ethics of language as performance in the *Analects:* (1) When the superior person "is heard to speak, his language is firm and decided"; (2) "The wise err neither in regard to their men nor to their words"; (3) "The virtuous will be sure to speak *correctly*, but those whose speech is good may not always be virtuous"; (4) "The superior man is modest in his speech, but exceeds in his actions"; and (5) Friendship with "the glib-tongued" is injurious.

Moral performance is an intentional act. It is an act based on "sincerity," which explains the nobility of success as well as the nobility of failure, both of which are equally heroic. For a person to be sincere, s/he must first *mean* what s/he says and then carry out in action what s/he says or promises to do. In performance-oriented Confucian philosophy, this is called the unity of knowledge and action: knowledge is the *beginning* of action and action is the *completion* (or consummation) of knowledge. Correlatively, the famous Confucian conception of the "rectification of names" (*cheng ming*) is addressed to the ethical power of speech in human conduct. Rectification implies the moral "uprightness" of humankind in the fulfillment of our humanity or humaneness (*jen*). In Book 13 of the *Analects*, there is the famous passage on the "rectification of names" as the moral foundation of all human conduct:

> If names be not correct, language is not in accordance with the truth of things. If language be not in accordance with the truth of things, affairs cannot be carried on to success. When affairs cannot be carried on to success, proprieties and music will not flourish. When proprieties and music do not flourish, punishments will not be properly awarded. When punishments are not properly awarded, the people do not know how to move hand or foot. Therefore a superior man considers it necessary that the names he uses may be spoken *appropriately*, and also that what he speaks may be carried out *appropriately*. What the superior man requires, is just that in his words there may be nothing incorrect.[53]

Being only half-real and half-true, as Wittgenstein put it, image-making (i.e., "seeing *as*") through media technology distorts the message and the ethics of language. Our age of verbalization often overlooks the language of silence and its function in human communication. The language of silence is not totally without a voice or performative efficacy. In the *Tao Te Ching*,[54] Lao Tzu made an astute observation that our very concern or preoccupation with the ethics of language itself is indicative of the fact that not all is well with our use of language, and he warned against the danger of insincere and excessive verbalization: a good person does not argue, and a person who argues is not a good person. The literature of silence is the voice of protest against the age in which the public relations, image-making, half-truths, deceptions, and lies of verbal language govern the norms of our everyday language games. Thus silence is the ultimate protest against verbal language, and it often points to "the frivolous insignificance of language."[55] In its deep sense, silence is not the nihilistic voice of reticent passivity and indifference, but rather the Zarathustrian power of no-saying against the mindless verbal behavior that fails miserably as the means of communication. Without much ado about the nature of silence and the role in the ontology of humankind,[56] let us note a few positive aspects of silence in human communication. Silence as the horizon of sound resides in the beginning, interlude, and ending of speech as verbal utterances. It is lack of utterance or enunciation but no lack of thought, words or intention to speak. As an interlude, silence works as a punctual interval between two "tones" of speech acts without breaking the continuity of conversation, dialogue or verbal discourse. In *Four Quartets*, T. S. Eliot says: "Words, after speech, reach/Into the silence." Norman O. Brown completes Eliot's thought by extending the reach of silence into meaning when he says: "The matrix in which the word is sown is silence. Silence is the mother tongue. . . . The meaning is not in the words but between the words, in the silence."[57] In "The Aesthetics of Silence," Susan Sontag summarily writes that "something takes place in time, a voice speaking which points to the before and to what comes after an utterance: silence. Silence, then, is both the precondition of speech and the result or aim of properly directed speech."[58] In short, silence and the uttered word as two continuous modes of communication work *diatactically*.

In a dialogue or conversation, there is no basic opposition between silence and utterance. Genuine dialogue demands the diatactics of speaking and listening as an exchange. For it is a coupling of saying utterance and silent listening: one who utters and the other who listens (silently), which are reversible or exchangeable. If there were no listening or silence, there would be no dialogue, and conversation would degenerate into an endlessly confused babble. The dialogical philosopher Martin Buber complained many years ago that good listening has become rare in our time. Wittgenstein's famed evocation of consigning to silence at the end of his *Tractatus Logico-Philosophicus*[59] is not the voice of negating the function of language. Rather, it is deep silence in a Taoistic and Zen bent that voices the limits of language considered in terms of the "propositions" or picturable facts that science, logic, and mathematics express. It affirms that there are important matters such as ethics, aesthetics, and metaphysics that are neither logical, nor mathematical, nor empirical, that is, of which propositional language cannot speak. Thus silence is a deep interlude in the transition from science, logic, and mathematics to ethics, aesthetics, and metaphysics. Ultimately, the latter *cannot be said* in propositional language but can only be *shown*. Therefore, it is wrong for us to ask "what Witt-

genstein is *saying*," but we must instead ask "what he is doing."[60]
What cannot be said must be shown or, better, done. For language
is in essence a form of life, that is, *doing* or *performing*. In Confucian philosophy, language is an *ethical* form of life. Only doing or
performing can fathom the depth of silence. Action is the embodiment of silence as the counterpart or correlative of the verbal in
communication. As John Keats says in "Ode to a Grecian Urn,"
"Heard melodies are sweet, but those unheard/Are sweeter."

V

In conclusion, a new theory of politics may be constructed in
terms of the centrality of language as performative utterances in
which rhetoric precedes grammatology.[61] In it the language of political actors precedes in both aim and meaning-genesis the language of political theorists: the everyday political life-world is the
founding and *funding* matrix of political theorizing, and the latter
is a special way of existing in the former.[62] In this essay, I have only
briefly considered a few points on how a new theory of politics
may be constructed, i.e., on the "genealogy" of political theory.
First, it requires an archaeological exploration of the nature of
(Homeric) oral poetry. For oral poetry is the "cradle" of language,
expression, and communication, and performance is central to it.
In oral poetry as in all performing arts (music, drama, and dance),
composition is done *in* and *for* performance. Here we are reminded
of a passage in John Dewey's classical work *The Public and Its
Problems:* "The connections of the ear with vital and out-going
thought and emotion are immensely closer and more varied than
those of the eye. Vision is a spectator; hearing is a participator."[63]
Second, McLuhan's invaluable contribution to the theory of communication lies in a critique of the domination of visualism in modern thought and in calling our attention to the importance of
electronic media that transformed a literate into a post-literate culture. However, his uncritical acceptance of electronic technology
and cybernation cloaked in the mystique of tacility as an ecumenical interplay of the human sensorium abandons the ethics of communication as *intentional act* in the phenomenological sense. The
"instrumental rationality" of technology breeds a banal insensitivity to morality whose results can be monstrously evil. Third, therefore, the idea of intentionality must be put back into political
rhetoric, for this alone gives it an ethical texture. To put it in a
Heideggerian perspective, the ethics of language becomes in the
end the way of thinking as *alētheia*—the disclosure of things both
natural and human as they *are*. To think morally is to think the way
of humankind as it really *is*.

NOTES

Chapter One

1. Kariel, "The Political Relevance of Behavioral and Existential Psychology," *American Political Science Review*, 61 (June 1967): 334–42, and Meehan, *Contemporary Political Thought* (Homewood: Dorsey Press, 1967), p. 383. Also cf. Arnold Brecht, *Political Theory* (Princeton: Princeton University Press, 1959), p. 383.

2. Heidegger, *Being and Time*, trans. John Macquarrie and Edward Robinson (New York: Harper & Brothers, 1962); Sartre, *Being and Nothingness*, trans. Hazel E. Barnes (New York Philosophical Library, 1956); Merleau-Ponty, *Phenomenology of Perception*, trans. Colin Smith (London: Routledge & Kegan Paul, 1962); Ricoeur, *Fallible Man*, trans. Charles Kelbley (Chicago: Regnery, 1965), and *Freedom and Nature*, trans. Erazim V. Kohák (Evanston: Northwestern University Press, 1966); Wild, *Existence and the World of Freedom* (Englewood Cliffs: Prentice-Hall, 1962). For a comprehensive survey of the development of phenomenology, see Herbert Spiegelberg, *The Phenomenological Movement*, 3rd rev. and enl. ed. (The Hague: Nijhoff, 1982).

3. Ricoeur, *Husserl*, trans. Edward G. Ballard and Lester E. Embree (Evanston: Northwestern University Press, 1967), p. 212.

4. See Alfred Schutz, "On Multiple Realities," in his *Collected Papers*, vol. 1:*The Problem of Social Reality*, ed. Maurice Natanson (The Hague: Nijhoff, 1962), pp. 207–59.

5. Husserl, *The Crisis of European Sciences and Transcendental Phenomenology*, trans. David Carr (Evanston: Northwestern University Press, 1970), p. 122.

6. See Wild, *Existence and the World of Freedom*, p. 54. Raymond Polin emphasizes that the phenomenological analysis of values is futile unless it contributes to the philosophy of action—see *La Création des valeurs*, 2nd ed. (Paris: Presses Universitaires de France, 1952), p. 3.

7. William James, *The Principles of Psychology*, 2 vols. (New York: Dover, 1950; originally published in 1890), vol. 2, p. 222. Cf. Eugene T. Gendlin, *Experiencing and the Creation of Meaning* (Glencoe: Free Press, 1962), p. 9.

8. On this point, see Paul Ricoeur, *History and Truth*, trans. Charles A. Kelbley (Evanston: Northwestern University Press, 1965), pp. 218–19.

9. Macmurray, *The Self as Agent* (London: Faber and Faber, 1957), p. 38.

10. In his Presidential Address to the Annual Meeting of the American Political Science Association in September, 1969, David Easton emphasized the idea of unity between political knowledge and action in what he called the "post-behavioral revolution"—see "The New Revolution in Political Science," *American Political Science Review,* 63 (December 1969): 1051–61. The theme of theory and practice is also discussed in Nicholas Lobkowicz, *Theory and Practice* (Notre Dame: University of Notre Dame Press, 1967), and Jürgen Habermas, *Theorie und Praxis,* 3rd ed. (Neuwied: Luchterhand, 1969).

11. For a detailed discussion of the interdependence between philosophy and the social sciences, see Maurice Merleau-Ponty, "The Philosophy and Sociology," in *Signs,* trans. Richard C. McCleary (Evanston: Northwestern University Press, 1964), pp. 98–113.

12. Schutz, *Collected Papers,* 1, p. 59. Cf. Merleau-Ponty, *Phenomenology of Perception,* pp. viii, ix: "The whole universe of science is built upon the world as directly experienced, and if we want to subject science itself to rigorous scrutiny and arrive at a precise assessment of its meaning and scope, we must begin by reawakening the basic experience of the world of which science is the second-order expression. . . . To return to things themselves is to return to that world which precedes knowledge, of which knowledge *speaks,* and in relation to which every scientific schematization is an abstract and derivative sign-language, as is geography in relation to the country-side in which we have learnt beforehand what a forest, a prairie or a river is."

13. The "empiricist" Robert A. Dahl criticizes many "trans-empiricists" for using "an unnatural vocabulary far removed from the ordinary language of politics"—*Modern Political Analysis* (Englewood Cliffs: Prentice-Hall, 1963), p. 105. In turn, the "trans-empiricist" Leo Strauss charges that while "the language of Aristotelian political science is identical with the language of political man" and "it hardly uses a term that did not originate in the market place and is not in common use there," nevertheless "the new political science cannot begin to speak without having elaborated an extensive technical vocabulary"—"An Epilogue," in *Essays on the Scientific Study of Politics,* ed. Herbert J. Storing (New York: Holt, Rinehart & Winston, 1962), p. 310. It is important to note that both Dahl and Strauss recognize the significance of the ordinary language of political humankind. Strauss recognizes the dependence of conceptual knowledge on preconceptual understanding. However, I have argued elsewhere (see Chapter 6 below) that while his intellectualism is guilty of self-contradiction, positivism, on the other hand, takes the preconceptual life-world for granted and may be charged with negligence.

14. An example of this approach is T. D. Weldon, *The Vocabulary of Politics* (Baltimore: Penguin Books, 1953). Following the logical positivist criteria of meaning, Weldon views the function of political philosophy as a linguistic therapeutic of political words. According to Felix E. Oppenheim, analytic political philosophy—both philosophy of political science and philosophy of political ethics—is concerned with the logical and linguistic analysis of factual and ethical statements about political phenomena (that is, with what is metafactual and metaethical)—see his *Moral*

Principles in Political Philosophy (New York: Random House, 1968), pp. 3–19. Similarly, Richard S. Rudner juxtaposes "substantive" and "methodological" issues in the study of social phenomena. For him, "social philosophy" and "philosophy of social science" deal with the former and the latter respectively: "The philosopher of social science is engaged not with the substance of any social theory nor with a view of what makes a good society but with the logic of any theory construction in social science and with the logic of justification of (any) social-science theory"—*Philosophy of Social Science* (Englewood Cliffs: Prentice-Hall, 1966), p. 3. For some incisive criticisms of the analytic conception of political philosophy for being too narrow and restrictive, see Peter Winch, *The Idea of a Social Science and Its Relation to Philosophy* (London: Routledge & Kegan Paul, 1958), pp. 3 ff., and Richard Wollheim, "Philosophie analytique et pensée politique," *Revue française de science politique*, 9 (June 1961): 295–308.

15. Downs, *An Economic Theory of Democracy* (New York: Harper & Row, 1957), particularly pp. 21–35.

16. J. L. Austin emphasizes that "ordinary language is *not* the last word: in principle it can everywhere be supplemented and improved upon and superseded. Only remember, it is the *first* word"—*Philosophical Papers*, ed. J. O. Urmson and G. J. Warnock (Oxford: Clarendon Press, 1961), p. 133. Moreover, Austin's exposition of "performative utterance" is significant for understanding political *words* in relation to political *action*. A "performative utterance" is not a report on what someone else says, but is the very execution of the act itself, as when a person says "I promise that . . . " (that is, the act of promising). It is then "doing" rather than "reporting" something. The spoken words of political actors are of this nature in many instances. See "Performative Utterances," *ibid.*, pp. 22–39, and Austin, *How to Do Things with Words* (New York: Oxford University Press, 1962).

17. Schutz, *Collected Papers*, 1, p. 59. For the relationship between phenomenology and the sociology of Max Weber, see Alfred Schutz, *The Phenomenology of the Social World*, trans. George Walsh and Frederick Lehnert (Evanston: Northwestern University Press, 1967), pp. 3–44.

18. See Eulau, *The Behavioral Persuasion in Politics* (New York: Random House, 1963); see further his *Micro-Macro Political Analysis* (Chicago: Aldine, 1969), pp. 148–65, 370–90.

19. Compare Eulau's views of scientific technology with those of the phenomenologist Hubert L. Dreyfus in *Alchemy and Artificial Intelligence*, RAND Paper P-3244 (Santa Monica: RAND Corporation, 1965).

20. For a phenomenology of human action, see Maurice Merleau-Ponty, *The Structure of Behavior*, trans. Alden L. Fisher (Boston: Beacon Press 1963); Jean-Paul Sartre, *Critique de la raison dialectique* (Paris: Gallimard, 1960); Alexander Pfänder, *Phenomenology of Willing and Motivation*, trans. Herbert Spiegelberg (Evanston: Northwestern University Press, 1967); Schutz, *Collected Papers*, 1, pp. 67–96, and *The Phenomenology of the Social World*; Ricoeur, *Freedom and Nature* and "Philosophy of Will and Action," in *Phenomenology of Will and Action*, ed. Erwin W. Straus and Richard M. Griffith (Pittsburgh: Duquesne University Press, 1966), pp. 7–33.

21. Ricoeur, *Freedom and Nature*, p. 46.

22. Downs, *An Economic Theory of Democracy*, p. 34.

23. Cf. James M. Buchanan and Gordon Tullock, *The Calculus of Consent* (Ann Arbor: University of Michigan Press, 1965), p. 27. Although William H. Riker is "eager to create specifically *political* theories of behavior to serve as a base for a future *political* science," there is nonetheless an economic overtone in his game theory. For him, "most of the decisions in economics and political life are made by persons acting in a fiduciary relation," and he equates "rational" behavior with "winning" behavior when he says that "politically rational man is the man who would rather win than lose, regardless of the particular stakes"—*The Theory of Political Coalitions* (New Haven: Yale University Press, 1962), p. ix. Yet as William T. Bluhm points out, " 'winning' as the political value par excellence is not for Riker an entirely selfish object, as the political object is for Downs"—*Theories of the Political System* (Englewood Cliffs: Prentice-Hall, 1965), p. 292.

24. For a discussion of diverse forms of rationality in social science, see Paul Diesing, *Reason in Society* (Urbana: University of Illinois Press, 1962). Sheldon S. Wolin argues that Locke and his successors hastened the decline of political theory; their "conviction that economics formed the proper study of mankind and economic activity the proper end . . . encouraged the imposition of economic categories onto political thought with the result that the role and status of political theory came to be usurped by economic theory"—*Politics and Vision* (Boston: Little, Brown, 1960), pp. 286–351. Similarly, C. B. Macpherson critically examined Hobbes and Locke, who based their political theory on the assumption that human beings are the infinite proprietors of their own interests, which is an economic claim—see *The Political Theory of Possessive Individualism* (Oxford: Clarendon Press, 1962).

25. Dewey, *Human Nature and Conduct* (New York: Modern Library, 1922), p. 115. For an excellent discussion of some philosophical presuppositions of analytic models, see William T. Bluhm, "Metaphysics, Ethics, and Political Science," *The Review of Politics*, 31 (January 1969): 66–87.

26. For a phenomenological theory of the human body, see Richard M. Zaner, *The Problem of Embodiment* (The Hague: Nijhoff, 1964).

27. Wild, "Foreword," in Merleau-Ponty, *The Structure of Behavior*, pp. xiv–xv.

28. R. D. Laing, *The Divided Self* (Baltimore: Penguin Books, 1965), p. 82.

29. See, e.g., Edward A. Tiryakian, *Sociologism and Existentialism* (Englewood Cliffs: Prentice-Hall, 1962), and Walter Odajnyk, *Marxism and Existentialism* (Garden City: Doubleday, 1965).

30. See Kierkegaard, *The Present Age*, trans. Alexander Dru (New York: Harper & Row, 1962). See also the present author's "Confucianism and Existentialism: Intersubjectivity as the Way of Man," *Philosophy and Phenomenological Research*, 30 (December 1969): 195–98. Among prolific existentialist writings on the subject of mass humanity in modern society, see particularly Karl Jaspers, *Man in the Modern Age*, trans. Eden and Cedar Paul (Garden City: Doubleday, 1957), and Gabriel Marcel, *Man Against Mass Society*, trans. G. S. Fraser (Chicago: Regnery, 1952).

31. Merleau-Ponty, *Sense and Non-Sense*, trans. Hubert L. Dreyfus and Patricia Allen Dreyfus (Evanston: Northwestern University Press, 1964), p. 152. For a phenomenological exposition of the "other," see Emmanuel Levinas, *Totality and Infinity,* trans. Alphonso Lingis (Pittsburgh: Duquesne University Press, 1969).

32. Dahl, *Modern Political Analysis,* p. 73. David B. Truman also says that "the activities of political interest groups imply controversy and conflict, the essence of politics. For those who abhor conflict in any form, who long for some past or future golden age of perfect harmony, these consequences of group activity are alone sufficient to provoke denunciation"— *The Governmental Process* (New York: Knopf, 1958), pp. 502–3. A balanced view of the political system as the concomitant process of conflict and integration is found in Maurice Duverger, *The Idea of Politics,* trans. Robert North and Ruth Murphy (Indianapolis: Bobbs-Merrill, 1966).

33. Schattschneider, *The Semi-Sovereign People* (New York: Holt, Rinehart & Winston, 1960).

Chapter Two

1. Easton, "The New Revolution in Political Science," *American Political Science Review,* 63 (December 1969): 1051–61.

2. Mill, *A System of Logic* (London: Logmans, Green, 1925).

3. Easton, *The Political System* (New York: Knopf, 1953).

4. It is interesting to observe that political behavioralists who ignore Mill's *A System of Logic* consider Graham Wallas's *Human Nature in Politics* (London: Constable, 1908) as one of the important source books for the origin of political behavioralism. In this work, Wallas is concerned with "psychological man" in the study of politics, and with psychological categories of human feelings, attitudes, and motivations, rather than with "institutions," in determining the basic parameters of political situations.

5. I find the most intemperate attack on Heidegger and existentialism in general in the political scientist Joseph Cropsey, one of the prominent students of Strauss, when he writes: "While Nietzsche spoke of the will to power, the overman, and the invitation of the eternal recurrence of the nauseous; and Heidegger proclaimed the authentic separation of *Dasein* from the dominance of the mass called Them or They (*der Man*) [*sic*] with an intention that was compatible with his own National Socialism, it cannot be doubted that the project of authentic existentialism is to harden— perhaps into petrification—the liberalized spirit of modern man and not to license it for petulant or hedonistic self-assertions. What exists among us now, as part of the extended regime that forms us and shapes our existence, is the ominous human discipline of high existentialism, passed through the medium of the liberalistic modernity it is intended to reform, and transformed by it into willfulness, consciousness-raising, and moral latitudinarianism. It would be morally wrong to pass from the subject of the vulgarization of existentialism without referring to the Nazism to which it lent itself, as well as to the attempts to turn it to the uses of communism that have an especial prestige in Europe"—*Political Philosophy and the Issues of Politics* (Chicago: University of Chicago Press, 1977), p. 11. In Cropsey's statement, there is a strong fear of anything modern.

6. For a hint of the "political Plato," see Hans-Georg Gadamer, *Dialogue and Dialectic: Eight Hermeneutical Studies on Plato*, trans. P. Christopher Smith (New Haven: Yale University Press, 1980), p. 125.

7. The following two works are crucial for understanding the "classical" position of Strauss: *What Is Political Philosophy? And Other Studies* (Glencoe: Free Press, 1959) and *Natural Right and History* (Chicago: University of Chicago Press, 1953).

8. For the critique of historicism that Strauss regarded as definitive, see Emil L. Fackenheim, *Metaphysics and Historicity* (Milwaukee: Marquette University Press, 1961); for a critique of historicism from the perspective of political science, see Eugene F. Miller, "Positivism, Historicism, and Political Inquiry," *American Political Science Review*, 66 (September 1972):796–817.

9. "An Epilogue," in Strauss, *Essays on the Scientific Study of Politics*, ed. Herbert J. Storing (New York: Holt, Rinehart & Winston, 1962).

10. *Ibid.*, p. 327. Strauss considers Machiavelli to be the founder of modern political science, and criticizes him for lowering the moral standard of classical political thought—see Strauss, *Thoughts on Machiavelli* (Glencoe: Free Press, 1958). In this connection, it is instructive to read Maurice Merleau-Ponty's sympathetic treatment of Machiavelli's politics and his sensitivity to the predicament of a collective life without moralizing politics in "A Note on Machiavelli," in *Signs*, trans. Richard C. McCleary (Evanston: Northwestern University Press, 1964), pp. 211–23.

11. For more on these themes, see Chapter 1 above and Chapters 3 and 6 below. Fred R. Dallmayr has also made a critical assessment of Strauss's "classical" formulation of political philosophy in his Inaugural Lecture entitled "Political Philosophy Today" for the Packey J. Dee Chair in political theory at the University of Notre Dame, March 21, 1980. The term "diatactics" is coined by Hayden White in *Tropics of Discourse: Essays in Cultural Criticism* (Baltimore: Johns Hopkins University Press, 1978), p. 4. White wishes to have the term "diatactics" replace the term "dialectics" in order to avoid the ideological overtone of Marx on the one hand and the transcendental overtone of Hegel on the other; diatactics is neither "paratactical" (conceptually underdetermined) nor "hypotactical" (conceptually overdetermined).

12. See *The Collected Works of Paul Valéry*, vol. 10; *History and Politics*, trans. Denise Folliot and Jackson Mathews (New York: Pantheon Books, 1962).

13. Strauss, *The City and Man* (Chicago: McNally, 1964), p. 12. A phenomenological treatment of Aristotle's practical and moral philosophy with a focus on his conception of *phronēsis* is found in J. Donald Monan, *Moral Knowledge and Its Methodology in Aristotle* (Oxford: Clarendon Press, 1968). Monan writes that "its [*phronēsis*'s] very distinctiveness makes him [Aristotle] solicitous to distinguish moral knowledge from the procedures of rigorous science. It has for object not a value perched in timeless immobility, but a value which exists only in concrete human conduct. Its origin lies not in a contemplative grasp of a good which has already been subjected to metaphysical elaboration, but rather in the concrete goods a person has realized in his own experiential *praxis*. Nor does it reach its term in grasping the relation between two abstract es-

sences, but in intuiting a human value within the 'sensory flow' of circumstances in which one must act morally. Lastly, being the fruit of both intellectual and moral virtue working in unison, moral knowledge contains an element of personal affective response to value which cannot be fitted into the same unimpassioned patterns as can purely scientific propositions" (*ibid.*, p. 88).

14. Gadamer, *Truth and Method*, ed. Garrett Barden and John Cumming (New York: Seabury Press, 1975), pp. 489–90.

15. Paul Ricoeur comments that "tradition . . . ,even understood as the transmission of a *depositum*, remains a dead tradition if it is not the continual interpretation of this deposit; our 'heritage' is not a sealed package we pass from hand to hand, without ever opening, but rather a treasure from which we draw by the handful and which by this very act is replenished. Every tradition lives by grace of interpretation, and it is at this price that it continues, that is, remains living"—*The Conflict of Interpretations: Essays in Hermeneutics*, ed. Don Ihde (Evanston: Northwestern University Press, 1974), p. 27. Strauss himself emphasizes that the classical tradition is of more than antiquarian interest for him, which is to say, it must be interpreted and reinterpreted to be kept alive. Adhering to the notion of universal truth as an intrinsic property of the ideas, however, the idealist or intellectualist tradition is in conflict with itself in its desire to keep its tradition alive by interpretation. Thus John O'Neill comments that "the universality and truth aimed at by theoretical consciousness is not an intrinsic property of the idea. It is an acquisition continuously established and reestablished in a community and tradition of knowledge called for and responded to by individuals in specific historical situations"—*Sociology as a Skin Trade: Towards a Reflexive Sociology* (New York: Harper & Row, 1972), p. 232. For Husserl, too, phenomenology always remained critique in that continual self-renewal is its *critical* spirit. He continuously regarded his own work as an "introduction" to phenomenology; phenomenology is an infinite task to be performed, and its ideas must be constantly challenged, rethought, and expanded in light of its own past.

16. In *The Ethics of Ambiguity*, trans. Bernard Frechtman (New York: Philosophical Library, 1948), Simone de Beauvoir proclaims the superiority of the "existentialist" ethics of fulfillment, based on the concept of ambiguity, over the "essentialist" ethics of principles. She writes that "existentialist doctrine permits the elaboration of an ethics, but it even appears to us as the only philosophy in which an ethics has its place. For, in a metaphysics of transcendence, in the classical sense of the term, evil is reduced to error; and in humanistic philosophies it is impossible to account for it, man being defined as complete in a complete world. Existentialism alone gives—like religions—a real role to evil, and it is this, perhaps, which make its judgments so gloomy. Men do not like to feel themselves in danger. Yet, it is because there are real dangers, real failures and real earthly damnation that words like victory, wisdom, or joy have meaning. Nothing is decided in advance, and it is because man has something to lose and because he can lose that he can also win" (p. 34). What de Beauvoir says of Hegel in the following passage is what we can also say of Strauss: "I remember having experienced a great feeling of calm on reading Hegel in the impersonal framework of the Bibliothèque Nationale in August, 1940. But once I got into the street again, into my life, out of the system, beneath a real sky, the system was no longer of any use to me; what

it had offered me, under a show of the infinite, was the consolations of death; and I again wanted to live in the midst of living men. I think that, inversely, existentialism does not offer to the reader the consolations of an abstract evasion; existentialism proposes no evasion. On the contrary, its ethics is experienced in the truth of life, and it then appears as the only proposition of salvation which one can address to men" (pp. 158–59).

17. For an excellent critique of the "methodism" of political behavioralism, see Sheldon S. Wolin, "Political Theory as a Vocation," *American Political Science Review*, 63 (December 1969): 1062–82.

18. A fact is the result of a comprehension of a thing or an event by a conscious, knowing subject. Michael Oakeshott thus declares: "Fact, whatever else it may be, is experience; without thought there can be no fact. Even a view which separates ideas from things must recognize that facts are ideas. Fact is what has been made or achieved; it is the product of judgment. And if there be an unalterable datum in experience, it certainly cannot consist of fact. Fact, then, is not what is given, it is what is achieved in experience. Facts are never merely observed, remembered or combined; they are always made. We cannot 'take' facts, because there are none to take until we have constructed them. And until a fact is established, that is, until it has achieved a place in a coherent world, it is no more than an hypothesis or a fiction"—*Experience and Its Modes* (Cambridge: University Press, 1933), p. 42.

19. For an extensive discussion of technology as autonomous *praxis* in the context of modern political thought, see Langdon Winner, *Autonomous Technology: Technics-out-of-Control as a Theme in Political Thought* (Cambridge: MIT Press, 1977).

20. See Husserl, *The Crisis of European Sciences and Transcendental Phenomenology*, trans. David Carr (Evanston: Northwestern University Press, 1970), *passim*. For an extended discussion of Husserl's theme of Galilean physics as the mathematization of nature, see Aron Gurwitsch, *Phenomenology and the Theory of Science*, ed. Lester Embree (Evanston: Northwestern University Press, 1974).

21. See Jacob Klein, *Greek Mathematical Thought and the Origin of Algebra*, trans. Eva Brann (Cambridge: MIT Press, 1968).

22. Husserl, *The Crisis of European Sciences and Transcendental Phenomenology*, pp. 62–63.

23. *Ibid.*, pp. 51–52.

24. Schutz, *Collected Papers, vol. 1: The Problem of Social Reality*, ed. Maurice Natanson (The Hague: Nijhoff, 1962), p. 58.

25. Schrag, *Radical Reflection and the Origin of the Human Sciences* (West Lafayette: Purdue University Press, 1980).

26. Richard Rorty writes that "the notion of philosophy as having foundations is as mistaken as that of knowledge having foundations. In this conception, 'philosophy' is not a name for a discipline which confronts permanent issues, and unfortunately keeps misstating them, or attacking them with clumsy dialectical instruments. Rather, it is a cultural genre, a 'voice in the conversation of mankind' (to use Michael Oakeshott's phrase), which centers on one topic rather than another at some given time not by dialectical necessity but as a result of various things happening else-

where in the conversation (the New Science, the French Revolution, the modern novel) or of individual men of genius who think of something new (Hegel, Marx, Frege, Freud, Wittgenstein, Heidegger), or perhaps of the resultant of several such forces. Interesting philosophical change (we might say 'philosophical progress,' but this would be question-begging) occurs not when a new way is found to deal with an old problem but when a new set of problems emerges and the old ones begin to fade away. The temptation (both in Descartes's time and in ours) is to think that the new problematic is the old one rightly seen. But, for all the reasons Kuhn and Feyerabend have offered in their criticisms of the 'textbook' approach to the history of inquiry, this temptation should be resisted"—*Philosophy and the Mirror of Nature* (Princeton: Princeton University Press, 1979), p. 264. The ideal model for the relation between philosophy and the social sciences that I wish to emulate is found in Maurice Merleau-Ponty, "The Philosopher and Sociology," in *Signs*, pp. 98–113.

27. Gadamer considers Vico's appeal to the *sensus communis* as integral to the Renaissance humanistic tradition. In addition to the cultivation of *prudentia* and *eloquentia*, the most important aspect of education is, according to him, "the training in the sensus communis, which is not nourished on the true, but on the probable. The main thing for our purposes is that sensus communis here obviously does not mean only that general faculty in all men, but the sense that founds community. According to Vico, what gives the human will its direction is not the abstract generality of reason, but the concrete generality that represents the community of a group, a people, a nation, or the whole human race. Hence the development of this sense of the community is of prime importance for living"— *Truth and Method*, pp. 20–21. For an excellent discussion of the Italian Renaissance humanistic tradition with a focus on the notion of rhetoric, see Ernesto Grassi, *Rhetoric as Philosophy: The Humanist Tradition*, trans. John Michael Krois and Azizeh Azodi (University Park: Pennsylvania State University Press, 1980). I wish simply to suggest rather than argue in detail here that by hermeneutics, I have in mind the model of oral hermeneutics (rhetoric) rather than that of written language (grammatology), for the text as an utterance or a set of utterances fixed by writing mummifies, calcifies, or monumentalizes the dynamic quality of language as speech acts. Thomas S. Kuhn points out that "textbooks" disguise, conceal, and distort the revolutionary dynamics of scientific research and discovery; that is to say, they make scientific revolutions "invisible"—see *The Structure of Scientific Revolutions*, 2nd rev. and enl. ed. (Chicago: University of Chicago Press, 1970), pp. 136–43. For similar points made from the standpoint of "reader-oriented" literary criticism today, see Stanley Fish, *Is There a Text in This Class?* (Cambridge: Harvard University Press, 1980), especially pp. 1–17, 21–67, 303–21.

28. See the present author's "A Hermeneutical Accent on the Conduct of Political Inquiry," *Human Studies*, 1 (1978): 48–83.

29. Schutz, *Collected Papers*, 1, pp. 65–66. Aron Gurwitsch too argues for the methodological significance of the sociocultural life-world as the basis for a phenomenological theory of the sciences and reaches the following conclusion, which I take to be more specific than Schutz's proposal: "All of the sciences, including the mathematical sciences of nature, find their place within the cultural world. For that reason, according to Husserl . . . , the cultural or human sciences prove to be all-encompassing, since they also comprise the natural sciences, since nature as conceived of

and constructed in modern natural science, i.e., mathematized nature, is itself a mental accomplishment, that is, a cultural phenomenon. The converse, however, is not true. The cultural sciences cannot be given a place among the natural sciences, any more than the cultural world can be reached beginning from mathematized nature or, for that matter, from the thing-world, while . . . by taking one's departure from the cultural world, one can arrive at the thing-world and the mathematized universe by means of abstraction, idealization, and formalization. In general, then, there is a possible transition from the concrete to the abstract, but not the reverse"— *Phenomenology and the Theory of Science*, pp. 148–49.

30. For the present author's more extensive treatment of phenomenology as a social critique of knowledge, see *The Crisis of Political Understanding: A Phenomenological Perspective in the Conduct of Political Inquiry* (Pittsburgh: Duquesne University Press, 1979), pp. 59–91.

31. Kuhn's groundbreaking work was first published in 1962.

32. See Kuhn, *The Essential Tension: Selected Studies in Scientific Tradition and Change* (Chicago: University of Chicago Press, 1977).

33. Gadamer, "Hermeneutics and Social Science," *Cultural Hermeneutics*, 2 (1975): 336.

34. Kuhn, *The Essential Tension*, p. 21.

35. Kuhn, *The Structure of Scientific Revolutions*, p. 210. Cf. Husserl, *The Crisis of European Sciences and Transcendental Phenomenology*, pp. 358–59: "One is conscious of civilization from the start as an immediate and mediate linguistic community. Clearly it is only through language and its far-reaching documentations, as possible communications, that the horizon of civilization can be an open and endless one, as it always is for men. What is privileged in consciousness as the horizon of civilization and as the linguistic community is mature normal civilization (taking away the abnormal and the world of children). In this sense civilization is, for every man whose we-horizon it is, a community of those who can reciprocally express themselves, normally, in a fully understandable fashion; and within this community everyone can talk about what is within the surrounding world of his civilization as objectively existing. Everything has its name, or is namable in the broadest sense, i.e., linguistically expressible. The objective world is from the start the world for all, the world which 'everyone' has as world-horizon. Its objective being presupposes men, understood as men with a common language. Language, for its part, as function and exercised capacity, is related correlatively to the world, the universe of objects which is linguistically expressible in its being and its being-such. Thus men as men, fellow men, world—the world of which men, of which we, always talk and can talk—and, on the other hand, language, are inseparably intertwined; and one is always certain of their inseparable relational unity, though usually only implicitly, in the manner of a horizon."

36. What Maurice Merleau-Ponty says of consciousness as institution is instructive here: "If the subject were taken not as a constituting but an instituting subject, it might be understood that the subject does not exist instantaneously and that the other person does not exist simply as a negative of myself. What I have begun at certain decisive moments would exist neither far off in the past as an objective memory nor be present like a

memory revived, but really between the two as the field of my becoming during that period. Likewise my relation to another person would not be reducible to a disjunction; an instituting subject could coexist with another because the one instituted is not the immediate reflection of the activity of the former and can be regained by himself or by others without involving anything like a total recreation. Thus the instituted subject exists between others and myself, between me and myself, like a hinge, the consequence and the guarantee of our belonging to a common world"—*Themes from the Lectures at the Collège de France, 1952–1960*, trans. John O'Neill (Evanston: Northwestern University Press, 1970), p. 40. In this spirit, John O'Neill considers reflexivity—the *critical* source of phenomenology—as institution rather than transcendental constitution: "By means of the notion of institution we may furnish a conception of reflexivity which, instead of resting upon a transcendental subjectivity, is given in a field of presence and coexistence which situates reflexivity and truth as sedimentation and search. We must think of reflexivity as tied to the textual structures of temporality and situation through which subjectivity and objectivity are constituted as the intentional unity and style of the world"—*Sociology as a Skin Trade*, p. 231.

37. See Ihde, *Experimental Phenomenology: An Introduction* (New York: G. P. Putnam's Sons, 1977), pp. 137–47.

38. Vico, *On the Study Methods of our Time*, trans. Elio Gianturco (Indianapolis: Bobbs-Merrill, 1965).

39. *Ibid.*, p. 33. In contemporary political theory, this Vichian sentiment of the "science of politics" is best conveyed, I think, in Michael Oakeshott, *On Human Conduct* (Oxford: Clarendon Press, 1975).

40. We would be remiss if we were to fail to notice the more recent debate between Hubert L. Dreyfus, Charles Taylor, and Richard Rorty on the nature of hermeneutics and its relation to the social and the natural sciences. See Dreyfus, "Holism and Hermeneutics"; Taylor, "Understanding in Human Science"; and Rorty, "A Reply to Dreyfus and Taylor; and a Discussion," *The Review of Metaphysics*, 34 (September 1980): 3–46. See also David Couzens Hoy, "Hermeneutics," *Social Research*, 42 (Winter 1980): 649–71.

41. For an excellent discussion of the nature of common sense in this connection, see Clifford Geertz, "Common Sense as a Cultural System," *Antioch Review*, 33 (Spring 1975): 5–27.

42. Vico writes: "This was the order of human institutions: first the forests, after that the huts, then the villages, next the cities, and finally the academies. This axiom is a great principle of etymology, for this sequence of human institutions sets the pattern for the histories of words in the various native languages. Thus we observe in the Latin language that almost the whole corpus of its words had sylvan or rustic origins. For example, *lex*. First it must have meant a collection of vegetables, from which the latter are called *legumina*. Later on, at a time when vulgar letters had not yet been invented for writing down the laws, *lex* by a necessity of civil nature must have meant a collection of citizens, or the public parliament; so that the presence of the people was the *lex*, or "law," that solemnized the wills that were made *calatis comitiis*, in the presence of the assembled *comitia*. Finally, collecting letters, and making, as it were a sheaf of them for each

word, was called *legere*, reading"—*The New Science of Giambattista Vico*, trans. Thomas Goddard Bergin and Max Harold Fisch (Ithaca: Cornell University Press, 1984), pars. 239–40, p. 78.

Chapter Three

1. Eulau, *The Behavioral Persuasion in Politics* (New York: Random House, 1963). See further his "Political Science," in *A Reader's Guide to the Social Sciences*, ed. Bert F. Hoselitz, rev. ed. (New York: Free Press, 1967), pp. 129–237; "Tradition and Innovation: On the Tension between Ancient and Modern Ways in the Study of Politics," in *Behavioralism in Political Science*, ed. Heinz Eulau (New York: Atherton, 1969), pp. 1–21; "The Behavioral Treatment of Politics" and "The Behavioral Movement in Political Science: A Personal Document," in *Micro-Macro Political Analysis* (Chicago: Aldine, 1969), pp. 148–65, 370–90; "Political Behavior," in *International Encyclopedia of the Social Sciences*, ed. David L. Sills (New York: Macmillan, 1968), vol. 12, pp. 203–14; and "Introduction" to *Political Behavior in America: New Directions*, ed. Heinz Eulau (New York: Random House, 1966), pp. 3–13.

2. For a body of literature relevant to my critique of political behavioralism, see particularly the following: Edmund Husserl, *The Crisis of European Sciences and Transcendental Phenomenology*, trans. David Carr (Evanston: Northwestern University Press, 1970); Martin Heidegger, *Being and Time*, trans. John Macquarrie and Edward Robinson (New York: Harper & Brothers, 1962); Jean-Paul Sartre, *Being and Nothingness*, trans. Hazel E. Barnes (New York: Philosophical Library, 1956), and *Critique de la raison dialectique*, vol. 1 (Paris: Gallimard, 1960); Maurice Merleau-Ponty, *Phenomenology of Perceptions*, trans. Colin Smith (London: Routledge & Kegan Paul, 1962), *The Structure of Behavior*, trans. Alden L. Fisher (Boston: Beacon Press, 1963), *The Primacy of Perception*, ed. James M. Edie and trans. William Cobb *et al.* (Evanston: Northwestern University Press, 1964), and *The Visible and the Invisible*, ed. Claude Lefort and trans. Alphonso Lingis (Evanston: Northwestern University Press, 1968); Paul Ricoeur, *Fallible Man*, trans. Charles Kelbley (Chicago: Regnery, 1965), *Freedom and Nature*, trans. Erazim Kohák (Evanston: Northwestern University Press, 1966), and *Freud and Philosophy*, trans. Denis Savage (New Haven: Yale University Press, 1970); John Wild, *Existence and the World of Freedom* (Englewood Cliffs: Prentice-Hall, 1963); Alfred Schutz, *Collected Papers*, 3 vols. (The Hague: Nijhoff, 1962–66), *The Phenomenology of the Social World*, trans. George Walsh and Frederick Lehnert (Evanston: Northwestern University Press, 1967), and *Reflections on the Problem of Relevance*, ed. Richard M. Zaner (New Haven: Yale University Press, 1970); Erwin W. Straus, *Phenomenological Psychology* (New York: Basic Books, 1966) and *The Primary World of Senses*, trans. Jacob Needleman (New York: Free Press, 1963); Maurice Natanson, *Literature, Philosophy, and the Social Sciences* (The Hague: Nijhoff, 1962) and *The Journeying Self* (Reading: Addison-Wesley, 1970); Calvin Schrag, *Experience and Being* (Evanston: Northwestern University Press, 1969); and *Patterns of the Life-World: Essays in Honor of John Wild*, ed. James M. Edie, Francis H. Parker, and Calvin O. Schrag (Evanston: Northwestern University Press, 1970). For a comprehensive survey of the development of phenomenology, see Herbert Spiegelberg, *The Phenomenological Movement*, 3rd rev. and enl. ed. (The Hague: Nijhoff, 1982).

3. Ricoeur, *Husserl: An Analysis of His Phenomenology,* trans. Edward G. Ballard and Lester E. Embree (Evanston: Northwestern University Press, 1967), p. 212.

4. Eulau, "Tradition and Innovation," p. 3.

5. For a phenomenological critique of the behavioralist conception of value, see the present author's "The Place of Valuation in the Theory of Politics: A Phenomenological Critique of Political Behavioralism," *Journal of Value Inquiry,* 14 (1974): 367–88.

6. Cavell, *Must We Mean What We Say?* (New York: Scribner, 1969), p. 22.

7. Maurice Merleau-Ponty, *Signs,* trans. Richard C. McCleary (Evanston: Northwestern University Press, 1964), p. 110 (italics added); see also Aron Gurwitsch, *Studies in Phenomenology and Psychology* (Evanston: Northwestern University Press, 1966), p. 68.

8. Dante Germino, *Beyond Ideology* (New York: Harper & Row, 1967), pp. 190–91.

9. *Ibid.,* p. 191 n. 5.

10. Eulau, "Tradition and Innovation," p. 19. See also *The Behavioral Persuasion in Politics,* pp. 7–8, and "Political Science," pp. 172–73. On the other hand, however, he is critical of William T. Bluhm's work, *Theories of the Political System,* 2d ed. (Englewood Cliffs: Prentice-Hall, 1971), for the reason that it is "a clever if malformed attempt at juxtaposing certain classical and contemporary writers that failed to be convincing because, in stressing continuities, it neglected to take account of the profound discontinuities that make for a very conspicuous separation of the ancients and moderns"—"Political Science," p. 178.

11. Dahl writes that "it [the behavioral mood] will gradually disappear. By this I mean only that it will slowly decay as a distinctive mood and outlook. For it will become, and in fact already is becoming, incorporated into the main body of the discipline. The behavioral mood will not disappear, then, because it has failed. It will disappear rather because it has succeeded. As a separate, somewhat sectarian, slightly factional outlook it will be the first victim of its own triumph"—"The Behavioral Approach in Political Science: Epitaph for a Monument to a Successful Protest," *American Political Science Review,* 55 (December, 1961): 770.

12. Eulau, "The Behavioral Treatment of Politics," p. 150.

13. Kuhn, *The Structure of Scientific Revolutions,* 2d rev. and enl. ed. (Chicago: University of Chicago Press, 1970).

14. Charles L. Stevenson says in *Facts and Values* (New Haven: Yale University Press, 1963), p. 32: "A 'persuasive' definition is one which gives a new conceptual meaning to a familiar word without substantially changing its emotive meaning, and which is used with the conscious or unconscious purpose of changing, by this means, the direction of people's interests."

15. Eulau, *The Behavioral Persuasion in Politics,* p. 5. Cf. Schutz, *Collected Papers,* vol. 1: *The Problem of Social Reality,* ed. Maurice Natanson (The Hague: Nijhoff, 1962), p. 50: "The world of nature, as explored by the natural scientists, does not 'mean' anything to molecules, atoms, and

electrons. But the observational field of the social scientists—social reality—has a specific meaning and relevance structure for the human beings, living, acting, and thinking within it."

16. Schutz, *Collected Papers*, 1, p. 66.

17. Eulau, "Political Behavior," p. 208.

18. Heidegger, *What Is a Thing?* trans. W. B. Barton, Jr. and Vera Deutsch (Chicago: Regnery, 1967).

19. See Heidegger, *Being and Time*, particularly pp. 78 ff.

20. Valéry, *History and Politics*, trans. Denise Folliot and Jackson Mathews (New York: Pantheon Books, 1962), pp. 103, 241.

21. *Political Behavior*, ed. Heinz Eulau, Samuel J. Eldersveld, and Morris Janowitz (Glencoe: Free Press, 1956), p. 3.

22. Eulau, "The Behavioral Treatment of Politics," p. 151.

23. Oppenheim, *Dimensions of Freedom* (New York: St. Martin's, 1961), p. 16.

24. Lane, *Political Thinking and Consciousness* (Chicago: Markham, 1969), pp. 312 ff., and Deutsch, "Mechanism, Teleology, and Mind: The Theory of Communications and Some Problems in Philosophy and Social Science," *Philosophy and Phenomenological Research*, 12 (December 1951): 185–223, which has been incorporated into his *The Nerves of Government* (New York: Free Press, 1966), in chaps. 2, 5, 6, and 8.

25. Deutsch, "Mechanism, Teleology, and Mind," p. 205.

26. Albert Camus, *The Rebel*, trans. Anthony Bower (New York: Knopf, 1956), p. 11.

27. Sartre, *Being and Nothingness*, p. 556 and *passim*.

28. Max Scheler, *Man's Place in Nature*, trans. Hans Meyerhoff (New York: Noonday Press, 1963), p. 29.

29. For the very reason of the existentialist thesis that the human being is incomplete in an incomplete world, Simone de Beauvoir suggests that existentialism is "the only philosophy in which an ethics has its place"— see *The Ethics of Ambiguity*, trans. Bernard Frechtman (New York: Philosophical Library, 1948), p. 34. For an existentialist critique of neoclassical natural law theory, see Chapter 6 below.

30. Merleau-Ponty, *Phenomenology of Perception*, p. 382.

31. Lifton, *Boundaries: Psychological Man in Revolution* (New York: Random House, 1970), pp. 37–63.

32. Etzioni, *The Active Society* (New York: Free Press, 1968).

33. Merleau-Ponty, *The Structure of Behavior*, p. 169.

34. Sartre, *Being and Nothingness*, p. 557.

35. May, *Psychology and the Human Dilemma* (Princeton: Van Nostrand, 1966), p. 220.

36. Straus, *Phenomenological Psychology*, pp. 197–98.

37. *Ibid.*, pp. 137–65.

38. For a phenomenological discussion of the nonverbal expressions of laughing and crying as uniquely human expression, see Helmuth Plessner, *Laughing and Crying*, trans. James S. Churchill and Marjorie Grene (Evanston: Northwestern University Press, 1970).

39. Laing, *The Divided Self* (New York: Pantheon Books, 1969), p. 86.

40. Marcel, *The Mystery of Being*, trans. G. S. Fraser (Chicago: Regnery, 1960), vol. 1, p. 124. See also "Existence and Objectivity," in his *Metaphysical Journal*, trans. Bernard Wall (London: Rockliff, 1952), pp. 319–39, and Maurice Merleau-Ponty, "Husserl et la notion de Nature (Notes prises au cours de Maurice Merleau-Ponty)," *Revue de metaphysique et de morale*, 70 (July–September 1965): 260–61.

41. Wild, Foreword to Merleau-Ponty, *The Structure of Behavior*, pp. xiv–xv.

42. See Husserl, *The Crisis of European Sciences and Transcendental Phenomenology*, pp. 23 ff.

43. Simon, *The Sciences of the Artificial* (Cambridge: MIT Press, 1969). "Artificiality," according to Simon, "connotes perceptual similarity but essential difference, resemblance from without rather than within" (p. 13).

44. Eulau, "Political Behavior," p. 208.

45. Cf. Charles Taylor, *The Explanation of Behavior* (New York: Humanities Press, 1964), p. 272.

46. Otto Neurath, "Sociology and Physicalism," trans. Morton Magnus and Ralph Raico, in *Logical Positivism*, ed. A. J. Ayer (Glencoe: Free Press, 1959), pp 282–317.

47. Barry, *Political Argument* (New York: Humanities Press, 1965), p. 290.

48. See Eulau, "Political Behavior," p. 203; Evron M. Kirkpatrick, "The Impact of the Behavioral Approach on Traditional Political Science," in *Essays on the Behavioral Study of Politics*, ed. Austin Ranney (Urbana: University of Illinois Press, 1962), p. 4; Deutsch, *The Nerves of Government*, p. 17; and Albert Somit and Joseph Tanenhaus, *The Development of American Political Science* (Boston: Allyn and Bacon, 1967), p. 177.

49. Downs, *An Economic Theory of Democracy* (New York: Harper & Row, 1957), pp. 3–20. The same methodological assumption ("methodological individualism") is made by James M. Buchanan, "An Individualistic Theory of Political Process," in *Varieties of Political Theory*, ed. David Easton (Englewood Cliffs: Prentice-Hall, 1966), pp. 25–37.

50. Milton Friedman, *Essays in Positive Economics* (Chicago: University of Chicago Press, 1953), pp. 8–9. In order to avoid the confusion of telling what will happen in the future and explaining an event that has already taken place, it may be useful to distinguish prediction (pre-dict the future) and postdiction (retro-dict the past). See Stephen Toulmin, *Foresight and Understanding* (New York: Harper & Row, 1963), p. 27,

and W. H. Walsh, *An Introduction to Philosophy of History* (London: Hutchinson, 1951), p. 41. Needless to say, so-called prediction in the social sciences has largely been of a postdictive rather than a predictive nature.

51. Toulmin challenges this predictivist thesis and denies the idea that prediction is "the kernel of science." Rather, prediction is a craft or technical application of science; "the predictive success of a theory is only one test of its explanatory power and neither a necessary nor a sufficient one"—*Foresight and Understanding*, pp. 35–36.

52. Ricoeur, *Fallible Man*, p. 109. Straus reminds us that "the logical form of a statement, the linkage with exact measurement, or the use of mathematical expressions are no guarantee of objectivity"—*Phenomenological Psychology*, p. 118.

53. Husserl, *The Crisis of European Sciences and Transcendental Phenomenology*, p. 226.

54. *Ibid.*, p. 127.

55. Merleau-Ponty, *Phenomenology of Perception*, p. viii (italics added).

56. By "social reality" Schutz means "the sum total of objects and occurrences within the social cultural world as experienced by the common-sense thinking of men living their daily lives among their fellow-men, connected with them in manifold relations in interaction"—*Collected Papers*, 1, p. 53. For other views of Schutz's phenomenology of the life-world and its implications for the social sciences, see Peter L. Berger and Thomas Luckmann, *The Social Construction of Reality* (New York: Doubleday, 1966), pp. 19–46, and Alfred Schutz and Thomas Luckmann, *The Structures of the Life-World*, trans. Richard M. Zaner and H. Tristram Engelhardt, Jr. (Evanston: Northwestern University Press, 1973).

57. Natanson, *The Journeying Self*, p. 97.

58. Concerning objectification in philosophy and science, Merleau-Ponty points out that "philosophical self-consciousness does not make science's effort at objectification futile; rather, philosophy pursues this effort at the human level, since all thought is inevitably objectification: only philosophy knows that on this level objectification cannot become carried away and makes us conquer the more fundamental relationship of co-existence. There can be no rivalry between scientific knowledge and the metaphysical knowing which continually confronts the former with its task. A science without philosophy would literally not know what it was talking about. A philosophy without methodical exploration of phenomena would end up with nothing but formal truths, which is to say, errors"—*Sense and Non-Sense*, trans. Hubert L. Dreyfus and Patricia Allen Dreyfus (Evanston: Northwestern University Press, 1964), p. 97.

59. Straus, *The Primary World of Senses*, pp. 111–12.

60. Michael Haas, "A Plea for Bridge Building in International Relations," in *Contending Approaches to International Politics*, ed. Klaus Knorr and James N. Rosenau (Princeton: Princeton University Press, 1969), pp. 168, 163.

61. The idea that scientific understanding necessarily presupposes common-sense understanding is the essential thesis of Schutz's philosophy of the social sciences. See especially "Common-Sense and Scientific Interpretation of Human Action," *Collected Papers*, 1, pp. 3–47, and cf. Harold Garfinkel, "The Rational Properties of Scientific and Common Sense Activities," in *Studies in Ethnomethodology* (Englewood Cliffs: Prentice-Hall, 1967), pp. 262–83.

62. Husserl, *The Crisis of European Sciences and Transcendental Phenomenology*, pp. 130–31.

63. See *Criticism and the Growth of Knowledge*, ed. Imre Lakatos and Alan Musgrave (Cambridge: University Press, 1970), and Israel Scheffler, *Science and Subjectivity* (Indianapolis: Bobbs-Merrill, 1967), pp. 1–19.

64. In asking questions concerning the nature of science and its growth, Kuhn comments that "already it should be clear that the explanation must, in the final analysis, be psychological or sociological. It must, that is, be a description of a value system, an ideology, together with an analysis of the institutions through which that system is transmitted and enforced. Knowing what scientists value, we may hope to understand what problems they will undertake and what choices they will make in particular circumstances of conflict. I doubt that there is another sort of answer to be found"–"Logic of Discovery or Psychology of Research?" in *Criticism and the Growth of Knowledge*, p. 21.

65. Kuhn, *The Structure of Scientific Revolutions*, pp. 111, 122.

66. Cf. Michael Polanyi, *Knowing and Being*, ed. Marjorie Grene (Chicago: University of Chicago Press, 1969), pp. 65–66.

67. Kuhn, *The Structure of Scientific Revolutions*, p. 146.

68. Eulau, "Political Science," p. 210.

69. See Carl G. Hempel, "Science and Human Values," in *Aspects of Scientific Explanation* (New York: Free Press, 1965), pp. 81–96, and Felix E. Oppenheim, *Moral Principles in Political Philosophy* (New York: Random House, 1968), pp. 8 ff. The "policy sciences" belong to the domain of scientific activity insofar as the value judgments they employ are purported to be "extrinsic" or "instrumental."

70. Austin, "Performative Utterances," in his *Philosophical Papers*, ed. J. O. Urmson and G. J. Warnock (Oxford: Clarendon Press, 1961), pp. 220–39, especially p. 222. See also "Performatif-Constatif," in *La Philosophie analytique*, Cahiers de Royaumont, Philosophie No. 4 (Paris: Minuit, 1862), pp. 271–81, and *How to Do Things with Words*, ed. J. O. Urmson (New York: Oxford University Press, 1965).

71. J. O. Urmson, *The Emotive Theory of Ethics* (New York: Oxford University Press, 1968), p. 147.

72. The term "personal" is used by Michael Polanyi, who rejects the idea of "scientific detachment" and considers scientific activity as the personal participation of the knower in the act of establishing contact with reality. Thus to be "personal" means to be neither subjective nor objective—see *Personal Knowledge: Towards a Post-Critical Philosophy* (Chicago: University of Chicago Press, 1958).

73. Gouldner, *The Coming Crisis of Western Sociology* (New York: Basic Books, 1970), p. 13. Cf. W. G. Runciman, *Social Science and Political Theory* (Cambridge: University Press, 1963), p. 174; E. H. Carr, *What Is History?"* (New York: Knopf, 1962), p. 51; and Isaiah Berlin, *Four Essays on Liberty* (New York: Oxford University Press, 1969), p. 92. It is extremely important to note that in rejecting the traditional dualism of subject and object, inner world and outer world, and body and mind, the physicist Werner Heisenberg declares that "even in science *the object of research is no longer nature itself, but man's investigation of nature.*"

What he says further on this matter is worthwhile quoting in some length: "When we speak of the picture of nature in the exact science of our age, we do not mean a picture of nature so much as *a picture of our relationships with nature.* The old division of the world into objective processes in space and time and the mind in which these processes are mirrored—in other words, the Cartesian difference between *res cogitans* and *res extensa*—is no longer a suitable starting point for our understanding of modern science. Science, we find, is now focused on the network of relationships between man and nature, on the framework which makes us as living beings dependent parts of nature, and which we as human beings have simultaneously made the object of our thoughts and actions. Science no longer confronts nature as an objective observer, but sees itself as an actor in this interplay between man and nature"—*The Physicist's Conception of Nature,* trans. Arnold J. Pomerans (New York: Harcourt, Brace, 1958), pp. 24, 28–29; italics Heisenberg's.

74. Paul Ricoeur, *History and Truth,* trans. Charles A. Kelbley (Evanston: Northwestern University Press, 1965), pp. 218–19.

75. Thus Merleau-Ponty declares that "to deal with given languages objectively is not enough. We must study the subject who is actually speaking. To the linguistic of language we must add the linguistic of the word"—*The Primacy of Perception,* p. 84.

76. Cf. C. F. von Weizsäcker, *The History of Nature* (Chicago: University of Chicago Press, 1949), p. 9. For the systematic treatment of knowing or thinking as a hermeneutical event, see particularly Hans-Georg Gadamer, *Truth and Method,* ed. Garrett Barden and John Cumming (New York: Seabury Press, 1975); Paul Ricoeur, *The Conflict of Interpretations,* ed. Don Ihde (Evanston: Northwestern University Press, 1974), and *Freud and Philosophy;* Edmund Husserl, *Logical Investigations,* trans. J. N. Findlay, 2 vols. (New York: Humanities Press, 1970); Jürgen Habermas, *Knowledge and Human Interests,* trans. Jeremy J. Shapiro (Boston: Beacon Press, 1971); and Charles Taylor, "Interpretation and the Sciences of Man," *The Review of Metaphysics,* 25 (September 1971): 3–51. For an excellent historical survey of hermeneutics in this connection, see Richard E. Palmer, *Hermeneutics* (Evanston: Northwestern University Press, 1969).

77. Ricoeur, *Fallible Man,* p. xxi.

78. Merleau-Ponty echoes this spirit when he writes that "because of the fact that the order of knowledge is not the only order, because it is not enclosed in itself, and because it contains at least the gaping chasm of the present, the whole of history is still action and action already history. History is the same whether we contemplate it as a spectacle or assume it as a responsibility"—*The Primacy of Perception,* p. 194.

79. Carr, *What Is History?* p. 9.

80. Oakeshott, *Experience and Its Modes* (Cambridge: University Press, 1933), p. 42.

81. Hanson, *Patterns of Discovery* (Cambridge: University Press, 1969), p. 31.

82. Kuhn, *The Structure of Scientific Revolutions*, p. 55.

83. Merleau-Ponty, *The Primacy of Perception*, pp. 54 ff.

84. Wolin, "Political Theory as a Vocation," *American Political Science Review*, 63 (December 1969): 1073.

85. James, *Principles of Psychology*, 2 vols. (New York: Dover, 1950), vol. 1, p. 222.

86. Eugene T. Gendlin, *Experiencing and the Creation of Meaning* (New York: Free Press, 1962), p. 11.

87. Ricoeur, *Fallible Man*, p. 129.

88. Marcel, *The Mystery of Being*, 1, pp. 127–53.

89. L. S. Vygotsky's genetic and developmental theory of thought and language is most poignant in making the idea of the inseparability between thought and affectivity clear. For him there is no sharp line of division between the inner and the outer since they are two moments of one process and every thought has an effective volitional basis. See his *Thought and Language*, ed. and trans. Eugenia Hanfmann and Gertrude Vakar (Cambridge: MIT Press, 1962). Vygotsky's distinction between "sense" and "meaning" parallels on the one hand James's distinction between knowledge by acquaintance and knowledge-about and Eugene Gendlin's distinction between felt meaning and symbolic meaning on the other.

90. Cf. Michael Polanyi, *The Tacit Dimension* (New York: Doubleday, 1966), p. 4.

91. Eulau, *The Behavioral Persuasion in Politics*, p. 32.

92. Eulau, "The Behavioral Treatment of Politics," p. 149. Eulau often endorses Morris R. Cohen's view of science and liberalism as two complementary systems of undogmatic attitudes; see Cohen, *The Faith of a Liberal* (New York: Holt, 1946), pp. 437–69. Interestingly enough, Eulau assigns to psychoanalysis the task of curing resistance to behavioralist techniques—see *The Behavioral Persuasion in Politics*, p. 32. It might also be suggested that an equally interesting task for psychoanalysis is to determine *why* science and technology have become thaumaturgy for modern humanity, including the intellectual and the layperson alike. In *The Psychology of Science* (Chicago: Regnery, 1966), Abraham Maslow remarks that "these 'good,' 'nice' scientific words—prediction, control, rigor, certainty, exactness, preciseness, neatness, orderliness, lawfulness, quantification, proof, explanation, validation, reliability, rationality, organization, etc.—are all capable of being pathologized when pushed to the extreme. All of them may be pressed into the service of the safety needs, that is, they may become primarily anxiety-avoiding and anxiety-controlling mechanisms" (p. 30).

93. Simon, *The Sciences of the Artificial*, p. 83. Cf. Gaston Bachelard, *La Formation de l'esprit scientifique: Contribution à une psychanalyse de la connaissance objective* (Paris: Vrin, 1947), pp. 250–51.

94. See Wiener, *Cybernetics*, 2d ed. (Cambridge: MIT Press, 1961), p. 164: "Whether our investigations in the social sciences be statistical or dynamic—and they should participate in the nature of both—they can never be good to more than a very few decimal places, and, in short, can never furnish us with a quantity of verifiable significant information which begins to compare with that which we have learned to expect in the natural sciences. We cannot afford to neglect them; neither should we build exaggerated expectations of their possibilities. There is much which we must leave, whether we like it or not, to the un-'scientific,' narrative method of the professional historian."

95. Deutsch, *The Nerves of Government*, p. 10.

96. Deutsch, "Mechanism, Teleology, and Mind," p. 192.

97. *Ibid.*, p. 222.

98. *Ibid.*, p. 216.

99. Deutsch, *The Nerves of Government*, p. 10, and "Mechanism, Teleology, and Mind," p. 221.

100. See Hubert L. Dreyfus, *Alchemy and Artificial Intelligence*, RAND Paper P-3244 (Santa Monica: RAND, December 1965); "Phenomenology and Artificial Intelligence," in *Phenomenology in America*, ed. James M. Edie (Chicago: Quandrangle, 1967), pp. 31–47; and "Why Computers Must Have Bodies in Order to Be Intelligent," *The Review of Metaphysics*, 21 (September 1967): 13–32. Dreyfus's most comprehensive critique of artificial reason is found in *What Computers Can't Do* (New York: Harper & Row, 1972).

101. Dreyfus, "Why Computers Must Have Bodies," p. 14.

102. Dreyfus, *Alchemy and Artificial Intelligence*, p. 66 (italics added).

103. It is extremely important to note that one of the most serious dilemmas that confronts the Cartesian notion of the human being as a *substance,* and thus the cybernetic model and the science of the human being as an artifact in relation to the *social* sciences, is that these concepts are incapable of rendering a philosophically consistent justification for intersubjectivity or sociality. For as Sartre rightly points out, once the self and the other are regarded as substances, which is to say, two separate substances, solipsism is inescapable—see *Being and Nothingness,* p. 233.

104. For an excellent criticism of cybernetics from a biological point of view, see Hans Jonas, "Cybernetics and Purpose: A Critique," in his *The Phenomenon of Life* (New York: Dell, 1966), pp. 108–34.

105. Simon, *The Sciences of the Artificial*, p. 52.

106. Merleau-Ponty, *The Primacy of Perception, p.* 99.

107. See Dreyfus, "Why Computers Must Have Bodies" and *What Computers Can't Do,* especially pp. 143 ff.

108. Dreyfus, "Why Computers Must Have Bodies," p. 31.

109. Dreyfus, *Alchemy and Artificial Intelligence*, p. 66.

110. Wittgenstein, *Tractatus Logico-Philosophicus*, trans. D. F. Pears and B. F. McGuinness (London: Routledge & Kegan Paul, 1961), p. 119.

111. See further Chapter 1 above.

Chapter Four

1. John O'Neill, *Five Bodies: The Human Shape of Human Society* (Ithaca: Cornell University Press, 1985), p. 12.

2. Martin Heidegger, *The Basic Problems of Phenomenology*, trans. Albert Hofstadter (Bloomington: Indiana University Press, 1982), p. 23.

3. Hayden White, *Tropics of Discourse* (Baltimore: Johns Hopkins University Press, 1978), p. 4. Etymologically speaking, dia/lectics is one of the very few words in philosophy that is auditory and verbal rather than visual. For this reason, I wish to preserve the auditory sense of dia/logue in Plato's writings in transplanting (dia-)"tactics." See also n. 1 to Chapter 10 below.

4. See José Ortega y Gasset, *Historical Reason*, trans. Philip W. Silver (New York: Norton, 1984), p. 102. Chinese philosophers call this logic the "logic of correlation" as opposed to the "logic of identity." The logic of correlation refers to the unity of two opposites—*yin* and *yang*—as complementary. See, for example, Chang Tung-sun, "A Chinese Philosopher's Theory of Knowledge," in *Our Language and Our World*, ed. S. I. Hayakawa (New York: Harper & Brothers, 1959), pp. 299–324. For a discussion of the dialectic as a "logic of correlation" in early Greek thought, see G. E. R. Lloyd, *Polarity and Analogy* (Cambridge: Cambridge University Press, 1966), pp. 1–171. In the Chinese philosophical tradition, the "logic of correlation" is exemplified in the *I Ching* or Book of Changes as the unity of *yin* and *yang* as complementary. In *Chi: A Neo-Taoist Approach to Life* (Cambridge: MIT Press, 1974), R. G. H. Siu writes that "in reality. . . . *yin* does not exist without *yang*, nor *yang* without *yin*. A truer model . . . would be one in which each of the actual *yin* and actual *yang* numbers is a resultant of many vectors, rather than being a singularity of its own. Thus, -1 may be the resultant of $(+7, -8)$, $(+8, -2 + 15, -22)$, and so on. One should not be surprised, therefore, to find contradictions within the same person or event. These are intrinsic to being. A is both A and not $-$A" (p. 289).

5. The historical semanticist Leo Spitzer has an extensive discussion on the subject in *Essays in Historical Semantics* (New York: S. F. Vanni, 1948), pp. 179–316.

6. See Hannah Arendt, *The Human Condition* (Chicago: University of Chicago Press, 1958). In discussing the Europeanization of Mesoamerica (and the Third World today), Tzvetan Todorov comments that "we want *equality* without its compelling us to accept identity; but also *differences* without its degenerating into superiority/inferiority. We aspire to reap the benefits of the egalitarian model *and* of the hierarchic model; we aspire to rediscover the meaning of the social without losing quality of the individual"—*The Conquest of America: The Question of the Other,* trans. Richard Howard (New York: Harper & Row, 1984), p. 249. This book is not a historical work but, as the subtitle suggests, a philosophical discussion of the self (Europeans) and the other (original Mesoamericans).

7. In *Totality and Infinity,* trans. Alphonso Lingis (Pittsburgh: Duquesne University Press, 1969), Emmanuel Levinas accentuates the principle of distinction when he says that pluralism is not a multiplicity of numbers, but is predicated upon a radical alterity of the other. Pluralism is for him an impossibility if the other were reduced to the Same. Thus the other is described not in terms of Totality, but in terms of Infinity, without which morality itself would be impossible. In his anthropological study, Robert Hertz conclusively documents the inequality in our treatment of the right and the left hand across different cultures: the right hand has been invariably right and noble, whereas the left hand has been wrong and servile. In brief, there is no perfect ambidexterity or symmetry in an anthropological and sociological sense—see *Death and the Right Hand,* trans. Rodney and Claudia Needham (Glencoe: Free Press, 1960), pp. 89–113. Hertz exclaims: "What resemblance more perfect than that between our two hands! And yet what a striking inequality there is!" (*ibid.,* p. 89).

8. See George Steiner, *After Babel: Aspects of Language and Translation* (New York: Oxford University Press, 1975).

9. In *What Is Called Thinking?* trans. Fred D. Wieck and J. Glenn Gray (New York: Harper & Row, 1968), Martin Heidegger has a marvelous passage about the many ways of the hand that culminate in thinking as a "handicraft": "The hand's gestures run everywhere through language, in their most perfect purity precisely when man speaks by being silent. And only when man speaks, does he think—not the other way around, as metaphysics still believes. Every motion of the hand in every one of its works carries itself through the element of thinking, every bearing of the hand bears itself in that element. All the work of the hand is rooted in thinking. Therefore, thinking itself is man's simplest, and for that reason hardest, handiwork, if it would be accomplished at its proper time" (pp. 16–17). Cf. David Sudnow's "sociology of the hand" in his *Ways of the Hand* (Cambridge: Harvard University Press, 1978) and *Talk's Body* (New York: Knopf, 1979), and cf. also n. 23 to Chapter 9 below.

10. In *The Visible and the Invisible,* ed. Claude Lefort and trans. Alphonso Lingis (Evanston: Northwestern University Press, 1968), Maurice Merleau-Ponty elevates the phenomenology of the body to the ontology of the flesh. He speaks of the flesh as an "element" in the same sense as water, air, earth, and fire. As "a general thing," it is called "an element of Being" (p. 139).

11. Elizabeth Sewell, *The Orphic Voice* (London: Routledge & Kegan Paul, 1961), pp. 35–36.

12. Concerning Cartesianism as an intellectual outline of the modern age and as the philosophical harbinger of scientific and technological rationality in alliance with Galileo, Bacon, Locke, and Newton, and concerning the deconstruction of the Cartesian paradigm toward a post-Cartesian movement, see particularly Edwin Arthur Burtt, *The Metaphysical Foundation of Modern Science* (Garden City: Doubleday, 1955); Philip J. Davis and Reuben Hersh, *Descartes' Dream* (San Diego: Harcourt Brace Jovanovich, 1986); Morris Berman, *The Reenchantment of the World* (Ithaca: Cornell University Press, 1981); Herman Josef Meyer, *Die Technisierung der Welt* (Tübingen: Max Niemeyer, 1961); William Barrett, *The Illusion of Technique* (Garden City: Doubleday, 1985); and Carolyn Merchant, *The Death of Nature* (New York: Harper & Row, 1980). In our critique of technological rationality in the social sciences, the 1984 Reith

Lectures of John Searle published as *Minds, Brains and Science* (Cambridge: Harvard University Press, 1984) should be singled out. The tenor of Searle's lectures reminds us of Alfred Schutz's social phenomenology or phenomenology of the social sciences. Searle refutes the thesis of artificial intelligence that the human brain is a digital computer and the human mind is a computer program. He maintains that there is a "radical discontinuity" between the human and the artificial. Searle blames the dualism of Descartes as a main source of the problems in modern philosophical discourse, and attempts to fill what he perceives to be a gap between mentalism and physicalism. He writes: "Now that leaves us apparently with a gap, a gap between the brain and the mind. And some of the greatest intellectual efforts of the twentieth century have been attempts to fill this gap, to get a science of human behavior which was not just commonsense grandmother psychology, but was not scientific neurophysiology either. Up to the present time, without exception, the gap-filling efforts have been failures. Behaviorism was the most spectacular failure, but in my lifetime I have lived through exaggerated claims made on half of and eventually disappointed by games theory, cybernetics, information theory, structuralism, sociobiology, and a bunch of others. To anticipate a bit, I am going to claim that all the gap-filling efforts fail because there isn't any gap to fill" (p. 42).

233
Notes

13. Quoted in Colin Murray Turbayne,*The Myth of Metaphor,* rev. ed. (Columbia: University of South Carolina Press, 1970), pp. 101–2.

14. See Jacob Klein, *Greek Mathematical Thought and the Origin of Algebra,* trans. Eva Brann (Cambridge: MIT Press, 1968), p. 123.

15. History repeats itself, indeed. The quarrel between the Cartesians, who are "analytical" and "exact," and the Viconians, who are "topical" and "inventive," has been reenacted in the contemporary controversy between "two cultures." For the quarrel between the Cartesians and the Viconians, see Michael Mooney, *Vico in the Tradition of Rhetoric* (Princeton: Princeton University Press, 1985), *passim.* By now Husserl's critique of scientism as "methodism" is well known. Scientism, according to him, is fallacious because it is foremost a conceptual garb (*Ideenkleid*) whereby what once was, or was intended to be, true in the mathematical formalization of nature *as a method* has gradually been taken, or indeed mistaken, for reality itself—see *The Crisis of European Sciences and Transcendental Phenomenology,* trans. David Carr (Evanston: Northwestern University Press, 1970). Thus the mathematical sedimentation of science since Galileo "is cast upon the life-world so as to conceal it to the point of being substituted for it. What in truth is a method and the result of that method comes to be taken for reality"—Aron Gurwitsch, "Comment on the Paper by H. Marcuse," in *Boston Studies in the Philosophy of Science,* vol. 2, ed. Robert S. Cohen and Marx W. Wartofsky (New York: Humanities Press, 1965), p. 300. For an extensive discussion on the subject, see further Aron Gurwitsch, *Phenomenology and the Theory of Science,* ed. Lester Embree (Evanston: Northwestern University Press, 1974).

16. René Descartes, *Philosophical Writings,* trans. Norman Kemp Smith (New York: Modern Library, 1958), pp. 239–40 (from the "Sixth Meditation" in *Meditations on First Philosophy*). Cf. *Oeuvres et Lettres de Descartes,* ed. André Bridoux (Paris: Éditions Gallimard, 1953), p. 326.

17. For a phenomenological critique of the Cartesian world of the senses, see Erwin Straus, *The Primary World of Senses,* trans. Jacob

Needleman (Glencoe: Free Press, 1963), *passim*. For a discussion of Descartes' dualism of mind and body, see C. A. Van Peursen, *Body, Soul, Spirit: A Survey of the Body-Mind Problem*, trans. Hubert H. Hoskins (London: Oxford University Press, 1966), pp. 18–33. In "The Other Descartes and Medicine," in *Phenomenology and the Understanding of Human Destiny*, ed. Stephen Skousgaard (Washington: Center for Advanced Research in Phenomenology and University Press of America, 1981), pp. 93–117, Richard M. Zaner discusses the implications of the Cartesian problematic of mind and body to medicine and the biomedical sciences. According to Albert William Levi, Descartes mirrors the vision of his age: "Descartes produced a philosophy which is at the same time a conception of the world, because the dualisms which haunt his thoughts are little more than the dilemmas of his age. . . . If Descartes is at once an idealist and a materialist (an idealist in metaphysics, a mechanistic materialist in science), this is but a mark of mind perfectly expressing the dilemma of the epoch. The seventeenth century lies between a dying feudalism and a rising bourgeoisie, between faith and science, theology and rational criticism, and this is perfectly expressed through that curious mixture in Descartes himself of prudence and audacity, timidity and assertiveness, impertinence and discretion, which are to be found so conspicuously in his response to the institutions of his time, in the letters he addresses to his contemporaries, and in the prefaces and prefatory materials of his major published works"—*Philosophy as Social Expression* (Chicago: University of Chicago Press, 1974), p. 218.

18. See Ortega y Gasset, *Historical Reason*, p. 122.

19. There is no one who argues against the egocentrism of the *Cogito* (the "I think") more vigorously and convincingly than John Macmurray. As the alternative, he offers the heterocentrism of the self as agent—see *The Self as Agent* (London: Faber and Faber, 1957) and *Persons in Relation* (London: Faber and Faber, 1961).

20. Laing, *The Divided Self* (New York: Pantheon Books, 1969), p. 86. Cf. Norman O. Brown, *Closing Time* (New York: Random House, 1973), p. 105: "Vico overcomes the disastrous dualism of the seventeenth century *res cogitans* and *res extensa.*"

21. Marcel, *The Mystery of Being*, trans. G. S. Fraser (Chicago: Regnery, 1960), vol. 1, p. 124. For a phenomenology of the body, see Richard M. Zaner, *The Problem of Embodiment* (The Hague: Nijhoff, 1964). In "Subjectivity," *The Review of Metaphysics*, 38 (1984): 227–73, Albert Shalom discusses the physical and metaphysical genesis of Cartesian dualism, the dualism of *res cogitans* and *res extensa*, as the result of positing the former in opposition to the latter as "matter" extended in space. Shalom points out that while Descartes was the first thinker who saw the philosophical consequences of seventeenth-century mechanism, he reached an impasse in resolving its difficulties, that is, he ended in contradiction in his attempt to resolve the body/mind dualism. To resolve the impasse of Cartesian dualism, Shalom suggests the conception of subjectivity as "personal identity" that would integrate body and mind.

22. Merleau-Ponty, *The Primacy of Perception*, ed. James M. Edie (Evanston: Northwestern University Press, 1964), p. 99. One of the best discussions on the role of habit in human conduct is found in John Dewey, *Human Nature and Conduct* (New York: Modern Library, 1957). At the end of his "Cartesian meditations"—including the fifth meditation on in-

tersubjectivity—Husserl approvingly quotes St. Augustine: "Do not wish to go out; go back into yourself. Truth dwells in the inner man"—*Cartesian Meditations*, trans. Dorion Cairns (The Hague: Nijhoff, 1960), p. 157. We know that an attempt to understand intersubjectivity or coexistence by "reducing" it (in the phenomenological sense of *epochē*) to the egological sphere (i.e., to treat it as transcendental constitution) is futile or leads us to a labyrinthine impasse. Thus Alfred Schutz long ago intimated that the social sciences, whose kernel is intersubjectivity, would find their true foundation *not* in transcendental phenomenology but in the "constitutive phenomenology of the natural attitude," and that intersubjectivity should be taken as a given datum (*Gegebenheit*) of the life-world as sociocultural reality. See Schutz, *Collected Papers*, vol. 1: *The Problem of Social Reality*, ed. Maurice Natanson (The Hague: Nijhoff, 1962), p. 149 *et passim*. Here let us also recall Maurice Merleau-Ponty's suggestion that "if the subject were taken not as a constituting but an instituting subject, it might be understood that the subject does not exist instantaneously and that the other person does not exist simply as a negative of myself. What I have begun at certain decisive moments would exist neither far off in the past as an objective memory nor be present like a memory revived, but really between the two as the field of my becoming during that period. Likewise my relation to another person would not be reducible to a disjunction: an instituting subject could coexist with another because the one instituted is not the immediate reflection of the activity of the former and can be regained by himself or by others without involving anything like a total recreation. Thus the instituted subject exists between others and myself, between me and myself, like a hinge, the consequence and the guarantee of our belonging to a common world"—*Themes from the Lectures at the Collège de France, 1952–1960*, trans. John O'Neill (Evanston: Northwestern University Press, 1970), p. 40. The implications of this passage for social and political philosophy are enormous.

23. Richard Rorty makes a conscious attempt to avoid visual allusions in philosophizing. Edifying philosophy, as he calls it, is "the attempt to prevent conversation from degenerating into inquiry—into an exchange of views"—*Philosophy and the Mirror of Nature* (Princeton: Princeton University Press, 1979), p. 372. In the proliferating literature on this issue, see particularly Walter J. Ong, *The Presence of the Word* (New Haven: Yale University Press, 1967). The famed literary critic Northrop Frye comments that "drama, like music, is an ensemble performance for an audience, and music and drama are most likely to flourish in a society with a strong consciousness of itself as a society, like Elizabethan England. When a society becomes individualized and competitive, like Victorian England, music and drama suffer accordingly, and the written word almost monopolizes literature"—*Anatomy of Criticism* (Princeton: Princeton University Press, 1957), p. 249.

24. Martin Heidegger, *The Question Concerning Technology and Other Essays*, trans. William Lovitt (New York: Harper & Row, 1977), especially "The Age of the World Picture," pp. 115–54. See also vol. 2 of Jean Beaufret, *Dialogue avec Heidegger*, 4 vols. (Paris: Éditions de Minuit, 1973–1985). Guy Debord, *Society of the Spectacle* (Detroit: Black and Red, 1983) is a Marxist critique of the spectacle as an autonomous ideology or *Weltanschauung*. Although it is suggestive rather than systematic, it strikes a sympathetic chord with the main thesis of the present essay when it is critical of the visualization of the world in terms of "representation," "objectification," "having," and monologic communication. Debord

echoes the Heideggerian critique of Western metaphysics when he writes in paragraph 19: "The spectacle inherits all the *weaknesses* of the Western philosophical project which undertook to comprehend activity in terms of the categories of *seeing;* furthermore, it is based on the incessant spread of the precise technical rationality which grew out of this thought. The spectacle does not realize philosophy, it philosophizes reality. The concrete life of everyone has been degraded into a *speculative* universe." For a discussion of Heidegger's *Being and Time* as a deconstruction of the Cartesian model of epistemology, see Charles B. Guignon, *Heidegger and the Problem of Knowledge* (Indianapolis: Hackett, 1983). For a critical study of Descartes's visual metaphysics, see Turbayne, *The Myth of Metaphor.* Concerning "objectivity"—the hallmark of social-scientific methodology—it is noteworthy that there is a family resemblance between "objective" and "optical": the former refers to that lens in an optical instrument which is nearest to the object.

25. See Michel Foucault, *Discipline and Punish,* trans. Alan Sheridan (New York: Pantheon Books, 1977), pp. 195–228. Thomas A. Spragen, *The Irony of Liberal Reason* (Chicago: University of Chicago Press, 1981), is a thoughtful critique of the schizophrenic tendencies of liberal reason from Descartes and Locke to present-day behavioralism and makes a convincing case for its network of technocracy coupled with value noncognitivism. Spragens refers to Bentham's Panopticon as "the paradigmatic institution of technocracy" (p. 119). When, Spragens reports, Edmund Burke saw Bentham's plan, he spoke of the Panopticon's keeper as "the spider in the web." I prefer "network" to "web" because in our age of technocracy, the former is a technocratic term while the latter is an organic one.

26. *The Works of Jeremy Bentham,* 11 vols., reprinted from the Bowering Edition of 1838–1843 (New York: Russell and Russell, 1962), vol. 4, p. 74.

27. See *ibid.,* pp. 44, 80, 79, respectively. In the context of the social and psychological dialectic of the visible and the invisible, it is worth mentioning that Ralph Ellison's *Invisible Man,* 30th Anniversary Edition (New York: Random House, 1982), is a dramatization of the American black in search of *visibility.*

28. Foucault, *Discipline and Punish,* pp. 201–2.

29. *Ibid.,* p. 217.

30. William T. Bluhm, *Force or Freedom?* (New Haven: Yale University Press, 1984) is a discerning critique of the ambiguous legacy of Descartes and its failure to achieve "a philosophy of freedom under law." Bluhm describes the central theme of his project: "It is from the puzzles, tensions, and ambiguities of Cartesian philosophy, I shall argue, that the ambivalences, tensions, and paradoxes of modern political thought . . . have arisen. The common currency of the diverse modern conceptions of individual freedom is found in the autonomy of Descartes's lone thinker, while the notion of force they share derives from the Cartesian view of body as mathematically structured matter whose motions are governed by necessary laws. Just as Cartesian dualism contains a fundamental ambiguity about the precise relationship between the free determinations of mind and will of the observer and political actor and the necessary movements of observed body (political behavior), so is there an ambiguity about

how subjective freedom of individual political choice can intelligibly be related to the objective necessities of a manipulable body politic" (pp. 25–26). In essence, Bluhm's force/freedom theme traces the political consequences of Descartes's body/mind problematic. Although he does not specifically mention or discuss Descartes, Stephen L. Newman, *Liberalism at Wits' End* (Ithaca: Cornell University Press, 1984) can be placed on the extended platform of Bluhm's thesis. For it is a critique of radical libertarianism (e.g., the libertarian ideology of Robert Nozick), whose politics of the apolitical demands the satisfaction of private desires, wishes, and dreams before the fulfillment of the public good, i.e., it aims at "the privatization of social existence."

31. See Julian Marias, *José Ortega y Gasset: Circumstance and Vocation,* trans. Frances M. Lopez-Morillas (Norman: University of Oklahoma Press, 1971), especially "The Idea of Circumstance," pp. 353–65; see also Philip W. Silver, *Ortega as Phenomenologist: The Genesis of Meditations on Quixote* (New York: Columbia University Press, 1978).

32. Ortega y Gasset, *Historical Reason,* p. 52. In this context, compare Ortega's thought with the following two passages from Merleau-Ponty: "The most important lesson which the reduction teaches us is the impossibility of a complete reduction," and "where empiricism was deficient was in any internal connection between the object and the act which it triggers off. What intellectualism lacks is contingency in the occasions of thought. In the first case consciousness is too poor, in the second too rich for any phenomenon to appeal compellingly to it. Empiricism cannot see that we need to know what we are looking for, otherwise we would not be looking for it, and intellectualism fails to see that we need to be ignorant of what we are looking for, or equally again we should not be searching"—*Phenomenology of Perception,* trans. Colin Smith (London: Routledge & Kegan Paul, 1962), pp. xiv, 28.

33. B. F. Skinner, *Beyond Freedom and Dignity* (New York: Knopf, 1971), p. 18.

34. For discussions of Descartes' theory of music, see Arthur W. Locke, "Descartes and Seventeenth-Century Music," *Music Quarterly,* 21 (1935): 423–31, and John Hollander, *The Untuning of the Sky* (Princeton: Princeton University Press, 1961). See also Erwin Panofsky, "Galileo as a Critic of the Arts: Aesthetic Attitude and Scientific Thought," *Isis,* 47 (1956): 3–15.

35. Hollander, *The Untuning of the Sky,* p. 179. Hollander then makes the following observation: "Descartes goes on to anticipate Pavlov to a certain extent, and to lay the groundwork for a notion of phonic norms established by means of conditioning . . . " (*ibid.*). We are well aware of Noam Chomsky's critique of Skinner. However, what is most interesting about Chomsky's "Cartesian linguistics" and Skinner's "verbal behaviorism" is a convergence in their "naturalistic" assumptions of language. George Steiner documents this convergence in an essay on "Tongues of Men," in his *Extraterritorial* (New York: Atheneum, 1976), pp. 102–25. Steiner quotes Yorick Wilks: "Chomsky's quarrel with Skinner is a trifle spurious. The dispute is not between a mechanistic model and a free or idealistic vision of the production of human speech, but between two alternative mechanistic theories: Skinner's the simple one, and Chomsky's the more complicated' " (*ibid.,* p. 120).

36. Charles J. Lumsden and Edward O. Wilson, *Promethean Fire: Reflections on the Origin of Mind* (Cambridge: Harvard University Press, 1983), p. 170.

37. *Ibid.*, p. 181.

38. *Ibid.*, p. 173.

39. *Ibid.*, p. 209.

40. In *The Mismeasure of Man* (New York: Norton, 1981), Stephen J. Gould comments on sociobiology as biological determinism: "The *biological* basis of human uniqueness leads us to reject biological determinism. Our large brain is the biological foundation of intelligence; intelligence is the ground of culture; and cultural transmission builds a new mode of evolution more effective than Darwinian processes in its limited realm—the 'inheritance' and modification of learned behavior. As philosopher Stephen Toulmin stated . . . 'Culture has the power to impose itself on nature from within' " (p. 325). See further Gould, *Ever Since Darwin* (New York: Norton, 1977), pp. 251–59.

41. See Marjorie Grene, "Sociobiology and the Human Mind," *Transaction*, 15 (September/October, 1978): 23–27. In *The Use and Abuse of Biology* (Ann Arbor: University of Michigan Press, 1976), Marshall Sahlins criticizes Wilson's sociobiology for reading certain cultural conditions into the conditions of nature. In this sense, sociobiology contains elements of anti-ethological anthropomorphism. To speak of the "selfish gene" is to anthropomorphize the biological. For a philosophy of biology favorable to phenomenological analysis, see Marjorie Grene, *Approaches to a Philosophical Biology* (New York: Basic Books, 1968). Speaking of Adolf Portmann's philosophical biology, Grene writes that "in the main tradition of modern naturalism, man must appear either as wholly alien to nature, like Galileo's 'living creature,' or as reduced to meaninglessness, simply one or more expression of the laws of matter in motion. The achievements of man, art, religion, legal and political institutions, science itself, *can* have no significance in a naturalistic one-level world, where there *is*, on principle, nothing but particles in a four-dimensional space-time continuum. Admittedly, if mechanism were true—if the book of the universe spread before us *were* Galilean—we should have to resign ourselves to this dismal fact: the only appropriate philosophy would be one of absurdism or of despair. Yet why should we so resign ourselves? In loyalty to the 'facts'? But the naturalist interpretation of man is itself in palpable contradiction of the 'facts' of our experience, even of living nature other than man, let alone of the massive human fact of consciousness, of the inner lives we do in fact lead. It seems intellectually justifiable, therefore, to try to revise our thinking about nature in such a way as to assimilate harmoniously to our basic view of things those aspects of our experience, so close to our deepest hopes and needs, which Galilean science must either deny or exile to some limbo of paradox and anomaly. And it is this more harmonious philosophy, this reintegration of man *into* nature, I believe, that Portmann's account of the characters of living things can help us to achieve" (p. 31).

42. Lumsden and Wilson, *Promethean Fire*, pp. 23–24.

43. Alfred North Whitehead, *Modes of Thought* (New York: Macmillan, 1938), p. 38.

44. Ortega y Gasset, *Historical Reason*, p. 96.

45. Sherry Turkle, *The Second Self: Computers and the Human Spirit* (New York: Simon & Schuster, 1984), p. 268. A phenomenological critique of artificial intelligence is found in Hubert L. Dreyfus, *What Computers Can't Do: The Limits of Artificial Intelligence,* rev. ed. (New York: Harper & Row, 1979).

46. Herbert A. Simon, *Reason in Human Affairs* (Stanford: Stanford University Press, 1983), p. 13.

47. *Ibid.,* p. 58.

48. *Ibid.,* p. 70.

49. See the present author's *The Crisis of Political Understanding* (Pittsburgh: Duquesne University Press, 1979), Chap. 6. "A Critique of the Cybernetic Model of Man in Political Science," pp. 109–29.

50. Herbert A. Simon, *The Sciences of the Artificial* (Cambridge: MIT Press, 1969), pp. 51–52.

51. *Ibid.,* p. 3.

52. Simon, *Reason in Human Affairs,* p. 93.

53. Marshall McLuhan, *Understanding Media* (New York: McGraw-Hill, 1964), p. 8. His critique of typographic humanity and of culture as mechanistic and visualistic is found in *The Gutenberg Galaxy: The Making of Typographic Man* (Toronto: University of Toronto Press, 1962).

54. McLuhan, *Understanding Media,* p. 18.

55. For a phenomenological critique of McLuhan, see the present author's "The Medium as Technology: A Phenomenological Critique of Marshall McLuhan," in *Phenomenology and the Understanding of Human Destiny,* pp. 45–80. For a collection of phenomenological essays on the philosophy of communication with a focus on technology, see *Communication Philosophy and the Technical Age,* ed. Michael J. Hyde (University: University of Alabama Press, 1982).

56. Cf. Langdon Winner's definition of "reverse adaptation" as the phenomenon in which "technical systems becomes severed from the ends originally set for them and, in effect, reprogram themselves and their environments to suit the special conditions of their own operation. The artificial slave gradually subverts the rule of its master"—*Autonomous Technology: Technics-out-of-Control as a Theme in Political Thought* (Cambridge: MIT Press, 1977), p. 227.

57. The main thesis of Ortega y Gasset, *The Revolt of the Masses* (New York: Norton, 1932) is often misunderstood as an elitist theory of politics. It must instead be understood as a critique of the anonymity of contemporary society, of the "lonely crowd," to use the expression of the American sociologist David Riesman.

58. Merleau-Ponty, *The Primacy of Perception,* p. 160. To *en/chant* the world, it is high time for us to *deconstruct* visual metaphors and models by means of auditory ones in order to explain the concept of sociality. For an outline of this new direction, see the present author's "Rhetoric, Grammatology, and Political Theory," *Reflections,* 4 (1983): 37–53. Alfred Schutz hinted at something very important: "A study of the social relationships connected with the musical process may lead to some insights valid

for many other forms of social intercourse, perhaps even to illumination of a certain aspect of the structure of social interaction as such that has not so far attracted from social scientists the attention it deserves"—*Collected Papers*, vol. 2: *Studies in Social Theory*, ed. Arvid Brodersen (The Hague: Nijhoff, 1964), pp. 159–60. See also Schutz, "Fragments on the Phenomenology of Music," ed. F. Kersten, *Music and Man*, 2 (1976): 5–71. In his critique of Ervin Goffman's "frame analysis," Avery Sharron comments that "the use of the theatrical analogy of society is limited, though. It focuses us to think in structural terms, such as script and set, because it describes a conceptualization of reality and not reality itself. A spatial-visual art is therefore a limited depiction of social reality. A temporal art, however, has to take time seriously and acknowledge its three dimensions. A musical analogy, for instance, in which the world is not a place (stage) but an abstract substance (sound), and all people make music, together or not, leaves a greater analytical freedom, illustrating the endless flow of social life"—"Frame Paralysis: When Time Stands Still," *Social Research*, 48 (1981): 516. I agree with the general emphasis on temporality as the key to the analysis of social reality except for the definition of sound as "an abstract substance."

Chapter Five

1. In recent years, the epistemology of anthropology has been focusing on this question of variance and invariance in terms of "rationality." For the most sustained debates on the subject, see *Rationality*, ed. Bryan R. Wilson (Oxford: Blackwell, 1970), and *Rationality and Relativism*, ed. Martin Hollis and Steven Lukes (Cambridge: MIT Press, 1982). In the thicket of these debates, Charles Taylor raises the question of ethnocentricity, makes an interesting point on the close connection between "understanding the order of things and being in attunement with it," and argues, albeit briefly, for the "transcultural judgments of rationality"—see "Rationality," in *Rationality and Relativism*, pp. 87–105. In *Beyond Objectivism and Relativism: Science, Hermeneutics, and Praxis* (Philadelphia: University of Pennsylvania Press, 1983), Richard J. Bernstein, too, points out that "relativists are suspicious of their opponents because, the relativists claim, all species of objectivism almost inevitably turn into vulgar or sophisticated forms of ethnocentrism in which some privileged understanding of rationality is falsely legitimated by claiming for it an unwarranted universality" (p. 19). In *Understanding* (Westport: Greenwood Press, 1982), G. B. Madison offers a third, phenomenological alternative to cross-cultural understanding, an alternative meant to avoid the extremes of absolutism and relativism. His critique of allegedly "value-free," "objective" scientific methodology as "reductionistic" continues the well-established tradition of phenomenology's critique of scientism. "In order to discern as best as we can the actual structure and mode of operation of human understanding," Madison writes, "we must apply the phenomenological reduction. We must suspend any prior conception we might have as to the ontological status of the objects of understanding (scientific, magical, or otherwise) and as to the relation between understanding and what is called reality so as to be able to analyze understanding and its various modes simply as they present themselves to our reflective scrutiny" (p. 64). As the suspension of all prior judgments, the phenomenological reduction (*epoché*) points in the right direction. The problem, however, does not end here. If, as Merleau-Ponty points out, we human beings are predisposed to

use predominantly only *one* language as the medium of thinking thought, understanding reality, and communicating with others, then there always is and always will be the problem of *translating* one language into another and one conception of reality into another. Be that as it may, one must of course challenge as a "prejudice" the conclusion that so-called scientific rationality is the paradigm of rationality, even if one might accept the distinction between science as "culturally emergent" and science as "culturally dependent." For example, the frequent characterization of the Orient as the paradise of "aesthetic sensibility" may signal weak rationality or irrationality and thereby tighten rather than loosen the iron grip of Western ethnocentrism on the Orient. In digging through the literature on the politics of literary interpretation, I came across the controversial work of Edward W. Said, *Orientalism* (New York: Pantheon Books, 1978). Inspired by Michel Foucault's "epistemic" approach and political radicalism, it attempts to reveal the hegemonic structures of Occidental over Oriental culture(s) with a focus on the Middle East.

2. For the question of interpretation and comparative politics, see Kazuhiko Okuda, "Kaishakugaku to Ibunka Rikai," in *Chiikikenkyu no Hoho to Chutogaku*, ed. Toshio Kuroda (Tokyo: Sanshu Sha, 1987), pp. 9–41. I have already begun the phenomenological exploration of comparative culture and politics in the following articles: (with Petee Jung), "The Hermeneutics of Political Ideology and Cultural Change: Maoism as the Sinicization of Marxism," *Cultural Hermeneutics*, 3 (1975): 165–98; (with Petee Jung), "Revolutionary Dialectics: Mao Tsetung and Maurice Merleau-Ponty," *Dialectical Anthropology*, 2 (1977): 35–56; (with Petee Jung), "Maoism, Psychoanalysis, and Hermeneutics: A Methodological Critique of the Interpretation of Cultures," *Asian Thought and Society*, 9 (1984): 143–67; "Misreading the Ideogram: From Fenollosa to Derrida and McLuhan," *Paideuma*, 13 (1984): 211–27; and "The Piety of Thinking: Heidegger's Pathway to Comparative Philosophy," in *Analecta Husserliana*, 21, ed. A. T. Tymieniecka (Dordrecht: Reidel, 1986), pp. 337–68.

3. Berger, Berger, and Kellner, *The Homeless Mind* (New York: Random House, 1973).

4. See Douglas, *Implicit Meanings* (London: Routledge & Kegan Paul, 1975) and *In the Active Voice* (London: Routledge & Kegan Paul, 1982).

5. See Geertz, *The Interpretation of Cultures* (New York: Basic Books, 1973) and *Local Knowledge* (New York: Basic Books, 1983).

6. Martin Heidegger, *Being and Time*, trans. John Macquarrie and Edward Robinson (New York: Harper & Brothers, 1962), p. 76. It seems likely that Heidegger read the writings of the French anthropologist Lucien Lévy-Bruhl on primitive mentality; see, for example, *How Natives Think*, trans. Lilian A. Clare (New York: Knopf, 1925). Cf. the present author's "The Logic of the Personal: John Macmurray and the Ancient Hebrew View of Life," *The Personalist*, 47 (Autumn 1966): 532–46.

7. Edmund Husserl, "Phenomenology and Anthropology," trans. Richard G. Schmitt, in *Realism and the Background of Phenomenology*, ed. Roderick M. Chisholm (Glencoe: Free Press, 1960), pp. 129–42.

8. Maurice Merleau-Ponty, *The Visible and the Invisible*, ed. Claude Lefort and trans. Alphonso Lingis (Evanston: Northwestern University Press, 1968), p. 212.

9. Donald M. Lowe, *History of Bourgeois Perception* (Chicago: University of Chicago Press, 1982).

10. Patrick A. Heelan, "Perception as a Hermeneutical Act," *The Review of Metaphysics*, 37 (September 1983): 61–75.

11. Here I am raising the question of research strategy rather than epistemology. In "Anti Anti-Relativism," *American Anthropologist*, 86 (June 1984): 253–78, Clifford Geertz proposes *not* to defend relativism but to attack the anti-relativism found particularly in the naturalism of "Human Nature" and the rationalism of "The Human Mind." While attacking anti-relativism, Geertz does not commit himself to a defense of relativism. I am grateful to my colleague Curt Keim for calling my attention to Geertz's article.

12. Maurice Merleau-Ponty, *Signs*, trans. Richard C. McCleary (Evanston: Northwestern University Press, 1964), p. 120.

13. *Ibid.*, p. 138.

14. *Ibid.*, p. 139 (italics added).

15. Hayden White, *Tropics of Discourse* (Baltimore: Johns Hopkins University Press, 1978), p. 4; see also n. 1 to Chapter 10 below.

16. Merleau-Ponty, *Signs*, p. 98.

17. David E. Apter, *Introduction to Political Analysis* (Cambridge: Winthrop, 1977), p. 537.

18. Charles Taylor, "Interpretation and the Sciences of Man," *The Review of Metaphysics*, 25 (September 1971): 34.

19. In placing phenomenology in the recent development of political science, it is noteworthy that the "positive political theorist" William H. Riker is the first President of the American Political Science Association to mention phenomenology and hermeneutics. In his 1982 Presidential Address, he said that "political science, which is my concern in this essay, has, however, often been said to have no history, which is of course merely a way of saying that it contains no accumulation of knowledge and that it is therefore not a branch of science. Many political scientists have been persuaded to believe this assertion, so that in despair they are inclined to abandon the search for scientific generalizations. (This despair is, I believe, the root of the movement toward phenomenology and hermeneutics and other efforts to turn political science into a belles-lettristic study)"—"The Two-Party System and Duverger's Law: An Essay on the History of Political Science," *American Political Science Review*, 76 (December 1982): 753. Without much ado, let me simply say that Riker is wrong when he dichotomizes "science" and the "belles-lettrism" of phenomenology and hermeneutics. Maurice Merleau-Ponty, for instance, speaks of "phenomenological positivism"—see *The Primacy of Perception*, ed. James M. Edie (Evanston: Northwestern University Press, 1964), p. 50.

20. Recall that in *Il Saggitore* Galileo wrote: "Philosophy is written in that vast book which stands forever open before our eyes, I mean the universe; but it cannot be read until we have learned the language and become familiar with the characters in which it is written. It is written in mathematical language, and the letters are triangles, circles, and other geometrical figures, without which means it is humanly impossible to comprehend

a single word"—quoted in Colin Murray Turbayne, *The Myth of Metaphor*, rev. ed. (Columbia: University of South Carolina Press, 1971), pp. 101–2.

21. See Roland Barthes, *L'Empire des signes* (Geneva: Skira, 1970), which has been translated into English by Richard Howard as *Empire of Signs* (New York: Hill & Wang, 1982) and into Japanese as *Hyocho no Teikoku* by So Sacon (Tokyo: Shincho, 1974). For the present author's detailed discussion of Barthes's work, see "The Joy of Textualizing Japan: A Metacommentary on Roland Barthes's *Empire of Signs*," in *Bucknell Review*, vol. 30: *Self, Sign, and Symbol*, ed. Mark Neuman and Michael Payne (Lewisburg: Bucknell University Press, 1987), pp. 144–67. Judging from the description on the cover of the Japanese translation, the Japanese consider Barthes's work as the "cultural criticism" of Japan. I am indebted to my friend Kazuhiko Okuda of the International University of Japan for sending me a copy of the Japanese translation of Barthes's book—*Hyocho no Teikoku*.

22. See Sontag, "Writing Itself: On Roland Barthes," in *A Barthes Reader*, ed. Susan Sontag (New York: Hill & Wang, 1982), p. xxiv.

23. Guy de Mallac, "Métaphores du vide: *L'Empire des signes* de Roland Barthes," *Sub-Stance*, 1 (1971): 31.

24. Culler, *Roland Barthes* (New York: Oxford University Press, 1983), p. 11. Of course, we should not take Culler's use of the term "touristic" as nonserious or supercilious. Rather, he seems to use it after a study fashioned by Dean MacCannell, *The Tourist: A New Theory of the Leisure Class* (New York: Schocken Books, 1976).

25. Barthes, *The Fashion System*, trans. Matthew Ward and Richard Howard (New York: Hill & Wang, 1973), p. 258.

26. Barthes, *Empire of Signs*, p. 29.

27. *Ibid.*, p. 4.

28. See Sontag, "The Aesthetics of Silence," in her *Styles of Radical Will* (New York: Farrar, Straus & Giroux, 1966), pp. 3–34.

29. Daisetz Teitaro Suzuki, *Zen and Japanese Culture* (New York: Pantheon Books, 1959).

30. Barthes, *Empire of Signs*, p. 75.

31. In relation to the importance of the surfacial, the following description by Liza Crihfield Dalby on *geisha* is relevant and appropriate: "Customers are expected to give a geisha an honorarium, but the cash (preferably a stiffly virgin 5,000-yen note or two) must be folded into a decorative envelope. A crumpled bill fished from a pocket would hardly do"—see "The Art of the Geisha," *Natural History*, 92 (February 1983): 49. For her complete treatment of Japanese *geisha* culture based on her anthropological fieldwork and personal experience as a *geisha*, see *Geisha* (Berkeley: University of California Press, 1983).

32. John Sturrock, "Roland Barthes," in *Structuralism and Since: From Lévi-Strauss to Derrida*, ed. John Sturrock (New York: Oxford University Press, 1979), p. 77.

33. *Ibid.*, p. 78.

34. Chang Tung-sun, "A Chinese Philosopher's Theory of Knowledge," in *Our Language and Our World*, ed. S. I. Hayakawa (New York: Harper & Brothers, 1959), pp. 299–324. During the course of modernization in the Meiji Restoration, whose acceleration was sloganized by a group of Japanese intellectuals as "America our mother, France our father," the Japanese unity of the inner (indigenous) and the outer (foreign) was expressed as "Eastern morality" and "Western science and technology." There may indeed be the difference here between the Eastern "logic of correlation" and the Western "logic of identity."

35. Cf. Dalby, who writes that "it is often said with justification that Japanese food is more a feast for the eyes than for the palate, so even if I didn't get to taste the banquets I witnessed, I at least got to view the beautifully orchestrated composition of dishes"—*Geisha*, p. 113.

36. Feld, *Sound and Sentiment: Birds, Weeping, Poetics, and Song in Kaluli Expression* (Philadelphia: University of Pennsylvania Press, 1982), p. 15.

37. It is heartening to come across *Writing Culture: The Poetics and Politics of Ethnography*, ed. James Clifford and George E. Marcus (Berkeley: University of California Press, 1986), which is a collection of interdisciplinary essays on reflexivity or auto-criticism on anthropological writings.

38. Richard M. Zaner, *The Way of Phenomenology: Criticism as a Philosophical Discipline* (New York: Pegasus, 1970), p. 188.

39. Tzvetan Todorov, *The Conquest of America*, trans. Richard Howard (New York: Harper & Row, 1984), is undoubtedly the most telling testimony for the atrocities committed by the Spanish *conquistadore* on the Mesoamerican population based on the undialogical (i.e., ethnocentric or Eurocentric) principle of the self and the other as alien. For the conception of the other with an accent on time, see Johannes Fabian, *Time and the Other: How Anthropology Makes Its Object* (New York: Columbia University Press, 1983).

40. Edward de Bono discusses the issue of lateral and vertical thinking in *New Think* (New York: Basic Books, 1968). "Lateral thinking," de Bono adds, "is not a substitute for vertical thinking but an addition: the two are complementary like two sides of a coin. Lateral thinking generates the ideas and vertical thinking develops them" (p. 6). In comparative civilization, the eighteenth-century Italian philosopher Giambattista Vico is one of the first, if not the first, of the lateral thinkers. According to Edward W. Said, *Beginnings: Intention and Method* (New York: Basic Books, 1975), one of the signposts of Vico's methodology is "an acute awareness not only of genealogical succession (except as its biological foundations obviously persist), but also of parallelism, adjacency, and complementarity—that is, all those relationships that emphasize the lateral and the dispersed rather than the linear and the sequential" (p. 357).

41. Jean-François Lyotard, *The Postmodern Condition: A Report on Knowledge*, trans. Geoff Bennington and Brian Massumi (Minneapolis: University of Minnesota Press, 1984), p. xxv.

42. In *Moral Relativity* (Berkeley: University of California Press, 1984), David B. Wong makes conscious efforts to include non-Western

(i.e., Chinese) philosophy in his discussion of morality and argues for the incommensurable cross-cultural differences between "virtue-centered" and "rights-centered" morality. He writes: "I have tried to connect the failure of absolutist theories to explain certain kinds of disagreements and apparent diversity in moral belief with the general difficulties I identified. . . . By making this connection, I am suggesting that the failure is likely to be incurable. Human beings have needs to resolve internal conflicts between requirements and to resolve interpersonal conflicts of interest. Morality is a social creation that evolved in response to these needs. There are constraints on what a morality could be like and still serve those needs. These constraints are derived from the physical environment, from human nature, and from standards of rationality, but they are not enough to eliminate all but one morality as meeting those needs. Moral relativity is an indication of the plasticity of human nature, of the power of ways of life to determine what constitutes a satisfactory resolution of the conflicts morality is intended to resolve" (p. 175).

43. See Claude Lévi-Strauss, *Structural Anthropology*, vol. 2, trans. Monique Layton (New York: Basic Books, 1976), p. 32.

44. Lévi-Strauss, *Myth and Meaning* (New York: Schocken Books, 1979), p. 45.

45. See George E. Marcus and Michael M. J. Fischer, *Anthropology as Cultural Critique: An Experimental Moment in the Human Sciences* (Chicago: University of Chicago Press, 1986).

46. Said, *The World, the Text, and the Critic* (Cambridge: Harvard University Press, 1983), p. 226.

47. In the literature of American anthropology there is a movement to abandon visual metaphors in favor of auditory ones. See Stephen A. Tyler, "Post-Modern Ethnography: From Document of the Occult to Occult Document," in *Writing Culture*, p. 137: "Perspective is the wrong metaphor. It conjures images appropriate to descriptive writing, writing in thought pictures or hieroglyphs. It is not a business of 'seeing' at all, for that is the metaphor of science, nor is it a 'doing'; that is the metaphor of politics. There is no attempt to go beyond language by means of vision and action. Polyphony is a better metaphor because it evokes sound and hearing and simultaneity and harmony, not pictures and seeing and sequence and line. Prose accomplishes at most only a kind of sequential polyphony until the reader adds his voice to it." Here too cf. Alfred Schutz, "Making Music Together," in his *Collected Papers*, vol. 2: *Studies in Social Theory,* ed. Arvid Brodersen (The Hague: Nijhoff, 1964), pp. 159–60: "A study of the social relationships connected with the musical process may lead to some insights valid for many other forms of social intercourse, perhaps even to illumination of a certain aspect of the structure of social interaction as such that has not so far attracted from social scientists the attention it deserves."

48. See Paul Ricoeur, *History and Truth*, trans. Charles A. Kelbley (Evanston: Northwestern University Press, 1965), pp. 271–84.

49. This is not Ricoeur's phrase. It is the title of Helmut R. Wagner's discussion of Alfred Schutz's phenomenological ontology—see "Toward an Anthropology of the Life-World: Alfred Schutz's Quest for the Ontological Justification of the Phenomenological Undertaking," *Human Studies,* 6 (1983): 239–46.

50. Herbert Spiegelberg, *Steppingstones Toward an Ethics for Fellow Existers: Essays 1944–1983* (Dordrecht: Nijhoff, 1986) contains some important pointers for constructing humanitarianism.

Chapter Six

1. Strauss, *Natural Right and History* (Chicago: University of Chicago Press, 1953).

2. Strauss, *The City and Man* (Chicago: McNally, 1964), p. 1.

3. Strauss, *What Is Political Philosophy? And Other Studies* (Glencoe: Free Press, 1959), p. 11.

4. Strauss, *Natural Rights and History*, pp. 81–82.

5. See particularly Strauss, "On Classical Political Philosophy," in *What Is Political Philosophy?* pp. 78–94, and "An Epilogue," in *Essays on the Scientific Study of Politics*, ed. Herbert J. Storing (New York: Holt, Rinehart & Winston, 1962), pp. 307–27.

6. Heidegger, *Being and Time*, trans. John Macquarrie and Edward Robinson (New York: Harper & Row, 1962); Sartre, *Being and Nothingness*, trans. Hazel E. Barnes (New York: Philosophical Library, 1956); Merleau-Ponty, *Phenomenology of Perception*, trans. Colin Smith (London: Routledge & Kegan Paul, 1962); Ricoeur, *History and Truth*, trans. Charles A. Kelbley (Evanston: Northwestern University Press, 1965); and Wild, *Existence and the World of Freedom* (Englewood Cliffs: Prentice Hall, 1963). Space does not allow me to discuss the relationship between existential philosophy and phenomenology. However, it should be noted that "existential phenomenology" is distinctively a philosophical style here to stay. The American sociologist Edward A. Tiryakian has noted the relevance of existential phenomenology to a theory of social existence in "Existential Phenomenology and the Sociological Tradition," *American Sociological Review*, 30 (October 1965): 674–88. Alfred Schultz's phenomenology has had great influence on the sociological writings of Harold Garfinkel and some influence on the political writings of Richard C. Snyder and his associates. See Garfinkel, "The Perception of the Other: A Study in Social Order" (Unpublished Ph.D. Thesis, Harvard University, 1952); "The Rational Properties of Scientific and Common Sense Activities," *Behavioral Science*, 5 (January 1960): 72–83; "Studies of the Routine Grounds of Everyday Activities," *Social Problems*, 11 (Winter 1964): 225–50; and "Common-Sense Knowledge of Social Structures: The Documentary Method of Interpretation," in *Theories of the Mind*, ed. Jordon M. Scher (New York: Free Press, 1962), pp. 689–712. See also Richard C. Snyder, H. W. Bruck, and Burton Sapin, "Decision-Making as an Approach to the Study of International Politics," in their *Foreign Policy Decision-Making* (Glencoe: Free Press, 1962), pp. 14–185.

7. Arendt, *The Human Condition* (Chicago: University of Chicago Press, 1958), p. 15.

8. Strauss, *What Is Political Philosophy?* p. 91.

9. *Ibid.*, p. 92.

10. Strauss, *Thoughts on Machiavelli* (Glencoe: Free Press, 1958), p. 295. Cf. *History of Political Philosophy*, ed. Leo Strauss and Joseph Cropsey (Chicago: McNally, 1963), p. 245.

11. Strauss, *Thoughts on Machiavelli*, p. 295.

12. Aristotle, *Politics*, trans. Ernest Barker (Oxford: Clarendon Press, 1948), p. 289.

13. Werner Marx, *The Meaning of Aristotle's "Ontology"* (The Hague: Nijhoff, 1954), p. 4.

14. *Ibid.*, p. 15.

15. *Ibid.*, p. 21.

16. *Ibid.*, p. 23.

17. *Ibid.*, p. 22.

18. *Ibid.*, p. 60.

19. Werner Marx says of Aristotle that "things *are* so ordered that, while accessible to all sorts of common-sense 'natural' acting and knowing, they also have a *qua* structure which makes them accessible, as *noeta*, to philosophical *noesis* that contemplates them *qua* be-ings. In seizing on the *qua* structure, the philosopher does not deny that they have other ways-to-be. . . . [T]here are two ways of acting and knowing, i.e., the natural way and the philosophical way. [Things] are so structured that they are accessible in two ways. This seems to us to be the Aristotelian position. They may be accessible in more than two ways, but man may not, or not yet, have developed the faculty by which to reach them"—*The Meaning of Aristotle's "Ontology,"* p. 26.

20. *The Basic Works of Aristotle*, ed. Richard McKeon (New York: Random House, 1941), p. 942.

21. Strauss, *On Tyranny*, rev. and enl. ed. (Glencoe: Free Press, 1963), p. 214.

22. Aristotle, *Politics*, p. 103.

23. Strauss, *The City and Man*, p. 49.

24. Aristotle, *Politics*, p. 289.

25. Strauss, *What Is Political Philosophy?* pp. 93–94.

26. Strauss, *On Tyranny*, p. 224.

27. Buber, *Eclipse of God* (New York: Harper & Brothers, 1952), pp. 40–41.

28. Macmurray, *Persons in Relation* (London: Faber and Faber, 1961), p. 215.

29. Kierkegaard, *Concluding Unscientific Postscript*, trans. David F. Swenson and Walter Lowrie (Princeton: Princeton University Press, 1941), p. 176.

30. Heschel, *Who Is Man?* (Stanford: Stanford University Press, 1965), p. 81.

31. Wild, "Christian Rationalism," in William Earle, James M. Edie, and John Wild, *Christianity and Existentialism* (Evanston: Northwestern University Press, 1963), p. 58.

32. Johann, "The Return to Experience," *The Review of Metaphysics*, 17 (March 1964): 339.

33. The terms "monological" and "dialogical" are Buber's. For the clarification of these terms, see particular *I and Thou*, trans. Ronald Gregor Smith, 2nd ed. (New York: Scribner's Sons, 1958); "Elements of the Interhuman," trans. Ronald Gregor Smith in *The Knowledge of Man*, ed. Maurice Friedman (London: Allen and Unwin, 1965), pp. 72–88; and *Philosophical Interrogations*, ed. Sydney and Beatrice Rome (New York: Holt, Rinehart & Winston, 1964), pp. 16–45. The terms "egocentric" and "heterocentric" are coined by John Macmurray, who is one of the outstanding "philosophers of action" today, and his philosophy is most closely related to Buber's "philosophy of dialogue." For the clarification of these terms, see particularly Macmurray, *The Self as Agent* (London: Faber and Faber, 1957), pp. 62–103 and *Persons in Relation*, pp. 15–43.

34. Macmurray, *Persons in Relation*, p. 128.

35. Weber, *The Theory of Social and Economic Organization*, trans. A. M. Henderson and Talcott Parsons (New York: Free Press, 1947), p. 112.

36. Let us recall how Strauss's critique of the scientific school of politics is highlighted, albeit in a rhetorical way, when he writes: "Only a great fool would call the new political science diabolic: it has no attributes peculiar to fallen angels. It is not even Machiavellian, for Machiavelli's teaching was graceful, subtle, and colorful. Nor is it Neronian. Nevertheless one may say of it that it fiddles while Rome burns. It is excused by two facts: it does not know that it fiddles, and it does not know that Rome burns"—"An Epilogue," p. 327. Eric Voegelin lists three principles of today's scientific creed: "(1) the assumption that the mathematized science of natural phenomena is a model science to which all other sciences ought to conform; (2) that all realms of being are accessible to the methods of the sciences of phenomena; and (3) that all reality which is not accessible to sciences of phenomena is either irrelevant or, in the more radical form of the dogma, illusionary"—"The Origins of Scientism," *Social Research*, 15 (December 1948): 462. Cf. John H. Hallowell, "Politics and Ethics," *American Political Science Review*, 38 (August 1944): 639–55.

37. Voegelin, *The New Science of Politics* (Chicago: University of Chicago Press, 1952), p. 8.

38. For example, see Frederick Patka, *Value and Existence* (New York: Philosophical Library, 1964).

39. Wild, *Existence and the World of Freedom*, p. 54.

40. John Wild, *Plato's Modern Enemies and the Theory of Natural Law* (Chicago: University of Chicago Press, 1953), pp. 157 ff.

41. Löwith, *Nature, History, and Existentialism*, ed. Arnold Levison (Evanston: Northwestern University Press, 1966), p. 36.

42. Wild, *Existence and the World of Freedom*, pp. 50–59, 66–79, 86–97.

43. Arnold Levison, "Editor's Introduction" to Löwith, *Nature, History, and Existentialism*, p. xx. Wild mentions four kinds of phenomena in the *Lebenswelt*, one of which is the realm of "nature," while the other three are "man himself," "other men and the realm of human culture," and "the transcendent"—*Philosophical Interrogations*, p. 177.

44. Strauss, "An Epilogue," p. 310.

45. *Ibid.*, p. 315.

46. Strauss, *The City and Man*, p. 12

47. Herbert Spiegelberg suggests that the two main areas of concern for post-Husserlian phenomenology are the life-world and intersubjectivity. Cf. his *The Phenomenological Movement*, 3rd rev. and enl. ed. (The Hague: Nijhoff, 1982), pp. 138, 144.

48. Edmund Husserl, *Cartesian Meditations*, trans. Dorion Cairns (The Hague: Nijhoff, 1960), p. 177.

49. Schutz, *Collected Papers*, vol. 1: *The Problem of Social Reality*, ed. Maurice Natanson (The Hague: Nijhoff, 1962), p. 53.

50. Husserl, *The Crisis of European Sciences and Transcendental Phenomenology*, trans. David Carr (Evanston: Northwestern University Press, 1970), pp. 121 ff.

51. Cf. John Wild, "Husserl's Life-World and the Lived Body," in *Phenomenology: Pure and Applied*, ed. Erwin W. Straus (Pittsburgh: Duquesne University Press, 1964), p. 10. For Heidegger's own discussion of "being-in-the-world," see *Being and Time*, pp. 78–224.

52. Löwith, *Nature, History, and Existentialism*, p. 56.

53. "Über den 'Humanismus,', " in *Platons Lehre von der Wahrheit* (Bern: Franke, 1954), p. 53.

54. Wild, "Is There an Existential *A Priori*?" (lecture delivered at Michigan State University, April, 1966), p. 10.

55. Strauss, *What Is Political Philosophy?* p. 17. In a seminar given in honor of the late Kurt Riezler, Strauss makes a few passing comments on the thought of Heidegger and says that "Heidegger surpasses all his contemporaries by far" (*ibid.*, p. 246). It might also be added that the Straussian leap to Plato and Aristotle is likened in spirit, although entirely different in aim and result, to Heidegger's return to the pre-Socratic Greek thinkers Parmenides and Heraclitus in search of the origins of the meaning of being in Western thought. I have briefly commented on this point in "A Post-Polemic," *American Political Science Review*, 58 (June 1964): 400–1.

56. Strauss, *Natural Right and History*, p. 79.

57. *Ibid.*, p. 77.

58. *Ibid.*

59. *Ibid.*, p. 79.

60. *Ibid.*, pp. 79–80.

61. Wild, *Existence and the World of Freedom*, p. 41.

62. Merleau-Ponty, *Phenomenology of Perception*, pp. ix, viii. Cf. his *The Primacy of Perception*, ed. James M. Edie (Evanston: Northwestern University Press, 1964), p. 13.

63. Strasser, *Phenomenology and the Human Sciences* (Pittsburgh: Duquesne University Press, 1963), p. 71.

64. Wild, "Is There an Existential *A Priori?*" p. 11.

65. Schutz, *Collected Papers*, vol. 2: *Studies in Social Theory*, ed. Arvid Brodersen (The Hague: Nijhoff, 1964), p. 21, and cf. *Collected Papers*, 1, pp. 6–7.

66. Schutz, *Collected Papers*, 1, p. 34.

67. *Ibid.*, p. 67.

68. See Alfred Schutz, *The Phenomenology of the Social World*, trans. George Walsh and Frederick Lehnert (Evanston: Northwestern University Press, 1967).

69. Weber, *The Theory of Social and Economic Organization*, pp. 103–4.

70. *Ibid.*, p. 104.

71. Schutz, *Collected Papers*, 1, p. 247.

72. *Philosophy of the Social Sciences: A Reader*, ed. Maurice Natanson (New York: Random House, 1963), p. 188.

73. Merleau-Ponty, *Phenomenology of Perception*, p. 347.

74. See John Macmurray, *Reason and Emotion*, 2nd ed. (New York: Barnes & Noble, 1962), p. 5, and cf. V. J. McGill, *Emotions and Reason* (Springfield: Thomas, 1954), pp. 25 ff.

75. Fackenheim, "Metaphysics, Historicity and Historicism," *The Personalist*, 46 (January 1965): 45. Fackenheim's argument is different from that of Strauss. Fackenheim argues that the doctrine of historicity presupposes the idea of self-making, that is, "in acting man makes or constitutes himself" and that the doctrine of self-making can develop into three different directions: (1) historicism, (2) Hegelianism, and (3) existentialism. The existentialist position, he comments, "is Hegelian and anti-historicist enough to assert that human being can rise to radical philosophical self-reflection, while at the same time being anti-Hegelian enough to deny the Hegelian transcendence of situatedness"—*ibid.*, pp. 47–48. According to Fackenheim, then, existentialism takes the middle ground between historicism and Hegelianism.

76. Strauss, *Natural Right and History*, p. 32.

77. Strauss, *What Is Political Philosophy?* p. 26. Strauss notes that positivism differs from historicism in that the latter has the following four characteristics: "(1) It abandons the distinction between facts and values, because every understanding, however theoretical, implies specific evaluations. (2) It denies the authoritative character of modern science, which appears as only one form among many of man's thinking orientation in the world. (3) It refuses to regard the historical process as fundamentally progressive, or, more generally stated, as reasonable. (4) It denies the relevance of evolutionist thesis by contending that the evolution of man out of nonman cannot make intelligible man's humanity" (*ibid*).

78. *Ibid.*, p. 57.

79. See Fackenheim, "Metaphysics, Historicity and Historicism," p. 45, and *Metaphysics and Historicity* (Milwaukee: Marquette University Press, 1961), p. 11.

80. Löwith, *Nature, History, and Existentialism*, p. 18. Cf. also Calvin O. Schrag, *Existence and Freedom* (Evanston: Northwestern University Press, 1961), pp. 6–17, 146, and George Joseph Seidel, O.S.B., *Martin Heidegger and the Pre-Socratics* (Lincoln: University of Nebraska Press, 1964), pp. 156, 15–26. For Heidegger's own analysis, see *Being and Time*, especially pp. 424 ff.

81. Strauss, *Natural Right and History*, pp. 30–31.

82. Sartre, *Existentialism*, trans. Bernard Frechtman (New York: Philosophical Library, 1947), p. 18.

83. John Wild, *The Challenge of Existentialism* (Bloomington: Indiana University Press, 1959), p. 256.

84. Löwith, *Nature, History, and Existentialism*, pp. 23, 135.

85. *Ibid.*, p. 137.

86. *The Basic Works Of Aristotle*, p. 1464.

87. Löwith, *Nature, History, and Existentialism*, p. 35.

88. Johann, "Love and Justice," in *Ethics and Society*, ed. Richard T. De George (Garden City: Doubleday, 1966), p. 34.

89. Scheler, *Man's Place in Nature*, trans. Hans Meyerhoff (New York: Noonday Press, 1961), p. 29. Cf. Macmurray, *Persons in Relation*, pp. 45, 128.

90. See Macmurray, *The Self as Agent*, pp. 131–35.

91. Alexandre Kojève, "Tyranny and Wisdom," in Strauss, *On Tyranny*, p. 164.

92. Wild, "Christian Rationalism," p. 59.

93. Strauss, *Natural Right and History*, p. 12.

94. See Jaspers, *The Perennial Scope of Philosophy*, trans. Ralph Manheim (New York: Philosophical Library, 1949), pp. 45–46; *Ways to Wisdom*, trans. Ralph Manheim (New Haven: Yale University Press, 1951), p. 27; and *Reason and Existenz*, trans. William Earle (New York: Noonday Press, 1955), pp. 77–106.

95. Buber, *I and Thou*, p. 63.

96. Strasser, *Phenomenology and the Human Sciences*, p. 231; cf. Merleau-Ponty, *The Primacy of Perception*, p. 13.

97. Merleau-Ponty, *In Praise of Philosophy*, trans. John Wild and James M. Edie (Evanston: Northwestern University Press, 1963), p. 59.

98. Wild, *The Challenge of Existentialism*, p. 272.

99. Husserl, *The Crisis of European Sciences and Transcendental Phenomenology*, p. 17.

100. Strauss, *On Tyranny*, p. 221.

101. Merleau-Ponty, *Phenomenology of Perception*, p. 382.

102. See John Wild, "Authentic Existence: A New Approach to 'Value Theory'," in *An Invitation to Phenomenology*, ed. James M. Edie (Chicago: Quadrangle Books, 1965), pp. 59, 70, 76.

103. Heidegger, *What Is Philosophy?* trans. William Kluback and Jean T. Wilde (New York: Twayne, 1958), p. 59.

Notes to Appendix

1. See the present Chapter 6 above. Miller's Straussian position is clearer in his "Political Philosophy and Human Nature," *The Personalist*, 53 (Summer 1972): 209–21.

2. See p. 130 above.

3. Simone de Beauvoir, *The Coming of Age*, trans. Patrick O'Brian (New York: Putnam's Sons, 1972), p. 361.

4. Miller, "Political Philosophy and Human Nature," p. 209.

5. *Ibid.*, p. 218.

6. Gabriel Marcel, *Being and Having*, trans. Katharine Farrer (Westminster: Dacre Press, 1949), p. 169.

7. See Martin Buber, *Eclipse of God* (New York: Harper & Brothers, 1952), p. 40.

8. Miller, "Political Philosophy and Human Nature," p. 219.

9. For a phenomenological critique of the behavioralist epistemology and ontology, see Chapter 3 above.

Chapter Seven

1. See Leszek Kolakowski, *Main Currents of Marxism*, trans. P. S. Falla, 3 vols. (Oxford: Clarendon Press, 1978), vol. 1, p. 6.

2. The best known treatises on the topic of phenomenology and Marxism are Tran-Duc-Thao, *Phénoménologie et matérialisme dialectique* (Paris: Minh-Tan, 1951), and Enzo Paci, *The Function of the Sciences and the Meaning of Man*, trans. Paul Piccone and James E. Hansen (Evanston: Northwestern University Press, 1972). For an excellent discussion of the subject, see also Fred. R. Dallmayr, "Phenomenology and Marxism: A Salute to Enzo Paci," in *Phenomenological Sociology*, ed. George Psathas (New York: Wiley, 1973), pp. 305–56.

3. Maurice Merleau-Ponty's "diacritical" injunction runs as follows: "Replace the notion of concept, idea, mind, representation with the notions of *dimensions*, articulations, level, hinges, pivots, configuration . . ." —*The Visible and the Invisible*, ed. Claude Lefort and trans. Alphonso Lingis (Evanston: Northwestern University Press, 1968), p. 224.

4. Maurice Merleau-Ponty, *Signs*, trans. Richard C. McCleary (Evanston: Northwestern University Press, 1964), p. 98.

5. Martin Heidegger writes that "the modern form of ontology is transcendental philosophy which becomes epistemology," and that "the

mere reverse side of the empirical-positivistic misinterpretation of episte-mology shows itself in the growing dominance of logistics"—*The End of Philosophy*, trans. Joan Stambaugh (New York: Harper & Row, 1973), pp. 88–89. Concerning the issue of scientism in the context of political in-quiry, see the present author's *The Crisis of Political Understanding: A Phenomenological Perspective in the Conduct of Political Inquiry* (Pitts-burgh: Duquesne University Press, 1979).

6. Paul Ricoeur, *The Conflict of Interpretations: Essays in Herme-neutics*, ed. Don Ihde (Evanston: Northwestern University Press, 1974), p. 246.

7. Max Scheler, *Man's Place in Nature*, trans. Hans Meyerhoff (New York: Noonday Press, 1962).

8. Merleau-Ponty, *Signs*, p. 131.

9. Maurice Merleau-Ponty, *Humanism and Terror*, trans. John O'Neill (Boston: Beacon Press, 1969), p. 153.

10. Martin Heidegger, *Basic Writings*, ed. David Farrell Krell (New York: Harper & Row, 1977), pp. 219–20. George Steiner points out that "it is difficult to imagine some of Heidegger's most representative pages on the depersonalization of twentieth-century urban man or on the exploit-ative, basically imperialist motivation in Western science and technology, without the immediate precedent of *Das Kapital* or Engels' indictments of industrial inhumanity"—*Martin Heidegger* (New York: Viking Press, 1979), pp. 147–48.

11. There are some notable exceptions. For example, see Lucien Gold-mann, *Lukács and Heidegger: Towards a New Philosophy*, trans. William Q. Boelbower (London: Routledge & Kegan Paul, 1977); Gajo Petrović, *Marx in the Mid-Twentieth Century* (Garden City: Doubleday, 1967); and Karel Kosík, *Dialectics of the Concrete: A Study on Problems of Man and World*, trans. Karel Kovanda with James Schmidt (Dordrecht: Reidel, 1976). Hans-Georg Gadamer writes that "we are still waiting for a Karl Marx who would resist treating Heidegger as Marx, though opposing him, resisted treating the great thinker, Hegel—as a 'dead dog' "—*Hegel's Dialectic: Five Hermeneutical Studies*, trans. P. Christopher Smith (New Haven: Yale University Press, 1976), p. 102.

12. Paci, *The Function of the Sciences and the Meaning of Man*, p. 55.

13. Karl Marx, *Capital*, ed. Friedrich Engels and trans. Samuel Moore and Edward Aveling, 3 vols. (New York: International Publishers, 1967), vol. 1, p. 372 n. 3.

14. Martin Heidegger, *Being and Time*, trans. John Macquarrie and Edward Robinson (New York: Harper & Brothers, 1962).

15. Karl Marx, *The Economic and Philosophic Manuscripts of 1844*, ed. Kirk J. Struik and trans. Martin Milligan (New York: International Publishers, 1964).

16. Kosík observes that "when Marx's early *Philosophical and Eco-nomic Manuscripts* [*sic*] were published in the thirties, they became a real sensation and inspired a vast literature. The publication of *Grundrisse*, which contain preparatory work for *Capital*, from Marx's *mature* period of late 1850s, and which form an extraordinary important link between

the *Manuscripts* and *Capital*, in turn passed virtually unnoticed. The significance of *Grundrisse* can hardly be exaggerated. They prove above all that Marx *never abandoned* the philosophical problematique, and that especially concepts of 'alienation,' 'reification,' 'totality,' the subject-object relationship, etc., which certain ignorant Marxologists would be happy to declare as sins of Marx's youth, were parts of the *permanent* conceptual equipment of Marx's theory. Without them, *Capital* would be incomprehensible"—*The Dialectics of the Concrete*, pp. 129–30 n. 29. For an excellent exposition of Marx's ontology of humankind based primarily on the *Grundrisse*, see Carol C. Gould, *Marx's Social Ontology: Individuality and Community in Marx's Theory of Social Reality* (Cambridge: MIT Press, 1978). In comparison with some other similar studies on Marx's thought, Gould claims that "my study goes beyond these interpretations in proposing that Marx is fundamentally philosophical not simply in the early work but in the later political economy as well. Furthermore, I attempt to work out Marx's distinctive synthesis of philosophy with social and political economic theory as a social ontology" (p. 180 n. 7).

17. Heidegger, *Being and Time*, p. 60.

18. Marx, *Capital*, 1, p. 19. In discussing "the method of political economy" in the *Grundrisse*, Marx also writes that "Hegel fell into the illusion of conceiving the real as the product of thought concentrating itself, probing its own depths, and unfolding itself out of itself, by itself . . ." —*Grundrisse: Foundation of the Critique of Political Economy*, trans. Martin Nicolaus (New York: Random House, 1973), p. 101. It should also be noted that a corollary of Marx's rejection of Hegel's idealism is the affirmation of the ontological priority of active real individuals over abstract entities; cf. Gould, *Marx's Social Ontology*, p. 28.

19. Karl Marx and Friedrich Engels, *The German Ideology*, ed. R. Pascal (New York: International Publishers, 1947), p. 15.

20. *Ibid.*, p. 14.

21. Kosík, *Dialectics of the Concrete*, p. 136.

22. *Ibid.*, p. 137.

23. Maurice Merleau-Ponty, "Philosophy and Non-Philosophy Since Hegel," *Telos*, No. 19 (Fall 1976): 43–105.

24. *Ibid.*, p. 92.

25. Marx, *Capital*, 1, p. 178. For an interesting discussion of time as a function of labor in Marx's thought that is related to Heidegger's thought, see Gould, *Marx's Social Ontology*, pp. 56 ff.

26. However, there is no "phenomenology of embodiment" in Marx because although he sees labor as an embodied activity, he is not directly concerned with the question of the body as *subject* and the medium of social intercourse.

27. Emmanuel Levinas, *Totality and Infinity*, trans. Alphonso Lingis (Pittsburgh: Duquesne University Press, 1969), p. 134.

28. Kosík, *Dialectics of the Concrete*, p. 63.

29. By now it is quite obvious that Marxists themselves—especially the critical theorists of the Frankfurt School such as Max Horkheimer,

Theodor W. Adorno, Herbert Marcuse, Jürgen Habermas, Albrecht Wellmer, and Alfred Schmidt—began to challenge explicitly or implicitly certain basic assumptions of Marx and focus on the issues of the autonomy of theory, technological rationality, mass culture industry, and scientism unforeseen by Marx himself.

30. Maurice Merleau-Ponty, *Phenomenology of Perception*, trans. Colin Smith (London: Routledge & Kegan Paul, 1962), p. 171 n. 1.

31. The Scottish philosopher John Macmurray, who is not free from Marx's influence, has worked out one of the most systematic, heterocentric philosophies of humanity in opposition to the egocentrism of thought-centered philosophy in *The Self as Agent* (London: Faber and Faber, 1957) and *Persons in Relation* (London: Faber and Faber, 1961). For example, Macmurray writes in *The Self as Agent:* "The traditional point of view is both theoretical and egocentric. It is theoretical in that it proceeds as though the Self were a pure *subject* for whom the world is *object*. This means that the point of view adopted by our philosophy is that of the Self in its moment of reflection, when its activity is directed towards the acquirement of knowledge. Since the Self in reflection is withdrawn from action, withdrawn into itself, withdrawn from participation in the life of the world into contemplation, this point of view is also egocentric. The Self in reflection is self-isolated from the world which it knows" (p. 11). In *Persons in Relation*, Macmurray writes: "A personal being is at once subject and object; but he is both because he is primarily agent. As subject he is 'I,' as object he is 'You,' since the 'You' is always 'the Other'. The unity of the personal is, then, to be sought in the community of the 'You and I,' and since persons are agents, this community is not merely matter of fact, but also matter of intention" (p. 27).

32. Jean-Paul Sartre, *Being and Nothingness*, trans. Hazel E. Barnes (New York: Philosophical Library, 1956), p. 233.

33. It is Sartre who defines sociality as the dialectic of the subjective and the objective in his existential Marxism—see *Search for a Method*, trans. Hazel E. Barnes (New York: Knopf, 1963), pp. 91 ff. Elsewhere he writes: "The individual interiorizes his social determinations: he interiorizes the relations of production, the family of his childhood, the historical past, the contemporary institutions, and he then re-exteriorizes these in acts and options which necessarily refer us back to them"—see Sartre, *Between Existentialism and Marxism*, trans. John Mathews (New York: Pantheon Books, 1974), p. 35.

34. Marx and Engels, *The German Ideology*, p. 19.

35. Adam Schaff attempts to bridge the missing link in Marx between language and cognition in *Language and Cognition*, ed. Robert S. Cohen and trans. Olgierd Wojtasiewicz (New York: McGraw-Hill, 1973).

36. The term "porous" is borrowed from Jürgen Habermas, "A Review of Gadamer's *Truth and Method*," in *Understanding and Social Inquiry*, ed. Fred R. Dallmayr and Thomas A. McCarthy (Notre Dame: University of Notre Dame Press, 1977), p. 341.

37. See V. N. Voloshinov, *Freudianism: A Marxist Critique*, trans. I. R. Titunik (New York: Academic Press, 1976), and *Marxism and the Philosophy of Language*, trans. Ladislav Matejka and I. R. Titunik (New York: Seminar Press, 1973). I should note that one of the most important

elements in Voloshinov's social conception of language is the interrelationship between *meaning* and *evaluation*. However, I will not pursue this important issue here. It should also be noted that the authorship of these two works by "V. N. Voloshinov" is now given to Mikhail Bakhtin (1895–1975). See Katerina Clark and Michael Holquist, *Mikhail Bakhtin* (Cambridge: Harvard University Press, 1983), pp. 146–85. See also "Translators' Preface, 1986" in a later printing of Voloshinov's *Marxism and the Philosophy of Language,* trans. Ladislav Matejka and I. R. Titunik (Cambridge: Harvard University Press, 1986), pp. vii–xii.

38. For discussions of language as the dialectic of signifying and signified from Marxian perspectives, see Fredric Jameson, *The Prison-House of Language: A Critical Account of Structuralism and Russian Formalism* (Princeton: Princeton University Press, 1972). See also Raymond Williams, who, echoing Voloshinov, writes that "this view [of language as the dialectic of signifying and signified] is . . . radically opposed to the construction of all acts of communication from pre-determined objective relationships and properties, within which no individual initiative, of a creative or self-generating kind, would be possible. It is thus a decisive theoretical rejection of mechanical, behaviourist, or Saussurean versions of an objective system which is beyond individual initiative or creative use. But it is also a theoretical rejection of subjectivist theories of language as individual expression, since what is internally constituted is the social fact of the sign, bearing a definite though never fixed or invariant social meaning and relationship"—*Marxism and Literature* (New York: Oxford University Press, 1977), pp. 40–41. For phenomenological accounts of this dialectic of language that seek, as does Voloshinov's Marxist philosophy, to overcome both "psychologism" and "objectivism," see particularly Ricoeur, "Structure, Word, Event," in *The Conflict of Interpretations,* pp. 79–96, and Merleau-Ponty, "On the Phenomenology of Language," in *Signs,* pp. 85–97. It may be said of this dialectic that ontogenetically the *parole* precedes the *langue,* whereas phylogenetically the reverse is true. Whether Ferdinand de Saussure's linguistics is a form of "sociologism" in the manner of Emile Durkheim, that is, an affirmation of *langue* at the expense of *parole,* is still a matter of debate and speculation. Roland Barthes notes that "a direct influence of Durkheim on Saussure has even been postulated; it has been alleged that Saussure had followed very closely the debate between Durkheim and [Gabriel] Tarde and that his conception of the language [*langue*] came from Durkheim while that of speech [*parole*] was a kind of concession to Tarde's idea on the individual element"—*Elements of Seminology,* trans. Annette Lavers and Colin Smith (New York: Hill & Wang, 1967), p. 23.

39. Voloshinov, *Marxism and the Philosophy of Language,* p. 11.

40. See Marvin Harris, *Cultural Materialism: The Struggle for a Science of Culture* (New York: Random House, 1979).

41. *Ibid.,* p. 30.

42. David-Hillel Ruben, *Marxism and Materialism: A Study in Marxist Theory of Knowledge* (Atlantic Highlands: Humanities Press, 1977).

43. *Ibid.,* p. 2.

44. *Ibid.,* p. 3.

45. *Ibid.,* p. 97.

46. Maurice Merleau-Ponty, *Adventures of the Dialectic*, trans. Joseph Bien (Evanston: Northwestern University Press, 1973), p. 65. The most devastating, psychoanalytical critique of this kind of bureaucratic politics is found in Gilles Deleuze and Félix Guattari, *Anti-Oedipus: Capitalism and Schizophrenia*, trans. Robert Hurley, Mark Seem, and Helen R. Lane (New York: Viking Press, 1977).

47. Merleau-Ponty, *Phenomenology of Perception*, p. 28.

48. Kosík, *Dialectics of the Concrete*, p. 105.

49. Hans-Georg Gadamer, *Truth and Method*, ed. Garrett Barden and John Cumming (New York: Seabury Press, 1975).

50. See Habermas, "A Review of Gadamer's *Truth and Method.*"

51. Hans-Georg Gadamer, *Philosophical Hermeneutics*, ed. and trans. David E. Linge (Berkeley: University of California Press, 1976), pp. 29–38. In his exposition of Gadamer's hermeneutics, David Couzens Hoy maintains that "hermeneutical theory does not exclude praxis. On the contrary, the value of the theory is its explanation of the possibility of praxis. The analysis demonstrates that a sharp separation between theory and praxis is itself a false picture. It can be questioned whether the status of this hermeneutical assertion that theory and praxis are intertwined is theoretical or practical"—*The Critical Circle: Literature and History in Contemporary Hermeneutics* (Berkeley: University of California Press, 1978), p. 112. Furthermore, Gadamer's hermeneutics, which has been influenced by Aristotle's "practical philosophy"—particularly his concept of *phronēsis*—cannot be too idealistic. For a discussion of Aristotle's "phenomenology" in this connection, see J. Donald Monan, *Moral Knowledge and Its Methodology in Aristotle* (Oxford: Clarendon Press, 1968).

52. Edmund Husserl, *The Crisis of European Sciences and Transcendental Phenomenology*, trans. David Carr (Evanston: Northwestern University Press, 1970).

53. Aron Gurwitsch, *Phenomenology and the Theory of Science*, ed. Lester Embree (Evanston: Northwestern University Press, 1974), p. 5. John Wild progmmatically sets forth the comprehensive role of phenomenology in investigating the various areas of the life-world when he says that "four different kinds of phenomena are found in the *Lebenswelt*, each of which is now the object of a distinct mode of scientific investigation: man himself, the realm of nature, other men and the realm of human culture, and finally, the transcendent. In each of these regions, however, foundational questions arise which involve first philosophy and the *Lebenswelt* as a whole and which cannot be settled by science alone. In the case of man himself, it has been shown that there are vast regions of lived experience hitherto dismissed by objective reason as 'subjective' which are absolutely essential to man and which can be described and understood by a disciplined phenomenology. Hence, in addition to psychology and what is now called anthropology, a philosophical anthropology which studies the total existence of man in his *Lebenswelt* is required. Some real light has been shed on these matters, and the further development and refinement of this discipline is of the first importance"—"The Interrogation of John Wild" (interview conducted by Henry B. Veatch), in *Philosophical Interrogations*, ed. Sydney and Beatrice Rome (New York: Holt, Rinehart & Winston, 1964), p. 177.

54. Merleau-Ponty, *Phenomenology of Perception*, p. viii.

55. Husserl, *The Crisis of European Sciences and Transcendental Phenomenology*, pp. 51–52.

56. Paci, *The Function of the Sciences and the Meaning of Man*, p. 323.

57. On this point and related matters, see the present author's critique of C. B. Macpherson—"Ontology and Technology: A Critique of C. B. Macpherson's Theory of Democratic Polity," in *The Crisis of Political Understanding*, pp. 130–44.

58. Herbert Marcuse, "On Science and Phenomenology," in *Boston Studies in the Philosophy of Science*, vol. 2, ed. Robert S. Cohen and Marx W. Wartofsky (New York: Humanities Press, 1965), pp. 286–87; cf. Martin Heidegger, who says that "modern science is grounded in the nature of technology"—*What Is Called Thinking?* trans. Fred D. Wieck and J. Glenn Gray (New York: Harper & Row, 1968), p. 135. However, there seems to be a radical difference between Marcuse's "instrumental" conception of technology (i.e., the *effects* of technology) and Heidegger's conception of the essence or nature (*Wesen*) of technology (*Technik*) as "framework" (*Gestell*).

59. Marcuse, "On Science and Phenomenology," p. 289.

60. See Aron Gurwitsch, "Comment on the Paper by H. Marcuse," in *Boston Studies in the Philosophy of Science*, vol. 2, pp. 219–306. If Husserl had been directly interested in disclosing the instrumental rationality of science, he would have analyzed Francis Bacon rather than Galileo. For a critical discussion on the modern "origin" of technological rationality in Bacon, see William Leiss, *The Domination of Nature* (New York: Braziller, 1972).

61. Gurwitsch, *Phenomenology and the Theory of Science*, p. 56.

62. Herbert Marcuse, *One Dimensional Man: Studies in the Ideology of Advanced Industrial Society* (Boston: Beacon Press, 1964), p. 175.

63. Kolakowski, *Main Currents of Marxism*, 3, p. 524.

64. The reference to "hedgehogs" pertains to the famous distinction between the "hedgehog" and the "fox" drawn by Isaiah Berlin in his 1953 study of Tolstoy, a distinction he used as a means to classify great thinkers into two paradigmatic groups—see *The Hedgehog and the Fox* (New York: Simon & Schuster, 1986), and cf. n. 73 to Chapter 9 below.

65. Søren Kierkegaard, *The Concept of Irony*, trans. Lee M. Capel (New York: Harper & Row, 1965), p. 47.

66. Ricoeur, *The Conflict of Interpretations*, p. 27.

67. Kolakowski, *Main Currents of Marxism*, 3, p. 530.

68. Martin Heidegger, "Modern Natural Science and Technology," *Research in Phenomenology*, 7 (1977): 3.

69. Michael E. Zimmerman, "Some Important Themes in Current Heidegger Research," *Research in Phenomenology*, 7 (1977): 275.

70. Merleau-Ponty's following comment on Marx is highly suggestive: "Marx's sketch of philosophy is essentially dialectical, i.e. nature,

man, and history are all understood, not as substances definable by a principal attribute, but as movements without a locatable discontinuity, where the other is always involved.—There is no cleavage between matter and idea, object and subject, nature and man, in-itself and for-itself, but a single Being where negativity works.—Therefore, nature will not be defined as a pure object, externality, but as the 'sensuous,' carnal nature in the way we see it. Natural beings have an internal relation where the relation between some of them and others is predetermined. Man will be defined neither as a pure subject nor as a fragment of nature, but by a sort of coupling of 'subject-object' with two sides; a relation to an object, or an active object, and also a relation essentially to another man, a generic being (*Gattungswesen*), 'society.' This latter relation is a transformation and a continuation of the natural relation of living beings with external being. History in this sense is the very flesh of man"—"Philosophy and Non-Philosophy Since Hegel," p. 101.

71. Heidegger, *Basic Writings*, p. 120. Heidegger's view on the essence of materialism and that of technology and on how they are related to the entire tradition of Western metaphysics as the "forgottenness of Being" requires an extensive treatment that I will not launch here. A glimpse of his representative thought on the matter is found in the following three passages: "This name [technology] includes all the areas of beings which equip the whole of beings: objectified nature, the business of culture, manufactured politics, and the gloss of ideals overlying everything. Thus 'technology' does not signify here the separate areas of the production and equipment of machines. The latter of course have a position of power, to be more closely defined, which is grounded in the precedence of matter as the supposedly elemental and primarily objective factor"—*The End of Philosophy*, p. 93; "Collapse and desolation find their adequate occurrence in the fact that metaphysical man, the *animal rationale*, gets fixed as the laboring animal. . . . The still hidden truth of Being is withheld from metaphysical humanity. The laboring animal is left to the giddy whirl of its products so that it may tear itself to pieces and annihilate itself in empty nothingness"—*ibid.*, pp. 86–87; and "What now *is*, is marked by the dominance of the active nature of modern technology. This dominance is already presenting itself in all areas of life, by various identifiable traits such as functionalization, systematic improvement, automation, bureaucratization, communications. Just as we call the idea of living things biology, just so the presentation and full articulation of all beings, dominated as they now are everywhere by the nature of the technical, may be called technology. The expression may serve as a term for the metaphysics of the atomic age. Viewed from the present and drawn from our insight into the present, the step back out of metaphysics into the essential nature of metaphysics is the stop out of technology and technological description and interpretation of the age, into the *essence* of modern technology which is still to be thought"—*Identity and Difference*, trans. Joan Stambaugh (New York: Harper & Row, 1969), pp. 51–52. It is well known that Heidegger showed a great interest in Ernst Jünger's *Der Arbeiter* (1932). Heidegger's own comment on Jünger is found in his *Zur Seinsfrage* (Frankfurt am Main: Klostermann, 1956), pp. 10 ff. An extensive account of the encounter between Heidegger and Jünger is given by Jean-Michel Palmier, *Les Écrits politiques de Heidegger* (Paris: Herne, 1968), pp. 167–212.

72. For a highly suggestive article on the possibility of an ontology of humankind that is neither anthropocentric nor biocentric, see Marjorie

Notes

Grene, "The Paradoxes of Historicity," *The Review of Mataphysics*, 22 (September 1968): 15–36.

73. The most comprehensive Heideggerian critique of Marx along this line is found in Kostas Axelos, *Alienation, Praxis, and Technē in the Thought of Karl Marx*, trans. Ronald Bruzina (Austin: University of Texas Press, 1976). For a critique of the utilitarian rationality of *homo laborans* and *homo faber*, see Hannah Arendt, *The Human Condition* (Chicago: University of Chicago Press, 1958). Heidegger's own critique of technology is found in a collection of essays in translation, *The Question Concerning Technology and Other Essays*, trans. William Lovitt (New York: Harper & Row, 1977), and in *Discourse on Thinking*, trans. John M. Anderson and E. Hans Freund (New York: Harper & Row, 1966).

74. For an outline of this new humanism, see Hwa Yol Jung and Petee Jung, "Toward a New Humanism: The Politics of Civility in a 'No-Growth' Society," *Man and World*, 9 (August 1976): 283–306.

Chapter Eight

1. Michel Foucault, *The Order of Things* (New York: Random House, 1970), p. 328.

2. Michel Foucault, "Politics and Ethics: An Interview," in *The Foucault Reader*, ed. Paul Rabinow (New York: Pantheon Books, 1984), p. 375.

3. Michel Foucault, "Afterword: The Subject and Power," in Hubert L. Dreyfus and Paul Rabinow, *Michel Foucault: Beyond Structuralism and Hermeneutics*, 2nd ed. (Chicago: University of Chicago Press, 1983), pp. 222–23.

4. Michel Foucault, *Power/Knowledge: Selected Interviews and Other Writings 1972–1977*, ed. Colin Gordon and trans. Colin Gordon, Leo Marshall, John Mepham, and Kate Soper (New York: Pantheon Books, 1980), p. 198.

5. Claude Lévi-Strauss, *The Savage Mind*, trans. George Weidenfeld (Chicago: University of Chicago Press, 1966).

6. Foucault, *The Order of Things*, p. 387.

7. Michel Foucault, *The Archaeology of Knowledge*, trans. A. M. Sheridan Smith (New York: Harper & Row, 1972), p. 12.

8. Many commentators on Foucault have come to view the idea of discontinuity as one of the most radical features of his thought. Foucault himself addresses the question of continuity and discontinuity in one of his interviews, "Power and Truth" (1977)—see *Power/Knowledge*, pp. 111–13. According to Paul Rabinow, Foucault is a philosopher of both continuity and discontinuity. Rabinow comments that "indeed, Foucault has often mistakenly been seen as a philosopher of discontinuity. The fault is partially his own; works such as *The Archaeology of Knowledge* and *The Order of Things* certainly do emphasize abrupt changes in the structures of discourse of the human sciences. But Foucault has also stressed, in other contexts, the longer-range continuities in cultural practices. The sharp lines of discursive discontinuity in the human sciences and the longer lines

of continuity in non-discursive practices provide Foucault with a powerful and flexible grid of interpretation with which to approach relations of knowledge and power. It should be underlined, however, that this is not a philosophy of history which for some mysterious reason glorifies discontinuity"—"Introduction," in *The Foucault Reader*, p. 9.

9. Maurice Merleau-Ponty, *Themes from the Lectures at the Collège de France, 1952–1960*, trans. John O'Neill (Evanston: Northwestern University Press, 1970), p. 40.

10. Hannah Arendt, *The Human Condition* (Chicago: University of Chicago Press, 1958), pp. 175–76.

11. Emmanuel Levinas, *Totality and Infinity*, trans. Alphonso Lingis (Pittsburgh: Duquesne University Press, 1969), *passim*.

12. Martin Heidegger, *The Basic Problems of Phenomenology*, trans. Albert Hofstadter (Bloomington: Indiana University Press, 1982), p. 23. This critical interchange of continuity and discontinuity is best worked out by Hans-Georg Gadamer in his philosophical hermeneutics and particularly in his notions of "historically effective consciousness" (*wirkungsgeschichtliches Bewusstsein*) and the "fusion of horizons" (*Horizontverschmelzung*). Gadamer insists that "obedience" to tradition is "neither blind nor slavish"—*Philosophical Hermenutics*, ed. and trans. David E. Linge (Berkeley: University of California Press, 1976), p. 34. Whatever unbridgeable differences there may exist between Jürgen Habermas and Gadamer, Habermas, who is critical of Gadamer's idea of tradition in particular and his hermeneutics in general as too conservative, also allows room for an interchange between continuity and discontinuity in language as well as communication when he asserts that language is "inwardly as well as outwardly porous"—see Jürgen Habermas, "A Review of Gadamer's *Truth and Method*," in *Understanding and Social Inquiry*, ed. Fred R. Dallmayr and Thomas A. McCarthy (Notre Dame: University of Notre Dame Press, 1977), p. 340.

13. Foucault, "Afterword: The Subject and Power," pp. 216, 212. Interestingly, Sartre's taped dialogue with Pierre Victor would be titled *Power and Freedom*—a treatise on morality that is, according to Sartre, the fulfillment of his promise in *Being and Nothingness;* see "Translator's Introduction," in Francis Jeanson, *Sartre and the Problem of Morality*, trans. Robert V. Stone (Bloomington: Indiana University Press, 1980), p. xxv.

14. See *Six Plays by Henrik Ibsen*, trans. Eva Le Gallienne (New York: Modern Library, 1957), pp. 458, 498. Ibsen's play is also alluded to in Paul de Man, *Blindness and Insight* (New York: Oxford University Press, 1971), p. 48.

15. See Martin Heidegger, *Schelling's Treatise on the Essence of Human Freedom*, trans. Joan Stambaugh (Athens: Ohio University Press, 1985), p. 17.

16. Maurice Merleau-Ponty, *Adventures of the Dialectic*, trans. Joseph Bien (Evanston: Northwestern University Press, 1973), p. 205.

17. Maurice Merleau-Ponty, *Consciousness and the Acquisition of Language*, trans. Hugh J. Silverman (Evanston: Northwestern University Press, 1973), p. 102.

18. Emile Benveniste, *Problems in General Linguistics*, trans. Mary Elizabeth Meek (Coral Gables: University of Miami Press, 1971), p. 225.

19. Paul Ricoeur, *The Conflict of Interpretations*, ed. Don Ihde (Evanston: Northwestern University Press, 1974), pp. 92, 261.

20. In this connection, let us also recall what Alfred Schutz says in "Making Music Together," *Collected Papers*, vol. 2: *Studies in Social Theory*, ed. Arvid Brodersen (The Hague: Nijhoff, 1964), pp. 159–60: "A study of the social relationships connected with the musical process may lead to some insights valid for many other forms of social intercourse, perhaps even to illumination of a certain aspect of the structure of social interaction as such that has not so attracted from social scientists the attention it deserves." This cardinal insight of Schutz has still not been tapped fully by the human sciences. Arguing against classical mechanics cloaked and masked in visual and spatial models, Milič Čapek proposes that auditory models are better suited to explain the dynamics of contemporary quantum physics. He writes: "In the musical experience of melody or polyphony, the situation is considerably different. The quality of a new tone, in spite of its irreducible individuality, is tinged by the whole antecedent musical context which, in turn, is retroactively changed by the emergence of a new musical quality. The individual tones are not externally related units of which the melody is additively built; neither is their individuality absorbed or dissolved in the undifferentiated unity of the musical whole. The musical phrase is a *successive differentiated whole* which remains a whole in spite of its dynamic wholeness. Like every dynamic whole it exhibits a synthesis of unity and multiplicity, of continuity and discontinuity; but it is not the unity of an undifferentiated simultaneous whole nor is it the plurality of juxtaposed units; it is neither continuity in the mathematical sense of infinite divisability nor is it the discontinuity of rigid atomic blocs"—*The Philosophical Impact of Contemporary Physics* (Princeton: Van Nostrand, 1961), pp. 371–72. In this context, and at the risk of going beyond Foucault's own intended formulation, let me extrapolate and speculate on the seminal insight of Foucault's analytics of power as a cluster or an ensemble of dynamic relations. For it transforms political thinking from the age of classical mechanics to that of quantum physics, from the closed, static, world to the infinite, dynamic universe of power. Foucault's is the quantum field of power whose dynamic quality derives from the temporalization (dynamization) of matter and motion, while classical mechanics was obsessed with "timeless" spatialization. Power associated with "free subjects" may be said to be a relational field of quanta governed by the principle of indeterminacy.

21. Jacques Derrida, *Margins of Philosophy*, trans. Alan Bass (Chicago: University of Chicago Press, 1982), p. xvii.

22. The neologism *otonomy* is patterned after Jacques Derrida's discussion of Nietzsche under the playful title "otobiographies" (oto/biographies) in place of "autobiographies." By using "otonomy," I wish on the one hand to preserve the homonymous sense of "autonomy," without being subjective, and on the other hand, to evoke the sensibility of the "associative ear" rather than the "collecting eye"—to use Eric Havelock's phrases. See Jacques Derrida, "Otobiographies: The Teaching of Nietzsche and the Politics of the Proper Name," trans. Avital Ronell, in *The Ear of the Other*, ed. Christie V. McDonald (New York: Schocken Books, 1985), pp. 1–38. Of course, we cannot afford to ignore the (musical) aestheticism of Fried-

rich Nietzsche in *The Birth of Tragedy,* trans. Walter Kaufmann (New York: Random House, 1967). Music is for Nietzsche one way to make the aesthetic intelligible and grasp it directly: "Quite generally, only music, placed beside the world, can give us an idea of what is meant by the justification of the world as an aesthetic phenomenon" (*ibid.,* p. 141). Social and political philosophy has yet to come to terms with the radical, immensely important implications of Nietzsche's transgression of Platonism, part of which is the opposition of *aesthesis* to *theōria.*

23. Martin Heidegger, *Nietzsche,* vol. 1: *The Will to Power as Art,* trans. David Farrell Krell (New York: Harper & Row, 1979), p. 99. In *Poetic Thinking: An Approach to Heidegger* (Chicago: University of Chicago Press, 1981), David Halliburton describes the encompassing circle of a musical performance that captures Heidegger's sense of mood, attunement, and proximity: "In the performance of a symphony, for example, responsibility may be seen in the interconnecting indebtedness of each constituent: the musicians, as users of equipment (instruments, chairs, music stands, and the like), together with their skills; the artisans responsible for the preparation of the equipment; the members of the audience, together with their capacity to hear and to sustain attention; the score, a being with a thingly character that allies it with equipment even as it carries an already constituted inclination (the totality of the composer's notations); the composer, as one who brings forth within the same order as the artisan; that artisan who is the printer of the score; the manner (in the sense of melody, timbre, tone) of the score as performed; the space of time in which that manner emerges through the concerted composure of performance; the space of time of the tradition without which the music could not move into its own articulation—without which, as the temporal structure that preserves the reciprocal responsibility of all the constituents, it would not be music; and finally, the space of time which is the world play's manner of moving, through all that is thus indebted, to its own disclosure" (p. 217).

24. For a detailed discussion of the nature of music as the organized movement of sound in time, see Victor Zuckerkandl, *Sound and Symbol* (Princeton: Princeton University Press, 1956). Cf. Marshall McLuhan and Quentin Fiore, *The Medium Is the Message* (New York: Bantam Books, 1967), p. 111: "The ear favors no particular 'point of view.' We are *enveloped* by sound. It forms a seamless web around us. We say, 'Music shall fill the air.' We never say, 'Music shall fill a particular segment of the air.' We hear sounds from everywhere, without having to focus. Sounds come from 'above,' from 'below,' from in 'front' of us, from 'behind' us, from our 'right,' from our 'left.' We can't shut out sound automatically. We simply are not equipped with earlids. Whereas a visual space is an organized continuum of a uniformed connected kind, the ear world is a world of simultaneous relationships."

25. For an extensive critical account of social ontology in the phenomenological movement, see Michael Theunissen, *The Other,* trans. Christopher Macann (Cambridge: MIT Press, 1984).

26. See Alfred Schutz, *The Phenomenology of the Social World,* trans. George Walsh and Frederick Lehnert (Evanston: Northwestern University Press, 1967). For the social ontology of Schutz, see Helmut R. Wagner, "Toward an Anthropology of the Life-World: Alfred Schutz's Quest for the Ontological Justification of the Phenomenological Undertaking,"

Human Studies, 6 (1983): 239–46, and "The Limitations of Phenomenology: Alfred Schutz's Critical Dialogue with Edmund Husserl," *Husserl Studies,* 1 (1984): 157–78. Incidentally, no one has thus far examined seriously the philosophical consequences of Schutz's proposal in his 1945 article on multiple realities: the idea of what he calls the *epoché* of the natural attitude, which—unlike transcendental reduction, which suspends our belief in the reality of the world—suspends doubt itself in the existence of the external world. In the *epoché* of the natural attitude, therefore, what is put in brackets is the doubt that the world and its objects might be otherwise than it appears to us. See Alfred Schutz, *Collected Papers,* vol. 1: *The Problem of Social Reality,* ed. Maurice Natanson (The Hague: Nijhoff, 1962), p. 229.

27. On the issue of proximity in recent French intellectual thought, see Joseph Libertson, *Proximity: Levinas, Blanchot, Bataille and Communication* (The Hague: Nijhoff, 1982). In the tradition of phenomenology, there are four philosophies of proximity: (1) cosmic, (2) linguistic, (3) ethical, and (4) political. Each has been worked out by, and is characteristic of, Heidegger, Gadamer, Levinas, and Arendt, respectively, although there is definitely some overlapping of each over the others. Heidegger's cosmic proximity is typified in his discussion of the fourfold unity (*das Geviert*) of earth, sky, gods, and mortals; see particularly *Poetry, Language, Thought,* trans. Albert Hofstadter (New York: Harper & Row, 1971). Hans-Georg Gadamer's linguistic proximity is found in, for example, *Truth and Method,* ed. Garrett Barden and John Cumming (New York: Seabury Press, 1972), and *Dialogue and Dialectic,* trans. P. Christopher Smith (New Haven: Yale University Press, 1980). For Levinas's ethical proximity, see *Totality and Infinity* and *Otherwise Than Being or Beyond Essence,* trans. Alphonso Lingis (The Hague: Nijhoff, 1981). And for Arendt's political proximity, see *The Human Condition.*

28. Denis Donoghue, *Ferocious Alphabets* (Boston: Little, Brown, 1981), p. 45.

29. Michel Foucault, *Discipline and Punish,* trans. Alan Sheridan (New York: Pantheon Books, 1977).

30. Katerina Clark and Michael Holquist, *Mikhail Bakhtin* (Cambridge: Harvard University Press, 1984), p. 175. The phrase quoted not only epitomizes what the term "body-subject" means here, but also aptly indicates the role of the lived body in Bakhtin's dialogical philosophy. For Bakhtin, dialogism is to monologism what Copernican heliocentrism is to Ptolemaic geocentrism. His sensitivity to the lived body, which is not unlike Merleau-Ponty's ontology of the flesh, is rooted deeply in Russian Orthodoxy's belief in the corporeality of Christ and kenosis of the potential holiness of matter. The implications of Bakhtin's dialogism for social, political, and moral philosophy is enormous, since as Clark and Holquist suggest, it "is not intended to be merely another theory of literature or even another philosophy of language, but is an account of relations between people and between persons and things that cuts across religious, political, and aesthetic boundaries"—*Mikhail Bakhtin,* p. 348.

31. See Emmanuel Levinas and Richard Kearney, "Dialogue with Emmanuel Levinas," in *Face to Face with Levinas,* ed. Richard A. Cohen (Albany: State University of New York Press, 1986), p. 20.

32. *Totality and Infinity,* p. 83. This work of Levinas is yet to be explored as a treatise on political philosophy.

33. "Dialogue with Levinas," p. 27.

34. Emmanuel Levinas, *Ethics and Infinity*, trans. Richard A. Cohen (Pittsburgh: Duquesne University Press, 1982), p. 95.

35. Martin Buber, *I and Thou*, trans. Ronald Gregor Smith, 2nd ed. (New York: Scribner's Sons, 1958), p. 4. It should be noted here that Levinas contends that Buber's "I-Thou" is the relation of "a symmetrical co-presence"—see "Dialogue with Levinas," p. 31. Levinas's contention should be clarified and may be called into question.

36. The German etymology clearly shows a familial circle of "word" (*Wort*), "answer" (*Antwort*), "to answer" (*antworten*), and "to be responsible for" (*verantworten*). See Martin Buber, *Between Man and Man*, trans. Ronald Gregor Smith (New York: Macmillan, 1965), p. 206 n. 2. For the phenomenological ethics of speaking as dialogical, see Georges Gusdorf, *Speaking*, trans. Paul T. Brockelman (Evanston: Northwestern University Press, 1965). One of the most thoroughgoing dialogisms has been developed by Mikhail Bakhtin. See particularly *The Dialogic Imagination*, ed. Michael Holquist and trans. Caryl Emerson and Michael Holquist (Austin: University of Texas Press, 1981), and two works published under the name V. N. Voloshinov: *Freudianism: A Marxist Critique*, trans. I. R. Titunik (New York: Academic Press, 1976), and *Marxism and the Philosophy of Language*, trans. Ladislav Matejka and I. R. Titunik (Cambridge: Harvard University Press, 1986). Tzvetan Todorov, *Mikhail Bakhtin: The Dialogical Principle*, trans. Wlad Godzich (Minneapolis: University of Minnesota Press, 1984), focuses on the implications of Bakhtin's dialogism on the philosophy of the human sciences.

37. Edith Wyschogrod, *Spirit in Ashes* (New Haven: Yale University Press, 1985), p. 207.

38. Levinas, *Totality and Infinity*, p. 395.

39. *Ibid.*, p. 199.

40. The subtitle of Elisabeth Young-Bruehl's intellectual biography of Arendt sums up, I think, Arendt's political ethics of proximity. See *Hannah Arendt: For Love of the World* (New Haven: Yale University Press, 1982).

41. For example, the trilogical thematics of Foucault's *The Order of Things* by way of life, labor, and language and Arendt's *The Human Condition* in the forms of labor, work, and action go beyond the casual matchings of their keywords. Foucault's *Discipline and Punish* and Arendt's *The Origins of Totalitarianism*, new ed. (New York: Harcourt, Brace & World, 1966), both pay attention to the totalitarian framework of power and to the political evils of Western society, particularly as they are sustained by means of the "instrumentalization" of the world and humanity.

42. Michel Foucault, *The History of Sexuality*, vol. 1: *An Introduction*, trans. Robert Hurley (New York: Pantheon Books, 1978), p. 92.

43. Søren Kierkegaard, *The Present Age*, trans. Alexander Dru (New York: Harper & Row, 1962), set the tone for existentialist concern for modern anonymity. The work in the same vein that is most familiar to political scientists is José Ortega y Gasset, *The Revolt of the Masses* (New York: Norton, 1932), whose central thesis, I might add, has quite often been misunderstood.

44. Hannah Arendt, *Eichmann in Jerusalem: A Report on the Banality of Evil*, rev. and enl. ed. (New York: Penguin Books, 1977), p. 279.

45. Hannah Arendt, *Crises of the Republic* (New York: Harcourt Brace Jovanovich, 1972), p. 179. Hans Jonas emphasizes the importance of Arendt's notion of natality because she introduced a new category into the philosophical doctrine of humanity. See his "Acting, Knowing, Thinking: Gleanings from Hannah Arendt's Philosophical Work," *Social Research*, 44 (Spring 1977): 30.

46. Levinas, *Totality and Infinity*, p. 83.

47. Arendt, *The Human Condition*, p. 245 n. 83.

48. *Ibid.*, p. 200.

49. *Ibid.*

50. Cf. Edward W. Said, *The World, the Text, and the Critic* (Cambridge: Harvard University Press, 1983), p. 188: "Perhaps his interest in rules is part of the reason why Foucault is unable to deal with, or provide an account of, historical change."

51. Simone de Beauvoir, *The Ethics of Ambiguity*, trans. Bernard Frechtman (New York: Citadel Press, 1962), is a rare and classical treatise in the development of existentialist ethics. By ambiguity, she means the existential condition of choice. She contends that "the existentialist doctrine permits the elaboration of an ethics, but it even appears to us as the only philosophy in which an ethics has its place. For, in a metaphysics or transcendence in the classical sense of the term, evil is reduced to error; and in humanistic philosophies it is impossible to account for it, man being defined as complete in a complete world. . . . Nothing is decided in advance, and it is because man has something to lose and because he can lose that he can also win" (*ibid.*, p. 34). In the context of Schelling's philosophy, Heidegger discusses the notion of freedom as the capacity of both good and evil: as he writes, "rather, freedom is freedom for good and evil. The 'and,' the possibility of this ambiguity and everything hidden in it is what is decisive. That means that the whole concept of freedom must change"— *Schelling's Treatise*, p. 97.

52. See Charles Taylor, "Self-Interpreting Animals," *Philosophical Papers*, 2 vols. (New York: Cambridge University Press, 1985), vol. 2: *Human Agency and Language*, pp. 45–76. Taylor writes that "human beings are self-interpreting animals. This is a widely echoing theme of contemporary philosophy. It is central to a thesis about the sciences of man, and what differentiates them from the sciences of nature, which passes through Dilthey and is very strong in the late twentieth century. It is one of the basic ideas of Heidegger's philosophy, early and late. Partly through his influence, it has been made the starting point for a new skein of connected conceptions of man, self-understanding and history, of which the most prominent protagonist has been Gadamer. At the same time, this conception of man as self-interpreting has been incorporated into the work of Habermas, the most important successor of the post-Marxist line of thought known somewhat strangely as critical theory" (*ibid.*, p. 45).

53. Cf. Maurice Merleau-Ponty, *In Praise of Philosophy*, trans. John Wild and James M. Edie (Evanston: Northwestern University Press, 1963), pp. 52–53: "History has no meaning, if this meaning is understood as that of a river which, under the influence of all-powerful causes, flows towards an ocean in which it disappears. Every appeal to universal history cuts off the meaning of the specific event, renders effective history insignificant, and is a nihilism in disguise."

266

RETHINKING
POLITICAL
THEORY

54. Cf. Perry Anderson, *In the Tracks of Historical Materialism* (London: Verso, 1983), p. 54: " . . . once structures were freed from any subject at all, delivered over totally to their own play, they would lose what *defines* them as structures—that is, any objective coordinates of organization at all. . . . Structure therewith, capsizes into its antithesis, and post-structuralism proper is born, or what can be defined as a subjectivism without a subject." In *Towards Deep Subjectivity* (New York: Harper & Row, 1972), Roger Poole, too, contends, albeit in a different context, that "positivism in fact weakens the case of objectivity by refusing to consider the hidden structures of subjectivity" (p. 75). In *Foucault, Marxism and History* (Cambridge: Polity Press, 1984), Mark Poster raises some important questions concerning Foucault's notion of the subject. For a general discussion of the subject in reference to literary theory, see David Carroll, *The Subject in Question* (Chicago: University of Chicago Press, 1982).

55. It may be said that everything—everything scholarly at any rate— becomes the matter of reading. What I have in mind is the phenomenology of reading or *Rezeptionsästhetik*, which has been exemplified particularly in the following works: Wolfgang Iser, *The Implied Reader* (Baltimore: John Hopkins University Press, 1974) and *The Act of Reading* (Baltimore: Johns Hopkins University Press, 1978); Hans Robert Jauss, *Toward an Aesthetic of Reception*, trans. Timothy Bahti (Minneapolis: University of Minnesota Press, 1982), and *Aesthetic Experience and Literary Hermeneutics*, trans. Michael Shaw (Minneapolis: University of Minnesota Press, 1982). For a classical text on the subject in American literary theory today, see Stanley Fish, *Is There a Text in This Class?* (Cambridge: Harvard University Press, 1980). Cf. the present author's "The Edification of Oral Hermeneutics and the Ecology of the Text," in *Proceedings of the Xth Congress of the International Comparative Literature Association*, vol. 2: *Comparative Poetics*, ed. Claudio Guillen and Peggy Escher (New York: Garland, 1986), pp. 539–50, and Mary Louise Pratt, "Interpretive Strategies/Strategic Interpretations: On Anglo-American Reader-Response Criticism," in *Postmodernism and Politics*, ed. Jonathan Arac (Minneapolis: University of Minnesota Press, 1986), pp. 26–54.

Chapter Nine

1. Todorov, *Mikhail Bakhtin*, trans. Wlad Godzich (Minneapolis: University of Minnesota Press, 1984), p. ix. My own fascination with Bakhtin began in 1978–1979 with reading V. N. Voloshinov, *Marxism and the Philosophy of Language*, trans. Ladislav Metejka and I. R. Titunik (New York: Seminar Press, 1973), and *Freudianism*, trans I. R. Titunik (New York: Academic press, 1976), while I was completing the essay entitled "Being, Praxis, and Truth: Toward a Dialogue Between Phenomenology and Marxism," with its focus on Heidegger and Marx (see Chapter 7 above). In reading Bakhtin for the first time, I found that his work struck a harmonious chord with the existential phenomenology of Merleau-Ponty. In *Mikhail Bakhtin* (Cambridge: Harvard University Press, 1984), Katerina Clark and Michael Holquist mention Bakhtin's affinity to Husserl, Heidegger, and Sartre. They do not mention, however, the existential phenomenology of Merleau-Ponty. A comparison between Bakhtin and Merleau-Ponty has yet to be written.

2. Clark and Holquist, *Mikhail Bakhtin*, p. 86.

3. *Ibid.*, p. 206, and cf. Michael Holquist, "The Surd Heard: Bakhtin and Derrida," in *Literature and History,* ed. Gary Saul Morson (Stanford: Stanford University Press, 1986), p. 148. Jacques Lacan's interpretation of Freud's psychoanalysis would enable us to inaugurate a new synthesis between Freud and Bakhtin. Speaking of Lacan's approach, Shoshana Felman writes: "The dialogue is analytical in that it is not equal to the sum of its parts; the knowledge for which the analytic dialogue is a vehicle is not reducible to the sum total of the knowledge of each of its two subjects. In Lacan's terminology, it is not a dialogue between two egos, it is not reducible to a dual relationship between *two* terms, but is constituted by a third term that is the meeting point in language between Lacan's and Freud's unconscious: a linguistic, signifying meeting place that is the focus of Lacan's insight but that Lacan does not master. Lacan's originality is thus the originality of a return in that it is irreducibly dialogic"—*Jacques Lacan and the Adventure of Insight* (Cambridge: Harvard University Press, 1987), p. 56. Again, she writes in a slightly different context: "Dialogue is thus the radical condition of learning and of knowledge, the analytically constitutive condition through which ignorance becomes structurally informative; knowledge is essentially, irreducibly dialogic" (*ibid.*, p. 83). And above all dialogue as performative *praxis* is first and foremost *ethical* for Freud/Lacan and Bakhtin.

4. Donoghue, *Ferocious Alphabets* (Boston: Little, Brown, 1981), p. 43.

5. Bakhtin, *The Dialogic Imagination,* ed. Michael Holquist and trans. Caryl Emerson and Michael Holquist (Austin: University of Texas Press, 1981), pp. 280–82.

6. See Martin Buber, *Between Man and Man,* trans. Ronald Gregory Smith (New York: Macmillan, 1965), p. 206 n. 2.

7. See Searle, *Minds, Brains and Science* (Cambridge: Harvard University Press, 1984).

8. See Schrag, *Communicative Praxis and the Space of Subjectivity* (Bloomington: Indiana University Press, 1986). Anthony Giddens also speaks of "the decentered subject" in summarizing his social "theory of structuration" which attempts to steer the rough waters between the Scylla of "subjectivism" and the Charybdis of "objectivism." He hints at a merger of social theory and literary theory within his theory of structuration, which would include such issues as practical consciousness, discourse, and the unconscious—see "Action, Subjectivity, and the Constitution of Meaning," *Social Research,* 53 (1986): 529–45, and *The Constitution of Society* (Berkeley: University of California Press, 1984). It should be pointed out here, moreover, that there is no one who is better than Fred R. Dallmayr at bridging the gap between political theory and postmodern philosophy; see his *Twilight of Subjectivity* (Amherst: University of Massachusetts Press, 1981) and his *Polis and Praxis* (Cambridge: MIT Press, 1984).

9. Barthes, *Empire of Signs,* trans Richard Howard (New York: Hill & Wang, 1982). Cf. the present author's "The Joy of Textualizing Japan: A Metacommentary on Roland Barthes's *Empire of Signs,*" in *Bucknell Review,* vol. 30: *Self, Sign and Symbol,* ed. Mark Neuman and Michael Payne (Lewisberg: Bucknell University Press, 1987), pp. 144–67, and cf. above, Chapter 5, section V. In an interview in 1970, Barthes stated that

there is a definite correlation (in Japan) between the sign system of cuisine (e.g., *sukiyaki*) and the (ideogrammic) language on the one hand and the Japanese mentality on the other. *Sukiyaki* is "an image of the plural"; its polycentricity is antipodal to Western monocentrism. See Barthes, *The Grain of the Voice*, trans. Linda Coverdale (New York: Hill & Wang, 1985), pp. 98–101.

10. See Bakhtin, *Speech Genres and Other Late Essays,* ed. Caryl Emerson and Michael Holquist and trans. Vern W. McGee (Austin: University of Texas Press, 1986), p. 167.

11. According to Clark and Holquist, Bakhtin's idea that the social is "conceived" rather than "given" is tied to the philosophical rallying cry of the Marburg Neo-Kantian school, especially of Hermann Cohen: *die Welt ist nicht gegeben aber aufgegeben* or (in Russian) *mir ne dan, a zadan.*

12. Merleau-Ponty, *Adventures of the Dialectic,* trans. Joseph Bien (Evanston: Northwestern University Press, 1973), p. 205.

13. Bakhtin, *The Dialogic Imagination,* p. 294.

14. The concept of institution is based on Merleau-Ponty, whose words bear repeating here: "If the subject were taken not as a constituting but an instituting subject, it might be understood that the subject does not exist instantaneously and that the other person does not exist simply as a negative of myself. What I have begun at certain decisive moments would exist neither far off in the past as an objective memory nor be present like a memory revived, but really between the two as the field of my becoming during that period. Likewise my relation to another person would not be reducible to a disjunction: an instituting subject could coexist with another because the one instituted is not the immediate reflection of the activity of the former and be regained by himself or by others without involving anything like a total recreation. Thus the instituted subject exists between others and myself, between me and myself, like a hinge, the consequence and the guarantee of our belonging to a common world"—*Themes from the Lectures at the Collège de France, 1952–1960,* trans. John O'Neill (Evanston: Northwestern University Press, 1970), p. 40. In *Institution and Interpretation* (Minneapolis: University of Minnesota Press, 1987), Samuel Weber touches on the question of institution in relation to literary interpretation. Ken Hirschkop, whose article begins with the statement that "revolution is a festival of the oppressed and exploited," is critical of Bakhtin, who allegedly privileges consciousness over institution—see his "Bakhtin, Discourse and Democracy," *New Left Review,* No. 158(1986): 92–113. His criticism is misguided, however, because it misses the genealogical basis of Bakhtin's attempt, where there is no denial of institutional importance. First of all, Hirschkop seems to have no understanding of the body as subject. The body without consciousness is the body only as objectified and leads blindly to the dualism of the two. Second, his notion of institution becomes reified without the human being as agent when he speaks of institution "beyond consciousness."

15. Arendt, *The Human Condition* (Chicago: University of Chicago Press, 1958), p. 23.

16. Heterarchy has a twofold meaning. On the one hand, it implies heterocentricity as opposed to egocentricity, that is, it is other-oriented in defining the relationships between the self and the other. In literary theory, it may be compared to "reader-response criticism." See *Reader-Response*

Criticism, ed. Jane P. Tompkins (Baltimore: Johns Hopkins University Press, 1980), and cf. the present author's "The Edification of Oral Hermeneutics and the Ecology of the Text," in *Proceedings of the Xth Congress of the International Comparative Literature Association*, vol. 2: *Comparative Poetics*, ed. Claudio Guillen and Peggy Escher (New York: Garland, 1985), pp. 539–50. On the other hand, heterarchy signifies "many." James Ogilvy uses heterarchy in the second sense in opposition to the "one-dimensional," of which Herbert Marcuse is extremely critical. See Ogilvy, *Many Dimensional Man* (New York: Oxford University Press, 1977), and Marcuse, *One Dimensional Man* (Boston: Beacon Press, 1964). I resisted the thought of employing the term *polyarchy* instead of heterarchy for two main reasons. First, polyarchy has already become the neologism of Robert Dahl, and in this sense refers to a democratic elitism grounded in naive empiricism. Second, I took seriously the following statement in Todorov, *The Conquest of America*, trans. Richard Howard (New York: Harper & Row, 1984), p. 251: "Heterology, which makes the differences of voices heard, is necessary; polylogy is insipid." Parenthetically, I see this work of Todorov as an attempt to realign the conception of the self and the other in which the imprint of Bakhtin's thought is subtle and incipient if not overarching. Cf. also Hans Joas, who focuses his attention on a concept that is central to George Herbert Mead's philosophy: the concept of sociality, which is the founding principle of the universe including the social world. Here sociality is defined as "the capacity of being several things at once" (i.e., of being polyphonic). See Joas, *G. H. Mead*, trans. Raymond Meyer (Cambridge: MIT Press, 1985), p. 182.

17. Arendt, *Crises of the Republic* (New York: Harcourt Brace Jovanovich, 1972), p. 179. Hans Jonas emphasizes the importance of Arendt's notion of natality because she introduced a new category into the philosophical doctrine of humanity. See his "Acting, Knowing, Thinking: Gleanings from Hannah Arendt's Philosophical Work," *Social Research*, 44 (Spring 1977): 25–43.

18. See Levinas, *Totality and Infinity*, trans. Alphonso Lingis (Pittsburgh: Duquesne University Press, 1969), p. 83.

19. Cf. Karl Marx and Friedrich Engels, who said: "Language is as old as consciousness, language is practical consciousness, as it exists for other men, and for that reason is really beginning to exist for me personally as well; for language, like consciousness, only arises from the need, the necessity, of intercourse with other men"—*The German Ideology*, ed. R. Pascal (New York: International Publishers, 1947), p. 19.

20. See Felman, *The Literary Speech Act*, trans. Catherine Porter (Ithaca: Cornell University Press, 1983).

21. Felman, *Jacques Lacan and the Adventure of Insight*, pp. 118–19. Cf. Donald P. Spence, *Narrative Truth and Historical Truth* (New York: Norton, 1982), p. 272: "A pragmatic statement is a certain kind of speech act, and it might be argued that the analyst making an interpretation is performing a certain kind of speech act in the analytic situation."

22. See White, *Tropics of Discourse* (Baltimore: Johns Hopkins University Press, 1978), p. 4. For an extensive discussion of the logic of diatactics as the unity of two opposites as complementary, see the present author's *The Question of Rationality and the Basic Grammar of Intercultural Texts* (Niigata: International University of Japan, 1989).

23. In Martin Heidegger, *What Is Called Thinking?* trans. Fred D. Wieck and J. Glenn Gray (New York: Harper & Row, 1968), there is a wonderful passage concerning the many ways of the hand that culminate in thinking as a "handicraft" (handy craft) in the same way that the use of language—both speaking and writing—is the *technē* (art) of the body: "We are trying to learn thinking. Perhaps thinking, too, is just something like building a cabinet. At any rate, it is a craft, a 'handicraft.' 'Craft' literally means the strength and skill in our hands. The hand is a peculiar thing. In the common view, the hand is part of our bodily organism. But the hand's essence can never be determined, or explained, by its being an organ which can grasp. Apes, too, have organs that can grasp, but they do not have hands. The hand is infinitely different from all grasping organs—paws, claws, or fangs—different by an abyss of essence. Only a being who can speak, that is, can have hands and can be handy in achieving works of handicraft. But the craft of the hand is richer than we commonly imagine. The hand does not only grasp and catch, or push and pull. The hand reaches and extends, receives, and welcomes—and not just things: the hand extends itself, and receives its own welcome in the hands of others. The hand holds. The hand carries. The hand designs and signs, presumably because man is a sign. Two hands fold into one, a gesture meant to carry man into the great oneness. The hand is all this, and this is the handicraft, and commonly we go no further. But the hand's gestures run everywhere through language, in their most perfect purity precisely when man speaks by being silent. And only when man speaks, does he think—not the other way around, as metaphysics still believes. Every motion of the hand in every one of its works carries itself through the element of thinking, every bearing of the hand bears itself in that element. All the work of the hand is rooted in thinking. Therefore, thinking itself is man's simplest, and for that reason hardest, handiwork, if it would be accomplished at its proper time" (pp. 16–17). We would be able to conclude that because it is diactactical, *thinking is the body politic par excellence.* See also David Sudnow's works, which are elegant discussions particularly on improvised piano playing (i.e., handiwork): *Ways of the Hand* (Cambridge: Harvard University Press, 1978) and *Talk's Body* (New York: Knopf, 1979). It is worth noting here that in his notes taken in 1970–71, Bakhtin made the distinction between dialogue and dialectics: "Take a dialogue and remove the voices (the partitioning of voices), remove the intonations (emotional and individualizing ones), carve out abstract concepts and judgments from living words and response, cram everything into one abstract consciousness—and that's how you get dialectics"—*Speech Genres and Other Late Essays*, p. 147. Here Bakhtin's dialogism reminds us of Kierkegaard's existential critique of Hegel. We may conclude, therefore, that dialectics is the outcome of the conceptual overdetermination of dialogue and that the transcription of fluid utterances into fixed writing corresponds to the movement from dialogue to dialectics. Hegel's dialectics puts too much conceptual garb on the naked body of dialogue. *Bakhtin's dialogism valorizes dialogue against dialectics.* In this regard, it may be likened to the Chinese logic of *yin* and *yang*, that is, to the idea of the open unity of the two opposites as complementary without finality or an ultimate fusion. For Lacan, too, knowledge is interminable, whereas the end of Hegel's dialectics is absolute knowledge or the identity of knowledge with itself, i.e., the exhaustion of all there is to know; see Felman, *Jacques Lacan and the Adventure of Insight*, p. 77. Interestingly, Caryl Emerson mentions the idea of "continuity without fusion" in reference to Bakhtin's thought—see Mikhail Bakhtin, *Problems of Dostoevsky's Poetics*, ed. and trans. Caryl

Emerson (Minneapolis: University of Minnesota Press, 1984), p. xxxiii. She comments on Bakhtin's passage on the distinction between dialogue and dialectics: "In place of the comfortable patterns of synthesis and *Aufhebung*, Bakhtin posits a dualistic universe of *permanent* dialogue. Life in language is in fact dependent upon the preservation of a gap. Two speakers must not, and never do, completely understand each other; they must remain only partially satisfied with each other's replies, because the continuation of dialogue is in large part dependent on neither party knowing exactly what the other means. Thus true communication never makes languages sound the same, never erases boundaries, never pretends to a perfect fit" (*ibid.*, pp. xxxii–xxxiii). In the tradition of Western thought, Bakhtin's paradigmatic model of dialogue is the Socratic-Platonic dialogue, not the dialectics of Hegel, whom Derrida calls "the first thinker of writing"—see Jacques Derrida, *Of Grammatology*, trans. Gayatri Chakrovorty Spivak (Baltimore: Johns Hopkins University Press, 1976), p. 26. For discussions of the nature of the Socratic-Platonic dialogues in this connection, see Hans-Georg Gadamer, *Dialogue and Dialectic*, trans. P. Christopher Smith (New Haven: Yale University Press, 1980).

24. Barthes, *The Grain of the Voice*, p. 4.

25. See *Performance in Postmodern Culture*, ed. Michael Benanou and Charles Caramello (Madison: Coda Press, 1977).

26. Concurring with the classical discussion by Johan Huizinga of *homo ludens*, Gadamer dwells on the notion of play as an elementary part of human life and considers that the aesthetic—and, for that matter, hermeneutics—is unimaginable without the play element. See *Truth and Method*, ed. Garrett Borden and John Cumming (New York: Seabury Press, 1975), and *The Relevance of the Beautiful and Other Essays*, ed. Robert Bernasconi and trans. Nicholas Walker (New York: Cambridge University Press, 1986).

27. Schechner, *Between Theatre and Anthropology* (Philadelphia: University of Pennsylvania Press, 1985), p. 23. Jerzy Grotowski's "poor theatre" emulates pantomime as its paradigm with minimal clothing (i.e., minimal masking) and the maximal economy of verbalism: "The costumes are bags full of holes covering naked bodies; through the holes one looks directly into a torn body"—Grotowski, *Toward a Poor Theatre* (New York: Simon & Schuster, 1968), p. 64. In his revisionist theory of Freud, Marcuse adds "the performance principle" to emphasize the pragmatic dimension of "the reality principle" and "the pleasure principle," that is, to call our attention to how they *perform* in different historical periods—see *Eros and Civilization* (Boston: Beacon Press, 1960).

28. Vico, *The New Science*, trans. Thomas Goddard Bergin and Max Harold Fisch (Ithaca: Cornell University Press, 1984), par. 1045, p. 393.

29. *Ibid.*, par. 237, p. 78. John O'Neill extensively explores the social implications of embodiment, including a chapter on "the body politic," in his *Five Bodies* (Ithaca: Cornell University Press, 1985).

30. Vico, *The New Science*, par. 405, p. 129. For an account of the affinity between Vico and Bakhtin, see the present author's "Vico and Bakhtin: A Prolegomenon to Any Future Comparison," *New Vico Studies*, 3 (1985): 157–65. In the tradition of Vico, Susan Sontag analyzes the use and misuse of metaphor in relation to the body's diseases in *Illness as Met-*

aphor (New York: Farrar, Straus & Giroux, 1978) and *AIDS and Its Metaphors* (New York: Farrar, Straus & Giroux, 1989).

31. Clark and Holquist, *Mikhail Bakhtin*, p. 87.

32. In *On Boxing* (Garden City: Doubleday, 1987), Joyce Carol Oates discusses the idea that a boxer *is* his body, that boxing is a theatrical performance, and that it *is* the body politic as dialogue. To quote an admirable passage from the work: "Because a boxing match is a story without words, this doesn't mean that it has no text or no language, that it is somehow 'brute,' 'primitive,' 'inarticulate,' only that the text is improvised in action; the language of a dialogue between the boxers of the most refined sort (one might say, as much neurological as psychological: a dialogue of split-second reflexes) in a joint response to the mysterious will of the audience which is always that the fight be a worthy one so that the crude paraphernalia of the setting—ring, lights, ropes, stained canvas, the staring onlookers themselves—be erased, forgotten. (As in the theater or the church, settings are erased by way, ideally, of transcendent action). Ringside announcers give to the wordless spectacle a narrative unity, yet boxing as performance is more clearly akin to dance or music than narrative" (p. 11).

33. Daisetz Teitaro Suzuki, *Zen and Japanese Culture* (New York: Pantheon Books, 1959), pp. 104–5, 178.

34. See Karlfried Graf von Dürckheim, *Hara: The Vital Center of Man*, trans. Sylvia-Monica von Kospoth (London: Allen and Unwin, 1962). Yasuo Yuasa, *The Body*, ed. T. P. Kasulis and trans. Shigenori Nagatomo and T. P. Kasulis (Albany: State University of New York Press, 1987), is an excellent account of an Eastern theory of the body-mind unity as *achievement*. It should be pointed out that the best part of Japanese philosophy is the production of the intertext that is at once Chinese, Indian, and Western as well as Japanese. Yuasa's *The Body* brings out not only what is unique and, I might add, phenomenological in Japanese thought, but also what is intertextual in the double sense of being (1) interdisciplinary and (2) intercultural. Yuasa writes that "in the East one starts from the experiential assumption that the mind-body modality changes through the training of the mind and body by means of cultivation (*shugyō*) or training (*keiko*). Only after assuming this experiential ground does one ask what the mind-body relation is. That is, the mind-body issue is not simply a theoretical speculation but it is originally a practical, lived experience (*taiken*), involving the mustering of one's whole mind and body. The theoretical is only a reflection on this lived experience" (p. 18). In this nondualistic account of the "molting" of body and mind, Dōgen (1200–1253), who founded Sōtō Zen in Japan, must be singled out. For him, humans have the natural propensity to view the mind as prior to the body, but they *acquired only by cultivation* (i.e., *zazen* or seated meditation) the knowledge that the body is prior to the mind.

35. Clark and Holquist, *Mikhail Bakhtin*, p. 175 (italics added).

36. Brown, *Love's Body* (New York: Knopf, 1966), p. 264.

37. *Ibid.*

38. The unconscious, according to Lacan, is "the discourse of the Other"—see Felman *Jacques Lacan and the Adventure of Insight*, pp. 122–23. In human communication, silence as the horizon of sound resides

in the beginning, interlude, and ending of speech as verbal utterances. It is lack of utterance or enunciation, but not lack of thought, lack of words, or lack of the intention to speak. As a beginning and ending of speech, it works like the "primordial" *Tao* that is "silent" (unspoken) and "empty" (unwritten). In a dialogue or conversation, there is no basic opposition or incompatibility between silence and utterance. Genuine dialogue demands the diatactics of speaking and listening as a transaction. For it is a doubling or coupling of saying utterance and silent listening: one who utters and the other who listens (silently), which are reversible or exchangeable. If there is no listening or silence, conversation would be a series of monologues rather than a dialogue. In brief, there is no basic opposition among silence, utterance, and action. For a phenomenological exposition concerning the philosophical implications of silence, see Bernard P. Dauenhauer, *Silence* (Bloomington: Indiana University Press, 1980).

39. For a discussion of Chinese ideography as human gestures, see Chang Cheng-ming, *L'Écriture chinoise et le geste humain* (Paris: Geuthner, 1929). Concerning the treatment of Chinese ideography in the Western literary circle, see the present author's "Misreading the Ideogram: From Fenollosa to Derrida and McLuhan," *Paideuma*, 13 (1984): 211–27. This is not an occasion to resolve the question of the ideographic nature of the Chinese language. Following the footsteps of Peter A. Boodberg, Peter S. DuPonceau, and J. M. Callery, John DeFrancis urges us to abandon or outlaw the "hallucinogenic" conception of the Chinese language as "ideographic" in favor of a "logographic," "lexigraphic," or "morphemic" conception because its signs represent *words, not ideas*. DeFrancis quotes the following passage of Wilhelm von Humboldt approvingly: "I think that the scholars who have almost let themselves be drawn into forgetting that Chinese is a spoken language have so exaggerated the influence of Chinese writing that they have, so to say, put the writing in place of the language"—cited in DeFrancis, *The Chinese Language* (Honolulu: University of Hawaii Press, 1984), p. 35.

40. The main reason for Michel Foucault's interest in the calligram is that it "aspires playfully to efface the oldest oppositions to our [Western] civilization: to show and to name; to shape and to say; to reproduce and to articulate; to imitate and to signify; to look and to read"—*This Is Not a Pipe*, ed. and trans. James Harkness (Berkeley: University of California Press, 1982), p. 21. See also Barthes's *Empire of Signs*, which textualizes in the ideogrammic tradition everything he witnessed in Japan during his brief visit. For a metacommentary on Barthes's textualization of Japan, see the present author's "The Joy of Textualizing Japan: A Metacommentary on Roland Barthes's *Empire of Signs*."

41. Suzi Gablik, *Margritte* (Greenwich: New York Graphic Society, 1970), p. 122.

42. Foucault, *This Is Not a Pipe*, p. 20.

43. *Ibid.*, pp. 57–58.

44. *The Writings of Jean-Paul Sartre*, vol. 2: *Selected Prose*, ed. Michel Contat and Michel Rybalka and trans. Richard McCleary (Evanston: Northwestern University Press, 1974), p. 67.

45. *Ibid.*, p. 70.

46. Levinas, *Totality and Infinity*, p. 199.

47. Levinas and Richard Kearney, "Dialogue with Emmanuel Levinas," in *Face to Face with Levinas,* ed. Richard A. Cohen (Albany: State University of New York Press, 1986), p. 20.

48. Levinas, *Totality and Infinity,* p. 395.

49. "Dialogue with Emmanual Levinas," p. 27.

50. Levinas, *Ethics and Infinity,* trans. Richard A. Cohen (Pittsburgh: Duquesne University Press, 1982), p. 95.

51. Leszek Kolakowski's dialectical juxtaposition in philosophical thought of the "priestly" and the "jesterly" parallels very closely Bakhtin's distinction between absolutistic monologism and relational dialogism. See Kolakowski, *Toward a Marxist Humanism,* trans. Jane Z. Peel (New York: Grove Press, 1968), p. 9–37.

52. Cf. Herbert Marcuse, *The Aesthetic Dimension* (Boston: Beacon Press, 1977), p. 9. An important point should be made here that the model of sound rather than that of sight is paradigmatic to Bakhtin's notion of dialogue and to his model of transforming the world into a playground of festivity, joy and laughter. First of all, vision is monistic and monophonic, that is, there is a fundamental narcissism and social amnesia of and in all vision, whereas sound is pluralistic and polyphonic. Second, dialogue is an intercourse of two *voices* that revolves around saying and listening punctuated with silence. "Ears," Bakhtin declares, " . . . are antiofficial"— *Speech Genres and Other Late Essays,* p. 141. Bakhtin's dialogism, which is vocal and pro/vocative, belongs to the tradition of Hermes, the god of eloquence, who was a "herald" or prophetic messenger (*keryx*) sent by Zeus to humanity. See Jacques Attali, who begins his discussion of music with the following statement: "For twenty-five centuries, Western knowledge has tried to look upon the world. It has failed to understand that the world is not for the beholding. It is for hearing. It is not legible, but audible"—*Noise,* trans. Brian Massumi (Minneapolis: University of Minnesota Press, 1985), p. 3. I have also discussed elsewhere the implications of sound (music) for social theory as juxtaposed to vision. Sound tends to socialize, unify, and synthesize, whereas sight tends to isolate, divide, and analyze. See "Rhetoric, Grammatology, and Political Theory," *Reflections,* 4 (1983): 37–53.

53. Albert Camus writes that "dialogue on the level of mankind is less costly than the gospel preached by totalitarian regimes in the form of monologue dictated from the top of a lonely mountain. On the stage as in reality, the monologue precedes death. Every rebel, solely by the movement that sets him in opposition to the oppressor, therefore pleads for life, undertakes to struggle against servitude, falsehood, and terror, and affirms, in a flash, that these three afflictions are the cause of silence between men, that they obscure them from one another and prevent them from rediscovering themselves in the only value that can save them from nihilism—the long complicity of men at grips with their destiny"—*The Rebel,* trans. Anthony Bower (New York: Knopf, 1956), pp. 283–84.

54. Martin Heidegger defines "destruction" as "a critical process in which the traditional concepts, which at first must necessarily be employed, are de-constructed down to the sources from which they were drawn"—*The Basic Problems of Phenomenology,* trans. Albert Hofstadter (Bloomington: Indiana University Press, 1982), p. 23.

55. Bakhtin, *Rabelais and His World*, trans. Hélène Iswolsky (Bloomington: Indiana University Press, 1984), pp. 285–86.

56. According to the playwright Luigi Pirandello, the Latin *humor* designates "a physical substance in the form of fluid, liquid, humidity or moisture" and humans are said to have four "humors"—blood, bile, phlegm and melancholy—see *On Humor*, trans. Antonio Illiano and Daniel P. Testa (Chapel Hill: University of North Carolina Press, 1974), p. 2. Because it is reputedly physical, it is associated, unfortunately, with "low culture" as opposed to the "high culture" of mind. Pirandello writes that " . . . cloth is . . . something that *composes* and *conceals,* two things which humor cannot stand" (*ibid.,* p. 144), and that "the humorist sees the world, not exactly in the nude but, so to speak, in shirt sleeves" (*ibid.,* p. 143). Humor as *negativa* uncloaks, unmasks, or exposes the "dirty bottom" of officialdom. For Pirandello, the *principium* of humor lies in edifying the "feeling of the opposite" in everything we do and think. By splitting every affirmative into a negative, humor triggers the *ingegno* (ingenuousness or spontaneous birth) of things.

57. While the term *playtext* emphasizes the play element of the body politic, John O'Neill's *homotext* (homotextuality) refers to style as "the corporeal bond between man and his text"—"Homotextuality: Barthes on Barthes, Fragments (RB), with a Footnote," in *Hermeneutics,* ed. Gary Shapiro and Alan Sica (Amherst: University of Massachusetts Press, 1984), p. 172.

58. Barthes, *The Fashion System,* trans. Matthew Ward and Richard Howard (New York: Hill & Wang, 1983), p. 258.

59. Clark and Holquist, *Mikhail Bakhtin,* p. 301.

60. *Ibid.*

61. Bakhtin, *Problems of Dosteovsky's Poetics,* p. 160.

62. Bakhtin, *Speech Genres and Other Late Essays,* pp. 134–35. Dominick LaCapra writes: "Bakhtin's dialogical and carnivalizing rendition of dialectics provides an alternative to the totalizing incentive of speculative dialectics, and it substitutes a Rabelaisian for a Hegelian Marx"— "Bakhtin, Marxism and the Carnivalesque," in his *Rethinking Intellectual History* (Ithaca: Cornell University Press, 1983), p. 323. It should be pointed out that LaCapra ably manages to relate Bakhtin with Marx without ever mentioning the latter's conception of revolution as the sole means of subverting and transforming the established regime.

63. Bakhtin, *Speech Genres and Other Late Essays,* p. 135.

64. Hegel laid the metaphysical foundation in his *Phenomenology of Spirit* for the justification of violence in modern thought when he viewed *recognition* as the life-and-death struggle between the self (master) and the other (slave). It is the idea of negation rather than *complementarity* that governs Hegel's notion of recognition.

65. In *Anonymity* (Bloomington: Indiana University Press, 1986), Maurice Natanson explores new dimensions of anonymity as "a feature of objectified meaning" based on the social phenomenology of Alfred Schutz, which he calls a "carnival of anonymity."

66. Camus, *The Rebel,* p. 22.

67. *Ibid.*, p. 11.

68. *Ibid.*, p. 252 (italics added).

69. See Marcuse, "Repressive Tolerance," in Robert Paul Wolff, Barrington Moore, Jr., and Herbert Marcuse, *A Critique of Pure Tolerance* (Boston: Beacon Press, 1965), pp. 81–117.

70. Merleau-Ponty, *Adventures of the Dialectic*, p. 207 (italics added).

71. Merleau-Ponty, *The Primacy of Perception*, ed. James M. Edie (Evanston: Northwestern University Press, 1964), p. 160. For an optimistic account of the cybernation of knowledge in postmodernity, see Jean-François Lyotard, *The Postmodern Condition*, trans. Geoff Bennington and Brian Massumi (Minneapolis: University of Minnesota Press, 1984). Herbert Marcuse is one of those few who had a clear vision of the "one-dimensionality" of technology when he observed: "The scientific method which led to the ever-more-effective domination of nature thus came to provide the pure concepts as well as the instrumentalities for the ever-more-effective domination of man by man *through* the domination of nature. Theoretical reason, remaining pure and neutral, entered into the service of practical reason. The merger proved beneficial to both. Today, domination perpetuates and extends itself not only through technology but *as* technology, and the latter provides the great legitimation of the expanding political power, which absorbs all spheres of culture"—*One Dimensional Man*, p. 158. Cf. Gilles Deleuze and Félix Guattari, *Anti-Oedipus*, trans Robert Hurley, Mark Seem, and Helen R. Lane (New York: Viking Press, 1977).

72. Clark and Holquist, *Mikhail Bakhtin*, pp. 349–50.

73. Edgar Wind, *Pagan Mysteries in the Renaissance*, rev. and enl. ed. (New York: Norton, 1968), p. 196. In this connection, it would be interesting to speculate whether Bakhtin is a "hedgehog" or a "fox." In his famous essay on Tolstoy's view of history, which was written in 1953, Isaiah Berlin divided great writers and thinkers into two different camps after the Greek poet Archilochus: "The fox knows many things, but the hedgehog knows one big thing"—see *The Hedgehog and the Fox* (New York: Simon & Schuster, 1986). Although Dostoevsky, who is Bakhtin's source for dialogism, is classified by Berlin as hedgehog, Bakhtin may bridge a "great chasm" between the two camps because while his dialogism is one big idea, it has many things in it. It is the recurring question in philosophy of the One (Pan) and the Many (Proteus).

Chapter Ten

1. Hayden White wishes to have the term "diatactics" replace the term "dialectics" in order to avoid the certain ideological overtone of Marx on the one hand and the transcendental overtone of Hegel's thought on the other: diatactics is neither "hypotactical" (conceptually overdetermined) nor "paratactical" (conceptually underdetermined); see his *Tropics of Discourse: Essays in Cultural Criticism* (Baltimore: Johns Hopkins University Press, 1978), p. 4. In our discussion, diatactics is used as a logic of correlation. First, it confirms any two disparate phenomena as *complementary*. Second, it is "tactical" to the extent to which it arouses the intimate sense of touch or "tactility" and emphasizes the *pragmatic* and *dialogical* side of

language-in-use. Third, there is strong evidence that diatactics as a logic of correlation originates in the auditory mind before the rise of visual consciousness. Julian Jaynes thus speculates: "It is interesting to note . . . that there is no hypostasis for hearing as there is for sight. Even today, we do not hear with the mind's ear as we see with the mind's eye. Nor do we refer to intelligent minds as loud, in the same way we say they are bright. This is probably because hearing was the very essence of the bicameral mind, and as such has those differences from vision. . . . The coming of consciousness can in a certain vague sense be construed as a shift from an auditory mind to a visual mind"—*The Origin of Consciousness in the Breakdown of the Bicameral Mind* (Boston: Houghton Mifflin, 1976), p. 269.

2. Heidegger, *What Is Called Thinking?* trans. Fred D. Wieck and J. Glenn Gray (New York: Harper & Row, 1968), p. 37.

3. Merleau-Ponty, *Themes from the Lectures at the Collège de France, 1952–1960,* trans. John O'Neill (Evanston: Northwestern University Press, 1970), p. 40. Elsewhere Maurice Merleau-Ponty stresses that "one could say about language in its relations with thought what one says of the life of the body in its relations with consciousness. Just as one could not place the body at the first level, just as one could not subordinate it or draw it out of its autonomy . . . ,one can say only that language makes thought, as much as it is made by thought. Thought inhabits language and language is its body. This mediation of the objective and the subjective, of the interior and of the exterior—what philosophy seeks to do—we can find in language if we succeed in getting close enough to it"—*Consciousness and the Acquisition of Language,* trans. Hugh J. Silverman (Evanston: Northwestern University Press, 1973), p. 102.

4. Merleau-Ponty, *Phenomenology of Perception,* trans. Colin Smith (London: Routledge & Kegan Paul, 1962), p. 189.

5. Snell, *The Discovery of the Mind,* trans. T. G. Rosenmeyer (Cambridge: Harvard University Press, 1953), p. 22 (italics added).

6. Merleau-Ponty speculates that "our language is less emotional than its rudimentary forms. There would not have been an initial difference between the act of speaking and the act of singing. . . . The initial form of language, therefore, would have been a kind of song. Men would have sung their feelings before communicating their thought. Just as writing was at first painting, language at first would have been song, which, if it analyzed itself, would have become a linguistic sign. It is through the exercise of this song that men would have tried out their power of expression"— *Consciousness and the Acquisition of Language,* p. 81. It is interesting to note in passing that the words *sing* and *sign* have equivalent anagrams. For discussions of oral language and poetry, see Milman Parry, *The Making of Homeric Verse: The Collected Papers of Milman Parry,* ed. Adam Parry (Oxford: Clarendon Press, 1970); Albert B. Lord, *The Singer of Tales* (Cambridge: Harvard University Press, 1960); Eric A. Havelock, *Prologue to Greek Literacy* (Cincinnati: University of Cincinnati Press, 1971) and *Preface to Plato* (Cambridge: Harvard University Press, 1963); Walter J. Ong, *The Presence of the Word: Some Prolegomena for Cultural and Religious History* (New Haven: Yale University Press, 1967); and Ruth Finnegan, *Oral Poetry: Its Nature, Significance and Social Context* (Cambridge: Cambridge University Press, 1977).

278

RETHINKING
POLITICAL
THEORY

7. Eliot, *The Use of Poetry and the Use of Criticism: Studies in the Relation of Criticism to Poetry in England* (London: Faber and Faber, 1933), p. 155. Comparing Vico with Joyce, Samuel Beckett writes that "the first men had to create matter by the force of their imagination, and 'poet' means 'creator.' Poetry was the first operation of the human mind, and without it thought could not exist"—"Dante . . . Bruno. Vico . . Joyce," in Samuel Beckett *et al., Our Exagmination Round His Factification for Incamination of Work in Progress* (London: Shakespeare, 1929), p. 9.

8. For expositions on Hermes relevant to our discussion here, see Norman O. Brown, *Hermes the Thief: The Revolution of a Myth* (New York: Random House, 1947), and Walter F. Otto, *The Homeric Gods: The Spiritual Significance of Greek Religion,* trans. Moses Hadas (New York: Pantheon Books, 1954), pp. 104–23. Cf. Richard E. Palmer, *Hermeneutics: Interpretation Theory in Schleiermacher, Dilthey, Heidegger, and Gadamer* (Evanston: Northwestern University Press, 1969), pp. 14–20.

9. Jaynes, *The Origin of Consciousness in the Breakdown of the Bicameral Mind,* p. 51.

10. Hassan, *The Dismemberment of Orpheus: Toward a Postmodern Literature* (New York: Oxford University Press, 1971), p. 5.

11. Lord, *The Singer of Tales,* p. 13.

12. Northrop Frye notes that "the world of social action and event, the world of time and process, has a particularly close association with the ear. The ear listens, and the ear translates what it hears into practical conduct. The world of individual thought and idea has a correspondingly close association with the eye, and nearly all our expressions for thought, from the Greek *theoria* down, are connected with visual metaphors"—*Anatomy of Criticism: Four Essays* (Princeton: Princeton University Press, 1957), p. 243.

13. Havelock, *Preface to Plato,* p. 14.

14. *Ibid.,* p. 155.

15. Jabès, *The Book of Questions,* trans. Rosemarie Waldrop (Middletown: Wesleyan University Press, 1976), p. 66.

16. It is interesting to note that the composer Igor Stravinsky and the poet T. S. Eliot employ the terms *poetics* and *music* as complementary to their respective arts; see Stravinsky, *Poetics of Music in the Form of Six Lessons,* trans. Arthur Knodel and Ingolf Dahl (Cambridge: Harvard University Press, 1947), and Eliot, *The Music of Poetry* (Glasgow: Jackson, 1942). For a crowning discussion on the "monogenesis" of language and music by the composer Leonard Bernstein, see *The Unanswered Question: Six Talks at Harvard* (Cambridge: Harvard University Press, 1976), especially pp. 3–49. For an extensive analysis of the relation between music and poetry from a historical perspective, see James Anderson Winn, *Unsuspected Eloquence: A History of the Relation Between Poetry and Music* (New Haven: Yale University Press, 1981).

17. In *Hebrew Thought Compared with Greek,* trans. Jules L. Moreau (Philadelphia: Westminster Press, 1960), p. 68, Thorlief Boman illustrates the interesting relation between the Hebrew *dabhar* and the Greek *logos* as follows:

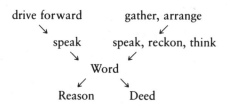

Dabhar   Logos

drive forward   gather, arrange

    speak   speak, reckon, think

      Word

    Reason   Deed

18. *The Collected Dialogues of Plato*, ed. Edith Hamilton and Huntington Cairns (New York: Pantheon Books, 1961), p. 1950.

19. See John Sallis, *Being and Logos: The Way of Platonic Dialogue* (Pittsburgh: Duquesne University Press, 1966), p. 19. For the best series of interpretive essays on the nature of Platonic dialogues, see Hans-Georg Gadamer, *Dialogue and Dialectic: Eight Hermeneutical Studies on Plato,* trans. P. Christopher Smith (New Haven: Yale University Press, 1980).

20. McLuhan, *Understanding Media: The Extensions of Man* (New York: McGraw-Hill, 1964), p. 8.

21. *Ibid.*, p. 111.

22. McLuhan, *The Gutenberg Galaxy* (Toronto: University of Toronto Press, 1962).

23. McLuhan, *Understanding Media*, p. 23.

24. *Ibid.*, p. 283.

25. *Ibid.*, p. 359.

26. *Ibid.*, p. 321.

27. McLuhan, *The Gutenberg Galaxy*, p. 50.

28. Innis, *The Bias of Communication* (Toronto: University of Toronto Press, 1951).

29. McLuhan, *Understanding Media*, p. 18.

30. *Ibid.*, p. 249.

31. *Ibid.*, p. 248.

32. For a more comprehensive critique of McLuhan's theory of communication, see the present author's "The Medium as Technology: A Phenomenological Critique of Marshall McLuhan," in *Phenomenology and the Understanding of Human Destiny*, ed. Stephen Skousgaard (Washington: Center for Advanced Research in Phenomenology and University Press of America, 1981), pp. 45–80.

33. See Chang Cheng-ming, *L'Écriture chinoise et le geste humain: Essai sur la formation de l'écriture chinoise* (Paris: Geuthner, 1937). Beckett perceptively writes that "the root of any word whatsoever can be traced back to some pre-lingual symbol. . . . Vico asserts the spontaneity of language and denies the dualism of poetry and language. Similarly, poetry is the foundation of writing. When language consisted of gesture, the spoken and the written were identical. . . . In such direct expression [as hieroglyphics], form and content are inseparable"—"Dante . . . Bruno. Vico . .

Joyce," pp. 11–12. In a similar vein, R. P. Blackmur writes that " . . . gesture is native to language, and if you cut it out you cut roots and get a sapless and gradually a rotting if indeed not a petrifying language"—*Language as Gesture: Essays in Poetry* (New York: Harcourt, Brace, 1952), p. 4.

34. McLuhan and Parker, *Through the Vanishing Point: Space in Poetry and Painting* (New York: Harper & Row, 1968), p. 39. In this connection, it ought to be noted that the nineteenth-century American Orientalist Ernest Fenollosa's interpretation of Chinese ideography has had considerable influence on Western literature, e.g., Ezra Pound's "ideogrammic method"—see Ernest Fenollosa, *The Chinese Written Character as a Medium for Poetry*, ed. Ezra Pound (San Francisco: City Lights Books, 1964). Of course, how much influence it has had on contemporary literary criticism would be an interesting study in its own right.

35. McLuhan, *The Gutenberg Galaxy*, p. 248.

36. *Ibid.*

37. Heidegger, *The Question Concerning Technology and Other Essays*, trans. William Lovitt (New York: Harper & Row, 1977), p. 116.

38. Winner, *Autonomous Technology: Technics-out-of-Control as a Theme in Political Thought* (Cambridge: MIT Press, 1977), p. 227.

39. Heidegger, *The Question Concerning Technology and Other Essays*, p. 134.

40. Wittgenstein, *Philosophical Investigations*, trans. G. E. M. Anscombe (Oxford: Blackwell, 1954), p. 197e.

41. Sontag, *On Photography* (New York: Dell, 1977). Cf. Roland Barthes, *Camera Lucida: Reflections on Photography*, trans. Richard Howard (New York: Hill & Wang, 1981).

42. Sontag, *On Photography*, p. 16.

43. Kosinski, *Being There* (New York: Harcourt Brace Jovanovich, 1970).

44. *Being There*, p. 5 (italics added).

45. *Ibid.*, pp. 78–79.

46. *Ibid.*, pp. 113–14.

47. *Ibid.*, p. 40.

48. *Ibid.*, p. 54.

49. Rousseau, *On the Origin of Language*, trans. John H. Moran and Alexander Gode (New York: Frederick Ungar, 1966), p. 53.

50. Gusdorf, *Speaking (La Parole)*, trans. Paul T. Brockelman (Evanston: Northwestern University Press, 1965), p. 9.

51. Arendt, "Thinking and Moral Considerations: A Lecture," *Social Research*, 38 (Autumn 1971): 417–18. Thinking is the most pervasive theme in the later thought of Heidegger who, as her teacher, has influenced Arendt's thought. For her tribute to Heidegger as a teacher and thinker, see "Martin Heidegger at Eighty," in *Heidegger and Modern Philosophy:*

Critical Essays, ed. Michael Murray (New Haven: Yale University Press, 1978), pp. 293–303.

52. See the present author's "Confucianism and Existentialism: Intersubjectivity as the Way of Man," *Philosophy and Phenomenological Research*, 30 (December 1969): 191–95. All quotations in the text from the *Analects* come from *The Chinese Classics*, vol. 1, trans. James Legge (Oxford: Oxford University Press, n.d.).

53. Maurice Merleau-Ponty contends that "for the child the thing is not known until it is named, the name is the essence of the thing and resides in it on the same footing as its colour and its form. For pre-scientific thinking, naming an object is causing it to exist or changing it"—*Phenomenology of Perception*, pp. 177–78.

54. See Chung-yuan Chang, *Tao: A New Way of Thinking* (New York: Harper & Row, 1978).

55. Barthes, *Camera Lucida*, p. 72.

56. For a detailed analysis of silence in the tradition of phenomenology, see Bernard P. Dauenhauer, *Silence: The Phenomenon and Its Ontological Significance* (Bloomington: Indiana University Press, 1980).

57. Brown, *Love's Body* (New York: Random House, 1966), pp. 264–65.

58. Sontag, *Styles of Radical Will* (New York: Farrar, Straus & Giroux, 1969), p. 23. Lik Kuen Tong notes that "in the context of Chinese philosophy, . . . speech and silence are correlative concepts. There is not speech without silence, and there is no silence without at least the possibility of speech. . . . We may say, in the metaphysical terminology of the *I Ching*, that speech is the *yang* of silence, and silence is the *yin* of speech. But 'one-*yin*-one-*yang* is called *Tao*'. The alternation of speech and silence is thus an instantiation of the cosmic law of *I*, the primordial process of Creativity which is the ultimate reality of the universe"—"The Meaning of Philosophical Silence: Some Reflections on the Use of Language in Chinese Thought," *Journal of Chinese Philosophy*, 3 (1976): 170. The ancient Pythagoreans are known to have thought that we do not hear the music of the heavenly bodies and are unable to distinguish it from silence because we hear it constantly from the very moment of our birth. By the same token, if the world were the constant flow of speech without the background of silence, that is, if speech were somehow not an interval of silence, it would be no speech. Merleau-Ponty emphasizes the diatactics of speech and silence in human expression and communication when he declares: "Our view of man will remain superficial so long as we fail to go back to that origin, so long as we fail to find, beneath the chatter of words, the primordial silence, and as long as we so not describe the action which breaks the silence"—*Phenomenology of Perception*, p. 184.

59. Wittgenstein, *Tractatus Logico-Philosophicus*, trans. D. F. Pears and B. F. McGuinness (London: Routledge & Kegan Paul, 1961).

60. See K. T. Fann, *Wittgenstein's Conception of Philosophy* (Berkeley: University of California Press, 1969).

61. In *Political Language and Rhetoric* (Austin: University of Texas Press, 1979), Paul E. Corcoran gives a descriptive and historical account of theories of rhetoric from oral and literate cultures to post-literate culture.

62. In *Radical Reflection and the Origin of the Human Sciences* (West Lafayette: Purdue University Press, 1980), Calvin O. Schrag spells out some important implications of defining the role of philosophy as a self-reflective search for the *origin* of the human sciences. Some implications of phenomenology as an archaeology for the philosophy of political science have been worked out in the present author's *The Crisis of Political Understanding: A Phenomenological Perspective in the Conduct of Political Inquiry* (Pittsburgh: Duquesne University Press, 1979).

63. Dewey, *The Public and Its Problems* (New York: Holt, 1927), pp. 218–19. The sixteenth-century French savant Michel de Montaigne wrote that "the most fruitful and natural exercise of our mind, in my opinion, is discussion [or conversation (*conférence*)]. I find it sweeter than any other action of our life; and that is the reason why, if I were right now forced to choose, I believe I would rather consent to lose my sight than my hearing or speech"—*The Complete Works of Montaigne*, trans. Donald M. Frame (Stanford: Stanford University Press, 1957), p. 704.

INDEX

Action, 4–5, 39, 51, 52, 53, 54, 55, 61, 115, 117, 118, 119, 122, 124, 128, 129, 130, 133, 170, 171, 179; and emotion, 125; and silence, 209; and sociality, 10; and value, 6; Arendt on, 170; as freedom and responsibility, 20–21; as heterocentric, 119, 129; ethics of, 125; meaning of, 15–18; political, 29, 62, 114, 116.

Alētheia, 116, 132, 209.

Almond, Gabriel, 47.

Althusser, Louis, 162.

Ambiguity, 32, 70, 75, 172, 186.

Anderson, Perry, 267n.54.

Anthropocentrism, 159, 188.

Anthropomorphism, 84.

Apollinaire, Guillaume, 182.

Apter, David E., *Introduction to Political Analysis*, 97.

Aquinas, Thomas, St., 114.

Archilochus, 157.

Arendt, Hannah, and Foucault on power, 169–72; *The Human Condition*, xvii, 163, 172, 179; on Eichmann, xvi–xvii, 170–71, 205–6; on *initium* and natality, 171–72, 179; on Nietzsche, 171–72; on Plato, 115–16; on plurality, xvi, 163–64, 179, 188.

Aristotle, 28, 31, 62, 120, 122, 127, 130, 216n.13, 247n.19; *Ethics*, 115, 117; on self-sufficiency (*autarkeia*), 117; *Poetics*, 127; *Politics*, 115, 117; Strauss on, 113–18, 121.

Artificial intelligence, 26; phenomenological critique of, 66–71. See also cybernetics.

Attali, Jacques, 275n.52.

Augustine, St., 235n.22.

Austin, John L., 156, 180, 213n.16; on descriptive fallacy, 63; on performative utterances, 63–64.

Averroism, 60–61.

Bachelard, Gaston, 108.

Bakhtin, Mikhail, xvi, 175–89, 264n.30, 269n.14, 275n.52; and Camus, 186–87; and Levinas compared, 183; and Mao, 184–85; as humanist, 189; dialogism of, 176–89, 271–72n.23, 276n.62; on language as embodied, 181–82; on Rabelais, 184, 185; on subject as *initium*, 178; on translinguistics (*metalingvistika*), 179–80.

Banality of evil, 170–71, 205–6. See also Eichmann.

Barry, Brian, 58.

Barthes, Roland, 162, 178, 180, 184; and semiology, 99–107; *Empire of Signs*, 99–107; *The Fashion System*, 101; on *haiku*, 104; on *satori*, 101–2, 104–5; on Saussure, 256n.38; on *sukiyaki*, 269n.9; on Zen, 101–2.

Basho, 105.

Bataille, Georges, 164.

Beauvoir, Simone de, xvii, 132–34, 172, 217–18n.16, 224n.29, 266n.51; *The Coming of Age*, 132.

Beckett, Samuel, 182, 279n.7, 280–81n.33.

Behavior, 58; and artificial intelligence, 70; defined by Merleau-Ponty, 53; political, 50–51; structure of, 49–56; Wild on, 17, 56.

Behavioralism (political), xiv, 26, 223n.11; as methodological determinism, 33; as scientism, 26, 33; fact and value in, 63; phenomenological critique of, 45–72. See also behaviorism (psychological).

Behaviorism (psychological), 26, 48, 55; Strauss on, 60–61. See also behavioralism (political).

Benedict, Ruth, 94.

Bentham, Jeremy, on Panopticon, 79–80.

Determinism, biological, 238–40; methodological, 33; ontological, 31, 32, 115, 126, 128, 129, 134.

Deutsch, Karl, cybernetic model of, 68–71; on consciousness, 51, 66.

Dewey, John, 17; on vision and hearing, 209; *The Public and Its Problems*, 209.

Dialogism, 175–89, 208, 275n.53.

Diatactics, 31, 74–76, 102, 105, 109, 180, 184, 192, 200, 201, 208; defined by White, 74–75, 96, 192, 216n.11.

Difference, *xvii*; as reciprocal and ethical, *xvi*; vs. identity, *xvi, xvii*.

Dilthey, Wilhelm, 28, 132, 147, 266n.52.

Donoghue, Denis, on conversation, 167, 176–77.

Douglas, Mary, 92.

Downs, Anthony, 16–17; on positive political science, 12; on rigor and positive politics, 58–59.

Dreyfus, Hubert, on artificial intelligence, 69–70.

Dualism, 118–19, 149–50, 228n.73, 234n.20, 234n.21, 236–37n.30; and dialectic, 150.

Dürckheim, Karl von, 104.

Durkheim, Emile, 256n.30; sociologism of, 27–28, 147.

Eagleton, Terry, *xviii*.

Easton, David, 47; on post-behavioral revolution, 26, 212n.10.

Eclecticism, 135.

Economics, positive, 58–59.

Ecopiety, 188.

Eichmann, Adolf, *xvi–xvii*, 170, 205–6. See also banality of evil.

Eidos, 32, 203.

Eliot, T. S., 194; *Four Quartets*, 208.

Ellison, Ralph, 107.

Embodiment, 66–71, 78–79. See also body.

Emerson, Caryl, 272n.23.

Emotion, 63–64, 125. See also feeling.

Empiricide, scientism as, 96–99.

Empiricism, 25, 30, 33, 151, 237n.32; logical, 57, 63; radical, 4, 7–10, 30.

Engels, Friedrich, 149, 253n.10, 270n.19.

Epireading, 176.

Epistēmē, 116, and *physis*, 116, 122.

Epistemology, 148–57; and behavioralism (political), 46–47.

Epochē, 136, 154, 155, 156, 237n.32.

Essence, and fact, 96–97, 133.

Essentialism, 113, 115–17, 118, 119, 122, 126, 128–29, 130, 131, 132, 133, 134, 217n.16; and existentialism, 115, 125, 127; as egocentric, 129.

Ethics, 161, 167–69, 180, 183, 189, 206–7; defined as responsibility, 168.

Ethnocentrism, 91–110.

Ethnography, 107–10; reflexivity in, 108.

Ethology, Mill on, 27–28; Uexküll on, 84.

Etzioni, Amitai, 53.

Eulau, Heinz, 57, 63, 67–68, 71, 223n.10; and phenomenology, 14–15; *The Behavioral Persuasion in Politics*, 45; on behavioralism (political), 46–48; on behaviorism (psychological), 50; politics defined by, 51–52.

Existentialism, 3, 4, 9–10, 18, 52, 115, 120, 125, 127, 128, 129, 130, 132, 133–34, 215n.5, 250n.76; and essentialism, 115, 125, 127; and positivism, 120; ethics of, 134, 217n.16, 224n.29, 266n.51.

Experience, *xiii*, 5, 7, 8, 30, 35, 59–60, 66, 67, 71, 96, 123, 153–54, 166; lived (*Erlebnis*), *xv*, 4, 7, 9, 15, 18, 21, 55, 61, 106, 107, 121, 133; meaningful (*Erfahrung*), 15.

Face, 182–83; and Levinas, 168–69, 183; aristocracy of, 182–83; as ethical, 183; as proximity, 167.

Fackenheim, Emil L., 125–26, 250n.75.

Fact, 9, 10, 33, 60, 66; and essence, 93, 96–97; and theory, 66; as hermeneutical, 97; defined by Oakeshott, 65–66; defined by Wild, 120–21. See also *factum*.

Factum, 85, 96, 98–99; and Ortega's *faciendum*, 85; and *verum*, *xiv*, 39, 138. See also fact.

Feeling, 51, 66, 82; and cognition, 66; and knowledge, 8–9, 49; and symbolizing, 9, 66, 67; as intentional, 66–67. See also emotion.

Feld, Steven, 107.

Felman, Shoshana, on Lacan, 180, 268n.3; on language, 180.

Feminism, *xvii*.

Feuerbach, Ludwig, 177; Copernican revolution of, *xv–xvi*, 176.

Feyerabend, Paul, 108, 219n.26.

Fiore, Quentin, 263n.24.

Fischer, Michael M. J., 109.

Forster, E. M., 3.

Foucault, Michel, 106, 160, 161–73, 182, 260–61n.8; and Arendt, 169–72; and phenomenology, 162–73;

intersubjectivity, 165; on language, 191, 192–93, 228n.75, 278n.6; on lateral universal, 95–96, 108; on life-world, 153, 212n.12; on Machiavelli, 216n.10; on Marx, 258–59n.70; on Marxism, 137, 141–42, 144–45; on objectification in science and philosophy, 226n.58; on phenomenological positivism, 60; on primacy of perception, 76; on reduction (*epochē*), 237n.32; on revolution, 186–87; on Sartre, 165; on science and ontology, 96–97; on *Wesensschau*, 66; on Western ethnocentrism, 94–96; *Phenomenology of Perception, xiv*, 144; *The Structure of Behavior*, 53; *The Visible and the Invisible*, 93–94.
Mersenne, Marin, 82.
Methodolatry, 33, 35–36, 49, 59, 60, 98.
Mill, John Stuart, *A System of Logic*, 26.
Miller, Eugene F., 131–34.
Mimēsis, 196.
Mnemosyne, 197.
Modernity, 28, 113–14.
Modernization, 92, 94.
Monan, J. Donald, on Aristotle's *phronēsis*, 216–17n.13.
Mood, 166.
Mozart, Wolfgang Amadeus, *Don Giovanni*, 196.
Mu, 101–2.
Music, 74, 82, 207; and language, 195; and power, 166; as *technē*, 196–97.

Natanson, Maurice, 124, 276n.65.
Natural attitude, 6, 117, 122, 123.
Natural law, theory of, 52, 128.
Nature, as mathematical manifold, 34.
Neurath, Otto, 58.
Newman, Stephen L., 237n.30.
Nietzsche, Friedrich, 158, 171–72, 179, 215n.5; on genealogy, 74; on music, 74, 263n.22.
Nihilism, 172, 185, 186, 208.
Nishida, Kitarō, 103.
Noema, 8, 30.
Noesis, 8, 30, 116.

Oakeshott, Michael, 218n.26; on fact, 65, 218n.18.
Oates, Joyce Carol, on boxing, 273n.32.
Objectivity, 9, 105; and phenomenology, 59–61.
Ocularcentrism, *xvi–xvii;* and *Cogito* (Cartesian), *xvi;* and philosophy, *xvii*.

O'Neill, John, 73, 217n.15, 221n.36, 276n.57.
Onnagata, 107.
Ontology, 50, 55, 77, 136–48, 208; and epistemology, 136, 148; and methodology, 34, 36; fallacy of misplaced, 148; social, 165–69, 172, 183.
Oppenheim, Felix, 51, 212n.14.
Oral poetry, 209; as origin of language, 194; Homeric, 194–97.
Orpheus, 195.
Ortega y Gasset, José, 73, 74, 75, 81, 89; *Meditations on Quixote, 81; on Cogito* (Cartesian), 81; on circumstance, 84–85.

Paci, Enzo, 138, 153, 154.
Pandora, 195.
Panopticon, 79–80, 168, 187, 236n.25; as Cartesian plot, 79; Foucault on, 79–80.
Parker, Harley, on ideography, 201.
Patočka, Jan, *xviii*.
Perception, 55, 78, 81, 93–94; and conception, 75–76; as hermeneutical, 94.
Performance, 180–82, 191; and body, 181; and oral poetry, 195–96; language as, 180–81.
Phenomenology, 4, 115, 121–22, 133, 135, 163–66, 242n.19, 257n.53; and comparative culture, 92–94; and human sciences, *xiv;* and language, 192–93; and Marxism compared, 151–60; and philosophy of political science, 10–15; and political philosophy, 21–23; and reflexivity, *xiii–xiv;* as archaeology, 30, 64, 72, 192; as critique of behavioralism, 45–72; as critique of politics, 25–41; as interdisciplinary, 40–41; as paradigm, *xiv;* as philosophical movement, *xiii*, 46; as radical empiricism, 7–10, 30; existential, 4, 21, 23, 46, 69, 115, 131, 132, 135, 137; hermeneutical, 36, 38, 107, 135, 165.
Philosophical anthropology, 92–94, 135, 136, 138, 139, 157, 176.
Phronēsis, 31–32, 216n.13.
Physicalism, 34, 52, 58, 72, 89; and cybernetics, 68, 85.
Physics, 48, 55, 57, 58, 71, 85; of power, 80.
Physis, 116–17, 120, 131–33; and *epistēmē*, 116.
Picasso, Pablo, *Swimmer* and *Acrobat* as anthropograms, 182.
Pico, Giovanni, 189.
Pirandello, Luigi, 27, 276n.56.

293

Index

A NOTE ABOUT THE AUTHOR

Hwa Yol Jung is Professor of Political Science at Moravian College, Bethlehem, Pennsylvania. His scholarly focus has been on the intersections between phenomenology, hermeneutics, and political theory. He has also written extensively on comparative philosophy, deep ecology, and literary and cultural theory. He is currently working on carnal hermeneutics/the body politic as a postmodern project. Most recently he edited a special double issue of *Human Studies* (1993) on "Postmodernity and the Question of the Other."